Politics and the Class Divide

In the Series
LABOR AND SOCIAL CHANGE
edited by Paula Rayman and Carmen Sirianni

Politics and

Temple University Press

PHILADELPHIA

the Class Divide

Working People
and the
Middle-Class Left

DAVID CROTEAU

To my parents, Laurette and Oliva.
They have taught me more than they know.

Temple University Press, Philadelphia 19122
Copyright © 1995 by Temple University
All rights reserved

Published 1995

The paper used in this publication meets the minimum require-
ments of American National Standard for Information Sciences—
Permanence of Paper for Printed Library Materials,
ANSI Z39.48-1984 ⊛

Printed in the United States of America

Figure App.1.1, page 233, is adapted from *Power in the Highest
Degree: Professionals and the Rise of a New Mandarin Order* by
Charles Derber, William A. Schwartz, and Yale Magrass. Copyright © 1990 by Oxford University Press, Inc. Reprinted by
permission.

Library of Congress Cataloging-in-Publication Data

Croteau, David.
    Politics and the class divide : working people and the middle class left
/ David Croteau.
        p.   cm.—(Labor and social change)
    Includes bibliographical references (p.   ) and index.
    ISBN 1-56639-254-3 (hc) : — ISBN 1-56639-255-1 (pbk.) :
        1. Political participation—United States.   2. Social movements—
United States.   3. Social classes—United States.   4. Working class—
United States—Political activity.   I. Title.   II. Series.
JK1764.C76   1995
323′.042′0973—dc20   94-37907

Contents

Preface

Bernice is a fifty-five-year-old factory worker. It was almost suppertime when we sat in the living room of her modest home, which she shares with her husband and elderly mother. She looked at me over her half-glasses, which were perched precariously on the tip of her nose, and as she spoke, her words hinted more of sadness than anger.

She said that working people are discouraged about politics. "I was raised to vote. Voting was your duty. You were proud to vote because it meant something about the way your country was run. Now, nobody bothers. 'Who cares?' 'What difference does it make?' 'They're all the same.' You hear all these things, so why bother? And *that* says a lot about how this country is run. People don't believe they have a say anymore, so they've given up."

Bernice is not alone. Growing numbers of Americans have come to feel that they have little or no voice in the world of politics; that they are powerless in the face of economic and political changes that threaten any stability they may have carved out for themselves and their children. While other parts of the world are struggling with the introduction of newly established democratic rights, U.S. academics and journalists have been writing works about the growing loss of faith in democracy at home. With titles such as *Why Americans Hate Politics* (Dionne 1991), *The Cynical Society* (Goldfarb 1991), and *Who Will Tell The People: The Betrayal of American Democracy* (Greider 1992), these works have explored the growing alienation and cynicism many U.S. citizens feel toward the political world.

Had Bernice been speaking a half-century earlier, she might have felt that her white working-class family was being represented in the politics of the Democratic Party and that perhaps their interests as workers were being promoted by the labor unions that were a central element of progressive politics. Now, like many other working people, she just feels discouraged.

In the electoral realm, today's workers often perceive a Democratic Party made up of an alliance between middle-class "limousine liberals" and the traditionally disenfranchised—the poor, racial minorities, gays and lesbians. Where, these workers ask themselves, do *they* fit in? In searching for a political home, these working people sometimes turn to the Republicans, who at least talk of values, responsibility for one's actions, hard work, patriotism, and the importance of family. But it's never a comfortable fit because the Republicans also represent the rich, the corporations, and the powerful elites. In the 1992 presidential election, some working people turned to Ross Perot, an apparently independent, plain-talking maverick who recognized the gridlock and corruption, who emphasized the importance of the "little guy," and who essentially ran on the politics of antipolitics. More often, though, these workers turn away from electoral politics altogether.

Workers find no comfort in other forms of politics either. The unions that once championed their cause are now often perceived as either ineffective or as having become greedy and—ironically—out of touch with regular working people. And those other groups that march and protest about a whole range of issues too often seem to be largely made up of middle-class throwbacks to the 1960s pursuing a politics of privilege. For the politically alienated members of America's white working class, there often seems no place to turn.

The Class Divide

This book examines the impact of class status on political participation and its implication for the future of democracy. More specifically, it is about the relative absence of white working-class participation in many liberal and left social movements.

Much of left politics in the United States was once primarily the domain of the working class. While always receiving crucial support from intellectuals, the labor movement—once a core element of left political life—was based in the lives and daily experiences of working people. But the situation has changed dramatically over the last half century. Now, the labor movement is beleaguered by dwindling membership and a hostile economic and political climate. Taking its place at the center of left politics has been an assortment of social movements—such as the environmental, peace, antinuclear, lesbian/gay, and women's movements—that sometimes are called "new social movements" (NSM).

One important defining characteristic of these "new" movements is that unlike the labor movement, NSMs supposedly do not work for class-specific goals. But the theoretical claim that such movements have "supraclass" agendas is contradicted by the empirical reality that these movements generally do not have substantial working-class participation and are, instead, distinctly *middle-class* movements.

This book explores the apparent contradiction: why are movements that are supposedly working for "universal" goals actually based in a particular class—the middle class?[1] "New" movements do exhibit characteristics that differentiate them from the "old" labor movement. However, I argue that the "new social movement" label is misleading insofar as it distracts from the continuing role of class in these movements. Thus, although I use *new social movements* in discussing the literature on the subject, elsewhere I generally refer to these movements as *middle class,* not *new.*

Many left movements are now middle class, and the working class in this country is usually no longer seen as a key source of left support. Instead, it is viewed as apparently conservative and largely quiescent. These images are primarily of a conservative *white* working class since workers of color are usually seen as allies of liberal and left civil-rights movements.

The situation leaves the left in a highly vulnerable position because its limited base of support often makes it politically ineffective. The emergence of working-class "Reagan Democrats"[2] has even been a threat to the viability of mildly liberal Democratic Party politics, influencing the party's 1992 presidential candidate to distance himself from the bogeymen special interests of racial minorities (embodied by the persona of Jesse Jackson) and unions (which most voters feel do not help and may actually hurt them).[3]

There are complex historical processes that have contributed to the middle-class nature of the contemporary Left. I briefly examine some of these processes in Part One of this work. My main focus, however, is on how activists and workers have come to understand this situation. I examine the political cultures of small numbers of white working people and of white, middle-class political activists who are part of liberal and left social movements. These are two groups that, in recent years, have been at odds on a whole range of issues. Yet they are groups that are linked by history. The democratic philosophy of left social movements envisions a politically active citizenry assuming responsibility for the future of their community. The Left, in other words, professes to struggle for the empowerment of people just like these white workers. For their part, working people often speak of distrusting government and politicians and of the need for fundamental political change in this country. In other words, they profess to want at least some of the political change being advocated by left social movements.

To someone totally unaware of recent political history, these two groups of citizens might seem destined to join forces. Yet there is a vast distance that separates political activists from most working people. I will argue that whereas each group sometimes recognizes similar problems, each has come to decidedly different conclusions about what is to be done and about what *can* be done to remedy those problems. I will also argue that a central reason this gap exists is that middle-class activists and disaffected workers are from opposite sides of a class divide. Each group speaks a different political language based in different experiences and reflecting different worldviews.

Political Culture and Social Class

One of the fundamental insights of sociology is that social structures can influence human behavior. Taking this idea seriously means looking beyond individual consciousness to explain social phenomena. But recognizing the potentially constraining nature of social structures is not to deny the role of human agency. Structures, which exist external to individuals, influence—but do not linearly determine—human behavior. The dynamic interaction between structural constraint and human agency forms a central line of inquiry within sociology.[4]

The relation between social structure and human behavior is at the heart of this work. The behaviors I am examining are political ones. The structural influences I am highlighting are those associated with class. As I explore in the first chapter, U.S. culture is often hostile to the discussion of class, in part because of its equivocal nature. Where do class boundaries start and stop? Who belongs to what class? How many classes are there? Such questions can turn discussions of the real-world impact of class into arcane debates filled with obscure jargon. I try to walk a fine line in this work by being clear about what I mean by "working class" and "middle class" without succumbing to overly pedantic definitions.

The basis for my distinguishing between working and middle class is loosely a manual/mental division. I explain this distinction in more detail in the first chapter (and review class theory in the appendix on class), but broadly speaking, for those who work outside the home, "working class" refers to those who rely largely on manual labor for their livelihood and usually work for an hourly wage. References to working class have traditionally conjured up images of blue-collared male factory workers, but working-class jobs are now more likely to be in the service sector than in manufacturing, and these service-sector employees are disproportionately female.

The label of "middle class" is used for those who earn their livelihood as a result of having particular credentials and knowledge-based expertise, and who are usually paid a salary, not an hourly wage. The "mental" work engaged in by the middle class usually requires a college education and often leads to the planning, supervision, or direction of other people's work.

The crucial division between working and middle class in the economic sphere also has an impact in the political realm. A common class position provides people with common material and cultural resources that facilitate a loosely shared perspective on the political world. Differing class cultures are crucial to the issue of political participation because the cultural "tools" that are part of different class cultures lend themselves to certain tasks, while making other tasks more difficult. You can pound a nail with a wrench, but success is more likely if you are equipped with a hammer. Similarly, the tools with which particular class cultures equip their members are more helpful for some tasks than for others. When it comes to political participation, the cultural divide between classes can be a significant one.

My emphasis here is on cultural aspects of the class divide. However, the structural sources of these differing cultures should not be overlooked. I am arguing that cultures most immediately influence political behavior, but it must be remembered that the differing cultures described in this work are, in part, the product of particular structural and historical conditions. In other words, the white working-class and social-movement cultures I describe here must be understood in their temporal and structural context. These cultures are neither universal nor eternal phenomena. In the last chapter I speculate about the possibility of change in current conditions.

The Role of Class: Some Cautions

While my emphasis here is on the class variable, it might appear at first glance that I am comparing apples and oranges—middle-class *activists* and working-class *nonparticipants*. The issue arises because of the presence of two variables: class and activism. One might well ask, shouldn't we control for the activism variable and compare activists from the middle class with activists from the working class?[5] Or shouldn't the comparison be of activists and nonactivists who are both from the middle class, thereby controlling for the class variable?

A more general study might well make such comparisons. But I am not exploring why a higher percentage of the middle class is not involved in such movements (which would suggest comparing activists and nonactivists from the middle class). Nor am I examining how middle-class and working-class activists compare. Both these issues are fair and interesting ones that deserve more research attention.

My question, though, is different, and it is delimited by my initial focus on "new" social movements that do not identify themselves as class-based and that do not pursue explicitly class-specific goals. My concern is with why such "new" social movements have little or no working-class participation. There is no self-evident reason that suggests working people are not concerned with peace, the environment, safe energy, or equality for women. A belief that such issues are "naturally" middle class warrants closer scrutiny and explanation.

Also, there is a unique relationship between left social-movement activists and working-class nonparticipants that must be taken into account. Often activists, either explicitly or implicitly, claim to speak on behalf of working people, and the two groups are therefore singularly linked. The Left, in fact, has tried to speak for democratic participation, and on behalf of those it sees as being excluded from the political process. More often than not, one central group of "excluded" players has been the working class.

Another point worth highlighting is that the dichotomy implied in this book between working- and middle-class cultures should not be overdrawn. Recognizing the inevitable variability within class cultures means that although I use "working class" and "middle class" throughout this work to describe differing orientations, it must be remembered that I am writing here of characteristics that tend to be more or less prevalent in particular classes.

That does not mean, for example, that political participation is a phenomenon found *exclusively* in the middle class or that *all* of the middle class is politically active. Clearly this is not the case. In fact, the type of left political activism that is the focus of this work is pursued by only a small segment of the middle class. And while those who *are* politically active *do* come disproportionately from the middle class, there are working-class activists who share in the efficacy and empowerment that I describe as characteristic of middle-class activists.

Similarly, some of the observations made about working-class disengagement can be applied to disaffected portions of the middle class.[6] Many in the middle class are alienated from political life. They do not follow current events in the media, nor do they take part in local civic life. Political disengagement, though, is *not* uniformly distributed throughout society. It has long been known that political nonparticipation is more prevalent amongst those with lower socioeconomic status; it is more prevalent among the working class than the middle class. The very nature of working-class life—with its connotations of limited resources, instability and insecurity, limited education, and relative powerlessness in the workplace—has exacerbated for workers the kind of political disengagement that sometimes reverberates well beyond the boundaries of the working class. As a result, working people are disproportionately represented among the nonvoters who have constituted nearly half of the electorate in recent years.[7]

Thus, pointing to cases of working-class activism or middle-class quiescence does not contradict the general thesis I am presenting here. As with all sociological analyses, the arguments in this book are presented in terms of aggregate tendencies, not universal laws.

Further, although this study focuses on class, the class division I describe is only one of several important cleavages in American society that affect political participation and orientation. In many cases, other factors such as race and gender surely play at least as important a role as class in conditioning political proclivities.

Is class the *only* influence on potential political participation? No. Do the cultural distinctions I describe adhere perfectly to clearly identified class boundaries? No. Does the examination of class tap a real and significant issue for social movements? Absolutely. We should be skeptical of analyses that neatly explain complex social phenomena with a single variable. This study highlights but one aspect of the intricate landscape that constitutes political life.

Overview

The story I tell in this work is divided into two parts. Part One provides some theoretical and historical context for the discussions that follow. In Chapter One, I introduce the idea of political participation and evolving democratic theory in brief historical context and discuss the unique relationship between the Left and democratic thought. In Chapter Two, I examine how left social movements have evolved as they seek to act on their democratic principles; again, I provide some brief historical context for the rise of "new social movements." In Chapter Three, I describe the concepts of class and culture as I use them in this work and explore their implications for participation in political life. (A more detailed theoretical discussion of class is presented in Appendix One, with an expanded discussion of culture in Appendix Two.)

Part Two, which forms the bulk of this work, is my retelling of experiences shared with me by a small number of people. As I describe more fully below, I spent several months listening to some working-class people while sharing in their daily work routines. I then conducted a series of interviews with both workers (coworkers and others) and with social-movement activists. Chapters Four through Ten are analyses largely based on what I saw and heard. The emphasis is on workers, but there are loosely comparative descriptions of key themes in the political cultures of the working people and middle-class activists interviewed for this study. These themes include mistrust and cynicism; efficacy; interest and motivation; material resources and constraint; cultural resources; the role of knowledge, information, and expertise in political life; and the notion of the private citizen.

Finally, Chapter Eleven explores the implications of this study's findings for future social-movement efforts, including an assessment of the potential for Left-worker alliances. I review the issue of diversity among social movements, as described to me by the activists I interviewed, and suggest some of the implications for the lack of class diversity found there.

Methods

A more detailed discussion of the methods used in this project is contained in Appendix Three. However, a few select comments are warranted here.

I have drawn from a variety of sources in writing this book. First, my own experiences traveling from a working-class background to middle-class, left social movements form a basis for my inquiry. This experience influenced the issues I chose to explore and gave me some "common ground" from which to discuss ideas with the people interviewed for this work. I explore my biographical positioning in more detail in the introduction.

Second, my analysis was partially developed during a five-month period of participant observation carried out at a nonunion printing plant and mailing house in a small New England city of eighty thousand people.[8] I will refer to this plant as Mail and Printing Services (MAPS), a fictitious name. I obtained employment at MAPS through a temporary employment agency, and I worked in the plant on a regular, full-time basis. I received no special treatment from management because my self-presentation had simply (and honestly) been that I was a graduate student looking for employment to pay bills while I finished work on my degree. I did not hide my status or my research interests from anyone. Permanent workers were accustomed to seeing temporary workers—including occasional college students—come and go because the company frequently used such short-term help. Since I gained access through the employment agency that the company regularly used, my arrival and departure five months later were not unusual. In fact, several other temporary workers came and left during the period that I was employed.[9]

The nature of much of the work I did at MAPS encouraged conversation as a diversion from the repetitive tasks being performed. As a result, I was able to spend literally hundreds of hours listening to workers converse on a wide array of subjects. These discussions would often go on nonstop for the entire two- to three-hour period between designated breaks. I would take part in the discussions as appropriate, but I tried never to initiate new topics of conversation. After work, I tape-recorded field notes, later transcribed these notes, and developed memoranda on my field experiences. Quotations from my notes are occasionally used in the text with appropriate citation. More information regarding the nature of this MAPS employment/participant observation is shared in the text and is discussed more fully in Appendix Three.

A third source of data, and one which is most visible in the text, is the forty-four individual interviews I conducted for this study. (A summary of interviewees' characteristics is provided in Appendix Three.) Half of the interviews were with working people (11 women, 11 men), half were with social-movement activists (10 women, 12 men). The interviewees were all white. Workers ranged in age from 23 to 62 (average 41.8, median 40) and included, among others, a mechanic, a salesperson, a data entry clerk, a janitor, a postal worker, a public works employee, a secretary, an electrician, a phone company employee, a cafeteria worker, and several factory workers. In nearly all cases, interviews were conducted in the homes of workers. Eleven of the worker interviews were done with coworkers from various parts of the MAPS plant after I had worked with them for over four months. The other workers were selected from a snowball sample initiated by the MAPS interviews.

Activists interviewed ranged in age from 24 to 74 (average 41.9, median 42) and included staffpeople and volunteers from, among others, environmental, peace, women's/feminist, anti-intervention, housing/homeless, antinuclear, and labor organizations. A couple of these activists are not from "new" movements but instead represented organizations that work in coalition efforts with "new" social-movement groups. About half of these interviews were conducted in the homes of activists; half were in or near the offices of movement organizations. Interviews with social-movement activists were developed from a snowball sample that began with personal contacts in such movements.

All the interviews were recorded and conducted with the understanding that anonymity would be maintained. Thus, all the names used here are pseudonyms, and some biographical details have been altered to protect the anonymity of the speakers. Interviews were loosely structured, lasting approximately two hours each. I transcribed the interview recordings and used Hyper-Research, a qualitative content-analysis software package, to code the transcripts for easier retrieval of relevant material. No attempt was made to quantify results. Excerpts from interviews are used extensively to highlight points in the text.

Finally, a couple of recent projects have aided in my understanding of some of the issues examined here. In 1990 I worked with Charlie Derber and Mary Murphy on a small exploratory project that included interviewing working- and middle-class residents in the Boston area about the role of government and about taxation policy. I also had the benefit of reading transcripts from forty small-group interviews with working-class people developed by William Gamson (1992) and his colleagues for a study published as *Talking Politics*.

I should remind the reader of the historical context in which this research was carried out. The participant observation and interviews for this work took place during 1990 and 1991 during the Bush administration. The economy, especially in New England, was under considerable strain, leaving workers concerned about their immediate economic future. For most, unions were an unlikely source of hope since they had just experienced their most devastating decade in over a half century. Internationally, Soviet influence over Eastern Europe was crumbling while U.S. involvement in the Persian Gulf was building, the latter leading to war in January of 1991. It was a rather bleak time in American political history; a bleakness that perhaps has been tempered a bit at this writing by the new Clinton administration and a stabilization in the economy. But the political and economic difficulties that face the nation have not been overcome by a changing of the presidential guard. There is little reason to believe that the views expressed during my interviews would be substantially different today.

The Consequences of Design

There are advantages and disadvantages to any method of social research. The type of fieldwork and interviewing conducted for this work provides, I believe, high validity. That is, the descriptions contained herein are likely to be a relatively accurate reflection of the small group of people under consideration. We must be more cautious, however, about the generalizability of the findings reported here. There is no reason to believe that the people interviewed for this project are anything but "typical" of their *particular subculture*. It is important to recognize, however, that the workers here are white, New England workers and that the activists here are similarly white and New England–based. In reporting findings, I do not discuss the percentage of workers or activists who responded a certain way to a particular question. To do so would imply the precise generalizability of such numbers, which clearly does not exist. However, I do use loosely descriptive terms such as "most" or "few" to discuss the prevalence of particular beliefs amongst my interviewees.

Is there any value in doing this sort of fieldwork and interviews with such a small group of people? I believe there is. One advantage of this research is its partially inductive approach. Although I clearly had an area of interest before embarking on my fieldwork, the five months I spent working at MAPS was largely devoted to listening and learning before I ever asked a single question. This experience helped to relocate me within a working-class culture and swept away some of the academic cobwebs that accumulate when relying too heavily on what workers derisively call "book learning." The questions I pursued in the interviews were different because of the experiences I had during my fieldwork.

My fieldwork with working people, though, was conducted primarily in the workplace. A word of caution is in order. Some research (Halle 1984) has shown that working people's sense of identity differs depending upon context. Working people have been found to have a stronger class identity in the context of the workplace than in their lives outside of work, where they may see themselves as part of an amorphous "middle class." Thus, I may have been privy to a context where class issues were more highlighted than they would have been outside of the workplace.

The relationships I developed during my fieldwork, I believe, made it easier for the coworkers I later interviewed to talk more freely than they otherwise would have. Similarly, my personal contacts with left-movement activists gave me a certain amount of credibility that academics rarely have in such circles. My contacts also served as references that at least one activist checked out before agreeing to my request for an interview. The process of identifying areas of potential inquiry and the relationship between researcher and interviewee are thus very different in this kind of work than those found in large-scale, quantitative survey research.

Arthur Sanders (1990: 167) notes that "close-ended, forced-choice questions do not lend themselves to an analysis of how people make sense of politics. We may be able to know what their opinion is on a particular issue or whether they like a particular candidate, but why that might be so is much harder to decipher." Thus, the use of open interviews is important in allowing for more textured and nuanced responses and for the pursuit of clarifying questions, both significant considerations when dealing with the complex issues addressed in this work. So although the results of such interviews cannot be precisely generalized, they are useful for filling in gaps left by more quantitative efforts, for allowing more complete and robust responses, for flagging issues that might be missed by closed-ended questionnaires, and for the exploration of apparently contradictory or idiosyncratic responses.

I have tried, in this work, to analyze some key issues in the political cultures of two distinct groups. One danger is that I have imposed on a complex world a coherence that may not exist. It is a hazard that haunts all of social science, since as Clifford (1986: 2) notes of ethnography, "it is always caught up in the invention, not the representation, of cultures." But I believe there is some significant truth in my tale; truth that may make some small contribution toward understanding the gulf that now exists between working people and the middle-class Left.

In telling this story, I make extensive use of quotations to share what I heard people saying. But it is important to remember that these quotes were extracted from hundreds of pages of transcripts. The people interviewed for this project are not "telling their own story," as is often claimed in this kind of work. I picked interviewees, asked questions, and chose quotations. In the end, I am the storyteller here, and it is the limited vision of a white male academic from a working-class background that is communicated in these pages.

Acknowledgments

Susan Griffin once observed that writing may be solitary but thinking is collective. I owe a great deal to the collective thinking that lies behind this effort. I would like to thank some of those who have contributed toward the completion of this book.

My debt to Cecelia Kirkman extends well beyond the confines of this work, but her insights, support, and good humor were especially appreciated in relation to this project. (And she didn't type a single word!) Her "front-line" efforts with working people are a continual reminder of some of the reasons for my own work, and of the luxuries involved in my intellectual endeavors.

A number of ideas incorporated into this work have resulted from the suggestions of friends and colleagues. I want to thank Charlie Derber, Bill Gamson, and Stephen Pfohl for their ongoing encouragement and help, and Eve Spangler for reading and commenting on an earlier version of this manuscript. Members of the Media Research and Action Project at Boston College gave me some helpful feedback early on, even though this project had precious little to do with media. Paul Joseph, who reviewed an earlier draft of this manuscript for Temple University Press, provided some useful suggestions. Special thanks to Bill Hoynes for all his help and optimism over the years on this and other projects. Thanks, too, for the comments and support of Charlotte Ryan and Sharon Kurtz.

The publication of this book involved the work of many people. Thanks to Paula Rayman for reading the manuscript and helping to get it published. I appreciate the efforts of Michael Ames and all those at Temple University Press who have helped produce this book. Thanks to Kenneth Plax for his meticulous copyediting.

My sincere appreciation to all the folks who took the time to talk with me for this project. Obviously this work would have been impossible without their help. I hope I have done justice to at least some of their ideas, and I hope the "book learning" hasn't gotten in the way of their insights.

Finally, I am indebted to the Boston College Graduate School of Arts and Sciences for its financial support of this project during the 1992–93 academic year.

Different Worlds

*No social study that does not come back to the problems of
biography, of history and of their intersections within a
society has completed its intellectual journey.*

C. WRIGHT MILLS, *The Sociological Imagination*

This work is closely related to my own biography. I grew up in a working-class family and have spent all of my adult life in and around middle-class social movements. My social, civic, and academic lives have all been organized around such political movements. My experiences in traveling from the world of my working-class origins to that of middle-class movements has been a central catalyst for this work. I begin, then, by telling some of this story.

Authors and Biographies

Although at first it may seem to be an act of confident presumptuousness, telling one's own story actually puts an author in an enormously vulnerable position. It is the kind of vulnerability that academics usually try very hard to avoid. There is something ironic about this, especially in sociology. The intersections of biography and history on a collective level, as Mills suggested, are the substance of the discipline. Yet usually, the individual biography of the sociologist is dismissed with a simple statement of institutional affiliation. As recently as 1971, Lewis Coser was able to write of even the "classic" sociologists, "There has been no sustained attempt to show how social origins, social position, social network, or audience found a reflection in the problems that a theorist addressed himself to or in the overall orientation of his life's work" (Coser 1971: xiv). It is only with the recent work of, for example, Gouldner (1970, 1985), Lepenies (1988) and Therborn (1976) that the insights of a sociology of knowledge have been applied, within the mainstream of the discipline, to the history of sociology itself.

Still, all too often, it seems that sociologists acknowledge the importance of social origins and social positions for everyone but themselves. Shulamit

Reinharz (1984: 24) makes the point well: "Sociologists claim that behavior is class bound, gender related, historically rooted, and situationally determined by expectations of others. To be consistent with this belief, sociologists' perceptions and behavior in their research activities must be considered bound to their social position. Their responsibility as sociologists, then, is to understand how their work is shaped by these factors." But in the real world of sociological research, this rarely happens.

Instead, while it is customary for authors to disclose the intellectual journeys that have led them to address the topic at hand, it is far less common to discuss the relationship between the researcher's personal biography and his or her subject matter. Perhaps some magnanimous sense of modesty pervades the discipline—but I doubt it. Instead, silence on the issue of biography is more likely a legacy of a particular approach to "science." "Science," in some circles, is seen as being predicated upon reduction and objectification. Knowledge and "truth" are supposedly the result of distancing the subjective observer from the object of investigation in order to reveal the transparent truth, unsoiled by the touch of the researcher. Of course, in its pure form, this is fantasy. But in most instances, an author's personal involvement with his or her topic is seen as a probable shortcoming, suggesting that the arguments contained in the work should be taken with a precautionary grain of salt.

Even those who have long ago dismissed the strictures of purely positivist science often continue to labor under the presumption that "distancing oneself" from the work provides for a sort of cover of objectivity. Perhaps that is why quantification is such a comfort. "Data" in quantified form appear to take on a life of their own, independent of the researcher, regardless of how central he or she was in choosing the topic, designing the study, gathering the data, and influencing the findings. At its worst, the apparently objective nature of "scientific" data has contributed to a form of domination based on the power and authority of scientific expertise (Aronowitz 1988).

It has always seemed peculiar to me to prize the attempt to sever researchers from their work. Sociologists understand the socially constructed nature of reality, and they, most of all, should accept and explore the relationship between authors and the stories they tell. Ideas are promoted by agents who occupy certain social positions, and we can better understand the origins of particular ideas if we better understand the social position of those who would advance them.

It would be disingenuous of me to examine the issues contained in this work without discussing my biographical relation to them. The questions raised and the issues explored in this work have concerned me for over fifteen years, and they continue to do so. To write of such things with a posture of pure intellectual distance would be tantamount to fraud. I leave it up to the reader to determine whether this personal involvement warrants the administering of a precautionary grain of salt.

The Story of the Author

I was born into a type of family that became a cultural stereotype shortly before it became an endangered species; the "traditional," white, "ethnic," blue-collar family. After brief periods as a logger and as a shipworker, my father worked in a paper mill for forty-four years, first as a towel-machine operator, then as a millwright. My mother, after stints as a domestic and a factory worker, toiled at home raising four children. Such arrangements were possible amongst significant sections of the working class during the post–World War II boom years. My father was a union member (United Paperworkers International Union) but inactive in union affairs. He earned what was considered to be good pay. My mother and he were able to build a modest home, raise a family, and live comfortably. They never had a credit card or a checking account. The family car was a used one, health care was dependent on union benefits (childhood photos show me with visibly decaying teeth—we had no dental insurance until I was a teen), and vacations were always within a half-day's drive; but there was always plenty of food and clothing, and the bills were paid on time.

The town in which I grew up was predominantly blue collar, heavily French Canadian and Irish, almost all white, and mostly Catholic. The local paper mill—whose towering smokestacks dominated the local landscape—was the primary source of employment. A now-abandoned shoe factory was a distant second. That paper mill played a central role in my life, not only because my father and other family members worked there, but because it served as a source of motivation for me. As long as I can remember, I was determined *not* to work in the mill. I cannot recall how I developed this determination, I just know it was a primary factor in motivating me to become the first member of my family to attend college. Education, in some vague fashion, was going to be my ticket out. If it did not work, it would at least provide a temporary reprieve from the mill.

What I wanted to get "out" of was a lifestyle centered on serving time in the mill; a lifestyle highlighted, as Studs Terkel (1972: xiii) once put it, by violence "to the spirit as well as to the body." Growing up in my town meant learning about the trade-offs that were involved in working at the mill. The good wages and benefits came at a high cost. Workers surrendered themselves for at least eight hours a day to become a cog in the always-churning paper machines. Many of the jobs were deathly boring and repetitive. Many were dangerous, loud, dirty, and hot. Rotating shifts were the norm—one week, "days" (8:00 A.M. to 4:00 P.M.), one week, "4 to 12," one week, "12 to 8." Days off were only occasionally contiguous and hardly ever on weekends. Most workers considered themselves lucky to have the opportunity for overtime pay and to "work a 16"—a sixteen-hour double shift. People did this regularly and counted on overtime pay for a substantial portion of their paychecks. Work weeks of forty-eight or fifty-six hours were not only common, they were the norm. Workers signed over their autonomy, almost all hope of interesting work, and in some cases their health for a regular paycheck and benefits. No one really loved it, but for many it was a tolerable deal; the best that could be had without college credentials. But it was a deal that I knew I did not want to make.

Neither did my older brother. We never talked about it, but it was clear that he hoped to avoid the mill as well. After two years in a local vocational school he got a job with a small general contractor, working as an electrician and doing carpentry. I can remember conversations between my concerned father and my brother about why he was forsaking the "security" and union benefits of the mill just for variety and "interesting" work. I do not think my father ever understood. Perhaps I was projecting my own interpretation onto my brother's actions, but in my mind they stood as a symbol of resistance to the pull of the all-powerful paper machines. I silently cheered him on.

About five years after I left my hometown, my mother phoned one day to tell me that my brother had applied at the mill and been hired. My parents hailed his decision as a sign of maturity and good judgment. I felt like crying.

Nearly ten years later my brother still works in the mill, though its future is uncertain. During the last few years, the mill has been up for sale as the industry shifts more of its operations to nonunion plants in the South. Conditions in the mill remain demanding. As a cost-cutting measure intended to save on overtime pay, the company introduced a new schedule of mandatory twelve-hour work shifts for nonsalaried employees.

By the time my brother entered the mill, I had already managed to leave my hometown. My father's union-scale salary and the fact that older siblings were already on their own combined to make it financially possible for me to sneak into college. (At the time, my oldest brother worked in a Connecticut defense plant, and my sister worked in a shoe factory. My sister has since been laid off four times by four separate companies that closed their plants. At this writing she has just started a job in yet another factory after having been unemployed for nearly two years. Meanwhile, the defense plant where my other brother works has been going through severe post–Cold War lay-offs, and his job is in jeopardy.) Neither of my parents had attended high school, let alone college, so I was left rudderless in choosing schools. The two part-time guidance counselors at my regional high school of more than seven hundred students were not helpful. One had suggested to me that perhaps, despite my excellent grades, welding would be more "practical" for someone with my "background." After applying to what in retrospect was an eclectic collection of schools, I made the only logical choice: the one that offered me the most scholarship money. It was an elite private college in the Boston area. Despite the fact that I had never touched a computer in my life, I told my parents I was going to be a computer scientist. Clean work, steady employment, decent pay; they understood that. The irony was that the high price of my education ticket out of town necessitated my working during the school year and then returning home during the summers to join the union and work in the paper mill. It is a cliché, but even in these relatively brief encounters I learned things from the mill and its workers that cannot really be taught in any college classroom.

From the very first day, my college education brought with it a new awareness of how different cultures could be. I have a vivid memory of the awkwardness and discomfort on my parents' faces when they met my assigned roommate and his obviously wealthy parents (both doctors) in the totally alien environment of a college dorm. (I was not feeling any better.) Cultures rarely confront each other so poignantly.

I shared my parents' discomfort as I learned lessons that would make it increasingly difficult for me to return to my working-class community. In both my formal and informal education I was immersed in middle-class culture. Employment expectations ("careers" not jobs), food ("ethnic" not meat-and-potatoes), dress (natural fibers not synthetic), music (folk and progressive/alternative rock not heavy metal), entertainment and leisure (something other than television and hockey)—it was all different from what I was accustomed to. Perhaps the most striking difference I encountered was the sense of entitlement shared by other students. For most of my middle-class peers, college seemed to be little more than a nuisance and an unexceptional part of their lives. Often choreographed by their parents, college was an expected step towards a larger world of broad opportunity. But for me school always seemed a luxury, and I had a strange sense that one day I would be told some terrible administrative error had been made and I would be sent packing back home to serve my time in the mill where I *really* belonged. (Years later, when I was a graduate student on a full scholarship, the feeling still lingered.)

On the whole, my experiences confirmed my earlier sense of the vast distance between "ordinary" people and the more privileged classes with whom I now interacted. Having strayed further and further from home, I saw and felt class differences more sharply than ever. The feelings were often unpleasant. During my first disorienting year at school I found solace by making friends with local working-class "townies" and frequently drinking to excess.

In the classroom, however, I discovered something fascinating. The world view that I had developed as an adolescent was in fact one that was shared by many people. I read voraciously and excitedly, not so much because I was discovering "new" ideas, but because for the first time in my life I was seeing "my" ideas and beliefs articulated more precisely and comprehensively than I could have ever dreamed possible. My vague political and intellectual leanings, which had led me to be suspicious of authority and resentful of elites (and which had resulted in brief peripheral involvement with the antinuclear Clamshell Alliance), were confirmed and deepened as I learned about traditions of progressive action and thought.

Computer science was quickly abandoned. I took courses in social movements, class and inequality, and international political economy. I wrote a senior thesis on the effect of disarmament on defense workers and the need for economic conversion planning. I regularly read left publications and attended lectures on political topics. I helped to start an alternative student political journal that became a magnet for others, especially foreign students, who felt alienated from mainstream campus life. I became involved in campus politics, refused to register for selective service (and thereby lost federal student aid my senior year), protested campus military funding and the U.S. invasion of Grenada, helped student feminist groups to stop the school-sponsored showing of pornographic films on campus, and worked with Boston-area peace and justice organizations. My faculty advisors in each of my two majors, sociology and English, were politically active and sympathetic to my efforts. During my senior year, despite departmental support, both of them were denied tenure by the new, incoming university president. I completed my undergraduate career by joining with other students and demonstrating at the graduation ceremonies, carrying balloons, ribbons, and a banner protesting the suspiciously political maneuverings that led to the tenure denials.

During the dawn of the "Reagan Revolution," I had been introduced to a part of left politics. But as I was learning to better analyze and understand the world in which I lived, I was drifting away from the world from which I had come. My education had equipped me with middle-class skills and had introduced me to middle-class values, attitudes, and ways of thinking. But I found it increasingly difficult to translate the issues and concerns of my college studies into a language that made sense to my family and friends back home. There was simply inadequate common ground. Ironically, my left political leanings only exacerbated the distance I felt from my working-class origins. The middle class was obviously not synonymous with the Left. But, as I discovered, much of the contemporary Left was distinctly middle class.

After college I went to work for several years for the national office of a "peace-and-justice" organization in New York City where I continued to be acutely aware of class issues. Once again, I was introduced to the experiences of a foreign culture; the New York Left and the national peace community. First, there was the fractious infighting amongst small left groups that was a source of constant amazement and sadness for me. Second, there were the dedicated, inspiring individuals who sometimes seemed utterly out of touch with the world outside of the insulated left community. Third, there was the money that flowed in and around the left community. One example stands out in my memory. As a staffperson, I was asked to attend the opening night of a fundraising SoHo art show that featured a forty-thousand-dollar de Kooning. ("Who?" I asked sheepishly). Nervously sipping my wine (not a beer in sight!), I looked around amazed at the wealth that surrounded me and wondered what this had to do with left politics.

There were other experiences that were so alien to me that they seemed almost unreal. Civil-disobedience actions are one example. I recall sitting with hundreds of others blocking the gates in front of the White House as part of a peace-and-justice demonstration. One of my coworkers whiled away the time waiting for arrest by reading a detective novel. Others passed around sections of the newspaper. But my first civil-disobedience arrest occurred in an anti-apartheid protest in front of the South African consulate in New York, and I sat next to Allen Ginsberg as he read a poem written especially for the occasion. I could not help thinking that the working-class kid from a small mill town had traveled a long, long way.

While I had a strong respect and affection for my fellow activists, it became startlingly apparent to me that many of them within this part of the Left often had no concrete referent in mind when they talked about "the working class." The peace group for which I worked, and most other left groups with which I came into contact, had an overwhelmingly white, middle-class constituency. The only visible working-class representation appeared in coalition efforts and consisted of members of the more progressive labor unions, an admirable but unfortunately tiny slice of the American working class. Consequently, activists' reified notions of "the working class" tended to fall at extreme poles: either workers were the gloriously idyllic proletariat (who one day would smarten up and start doing their revolutionary duty), or they were stupid, fascistic hard hats for whom there was no hope (and who were the easy target of ridicule). Either way *their* working class bore little resemblance to the working class I knew. When I questioned the absence of working-class participation in the Left, I was often met with heroic tales of militant working-class activists. As middle-class activists often made clear, some of their best friends were from the working class.

The working people I grew up among were not the militant trade unionists so often romanticized by leftists, but neither were they the right-wing "hard hats" that others so often disparaged. But I found it very difficult to explain this to my fellow activists. My experience of class did not fit their ideological mold.

In a study of social mobility, David Karp (1986: 23) has commented that "Class background does not fall away like a snake's old skin once professional status is achieved." The image is a good one and it holds true for my travels to the middle-class Left. I found myself straddling a fence. I had a full set of middle-class educational credentials and was part of a middle-class movement, but I still had strong attachments to my roots and to my working-class family and friends. I had a foot in each world but was completely comfortable in neither of them. Having been socialized into two different classes, I was constantly aware—sometimes painfully so—of the differences between these cultures.

Perhaps these differences revealed themselves most clearly when I went back "home" to visit family and friends and tried to talk about my work in the peace movement. It was an awkward and difficult task. The difficulty was not primarily related to potential agreement with my positions. Instead, the experiences I was having in the peace movement, the ideas with which I was grappling, and the way I was learning to see the world were simply different from anything that my family and friends had ever encountered; they were ideas of a foreign culture—of a different world.

The issues I was learning to analyze and address were *not* the issues of primary concern to my family and friends. The issues that *did* concern them were either only vaguely addressed or completely ignored by the middle-class Left's agenda. More important, the idea that politics was a sphere of life worthy of extensive involvement and accessible to people like themselves seemed inconceivable to them. I was learning about politics and discussing it in a way that simply did not resonate with their experiences and concerns. I was confronted with the undeniable reality of a class divide that separated the cultures of the working-class world from which I had come from that of the middle-class, political Left to which I had traveled. I ended up feeling a bit silly and naive for somehow believing that a working-class kid had any business getting involved in the machinations of politics.

A return to graduate school allowed me to explore the issue on more or less my own terms. I knew my own story, but I also came to learn the stories academics told about social movements and working people. Some of it made sense, some of it did not, much of it seemed totally irrelevant.[1]

The two worlds I continued to straddle met in 1987 when the twelve hundred paperworkers at International Paper's mill in Jay, Maine, went on strike. A caravan of striking millworkers later came to Boston, and several workers came to a social economy class I was taking at the time. The experience was almost surreal for me. The workers could have been my parents, my siblings, or friends from high school. And here they were, visibly uncomfortable, sitting in a college classroom, talking movingly to graduate students about their struggle. Cultures were clashing once again, and I could not help but think of my parents in that dorm room nearly ten years earlier.

I wrote a paper on the Jay strike for the course. I traveled up to the mill to speak with strikers and went back to my hometown to talk to a local union official about his take on the strike. Not to worry, he assured me, the company that owned *his* mill did not see the union as the enemy. His thirteen-hundred-member local had a "good rapport" with the company because the union and owners were in a "partnership" and were competing against other companies, not each other. I left the interview once again having been reminded of the vast gulf between my middle-class political life and even the organized segments of the working class. It is a topic that seems to constantly shadow my experiences.

This book is the result of subsequent research and reflection aimed at better understanding the roots and political consequences of this gulf. Such a confrontation of cultures is fertile ground for sociological analysis. That is what my professional training has taught me. My lived experience of this class divide has, for me, made it more than an academic question.

PART ONE

Democracy, Social Movements, and Class

CHAPTER 1

The Promise of Democracy

*[D]emocracy, both in ancient Greece and in the politics of
the past two centuries, has never been achieved without
a struggle, and that struggle has always been,
in good part, a type of class struggle.*

ANTHONY ARBLASTER, *Democracy*

American democracy has never lived up to its promise. Instead, under the
banner of a democratic society, indigenous nations were slaughtered or displaced, Africans and others were enslaved, and women were often relegated to
the status of cheap or unpaid labor. With varying degrees of blatant and often
violent circumscription, people of color, women, and even the white men who
did not own property were excluded from the promise that "all men are created
equal." For much of the country's history, the majority of Americans were
excluded from sharing in even the most basic of democratic rights, the right to
vote. Thus, citizens have always faced enormous barriers to participating in the
American promise of democracy.

But while the picture has often been bleak, much of American history has
been marked by the expansion of basic rights to growing numbers of citizens.
Frederick Douglass's contention that "Power concedes nothing without demand" has surely been an accurate characterization of this slow, arduous, and
incomplete progress. Slave revolts, the abolition movement, the struggle of
native peoples, the rise of organized labor, poor people's movements, women's
movements, the civil rights movement, and the struggle for gay and lesbian
rights, among others, have marked advances in the extension of basic democratic rights and protections to American citizens.

Martin Luther King (1986: 314) once wrote of this slow progress, "While
it is a bitter fact that in America in 1968, I am denied equality solely because I
am black, yet I am not a chattel slave. Millions of people have fought thousands
of battles to enlarge my freedom; restricted as it still is, progress has been made.

This is why I remain an optimist, though I am also a realist, about the barriers before us."

However, as the twentieth century draws to a close, King's sense of realistic optimism has largely left our political discourse. The beliefs that democracy can be revitalized and expanded, that justice can be slowly but surely extended to more of our citizens, are badly tattered. Instead, there is a growing sense of foreboding regarding American democracy. While many people abroad struggle to increase their participation in public life, to strengthen fledgling democracies, and to redevelop civil society, many Americans seem to have abandoned any hope of invigorating democracy at home. The reigning political mood in America is a combination of disenchantment, cynicism, and alienation. Although many who have been excluded from democracy's promise have known this all along, many more Americans are becoming aware that something is terribly wrong with our political and social systems.

The current state of affairs poses a special challenge to the Left, for historically it has been the Left that has agitated most directly for the expansion of democracy. But whereas the American Left at one time carried the flag of change on behalf of working people, with the significant participation of working people, in the last few decades this has no longer been the case. Much of the Left has become distinctly middle class, and the Left's central vision of robust and diverse democratic participation seems further away than ever. This chapter and the next examine how this state of affairs has come about.

Evolving Notions of Democracy

"Democracy," as Arblaster (1987: 62) observes, was originally understood to mean "the people govern themselves, without mediation through chosen representatives, directly or, if necessary, by the rotation of governing offices among citizens." But over time, democracy has been interpreted in many ways.

In the classical Greek sense, democracy is the idea of popular "power," derived from the Latin *potere* meaning "to be able." Politics can be said to be the social organization of power in a society, so democratic politics is the organization of power such that the citizenry is able to act and participate in the decisions that affect their lives. In other words, democracy suggests that it is "the people" who hold ultimate authority. Greek democracy was what we have since come to label "direct" democracy, where many public offices were filled by lot, not election, and direct citizen participation in decision making was the norm. But the often romanticized vision of Greece as the "cradle of democracy" ignores the fact that citizenship was denied to women, slaves, and foreign residents and, as a result, was limited to a quarter or less of the adult population.

As the example of Greek democracy shows, the evolution of democratic thinking has been a long and circuitous one with a more checkered history than is often acknowledged.[1] This history is far beyond the scope of this work, but it has included repeated attempts by left movements to expand democratic freedoms and full citizenship.

In the United States, after long struggles, the protections of citizenship were often still limited to white men, but the expansion of democracy eventually resulted in increased suffrage rights, trade union rights, and basic freedoms of press, assembly, speech, and religion. But during the struggle for these rights, a new questioning of democracy began. For example, questions arose as to the centrality of elections in guiding democracies. Vilfredo Pareto (1935), Robert Michels (1949), Gaetano Mosca (1939), among others, began arguing that democracy was at heart a fraud and a delusion. Modern governments were, in fact, bureaucratic oligarchies resistant to control by the ballot box. Government could be *for* the people, but it could not be *by* the people.

The impact of such arguments was minimized by the intervention of the war that Wilson argued was being fought to make the world "safe for democracy." The propagandistic attempts to drum up support for the First World War saw "democracy" being touted like never before. Later, the need to defend against fascist attacks on democracy would be cited as one justification for Allied involvement in the Second World War. But after the war, it was impossible not to recognize the gap between democratic theory and Western reality. In response, theorists tried to redefine democracy. Joseph Schumpeter (1950: 250, 269) argued that we could no longer pretend that democracy meant that "the people itself decide issues through the election of individuals who are to assemble in order to carry out its will." This elaborate fiction needed to be replaced by the realization that democracy "is that institutional arrangement for arriving at political decisions in which individuals acquire that power to decide by means of a competitive struggle for the people's vote." Thus, "democracy is the rule of the politician." Robert Dahl (1967) argued that popular rule in the classical sense was a fallacy since it was a multitude of fragmented groups who contested for power and influence. Thus, diverse and pluralistic societies developed competing interest and pressure groups.

According to Schumpeter, significant portions of the population exhibited signs of ignorance and apathy, and consequently democracy as government by the people was not only impossible but undesirable as well. Other theorists concurred. Seymour Martin Lipset (1959: 14) argued that "The belief that a very high level of participation is always good for democracy is not valid." Bernard Berelson (1952: 317) argued that apathy was a welcome " 'cushion' to absorb the intense action of highly motivated partisans." It protected against "the danger of total politics." Apathy and acquiescence on the part of the electorate could be seen as positive virtues since they contributed to political stability.

Despite the fact that Western societies wrap themselves in the mantle of "democracy," political theorists have come to realize that the claims of "democratic" societies are often suspect. Edmund Morgan (1988: 65) has argued that the idea of democratic rule was a fallacy from its inception. He suggests that the "sovereignty of the people" was as much a fiction as the earlier notion of the divine right of kings. In fact, he argues that English Parliament's recognition of the authority of citizens in the mid-1600s was an astute political maneuver. "In endowing the people with supreme authority," he writes, "Parliament intended only to endow itself." Popular sovereignty in England, according to Morgan (1988: 148), "became the prevailing fiction in a society where government was traditionally the province of a relatively small elite. Although the new fiction slowly widened popular participation in the governing process, those who made use of it generally belonged to that elite and employed it in contests with other members. In doing so they had to be cautious lest they invite a wider participation than they had bargained for." Despite the fact that it was largely run by traditional elites, government "by the people" gained power and legitimacy by the very fact that it supposedly had the authorization of citizens.

Morgan argues that democracy in the United States was built on a similar deception. The image of the "noble," small-landholding (yeoman) farmer as the basis of the early republic was a useful myth that helped large-landholding "gentlemen" to maintain political influence, since yeoman farmers were expected to defer to the "better" judgment of "gentlemen." Part of the motivation for touting the virtues of the "common" landowner was, ironically, to limit the spread of democratic participation. Morgan (1988: 168, 173) points out:

> The glorification of the yeoman had begun with a denigration of the peasant and carried on with a denigration of paupers and landless laborers, who spent their earnings on drink and went on relief when the jobs gave out, people whom landowners had to support with taxes that ate away at their property. Nor did glorification of the yeoman involve much sympathy with the slaves who manned the American plantations of the South. When Thomas Jefferson talked about those who labored in the earth being the chosen people of God, he did not mean slaves . . . . The fiction of the invincible yeoman thus embodied the same ambiguities as the larger fiction it supported: it sustained the government of the many by the few, even while it elevated and glorified the many.

But even democracy as a fiction proved to be an influential idea. Morgan (1988: 152) writes, "The history of popular sovereignty in both England and America after 1689 can be read as a history of the successive efforts of different generations to bring the facts into closer conformity with the fiction, efforts that have gradually transformed the very structure of society."

It is these efforts that have been at the core of the left tradition. It has been left movements that, in many different ways, have argued most persuasively for the expansion of democracy and the empowerment of citizens. The Left has often struggled to bring substance to the theory of democracy. But the inclusiveness that usually characterizes left philosophy has *itself* been contradicted by the reality of the Left's limited social base. Thus, like the history of democracy itself, the Left's history has often been a process of trying to bring the fact of democratic participation into closer conformity with the fiction.

Democracy and the Left

Disparate social movements can be grouped under the broad umbrella of the "Left" because of their common belief in democratic participation by as many people as possible. Richard Flacks (1988: 7) describes left history this way:

> Radical democracy, populism, socialism, communism, syndicalism, anarcho-communism, pacifism—all of these are labels for ideologies and organized political forces that, despite their manifold differences and mutual hostilities, have espoused a common idea. This idea is that the people are capable of and ought to be making their own history, that the making of history ought to be integrated with everyday life, that all social arrangements that perpetuate separations of history making from daily life can and must be replaced by frameworks that permit routine access and participation by all in the decisions that affect their lives.

Thus, for Flacks (1988: 7) the "tradition of the left" includes "all forces in our society that have sought to democratize politics, institutions, or culture and have sought to encourage relatively powerless groups to intervene in history."

Flacks draws a useful distinction between "making life"—the day-to-day routines that are necessary for the sustenance of life—and "making history"— the pursuit of activities that have a broader social and political impact. Making history includes (1988: 3) "activities that have the effect of changing one or more features of the patterned everyday ways of life characteristic of a community or a society." The heart of the left tradition, he contends, lies in expanding access to history making. It is a tradition that (1988: 101) "includes all those who have said that they wanted to replace decision making controlled by private profit and elite domination with processes based on popular voice." Clearly not all left movements have lived up to this ideal. Some have deteriorated into structures of centralized power that violate the philosophical basis of left politics. However, movements that have remained consistent with a democratic vision have struggled to expand popular participation in history making.

Some left movements, for example, women's organizations, labor unions, or civil rights groups, work for the inclusion of particular segments of the population that have been traditionally excluded from political and economic decision making. Other movements, such as peace and environmental groups, seek the inclusion of a more generalized "public" in areas of decision making that have traditionally been the sole domain of government, scientific, and corporate elites. What all these groups share, however, is a commitment to work for the inclusion of all in the "making of history."

The Nature of Liberty and the Influence of Capitalism

Associating the Left with the promotion of democracy is not to say that the Right is necessarily characterized by an elitist, antipopulist orientation. Such a belief can blind us to the appeal that right-wing ideology holds for some people who could not—by any stretch of the imagination—be called powerful elites. Instead, the Right nurtures support among regular citizens by promoting liberty as an alternative to the Left's vision of democracy.[2]

Liberty represents freedom from constraint and a generalized belief in the superiority of an individual's rights in the face of encroaching government. It suggests lower taxes, smaller government, deregulation, and other measures intended to shield the individual from the impact of government. Unlike democracy, liberty does not necessarily require the active engagement of citizens in political or social spheres.

Whereas a belief in democracy brings with it a commitment to the facilitation and encouragement of political participation, Flacks (1988: 102) argues that "Right-wing ideology is inherently incongruent with political activism." He explains, "To the degree that one favors keeping social initiative away from the political process then it seems contradictory to commit oneself to politics, except when necessary to resist state encroachment." The Left's vision, then, is one of shared participation and responsibility—a public collective vision. With some significant exceptions, in most cases, the Right wants to guarantee a person's freedom to be left alone—a decidedly private vision.

Both perspectives promote empowerment by which people will be able to control their own lives. Left efforts are aimed at advancing social and political processes that enable people to make history. The Right focuses on creating enclaves of private space that people are able to control, free of government intervention.

The exceptions to this general orientation include the call by some on the right for government intervention to enforce moral codes, especially in the area of sexuality, through restrictions on abortion, antihomosexual initiatives, and antiobscenity laws. These are usually justified in the name of local control and community standards. Elements of the Right also call for *increased* government intervention in policing some segments of society—especially people of color and the poor. Finally, there are cases of right-wing and fascist movements promoting aspects of a collective political and social vision.

A belief in the existence of distinct "private" spaces, separate from political state intervention, is essential for the Right because it serves to buttress a belief in the adequacy of capitalism. The Right draws upon traditional liberal democratic thinking in suggesting that the enlightened *individual* self-interest at the heart of capitalist, market-based thinking is sufficient to determine the *collective* good as well. Thus, in this vision, capitalism and democracy are entirely compatible. Government need not intervene in the "private" realm of the market since to do so would suggest a claim to knowing what is best for people—a knowledge possessed only by the individual pursuing his or her own self-interest.

The left tradition, however, which draws from Marx, suggests a different analysis. It denies the existence of a separate state, totally independent of the economic realm. Most important, this tradition argues that the inequalities in distribution of resources, which characterize capitalism, significantly affect the exercise of political rights that may exist *in theory* but that are denied *in practice* (Cohen and Rogers 1983: 50–51). Thus, state intervention into the market is essential for the redressing of inequalities developed there that, in effect, threaten to undermine democracy.

If the Right's notion of liberty is carried to its logical extreme—that is, if government essentially withdraws from the lives of its citizens—then at least two developments are possible. First, inequalities that have developed over centuries, based on the accumulation of wealth and resources or based on characteristics such as race and sex, are allowed to continue unabated. There is no need, in the Right's worldview, for government intervention to alleviate the harmful effects of these or other inequalities. Second, the withdrawal of popular participation in the political and social sphere by a populace concerned solely with liberty, without the corresponding dismantling of the state, means that central realms of political and economic power are abandoned to the potential control of interested elites. The legitimacy of these elites is contingent upon their willingness to check their explicit intervention in the personal lives of citizens (through deregulation, lower taxes, etc.). As long as the elites deliver the primary good of liberty, personal freedom, their control of the central institutions of power are apparently of little concern to adherents of the Right. These elites, then, are free to govern within these constraints.

The Left, however, pursues a different vision and faces a much more complicated dilemma. Carrying forth the left vision to its logical extreme requires the opportunity for active political participation by all. Liberty can flourish merely through the absence of constraint. Democracy, however, requires processes that provide for ongoing meaningful participation from citizens. A powerful left elite is no Left at all. The moment power becomes concentrated in the hands of a few, even if these few espouse leftist beliefs, the left vision is betrayed. Disastrous experiments in state socialism have revealed this fact all too clearly.

Thus, left social movements are faced with the difficulty of facilitating and promoting broad-based political and social participation. Failure to achieve such participation is tantamount to the failure of the left project as a whole. Left democratic theory, then, is based on the assumption that people either want to participate in history-making efforts or they can be convinced of the need for such participation since true empowerment cannot occur in the shadow of elite power structures.

A left perspective on the environment, for example, includes not only calls for the preservation of natural resources and the promotion of appropriate technology but also demands for active participation in the decision making surrounding the use of resources and technology. Such popular decision making, it is understood, may result in the elevating of community values over the rights of individual private property. Such themes of collective community control, whether directly or through elected representatives, form a staple of the Left's approach.

Conceptualizing Democratic Participation

The form that democratic participation may take varies. One obvious possibility is representative democracy, as advocated by many liberal democratic thinkers. But Flacks (1988: 216) observes, "The tradition of the left is realized . . . only and whenever the people are making their own history, not when history is being made in their name or with their consent. Thus, the representational mode, however necessary it may be at a given historical juncture, cannot be the defining strategy of leftists if they mean to achieve in history what they say they are about." In addition, true democracy refers to the structuring of power in a *society,* not just in a *government.* Representative government, by itself, is not full democracy.

Activists, too, recognize that politics—the social organization of power—is a battle fought not only in governmental arenas but in more immediate social and cultural spheres as well. Accordingly, the left vision goes well beyond the strict confines of electoral politics and government structures. The personal *is* political. The organization of "private" life has significant political ramifications, whether it be the politics of the bedroom or the culture of consumption. Sociologists and political scientists have long been commenting on the erosion of distinction between "political" and "private" life that has led to a reconceptualization of politics.[3] The Left and the Right have related to this development in starkly different ways.

The neoconservative movements of the 1980s saw the state's overextension into the lives of individuals as the source of the emerging crisis of legitimacy of the state. The Right thus wishes to shore up the state's legitimacy by pulling in the government's tentacles. It wants to restore "private," nonpolitical spheres of life, such as the family, promote private school "choice" as an alternative to government schools, and protect private property and market rights from state intervention. (Again, some efforts by the Right are stark exceptions to this trend.)

The Left, by contrast, has also recognized the legitimacy problems of the state. One response has been to attempt to influence state policy by participating more actively in the electoral process and by running progressive candidates. But some left social movements have a different response. They argue that the premise that allowed for the equation of democracy with representative government no longer exists. As Arblaster (1987: 64) notes, "The belief that democracy meant government by the people, or at least by their accountable representatives, was premised on the assumption that governmental power was *the* power in society, that politics dominated over social and economic life, and that no factional power or interest group could successfully resist the legitimate might of the popular will." But power in contemporary society has in many cases escaped state control. That is, government is no longer *the* power in society. Multinational corporations are the clearest example, shuffling capital and jobs from country to country to elude government restrictions and exploit corporate-friendly environments.

While some argue that economic powers have grown so influential as to subvert efforts of governments, others have argued that power does not have a single base in the economy or politics but is instead diffuse, permeating society and taking different forms in different sites. As a result, political struggles must be carried out in the broader battleground of culture and society as a whole, not simply in the narrow confines of electoral politics. Some social movements have consequently focused on politicizing the institutions of social life or "civil society" rather than privileging the contest for state power. Such movements wish to reconstitute an independent, politicized, democratic civil society to act as a counterweight to state influence. While the Right wants to separate the state from social life, some on the left want to create democratic institutions that blur the line between government and the governed. In essence, the Left wants to socialize the state and politicize society.

One group of left movements that has pursued such a strategy are the so-called new social movements (as distinct from the "old" class-based labor movement) that are the focus of this work. Habermas's (1981: 33–34) very definition of new social movements is based on their existence as remaining fragments of civil society struggling against the institutionalized state and corporate structures. For Habermas, the tension between civil society and the state is sufficient to fuel discord, making it unnecessary to resort to a model of class conflict to explain political and social divisions. Thus, class takes on a much less significant role in New Movement theory than it has in the past. This new mode of diffuse conflict, according to Habermas, takes the form of the struggle between the overinstitutionalized "center" of society "composed of strata directly involved in the production process" (including state, corporations, media, political parties, military, and even unions) and the forces supposedly "on the periphery" that make up new social movements (women, people of color, environmentalists, peace activists, etc.).

But Habermas is misleading in his romanticized vision of the "peripheral" forces of new social movements. As Habermas (1981: 33) himself acknowledges, inspection of the actual participants in these movements reveals that they are not the inhabitants of "outsider groups" but are primarily "the new middle class, the younger generation, and those groups with higher levels of formal education." Dieter Rucht (1988: 317), for example, concludes that "the social cores of NSMs are neither socially marginal nor economically threatened."

The middle-class constituency of these left movements once again reminds us of a central dilemma of democracy and leads to an important question: Why is it that social movements that espouse a democratic philosophy of inclusive participation and that claim to speak on behalf of the disempowered on issues that are not class-specific have constituents that are overwhelmingly from middle-class backgrounds?

The question is an important one because the relative nonparticipation of the working class in NSMs contradicts the Left's core philosophy of broad democratic participation. Progressive left movements have positioned themselves as the voice of the disadvantaged and disenfranchised, those who are locked out of meaningful political participation. But as with many earlier experiments in democracy, there is a gap between the Left's rhetoric and the fundamental fact that the vast majority of the NSM Left is middle class, while the majority of Americans are working class.

In the past, the Left has sometimes tried to theorize itself out of this dilemma. In the 1960s when the student and antiwar movements found themselves with little visible working-class support, segments of the movement simply adopted a reformulated notion of working class and claimed that *they* were the "new working class." Those in the privileged halls of academia were producing tracts that painted students as the oppressed victims of a changing society. Some envisioned students as workers in the intellectual factories of university life, while others saw *The Student as Nigger* (Farber 1969), as one popular work was titled.

Another strategy for dealing with the lack of working-class participation in left movements has been to simply assert that class is no longer a significant cleavage in contemporary society. Instead, some theorize, new forms of "identity politics" have largely displaced class as the basis of significant social-change efforts. Such an approach undergirds much NSM theory. Women, people of color, lesbians and gays, environmentalists, and peace activists all make up segments of such "new social movements" that are, in part, defined by their formation around supraclass issues. While these movements have served as a needed corrective to a class-based politics that too often had been only white and male, the rise of NSMs has led some to see class as archaic and increasingly irrelevant to progressive concerns. But rather than overcoming "outdated" class identities, middle-class new social movements have, in fact, organized themselves along a new class cleavage that separates them from the "old" working class. Theoretical reports of the death of class have, in reality, been greatly exaggerated.

Conclusion

The question of working-class nonparticipation should be of vital interest to progressive social movements, but it should also be of concern to anyone interested in the reinvigoration of American political life. As long as working people are largely nonparticipants in our political system, American democracy will remain a mirage whose legitimacy is, at best, in question. Societies with stark differential class participation will never produce justice.

The Left's vision of democratic participation has not been adequate in overcoming the appeal of the Right's advancement of a more limited vision of liberty. In the end, we must admit that we have yet to create a truly democratic society. Perhaps more surprisingly, we must also admit that the new-social-movement Left has largely failed to create organizations that can reach out beyond their middle-class base.

In order to understand why working people by and large do not participate politically, especially in left movements, it is necessary to better understand how working people relate to the world of politics more broadly. It is also important not just to ask what's "wrong" with working people for not participating in left politics, but to ask what might be "wrong" with the political system and with what left movements are doing—or not doing—that makes democratic participation unattractive to working people. As the next chapter suggests, the current state of affairs has not always existed.

CHAPTER 2

The Changing Face
of Social Movements

*To generations of radicals, the working class has been the
bearer of socialism, the agent of both progressive social
reform and revolution. But in the United States in the last
two decades, the left has been concentrated most heavily
among people who feel themselves to be "middle-class,"
while the working class has appeared relatively quiescent.
This "middle-class" left . . . is not a minority within a
mass working class (or peasant) movement; it is,
to a very large extent, the left itself.*

BARBARA AND JOHN EHRENREICH,
The Professional-Managerial Class

By and large, U.S. movements for social change in the late twentieth century do
not carry a union label. Attacked from both the private and public sectors,
unions have been unable to hold on to their former gains, let alone expand their
efforts. Even relatively high-paid industrial workers, who at one time represented a sort of working-class aristocracy, have seen the "deindustrialization"
of America pull the economic rug out from under them. Led, ironically, by the
first former labor union president ever to inhabit the White House, the assault
on organized labor in the 1980s (which actually was well under way with
Carter's deregulation policies) took a dramatic toll on already moribund
unions that had failed to make significant inroads with women and workers of
color who, in recent decades, heavily populated the growing service and "pink
collar" job sectors.

Unions have been unable or unwilling to adapt to a changing economy and
changing work force. But the seeds of labor's decline were planted long before
the economic and political changes of the 1970s and 1980s. In a post–World
War II compromise with management, unions largely gave up their broader
social vision in exchange for corporate recognition of their right to exist, and

for higher wages and benefits for their members. The security and stability of this arrangement brought relative prosperity to the largely male industrial and craft workers who benefited from it. But the benefits for this section of the working class continued only as long as the postwar economic growth continued and only as long as corporate America stuck to its end of the bargain. Both of those conditions changed in the 1970s and 1980s.

As jobs were lost in the industrial sector, the well-established unions located primarily in these basic industries could no longer be relied upon to sustain the labor movement. In 1980, 23 percent of the U.S. work force belonged to a union. By 1992, that percentage had dropped to 16.1. In the private sector, unions are even weaker, representing just 11.9 percent of workers.[1] In the 1980s, goods-producing, private-sector unionization rates fell a full third, from 30.5 percent in 1980 to 20.4 percent in 1989. The extent of the hemorrhaging of overall union membership has been obscured by growth in membership amongst the public sector. From 1980 to 1989, the percentage of unionized workers in the American private sector fell from 20.1 to 12.4 percent while the percentage of unionized government workers increased slightly from 35.9 to 36.7 percent. In 1980, government employees made up 28.7 percent of all union members (up from 17.5 percent in 1968), but by 1989 they made up a full 37.9 percent (Chaison and Rose 1991: 15). More than a third of union salaries, then, are paid for by taxpayer money.

Declining union membership has translated into declining influence. Encouraging signs of fledgling union democracy movements, such as the UAW's New Directions, or the Teamsters for a Democratic Union, have come in part from a recognition of the failure of traditional unionism in a changing economic and political climate. The weakness of unions has prevented even progressive factions from effectively taking the lead in addressing contemporary issues of economic and social justice. Instead, the most prominent banners of social change have been passed on to a different and diverse group of "new social movements."

In this chapter, by considering the changing nature of the social movement terrain, I briefly explore how this complex state of affairs came into being. I will argue that the decline of organized labor does not mean that class becomes irrelevant for understanding contemporary social movements. Instead, although the class compositions of today's movements are different from those that characterized the class struggles of the past, the importance of class as an issue that affects political participation remains.

The Left and Working-People's Movements

The rise of new social movements is by no means a clear and sharp rupture in the history of the Left. The lines are blurred between "old" and "new" social movements, and clearly, both kinds continue to exist. But some broad generalizations can be made that suggest a change of direction, character, and class composition in major social movements.

Though often receiving support and key leadership from the middle class, most of the major social movements of the last century—until the late 1950s—were composed largely of working and poor people who were responding to the onerous conditions of industrial capitalism.[2] While important movements based on race, gender, and issues such as antimilitarism existed, for nearly a century the highly visible Left was virtually synonymous with worker movements. The clearest involvement of working people occurred, of course, in the labor movement itself, but working people have also played a central role in other movements.[3]

The Labor Movement

The United States began its second century with what became known as the "Great Uprising of 1877" (Foner 1977). In that year, the presidents of the nation's four largest railroads announced pay cuts for their employees. Although only one in a series, this particular cut led to a spontaneous strike at the B&O yards in Martinsburg, Virginia, that spread into a national strike affecting fourteen states from coast to coast and that, at its height, stopped fully half of the nation's rail freight. The following two weeks of confrontations between strikers and the troops who were called to "restore order" left over a hundred people dead, a thousand in jails, and millions of dollars worth of property destroyed. The Great Uprising was "the first truly national strike in American history and the first in which the federal government had placed its full power (in the form of the army) on the side of business" (American Social History Project [ASHP] 1992: xxviii). The Uprising shocked Americans into realizing that the United States would not escape the kinds of class conflict that had plagued Europe since the birth of industrial capitalism. But the limited gains of the strikers also showed working people that "they were not united enough, not powerful enough, to defeat the combination of private capital and government power (Zinn 1980: 246)."

Class-based conflict continued to be the hallmark of American politics for many years. Although the labor movement has taken different forms, they have all centered on the struggles of working people for a better standard of living and for more social, political, and economic rights. But as with the history of democracy, the history of the labor movement has included much debate about who should be included. The early Federation of Organized Trades and Labor Unions was concerned with only skilled workers and at its peak in 1886 included only 3 percent of nonagricultural workers. The Knights of Labor received broad-based support by calling for an organization to bring together all workers, regardless of skill, race, or nationality. Although never totally free of discriminatory practices, the Knights became the home of immigrant factory workers, southern blacks, and women (but it retained blatantly racist policies towards Chinese workers). It mobilized, for example, for equal pay and equal rights for women and had both all-black and integrated local assemblies. By 1886, nearly 10 percent of nonagricultural workers were members of the Knights, by far the highest percentage for an American union up to that time (ASHP 1992: 118).

The Knights, along with the craft unions, were at the center of a series of strikes and boycotts in 1886 that became known as the "Great Upheaval." In that year, over fifteen hundred strikes took place nationwide, many of them calling for a standard eight-hour work day, and various labor-based parties won seats as mayors, aldermen, and school board officials in over two hundred cities and towns.

Employers responded to the workers' uprising with a counteroffensive that included firing and blacklisting union members, using the courts to break strikes and limit the rights of workers, and enlisting the growing Pinkerton Detective Agency to infiltrate and attack unions. In the wake of this repression national unions began to constrict their vision of their role as labor unions. A new alliance of independent national unions, the American Federation of Labor (AFL), was formed under the leadership of Samuel Gompers.

What was unique about the AFL was that it practiced "business union-ism," avoiding involvement in broad-based political movements, and tacitly accepting capitalism and the political and social status quo. In contrast to the Knights' broad social vision, the AFL concentrated on organizing skilled workers by establishing exclusive rights to a specific craft and by controlling large strike funds that were developed from high membership dues. It also focused on collective bargaining as a strategy for winning better pay and conditions. But by its exclusionary practices, the AFL represented a step back for the breadth of participation in the labor movement.

The ensuing years saw numerous efforts to broaden labor's constituency once more. The United Mine Workers created an effective, racially integrated organization in the 1890s. The American Railway Union, under the leadership of Eugene Debs, was open to railway workers of all skills (but black workers were not allowed to join).

Between 1905 and 1917 semi- and unskilled workers took the lead in fighting for greater rights. In 1905, Debs joined others in forming the Industrial Workers of the World (IWW, or Wobblies). Unlike many socialists, the IWW was syndicalist, believing that radical economic and social change would come from a revolutionary union, not a working-class political party. The Wobblies were committed to organizing the most impoverished of workers, who were often left out of other unions, and its belief in "one big union" made it open to everyone including women and workers of all races. The IWW headed such famous struggles as the 1912 "Bread and Roses" textile strike in Lawrence, Massachusetts, and the 1913 silk mill strikes in Paterson, New Jersey, signaling the growing importance of semiskilled workers to the labor movement.

Workers were having an impact in the electoral realm as well. In 1911, the

Socialist Party won seventy-three mayoral seats and twelve hundred other offices in nearly 350 cities and towns across the country (ASHP 1992: 191).

Mobilization for World War I deeply divided the labor movement. The government rewarded unions that supported the war—like Gompers's AFL—and repressed those that did not—especially the IWW. In the 1920s, workers experienced a slow rise in their standard of living but a significant loss of control in the workplace as employers introduced changes based on Taylorist principles. The downturn in workers' fortunes reached epidemic proportions with the Great Depression. By 1933 nearly a third of the nation's labor force was unemployed. Union membership had plummeted to less than 10 percent of the workforce, about three million workers (ASHP 1992: 319, 355).

With help from Section 7a of the National Industrial Recovery Act (1933), which affirmed—at least in theory—that workers had the right to organize and bargain collectively through their own representatives, union organization grew immensely. In 1935 the Wagner Act was passed, affirming the right of workers to select a union by majority vote, the right to strike, boycott, and picket, and it identified unfair labor practices, including establishing company unions, arbitrarily dismissing union activists, blacklisting, and employing spies. The act, though, exempted agricultural and domestic workers, the majority of whom were women and workers of color.

A series of dramatic actions in 1934, including the first sit-down strike, which took place at the Akron rubber factories, showed that many workers were ready to be organized on a broad industrial basis, despite the AFL's reluctance to reach beyond highly skilled, relatively well-paid, white, male workers. In 1935, the UMWA's John L. Lewis led an effort to begin organizing by industry, not by craft. Along with the heads of the International Ladies Garment Workers Union (ILGWU), the Amalgamated Clothing Workers Union (ACWU), and others, Lewis formed the Committee for Industrial Organization within the AFL. The move met with disapproval from AFL leaders, who demanded the new committee be dissolved. When the committee refused, the member unions were expelled from the AFL. In the next few years, after a slow start, the newly dubbed Congress of Industrial Organizations (CIO) went on to organize workers who had been shunned by the AFL. The CIO launched dramatic drives among auto, steel, rubber, meatpacking, textile, trucking, and dock workers in what is often considered the heyday of the labor movement. In 1937, 4.7 million workers took part in strike actions. The CIO had 3.7 million members, and the AFL had grown to over 7 million. But the growth would not last. A new economic downturn and a renewed antiunion effort on the part of industry marked another period of stagnation for the movement.

World War II resulted in another labor shortage. But Roosevelt used the need for national preparedness to team up with conservative labor leaders in containing labor unrest. Most labor leaders agreed to a "no strike pledge" for the duration of the war. Ironically, this made union membership less attractive to workers, since it was unclear what benefit they would receive by joining.

Membership began dropping. The War Labor Board, which liked the stability created by the no-strike pledge, intervened to virtually require that all workers in unionized factories had to join the union. Consequently, as war production grew, so did union membership, by almost 50 percent to 15 million workers. By 1943 wartime production demands, coupled with the siphoning off of workers through the draft, resulted in virtual full employment. Wages increased substantially, and the availability of virtually limitless overtime work meant that workers' paychecks were much larger.

But higher wages did not compensate for the increased encroachment of management as they set higher production standards and piece rates and disciplined employees without fear of union response. The result was a steady increase of small wildcat job actions in defiance of union leadership.

The peak of labor activity, however, occurred in 1946 as the postwar economy generated waves of inflation that combined with reduced working hours to slash workers' real income. More strikes took place in 1946 than in any other year, with the exception of 1919. But the strikes produced mixed results for labor. In contrast to its policy during prewar strikes, industry now readily agreed to negotiate with unions and provided some wage increases. But it also demanded, and won, contract clauses that established management's rights to set production standards and limit the influence of union stewards.

The increasingly hostile environment of post–New Deal Washington was made clear by the 1947 Taft-Hartley Act, which stripped foremen of Wagner Act protections, made sympathy strikes and boycotts more difficult, and allowed states to ban union shops. In a clause that reflected the new Cold War obsession, it also required unions to renounce communism in order to take part in NLRB elections.

The communist hysteria helped to tear the labor movement apart. The recent war, coupled with the growing number of workers who were third-generation Americans, resulted in much stronger worker identification as "patriotic" Americans. Radical critiques of this country, as propagated by socialists and communists, came increasingly to be seen as distinctly "un-American" in the context of growing anti-immigrant sentiment. Unions began ejecting communists from their ranks. The CIO expelled nine unions totaling nine hundred thousand workers in order to distance themselves from communist organizers. Anticommunism was an instrumental force in transforming unions from organizations that pursued broad social goals into groups that worked for a much narrower and limited set of goals.

The growing economic pie in the postwar boom years virtually silenced the call for the redistribution of wealth. Distribution remained the same, but most white workers were enjoying standard of living increases. (The exclusion of black prosperity in this period was an important element of the rise of the civil rights movement.) This overall growth in prosperity resulted in an important labor-management compact. Companies dealing with a unionized work force guaranteed good wages to established unions and protected their right to exist.

In return, unions largely abandoned attempts to influence the organization of production and the business strategies of corporations. They also abandoned larger political and social goals in favor of narrow business unionism.

The new accommodation meant a decline of activism and democratic participation in unions because grievances were now handled through established channels, collective-bargain agreements resulted in contracts of longer duration, and union officials took on the role of "policing" contracts and preventing wildcat strikes. The new accommodationist spirit was exemplified by the 1955 merger of the AFL and CIO, who, with the CIO's abandonment of a broader social vision, found themselves with few substantive political differences. The AFL's membership was nearly double that of the CIO, and its more accommodationist approach prevailed.

The AFL-CIO merger marked the symbolic end of labor unions as broad social movements and signaled their reconstitution as special-interest groups that held a junior partnership in the newly formed labor-management accord. National unions no longer represented a movement with the powerfully unique characteristics of both a broad social vision and a working-class constituency. Although there have always been union activists and particular unions that have kept the flame of social change alive, after the 1950s the main impetus for broad social change would no longer come from the national labor movement but from a host of newly developing social movements. With the economic and political changes of the last two decades, even unions' narrow gains in wages and benefits have been drastically eroded.

Populists

During the labor movement's struggle, other social movements developed that featured significant working-class participation. In the 1890s, labor was temporarily eclipsed by what became known as the "Populist" movement. The Populists were rooted in the Farmer's Alliance, which had been formed by farmers to buy and sell cooperatively in large scale. Buying and selling thus meant farmers were able to avoid the exorbitant interest charges of local merchants and to manage the high costs of the increasingly centralized transportation system. The cooperation developed through these efforts led to a populist explosion in the South and West that included the establishment of more than a thousand populist newspapers, an extensive lecture circuit, and numerous revival-like encampments. When banks began refusing credit for their efforts, the Alliance entered the political arena in an attempt to change government policy.

The Alliance, however, had naturally appealed mostly to landowners, and it excluded African Americans, who developed their own Colored Farmer's Alliance. Still, the Farmer's Alliance entered politics in 1890 in a major way, electing four governors, more than forty congressmen, and taking control of eight state legislatures. In 1892 the resulting People's Party—more commonly known as the Populists—was formalized in what some call "the last truly serious challenge to the two-party system in American political history" (Boyte 1989: 30).

Although farmers were the focus of the effort of the Populists, their party platform included the call for direct election of U.S. senators (who were still elected by state legislatures), a single-term limitation for the president, and the availability of initiative and referendum efforts to ensure democratic participation. Significantly for workers, it also advocated a shorter working day and called for a restriction on immigration (ASHP 1992: 148).

After only modest success in 1892, the Populists garnered a 50 percent increase in support in 1894, to 1.5 million votes. But the strength of the party lay overwhelmingly in rural votes, and it failed to reach significant numbers of urban workers whose disgust with the Democratic Party for ignoring worker concerns led many, instead, to vote Republican. The AFL had refused to give the Populists much support, but the high Republican vote amongst workers led to an intense internal debate regarding the AFL's possible adoption of a socialist program that would bring together workers and farmers. But Gompers and his allies prevailed, and their vision of business unionism remained intact. Meanwhile, in 1896, the Populists were outmaneuvered by the Democrats who adopted the call for free coinage of silver with William Jennings Bryan's delivery of his famous "Cross of Gold" speech. The Populists crumbled in the face of the co-optation of their favorite issue.

Progressives and the Women's Movement

Militant labor struggles such as the UMWA's 1914 strike against John D. Rockefeller's Colorado Fuel and Iron Company, which resulted in the infamous Ludlow massacre, and the tragic 1911 Triangle Shirtwaist Company fire on New York's Lower East Side, helped to bring together working people and middle-class reformers who were convinced that regulation of industrial capitalism was necessary. The so-called Progressives of the early 1900s were most often drawn from the white, Protestant middle class and included alliances among members of the newly emerging "professional" class. But the concerns of Progressives were the result of the efforts and plight of working people. Progressives, however, saw the problems of workers as arising, not from industrial capitalism per se, but from the chaotic manner in which it developed. The Progressive movement in the Midwest teamed up with unions to open the political process to the working class. Together, they supported direct primaries for candidates, the establishment of citizen-sponsored initiatives and referendums, and the popular election of U.S. senators (issues that had been promoted earlier by the Populists).

But the Progressive movement in the South and on the East Coast was dominated by businesspeople and professional elites. Their goals were to make government more efficient through the dismantling of local party machines. Rather than struggle on behalf of workers, these Progressives saw workers as part of the problem. They organized to introduce "expertise" into government via city managers and city commissions, thus undermining the power of working-class communities.

During these same years, the women's movement was also shaped by class conflict. Along with its support for equal pay for women, the Knights of Labor had championed the cause of suffrage for women in the 1880s. The movement for women's right to vote, however, was conducted largely by middle-class women. Some, most notably Elizabeth Cady Stanton and Susan B. Anthony, saw labor issues such as the eight-hour day as being an integral part of the struggle for women's rights. Most, though, did not incorporate into their vision the concerns of wage-earning women. By 1890, this more narrowly formulated women's movement had pushed to the background the more inclusive vision of Stanton and Anthony, and as a consequence the movement was stagnating. In the late 1880s through the early 1900s, middle-class feminists would come into contact with working women through the "settlement house" movement associated with the Progressive era. These reformers worked to support striking women shirtwaistmakers in 1909, and, in turn, working women began marching in suffrage parades, bringing new life to the suffrage movement.

The varied coalitions produced by the Progressive era did help to bring some needed reform, such as laws regulating child labor and maximum hours for women workers, although these reforms applied to only a small percentage of workers. Still, the movement was significant in establishing a role for government in economic and social affairs. The Progressives, however, were overwhelmed by the powerful conservative efforts unleashed to produce a consensus for war (ASHP 1992: 246).

The Limits of Labor's Vision and the Rise of the Civil Rights Movement

While the important legacy of labor needs to be remembered, we should do well to also recall that union struggles in this country were often carried out on behalf of a minority of workers and were always carried out by a small percentage of workers. The strategic differences between craft versus industrial unions marked an important dividing line in the labor movement. But even more important were the millions of workers largely left out of most unions' vision. With important exceptions, women and workers of color were almost never afforded equal status within the labor movement. They were sometimes banned from inclusion in unions, or else they faced discrimination much as they did in broader society.

However, the union movement benefited more than just union members. The rising wages and improved working conditions resulting from union efforts often had a spillover effect into nonunion workplaces as, ironically, employers met some worker demands in order to stave off the introduction of full-fledged unions. Union political power exerted to influence legislation affecting workplaces could also impact workers well beyond actual union membership. Women and people of color outside of unions, therefore, often benefited indirectly from union victories. Also, barriers to greater participation in unions were lowered somewhat as women and people of color gained greater freedoms in society as a whole.

This was little consolation, though, for African Americans, some of whom had fought in World War II and had experienced a desegregated Europe. The civil rights movement of the 1950s and 1960s, which drew upon tactics developed during the earlier labor struggles, marks the most recent major social movement that was carried out primarily by working-class Americans. Though clearly civil rights leaders such as Martin Luther King were quintessential middle-class spokespeople, the rank and file of the movement was made up overwhelmingly of working people, the vast majority of whom were not part of any labor organization.

The civil rights movement, however, was also a watershed in the development of social movements. It was in many ways a transition between the "old" social movements based in the working class and the "new" social movements of subsequent years (Eyerman and Jamison 1991: 6). It pointed the way for a shift from primarily class-based politics to movements based on other social cleavages that were not being adequately addressed by labor. Clearly, as the early women's movement shows, this was not the first time a movement was based on something other than class. However, the civil rights movement marked the turning point for the ascendancy of ostensibly supraclass movements. The most prominent movements between the 1870s and the 1950s were responses to the development of industrial capitalism and were largely carried out on behalf of a particular class, the working class. The labor movement, the Populist movement, and the Progressives were all reacting to economic and social conditions that were directly related to issues of production. They often were attempts at bringing the fruits of increased productivity to a wider circle of people. The emphasis was on the reorganization and control of the production process, increasingly through government intervention, as a solution to the economic and social ills facing working people of the day.

By the 1950s, however, the labor movement had given up its attempt to fundamentally reorganize and control the direction of production and instead was content to let its existing members ride the wave of postwar prosperity. Perhaps labor's last significant attempt at influencing the direction of production occurred in the immediate aftermath of World War II, when the CIO tried to convince government to convert federally owned war-production facilities into plants for the manufacture of low-cost housing. In a sign of things to come, Washington instead sold the taxpayer-financed plants to major corporations at bargain-basement prices. Subsequently, as a result of labor's circumscribed social vision and changing economic conditions, unions would no longer lead in efforts for progressive social change.

In the past few decades, left social movements in the United States have changed in character and substance. Their areas of concern have shifted away from the workplace and working-class issues, and their membership is no longer drawn primarily from the working classes. The labor movement, which formed the heart of the left project for nearly a century, has been eclipsed by a constellation of movements that have come to be known as "new social movements."

New Social Movements: Why New? Why Now?

It would be a mistake to consider NSMs as a consistent monolithic block. In fact both the movements and the theories developed to explain them span a wide range. Some have even argued that there really is nothing "new" about "new social movements" at all (D'Anieri, Ernst, and Keir 1990; Fuentes and Frank 1989; Huber 1989). However, nearly all observers recognize something different in the notion of new social movements. As Timothy Luke (1989: 207–8) puts it, "Most observers cannot define what a new social movement is, but they seem to know one when they see one." On the left, the environmental movement, the women's movement, race-based movements, the peace movement and anti-intervention movements, the antinuclear movement, and the movement for lesbian and gay rights generally are seen as among the core of what are identified as new social movements.

The tasks remain, however, of describing the common characteristics that hold such disparate movements together and of suggesting the sources of their identity that are distinct from those in the labor movement. What follows is a brief sketch of these characteristics. As Rucht (1988: 307) notes, "If we use the term NSMs as an analytical concept, we should not forget that empirically there are considerable differences between the various groups and movements." Thus, the discussion that follows is a description of NSMs that would not elicit agreement from all theorists, nor would it completely describe the variety of movements that sometime fall under the NSM label. It does, however, highlight what many theorists see as some of the central features of NSMs.[4] In drawing such a sketch, I will emphasize five dimensions that are used in distinguishing between "old" and "new" social movements: (1) structural sources, (2) form and actions, (3) issues and goals, (4) values, and (5) agents.

Structural Sources

It is ironic that some theorists rely on a distinctly old method of analysis for explaining the emergence of new social movements. These theorists see NSMs as arising in response to new grievances that develop from the structural strains of contemporary postindustrial society. The issue of why people mobilize had been underemphasized by resource-mobilization theory, which took for granted the existence of shared grievances. Drawing from the work of Durkheim, earlier collective behaviorists, though, had emphasized structural strains as the source of social movements.[5] For NSM theorists, however, the passing of modernity and the emergence of a postmodern condition serve as the structural catalysts for the new movements that emphasize different social cleavages.

The eighteenth century was the origin of what Habermas (1983) calls the "project of modernity." Although amorphous in nature, modernity is "generally perceived as positivistic, technocentric, and rationalistic." It "has been identified with the belief in linear progress, absolute truths, the rational planning of ideal social orders, and the standardization of knowledge and production" (in Harvey 1989: 9). Modernity was characterized by the endless destruction of old methods of thinking and organizing life. For Marx, this perpetual upheaval was one of the great achievements of the bourgeoisie since it allowed for the liberation of human capacity and encouraged the drive for development. After centuries of slow evolution, industrial forces and new ways of thinking were changing the world at an unprecedented pace.

The development of both scientific knowledge and of industrialism held out the promise of material abundance and the elimination of want through the scientific domination of nature. Labor-based social movements, which formed the core of the Left in the period of modernity, generally accepted the notion that continued economic growth was necessary for the inclusion of ever growing numbers of people in the fruits of industrial progress. Accordingly, class concerns, as played out through the production and distribution of material goods, were the central focus of these movements.

As a result of continued productive growth and the success of labor-based movements, some parts of labor-based social-reform programs were incorporated within the ever growing welfare state, itself a unique feature of modernity. The welfare state's mildly redistributive policies helped to mediate between the disparities of rich and poor, and ongoing economic growth allowed for the inclusion of ever growing numbers of people in the developing postwar consumer society.

The postwar compact between labor and capital relied upon state intervention and the institutionalized and bureaucratized welfare state. Although necessary for the functioning of such a system, these mechanisms created problems of their own. Growing interest in the regulation of consumption and social relations resulted in more direct intervention into citizens' lives in the form of new laws and regulations and in the levying of a heavier tax burden. NSMs are, in part, a response to the resulting encroachment of centralized bureaucratic institutions on the life spaces of individuals and local communities.

NSMs are also responding to economic changes—but in a way that differs from the labor movement. The scale of economies has changed dramatically in the postindustrial period, resulting in "global" or "supranational" economies. Such a development "weakens the nation-state's ability to control its own economic destiny, and this produces a public impatience with other countries that reveals itself in a growing political nationalism and support for protectionist economic policies" (Wachtel 1986: 15). This growing nationalism and the related issues of militarism provide yet further territory on which NSMs stake a claim.

Sometimes these new claims come into direct conflict with the labor movement. For example, the growth of the military-industrial complex served as a Keynesian device for government intervention in the economy while at the same time avoiding state-sponsored competition in the field of consumer goods. The result was millions of government-sponsored, good-paying, and usually union jobs. The costs, however, eventually included a world bristling with more than fifty thousand nuclear weapons (with resulting nuclear waste) and a system of "Pentagon capitalism" that resulted in a "permanent war economy" (Melman 1970, 1974). For five decades, this war economy has siphoned national resources away from meeting the society's needs for better housing, transportation, and other infrastructure development towards the most costly stockpiling of redundant weaponry the earth has ever seen. Thus, a single institutional arrangement was, in a narrow sense, meeting the needs of "old" labor-based movements for good-paying, secure employment while opening the door to the creation of new grievances from environmentalists, peace activists, and other critics of military spending.

Thus, in the last few decades, a whole host of changes, primarily in the economic and technological structuring of societies, has created new conditions that are not centrally addressed by the labor movement and which consequently serve as fertile ground for "new social movements."

These structural changes have also contributed to the decline of organized labor and, consequently, to the erosion of an active working-class culture. The postwar compact between industry and labor resulted in a comfortable and stagnant labor movement: comfortable in the sense that it provided good wages and benefits for those (often white, male workers) who belonged; stagnant in the sense that labor "success" often resulted in a bloated bureaucratic organization that responded too slowly, if at all, to the changing economic climate, and as a result failed to evolve with the growing service sector and the changing race and gender composition of the work force.

The stagnation and decline of unions also meant the loss of an indigenous political infrastructure for working people. Working people no longer looked to unions as a source of political or cultural support. The local union hall that had at one time served as a focal point of community activities for many became increasingly irrelevant to workers' lives. Union membership became a sort of insurance policy, with union dues "paying off" in higher wages and benefits, but requiring no further participation on the part of the rank and file. The higher wages provided to members allowed many to move away from urban, working-class neighborhoods to the suburbs and join in mass consumer culture. The union-sponsored libraries, dances, writing contests, and other cultural events that once marked the union local as the hub of working-class activity were replaced as working-class neighborhoods crumbled and mass privatized culture, especially television, became widely available.

The structural changes, then, that facilitated the rise of NSMs simultaneously contributed to the decline of a vibrant working-class culture.

Issues and Goals

The old social movements were primarily concerned with the issues of economic growth and material distribution. As noted above, the labor movement made a strategic decision not to pursue a broader agenda in order to maintain the postwar management-labor accord. But, "unlike their nineteenth-century counterparts, contemporary social movements are not preoccupied with struggles over the production and distribution of material goods and resources" (Keane and Mier 1989: 5). In fact, many new movements reject the premise of growth that is at the heart of the postwar compromise between labor and capital. The agenda of new social movements is therefore largely devoid of production issues but filled with "quality of life" issues.

NSM theory critiques Marxism for failing, as Boggs (1986: 59) puts it, "to confront the problem of domination in its multiple forms." Instead, NSM theory favors the recognition of multiple sites of economic, political, and cultural struggle. The multiple orientations of new social movements are said to reflect the fragmentation of power and resistance in postmodern societies. Melucci (1980: 217) notes, "In comparison with the industrial phase of capitalism, the production characteristic of advanced societies requires that control reach beyond the productive structure into the areas of consumption, services, and social relations." Foucault (1972) has produced the best-known articulation of this position, arguing that the connection between power and knowledge is fundamental. Power is exerted beginning with the "infinitesimal mechanisms" of daily life. Rather than identify any single source of power, Foucault argues for an analysis that reveals the multiple "discourses," or systems of knowledge, that codify specialized techniques and practices in order to exert power, control, and domination within particular arenas. These multiple sites of domination cannot be connected by some overarching analysis of power, such as Marxism. Instead, the human body serves as the only constant within these arenas because it is the ultimate site toward which social control is directed.

As Harvey (1989: 9) observes, postmodernism signals a "rejection of 'meta-narratives' (large-scale theoretical interpretations purportedly of universal application)." Thus, the Marxist contention that class conflict is the single engine of history is rejected in favor of multiple analyses adapted for particular and varied contexts. There is no longer a sense that some single cleavage has primacy over others. Consequently, whereas old social movements were recognized as being "class movements" aimed at gaining power or benefits for a particular group of people who shared a similar economic status, new social movements are often said to be "universal movements" that claim that nearly everyone will benefit if their goals are achieved.

Foucault's pessimism at ever escaping the power-knowledge relation echoes Weber's own belief in humanity's inability to escape the "iron cage" of repressive bureaucratic-technical rationality. For Foucault, however, there are "no relations of power without resistances." However, any challenge to the existing order needs to be carried out in separate and multifaceted ways, without resorting to any single tactic or agent. In addition, the important link between power and knowledge and the multiple discourses of which Foucault speaks argues for the emergence of culture as a site of contention.

The result is a plethora of social movements, each addressing one or more of a variety of issues. Central among these issues are the development and affirmation of identity and autonomy. Melucci (1980: 219) writes, "Sexuality and the body, leisure, consumer goods, one's relationship to nature—these are no longer loci of private rewards but areas of collective resistance, of demands for expression and pleasure which are raised in opposition to the instrumental rationality of the apparatuses of order."

Melucci (1988: 342) argues that the central task of new social movements has become the development of collective identity. Thus, collective identity serves as a connection between the individual and the social and political world. It also signals the "requirements" for belonging to a social-movement collective. Or as Friedman and McAdam (1992: 157) put it, "The collective identity of a social movement organization (SMO) is a shorthand designation announcing a status—a set of attitudes, commitments, and rules for behavior—that those who assume the identity can be expected to subscribe to."

Melucci contends that earlier resource-mobilization theory is limited in that it assumes the existence of a collective identity, rather than explaining the process of constructing this identity. According to Melucci (1989: 73) the necessity of developing a collective identity is one of the characteristics that makes these movements "new." For movement participants, developing a collective identity involves a negotiation of who "we" are by creating new social identities linked to efforts for change.

The development of collective identity is all the more important, according to Melucci (1989: 89), because class is no longer a central defining characteristic. During industrial capitalism, "there was a close correspondence between the position occupied within productive relations and the cultures of the various social groups." For Melucci, the modernization of complex societies has severed this connection between class and cultural identity, leaving open the opportunity for the development of new forms of collective identity. The main agents in new social movements, according to Melucci (1989: 185), "are no longer groups defined by class consciousness, religious affiliation or ethnicity, but—potentially at least—individuals who strive to individuate themselves by participating in, and giving meaning to, various forms of social action."

But such an analysis is not complete. There are other issues that have contributed to the decline of class-based political identity. For example, Melucci tends to downplay the political repression that, especially in the American context, was an important factor in the decline of working-class political movements (Sexton 1991). His claims, too, are overly broad. For example, ethnicity continues to be a fundamentally divisive issue in both European and American society. In addition, a subset of working people has always developed a sense of collective identity from involvement in the labor movement. This is not a unique feature of "new" movements. However, new social movements can serve as a space for the emergence of new identities *within the white middle class*—and joining an activist community associated with an NSM becomes, in part, an end in itself.

Changing issues and goals have also meant that in many cases resistance actions aimed at creating free spaces in civil society have become more important than a struggle for state power. Cohen (1985: 670) argues that in NSMs "democratically structured associations and public spaces, a plurality of types of political actors and action within *civil society*, are viewed as ends in themselves."

Ironically, for many working people, the labor movement once served as just such a public space providing a base for political action and serving as a cultural resource and support network. What NSMs sometimes seem to be struggling to achieve for their members is, in part, the role that unions once served for workers.

Values

New social movements also represent a departure from the old movements' emphasis on freedom and security through private consumption and material progress. The new values found within NSMs amount to what Inglehart (1977) has called a "silent revolution" in changing values and styles that form the basis for the pursuit of new issues and goals described above.

Despite the rapid changes of modernity, NSM theorists argue that "Only in the postwar years have the old, traditional bonds tying people to their immediate social environment been severed completely; only quite recently have people really been freed from traditional ties of class, religion, and family (Kriesi 1988: 356)." Some of these changes have occurred because of the physical changes that have marked contemporary life. Social needs that used to be met by networks of family and neighbors who lived in one area for long periods of time have now often become commercialized as people move more frequently and come to rely on commercial services for babysitting, for home and auto repairs, and even for counseling. The market economy has in many ways become the market society.

The severance from traditional bonds and communities, therefore, has not necessarily produced new autonomy. Instead, it has resulted in renewed dependence on institutional structures for support and has created, for some, a vacuum in identities. Consequently, the new values espoused by NSMs include a renewed emphasis on the importance of personal autonomy and the development of identity, with some NSMs organized primarily around "lifestyle" issues.

The environmental movement, for example, emphasizes a need for *reduced* consumer demand and for changes in consumer lifestyles. Thus, production is measured in terms of the quality and utility of goods instead of merely the quantity, resulting in an emphasis on "natural" products and "environment-friendly" consumer goods. Ironically, identification with such lifestyle values has proven quite profitable for some companies that position themselves as producers of "natural" and alternative products.

In the area of social welfare, some NSMs reject the more traditional reliance on the state to meet social needs. Instead, they promote the establishment of cooperative or autonomous economic enclaves in the form of consumer cooperatives and community development corporations as a desirable alternative to the expansion of state programs. Such development represents a shift away from exclusive reliance upon government to address social needs and is indicative of strategies that often emphasize local and decentralized solutions.

Form and Actions

Melucci (1985: 801) contends that "The form of the movement is the message." The forms and actions of new social movements are significantly different than those that characterize "old" social movements. Old labor-based movements were usually large-scale formal organizations structured in highly rigid hierarchies, often with limited internal democracy. In recent decades, participation of organized labor in the political sphere has been achieved in large measure through established political parties.

Although variations exist, new social movements tend to be much less institutionalized. They are more informal and feature a relatively low degree of horizontal and vertical differentiation. Their involvement in politics tends to take the form of protest politics with a strong emphasis on negative actions, in other words, preventing or protesting policies and actions, rather than attempting to gain power. As Cohen (1985: 667) summarizes, "Instead of forming unions or political parties of the socialist, social democratic, or communist type, [NSMs] focus on grass-roots politics and create horizontal, directly democratic associations that are loosely federated on national levels."

Such structures do not provide for the stability, continuity, and resources available to unions. However, they do provide for a more flexible, responsive organization structure that often depends more on active member-participation for success than unions do.

Agents

New social movement theorists argue that with structural conditions and values shifting, it is not surprising to find that the actors involved in confrontations with power are also changing. Some observers argue that new social movements represent the emergence of new, middle-class actors (Gouldner 1979; Kriesi 1989). But most NSM theorists take a different approach.

Some new social movements organize people based on characteristics such as gender, race, or sexual orientation. Aronowitz (1992: 15) notes that as a result "the last two decades have been marked, in nearly all major countries of the late capitalist West, by a discernible decline in politics in which class, rather than race, gender, or ethnicity, was a crucial element."

Other movements are seen as exhibiting what Dieter Rucht (1988) calls "expressive logic," as opposed to more "instrumental logic," and thus develop and assert an identity through the process of participating in NSMs. Joining the activist community associated with a NSM becomes, in part, an end in itself.

Claus Offe (1985: 835) writes that the NSM pattern of social and political conflict moves beyond class conflict in that, first, conflict is not staged by one class but by alliances that cut across class lines; second, contemporary struggles are not carried out by the principal economic agents but by an alliance that excludes these principal classes; and third, demands are not class specific but rather are universal goods.

But merely claiming that the theoretical frame of a movement crosses class boundaries does not automatically make it so. As Offe (1985: 831) remarks, "the insistence upon the irrelevance of socioeconomic codes (such as class) and political codes (ideologies) that we find on the level of self-identification of new social movements (and often of their opponents), and which is part of their very 'newness' (and distinguishes them from 'old' social movements), by no means implies that the social base and political practice of these movements is in fact as amorphous and heterogeneous in class and ideological terms." A closer look at new social movements reveals that while participation may not be explicitly *on behalf* of a class, it clearly is conducted *by* a class. As Kriesi (1989: 1080) observes, the mobilization potential of new social movements "is primarily located in parts of the new middle class."

Aronowitz (1992: 34) argues that new social movement leadership is typically "drawn from the ranks of various strata of technical, scientific, and cultural intellectuals. . . . Even if many of the movements are situated, not at the workplace, but in the sphere of social and cultural life, of which consumption occupies considerable space, the emergence of these movements can hardly be separated from their social composition."

In fact, as I will elaborate below, empirical evidence has repeatedly shown that new social movements are not heterogeneous in composition but rather have relatively clear and consistent constituencies. Studies of peace movements, environmental movements, feminist movements, student movements, and various "green" coalitions have all shown that the substantial core of activists and supporters of such movements shares the structural characteristics of the "new" or "professional" middle class (PMC). These characteristics include "high educational status, relative economic security (and, in particular, experience of such security in their 'formative years'), and employment in personal-service occupations" (Offe 1985: 833). So while new social movements may not be rooted in the traditional working class, as the "old" movements were, they *are* rooted in a class—the PMC.

For example, in Rucht's (1988: 308) comparative study of the German feminist and environmental movements, he found that "the core groups of these movements are relatively homogeneous. Activists are essentially younger middle-class people with an above-average education, among whom are many employees of the social service sector." He (1988: 316) goes on to say that the "vanguard" of these movements is the "new middle class." "Not directly involved in the industrial sphere of production, economically secure, sensitive to questions concerning the quality of life, and capable of articulating its views in public, this class is crucial to the promotion of social change."

Referring to peace, antinuclear, women's, and squatter's movements in the Netherlands, Kreisi (1989: 1102) observes, "we can conclude that the NSMs are supported by broad parts of the population but that their active participants and their leaders in particular have their social-structural roots mainly in the segments of the new middle class that are most closely associated with the new class as conceptualized here—the specialists in social and cultural services."

Summarizing research on the British Campaign for Nuclear Disarmament (CND), Mattausch (1989: 218) observes that its constituency is "socially unrepresentative" with "a striking absence of support from the mass of British working people." Parkin (1968) had labeled CND as an example of "middle class radicalism" over twenty years earlier. Klandermans and Oegema (1987: 529) found that the Dutch peace movement is made up of participants who are "young, highly educated, and professionals."

The significance of the European origin of NSM theory should not be overlooked. It is, in part, the result of a unique political climate for left social movements. Among other things, many European nations have strong union movements and labor-based electoral parties, whereas the United States has, instead, a history of particularly intense labor repression, no labor-based party, and the legacy of anticommunism. Thus, "new" movements in Europe are responding, in part, to a strongly entrenched labor establishment that is very different from the labor movement in the United States.[6]

Still, although most NSM theory and research has been conducted in Europe, U.S. examples confirm the middle-class base of NSMs. Although concern for the environment is now broad-based in the United States, member-ship in most environmental groups is firmly a middle-class affair.[7] For example, a membership survey of the mainstream Sierra Club revealed that nearly three out of four members is employed in managerial, professional, or technical positions, more than double the national rate. Half of the the Sierra Club's members have annual incomes of more than $50,000, and one out of six has an annual income of over $100,000. The average member has a home valued at $187,300, more than twice that of the national average (King 1989: 22). An important exception to the environmental case is local defensive or "NIMBY" (not in my backyard) efforts, which tend to have broader class and race diversity among participants. But even participation in local environmental efforts is associated with whites who have PMC employment and education

(Agyeman 1988). More generally, research has shown that environmental activists have relatively high levels of social and economic status (Mitchell 1978: 6). The emerging environmental justice movement has attracted so much attention precisely because it is the exception to the white, middle-class environmental norm (Bullard 1990; Di Chiro 1992; Gottlieb 1992).

Verta Taylor and Nancy E. Whittier (1993: 540–41) observe that the American women's movement of the last twenty-five years has attracted "primarily white middle-class women" and that "the class bias of the women's movement has made working-class and poor women unlikely to participate in sizable numbers." In their interviews with lesbian feminist activists, Taylor and Whittier (1992: 106) note that "the majority are from middle-class backgrounds."

The student movement and the broader New Left in the United States provides another well-researched American example. Flacks (1988: 133), himself an early member of SDS, writes:

> The founders of SDS had been reared in families of at least middle-class comfort—and quite a few were very well-off. These were the sorts of families that provided their children with a richness of cultural resources. They were excellently schooled; they had private lessons and went to progressive summer camps; they had traveled widely and lived in stimulating and self-consciously caring family surroundings. Most SDS founders, and others in the early New Left, had all the benefits to self-esteem that come from academic success. Most of them did not lack opportunities for self-expression. They had been encouraged to develop their artistic talents, they had been leaders of their classmates. . . . Most were enrolled in elite colleges and universities and had little doubt that any careers they might choose were readily accessible to them.

In the end, according to Flacks (1972: 259), the student movement and the New Left "failed very largely to break out of its isolation as a movement of the young, and particularly of the relatively advantaged young."

The middle-class base of the New Left and later new social movements is a significant change in left social-movement history. Kahn (1986: 59) observes:

> American radicals have frequently been members of the middle class but have also consistently identified their aspirations and frustrations with other classes, particularly farmers and the working class. They generally condemned their own class as "bourgeois," either complicit in the social injustices that make for inequality or complacent in the fact of social oppression begotten by elites and suffered by lower classes. Occasionally, American radicals such as Morris Hillquit of the old Socialist Party believed that the proletarian struggle might absorb some middle-class elements, but virtually no serious radical looked to the middle class itself as the social base for change in America.

All of this changed with the rise of the New Left. Whereas Isserman (1987) has pointed out the many threads linking the "Old" and "New" Left, Boyte (1989: 71) argues that the SDS and the New Left were still a break from the earlier left efforts. He writes, "In the Port Huron Statement there is virtually no reference to American antecedents of its quest for 'participatory democracy,' no recitation of prior movements, or mention of the aspirations of those who had gone before. Instead, the document expresses disillusionment mingled with arrogance."

The New Left approach to social change, as outlined in SDS's Port Huron Statement, suggested (Kahn 1986: 60) that "Social change would not likely come from a labor movement that was 'too quiescent to be counted on with enthusiasm.' Nor was it likely to come from minorities who were 'too poor and socially slighted.' However, change might come by mobilizing the affluent white youth of the middle class who had the sense of efficacy to believe that 'something can be done to change circumstance' and the potential power to make that change." And thus, we have the beginning of "middle-class" left movements that are firmly rooted in the contradiction of calling for a generalized "participatory democracy" while seeing the catalyst for change as being primarily the "affluent white youth of the middle class."

The middle-class bias of NSMs created problems for the Left. As Derber, Schwartz, and Magrass (1990: 188) point out, "Ignorance of, if not contempt for, the working class was rampant in New Left circles. Radical students borrowed Marx's rhetoric, but many had never walked into a factory. Working-class activists often found their movement compatriots from professional backgrounds intolerably arrogant and hostile." Indeed, in the ensuing years, the new social movements of the Left have increasingly been associated with this middle-class constituency, and they have increasingly been criticized by the Right for representing the politics of privilege.

Portions of the New Left can be seen more as precursors to new social movements than as actual new social movements. That is because these segments of the New Left still clung to the notion of classes as the primary agents of change. Mostly, they dealt with the distinctly middle-class composition of their own movement in one of two ways. First, some groups identified themselves as being bourgeois and thus needing to subordinate their issues to those of the working class or of "third-world" revolutionaries. Second, some in the New Left tried to achieve self-legitimation by reconceptualizing the working class to include knowledge workers as part of a "new working class." For the most part, though, the Left became populated by distinctly middle-class movements.

Recent studies of social activists have continued to document the uniquely middle-class nature of left activism. Kahn (1986: 16–17) has explored one quintessential middle-class activist community in Santa Monica, California.

Santa Monica's leftwing activists were both middle class and radical. They generally come from middle to upper middle class homes. They are highly educated and credentialed, extraordinarily articulate in the spoken and written word, and comfortable when dealing with major political figures, public audiences, and the media. . . . They are professionals at what they do, well-connected to other professionals, and they rise to managerial positions in relatively large organizations. . . . [O]ne must at least surmise that their middle class backgrounds, lifestyles, and successes are somehow sources of their radicalism rather than something alien to it.

Although the group Kahn studied may be an extreme case, his call to recognize a possible affinity between middle-class status and left politics is an important one. In contemporary society, being from a middle-class background facilitates political participation by providing members with the material and cultural tools necessary for participation in the political realm, as currently structured. In today's political environment, the material constraints and the orientation of contemporary working-class culture does not offer such advantages.

Conclusion

There have always been some members of the middle class who have been attracted to left politics. The labor movement, for example, has benefited from the participation of middle-class intellectuals and professionals. But increasingly, the Left as a whole has become middle class while the participation of working people has declined.

In the particular political context of the United States, the emergence of middle-class new social movements can be seen, in part, as a response to the void that was partially created by the labor movement's abandonment of a broader social vision in the postwar years. (This is not true of some European countries where NSM issues were incorporated into stronger working-class movements and parties [Eyerman and Jamison 1991].)

Unions have been unwilling or unable to be at the forefront of the struggle for equality for groups that have been historically discriminated against. Thus, the civil rights movement, the modern women's movement, the movement of disabled people, and the gay and lesbian rights movement have taken on these tasks. The labor movement has also largely abandoned its efforts on behalf of workers outside of the workplace; thus, tenants' rights groups and consumer groups have arisen to take on these struggles. With the rise of mass-culture technologies and the growth of suburbanization, labor unions no longer serve as the cultural and social hub of working-class communities. Meanwhile, NSMs have tried to serve as a cultural as well as a political home for their members. Finally, the labor movement has abandoned most claims to influence the direction in which workers' productive capacity will be steered. Thus, new social movements such as the environmental, the peace, and the antinuclear movements, which often find themselves opposing undertakings—such as nuclear power plants or military projects—that are seen by labor as the attractive source of well-paying union jobs, have arisen. As the U.S. industrial base continues its dramatic erosion, these conflicts become all the more intense. Labor is accused of selling its soul for wages, benefits, and working conditions and of not caring about the potentially devastating impact of such projects. In turn, environmental groups and peace groups are accused of occupying positions of privilege and wanting to sacrifice workers and their families for the sake of utopian environmental visions or, worse, distinctly naive and anti-American notions of global harmony.

But working-class nonparticipation in NSMs should not necessarily be equated with a lack of support for the goals of NSMs. Innumerable survey data show that some new social movement concerns reach beyond class lines. In empirical studies, "mobilization potential" (Klandermans and Oegema 1987) has been shown also to cut across class lines, but membership and participation in new social movements is class specific. One question to be examined then is why class intervenes in the actual mobilization of new social movement constituencies.

Of course unions and other labor-based movement organizations continue to function, and as I will explore in the final chapter, they retain the potential for playing a crucial role in social-change efforts. But the Left in the United States, into the next century, will continue to be led by new social movement efforts. The distinctly middle-class composition of these new movements should alert us to the fact that class will also continue to play a fundamental role in the future of these movements.

CHAPTER 3

Class and Politics

What I want to see above all else is that this remains a country where someone can always get rich.

RONALD REAGAN, quoted in Lewis Lapham,
Money and Class in America

There is a good deal of appeal to the belief that we live in a highly permeable society where anyone can grow up to be president and, perhaps more important, "someone can always get rich." Partly due to American "exceptionalism"—the absence of a labor-based political party and the relative weakness of the union movement in this country—mainstream political culture has often harbored this myth of a classless America. Indeed, irregular forays into explicit class-based politics are often portrayed in the popular press as divisive and largely illegitimate endeavors. Instead, with the exception of welfare bashing, political agents have generally steered clear of any pointed use of class, opting instead for reference to an amorphous American "middle class" that sometimes seems to include virtually all of the population.

But the fact that American political culture has not developed a significant discourse on class does not mean that people are unaware of class difference. In fact, there is clear and widespread recognition of class in the United States (see Vanneman and Cannon). When Americans talk about political and social life, such discussion is likely to include references to "working people," the "average person," the "regular guy," the "middle class," the "rich," the "big shots," and so on. There is a commonsense understanding among most people that some citizens are in very different economic circumstances than others and that these different circumstances result in different amounts of power and foster very different attitudes and lifestyles. But whereas most people have a sense of class, the popular discourse on the subject is often muddled and contradictory. The scholarly discourse on class has often been of little help. Academics have filled countless, and often arcane, volumes trying to tell a coherent story about class.

Part of the problem for all types of class discourse is that, on an individual basis, class is more ambiguous than the other characteristics by which we commonly group people. For example, it is usually clearer to which sex or race one belongs than to which class. The ambiguities of class mean that it is often very difficult to agree even on what we mean by "working class," "middle class," and so on.

It is doubly difficult to ascribe any explanatory power to membership in a particular class. Thus, the caution of Barbara and John Ehrenreich (1979: 11–12) is warranted. They write, "class is an analytic abstraction, a way of putting some order into an otherwise bewildering array of individual and group characteristics and interrelationships. It describes a phenomenon existing most clearly at the level of society as a whole. When, however, the notion of class is called on to explain or predict infallibly the actions, ideas and relationships of every individual, it ceases to be very useful."

The reason for such caution is clear. Classes are made up of real people who exhibit endless varieties and gradations of characteristics. As Paul Sweezy (Ehrenreich and Ehrenreich 1979: 13) once noted, "It would be a mistake to think of a class as perfectly homogeneous internally and sharply marked off from other classes. Actually there is variety within the class; and one class sometimes shades off very gradually, almost imperceptibly, into another." These shadings make it impossible to speak of class with thorough certainty. The ambiguities of class have also allowed the concept to be absorbed into different discourses with substantially different meaning. As Erik Olin Wright (1979: 3) observes, class "is a chameleon which blends into virtually every sociological tradition."

But being from a particular class *can* have profound impact on someone's life experiences—and consequently on their political experiences. Political scientists have known this for a long time. Higher socioeconomic status is strongly correlated with higher rates of political participation as measured by voting behavior and membership in voluntary associations. This trend is, in fact, more pronounced in the United States than elsewhere. In their classic study of participation, Sidney Verba and Norman Nie (1972: 133) noted: "The United States is often contrasted with other countries as being a society where class and status matter relatively little in political life. But in regard to the relationship between social status and political participation, the United States clearly has a class-biased pattern. Indeed, . . . the U.S. pattern shows more class bias than almost all other countries for which comparable data exist." So although it may be difficult to talk about class, it is important to include it in our analysis if we are to get a clearer picture of the dynamics of American political life.

This chapter reviews the concept of class and examines the contemporary reality of American political participation. It *is* possible to speak of class in a way that helps us to better understand differential participation. To do so, however, we must disentangle some of the components associated with the idea of class.

The Concept of Class

In order to assess the impact of class on political life, we should distinguish between some of the different usages of the term "class." There are three important aspects of class that must be differentiated. First, class is a theoretical device useful in analyzing the terrain of macrosocial cleavages. Second, class suggests shared social conditions. Third, shared conditions can help foster particular orientations, beliefs, and daily life practices that are widely held within a class and which constitute what I mean by "class culture."[1]

Class Structure

One facet of class is its structuring. Class is fundamentally a characteristic of the organization of production within a society. Every form of production requires three central resources: capital, knowledge, and labor. In capitalist society, these three resources are both the foundation of production and the basis of class divisions. In making their living, different groups relate differently to the process of production, and groups that share in a common relation to the means of production are classes.[2] Capitalists, the professional middle class (PMC),[3] and the working class form the basic classes of American society.[4]

Classes are not merely different, they are unequal. This inequality stems from the fact that classes are created through *relations*. In a capitalist system, capitalists are able to benefit from the labor of others because they pay workers—both "knowledge" workers and laborers—less than the value their labor produces. By appropriating this "surplus value" capitalists exploit workers. Capitalists as a distinct class cannot exist without workers. Their identity is formed by their relation to workers. Similarly, speaking of workers in a capitalist system intimates the existence of capitalists. Without them, the system is no longer a capitalist one.

Power, among classes, is unevenly distributed. The key to accruing power in class relations is the control of *property* (Derber, Schwartz, and Magrass 1990). Something can become property only when access to it is denied to nonowners—a process that Weber called "social closure." Air used for breathing cannot (yet!) be "owned" because, with variations in quality, everyone has equal access to it. Land, however, is dubbed "property" because legal titles and enforcement mechanisms have been established to limit access to and use of it. Airwaves for communication purposes have similarly been turned into "property" through the Federal Communications Commission, which limits access to them and regulates their use.

Under capitalism, each class derives its power from maintaining control over one of the necessary productive resources, capital, knowledge, or labor. Capital is power only when money is scarce and controllable. If workers had the ability and resources to invest and buy their own machinery, equipment, and distribution facilities, the power of capitalists as a distinct class would be greatly diminished or eliminated. Socialism is, in part, the elimination of capital as a form of property.

Similarly, knowledge translates into power for the professional-middle class only insofar as it is a scarce and controllable commodity. If huge numbers of people knew how to decipher the maze of jargon and archaic procedures that characterizes our legal system, lawyers would not be able to extract the high fees and comfortable working conditions that they have.[5] Instead, elaborate educational requirements and licensing procedures limit the number of people deemed qualified to practice law (or any other profession). It is in the interest of lawyers to prevent the legal system from being simplified and made more accessible. Such a development would begin to render their services obsolete.

Labor, too, is property insofar as it is scarce and controllable. A strike by workers is simply the removal of workers' property—their labor—from the process of production. Laws prohibiting the use of so-called replacement workers ("scabs") would strengthen the position of workers by limiting the labor available to capitalists and by facilitating union regulation of available labor. The existence of a pool of under- and unemployed workers, however, undermines the value of a worker's "property" since replacement labor is readily available. It is in the interest of each of the three classes therefore to limit access to the primary form of property it possesses—in other words to ensure social closure of its class property.

It should be noted that although each class is associated with a principal type of property, each class also has some degree of the other classes' property available to it. For example, while workers primarily control labor, they also have varying degrees of knowledge regarding the organization of production. The de-skilling of workers through Taylorist schemes brought the working class into direct conflict with the newly emerging managerial middle class as knowledge was wrenched from one class and concentrated in another (Braverman 1974). Also, workers can collectively control considerable capital, for example, in the form of union pension funds.

The power of each class is also related to the dominant productive technologies of an era. Capitalists grew in influence when the Industrial Revolution made large sums of investment capital necessary for the purchase of machinery and equipment. Similarly, in postindustrial societies, the knowledge class has experienced a growth in influence that has paralleled the flowering of scientifically based industries and communication and information technologies. These technologies have in turn undermined the position of skilled workers. The proliferation of relatively low-cost, computerized desktop publishing, for example, has had the effect of widely distributing the once scarce and highly valued knowledge of printers, typesetters, and layout artists—only to strengthen the power and influence of software designers. A similar process has occurred as highly skilled machinists have been replaced with computer-controlled equipment.

Most "knowledge" workers are still ultimately beholden to the capitalists who pay their salaries, own their labs, fund their research, and contribute to their universities, but the importance of knowledge in the contemporary economy has allowed the professional-middle class to carve out an uneasy but relatively comfortable niche in capitalist society.

By looking at class on this macrolevel, one type of class conflict becomes apparent; it is in the interest of members of one class to prevent outsiders from gaining access to their class's property. Thus, capitalists work the political system to maintain unrestricted control of capital while limiting others' access to it. Members of the professional-middle class usually try to regulate access to knowledge property via controls on education, skills training, credentialing, and licensing (Collins 1977; Derber, Schwartz, and Magrass 1990). Organized workers try to hold on to the jobs they have by limiting the availability of competing labor. Tactics that unions have pursued over the years include calls for limiting immigration, discriminatory exclusion of workers on the basis of race and sex, elaborate apprenticeship systems, job-security provisions in negotiated contracts, and support for antiscab legislation. The relative absence of working-class power over *other* classes has meant that control efforts of organized labor have often been aimed at the unorganized members of the working class, thus creating deep and long-term internal class conflict, often established along racial, ethnic, and gender lines.

Differing interests are conflictual. Although they may have aspirations to middle-class incomes, workers in the United States have repeatedly been found to generally dislike the professional-middle class. (A fact not lost on Dan Quayle as shown by his 1992 campaign attacks on lawyers and "cultural elites.") For example, in his study of chemical plant workers, David Halle (1984: 208) found that the dominant attitude towards middle-class professionals was "mistrust and often hostility, rooted in a belief that part or all of their activity is in some way unproductive." The PMC is the class that—through its "professional" skills, knowledge, and expertise—manages, controls, and has authority over labor. According to the Ehrenreichs (1979: 17), the PMC has a relationship with the working class that is "fundamentally antagonistic." They write that, "The functions and interests of the two classes are not merely different; they are mutually contradictory." In fact, most working people experience the PMC primarily in their regulatory roles as teachers, bosses, and "expert" professionals.

Earlier Marxist assumptions of the unique revolutionary role of the working class were predicated upon the belief that it was the only alternative to capitalists. But conceptualizing class structure to include a third middle class means that the working class is not the only rival of capitalists for class power in capitalist society—nor are capitalists the only potential opponents of workers.

Class as Lived Experience

A macrolevel class analysis is a set of abstract notions conceived by theorists to help explain social phenomena. It is what Bourdieu (1985: 725) calls "classes on paper," and it is helpful in understanding mechanisms of power in a society.

But, strictly speaking, classes cannot act; they are theoretical constructs. In the real world, classes are made up of real people who, as a result of their common class position, often share common material and social conditions such as work experiences, lifestyles, educational backgrounds, and consumption patterns. Class, then, manifests itself in people's lives, in part, as these material and social conditions of daily life both in *and* outside the workplace.[6] In order to move beyond the faceless abstractions of class theory and examine the ramifications of class in all their real-world diversity, we must consider class as it is encountered in these lived experiences of daily life.[7] When considering politics, after all, it is individuals, not classes, who must ultimately decide both the extent and the nature of their activity. People from identical class backgrounds sometimes make startlingly different choices regarding their political actions. Thus, in talking about class, we are painting with a necessarily broad brush.

Lived experience covers a broad range of territory, and I will examine some aspects of it in more detail in Part Two. For now, I merely wish to highlight some key elements of lived experience that are most influenced by class membership. Let me take the example of the working class. Wright (1989b) suggests that under capitalism workers share in at least three fundamental lived experiences.[8]

First, by definition, workers are forced to sell their labor in order to earn a living. "Showing up at the factory gate, being unable to reproduce oneself without entering the labor market, does not simply define a set of material interests of actors, but a set of experiences as well" (Wright 1989b: 289).[9] Clearly this experience is different from that of capitalists. It may have more in common with the experiences of salaried knowledge professionals, but it differs dramatically from those professionals who are self-employed.

Second, within the production process itself—"on the job" if you will—workers are dominated. "Under a set of production conditions in which the critical task for employers is to extract surplus labor from their employees—to turn labor power into effective labor—experiences of domination will be an inherent aspect of the class relation itself" (Wright 1989b: 289). Again, this is different from the experiences of capitalists who do not have "bosses" per se. Significantly, it is also different from the experience of many knowledge professionals who, by virtue of their "expertise," are often given significant freedom to at least organize and carry out their work, if not decide which direction that work will take. Most important, while the ultimate beneficiaries of worker domination may be capitalists, the day-to-day implementation of this domination is usually carried out by members of the professional-managerial class.

Third, since workers are paid a fixed wage, they do not have any control over the "social surplus" that results from their labor. They cannot make the decisions that direct the amount and type of economic development that is to be pursued. Perhaps most significant for social movements, "Because of the centrality of investments to a broad range of social goals, the control over the surplus can also be considered a central mechanism constraining social and political alternatives in general" (Wright 1989b: 283). Workers do not share in the political and social power that accrues from being in the position to make economic decisions. Consequently, this "generates a certain kind of lived experience—the experience of powerlessness in the face of social forces that shape one's destiny" (Wright 1989b: 289). Once again, this differs completely from capitalists and significantly from knowledge professionals. The latter do not directly control social surplus but they do have skills and expertise that can be influential in the political realm.

Like working people, other classes also share in common life experiences. Using slightly different terms than I employ, Barbara Ehrenreich (1989: 13) writes that the professional-middle class shares in at least four "points of commonality." First, like the working class, members of the PMC must work for a living, but PMC occupations are distinct from working-class jobs. "Today both may wear white (or pink) collars and participate in what might loosely be called 'mental work'. . . the professional or manager is granted far more autonomy in his or her work and is expected to be fairly self-directing much of the time. In fact, his or her job is often to define the work of others: to conceptualize—and command."

Second, the PMC shares in "defining experiences," the most significant of which is higher education and training. Ehrenreich (1989: 13–14) believes that "The period of study and apprenticeship—which may extend nearly to mid-life—is essential to the social cohesion of the middle class." She points out that "It is in college or graduate school that the young often find their future spouses and lifelong friends."

Third, the PMC shares in its ability to earn "upper-middle" incomes that allow people to own a home, provide their children with college educations, and pay for "such enriching experiences as vacation trips, psychotherapy, fitness training, summer camp, and the consumption of 'culture' in various forms" (Ehrenreich 1989: 14). Being able to afford homes in "good" suburbs or neighborhoods also enables the children of the PMC to attend quality schools, or in some cases even private schools. Such quality education is an essential part of reproducing the class.

Finally, Ehrenreich (1989: 14) notes that "all of the above shape a rough commonality of lifestyle and consumer tastes" that are used to "establish its status, especially relative to the working class. Typically this has meant an emphasis on things 'authentic,' 'natural,' and frequently imported. Such tastes provide the class cues by which middle-class people recognize each other outside of their occupational settings."

Capitalists, too, share in basic lived experiences that result from their wealth and influence, though their power has largely shielded them from ethnographic accounts (Domhoff 1978, 1983; Mills 1956).

Class, then, structures for its members a loose set of shared experiences that are grounded in similar material conditions. But as with all experience, class experiences must be interpreted by the individual in order to give material experience its meaning. This interaction between material conditions and the social construction of meaning is the terrain of class culture.

Class Culture

Dick Hebdige (1979: 5) begins his study of subcultures by acknowledging that "Culture is a notoriously ambiguous concept. . . . Refracted through centuries of usage, the word has acquired a number of quite different, often contradictory, meanings." Indeed, "culture" is perhaps one of the few sociological terms that has an even wider range of meanings than "class." Yet, like class, the concept of culture continues to serve a valuable function, alerting us to the symbolic and expressive dimension of practices and beliefs.

There was a time in the history of anthropology and sociology when culture was taken to mean nothing less than a people's entire way of life (Geertz 1973). But as Roger Keesing (1974: 73) points out, "The challenge in recent years has been to narrow the concept of 'culture' so that it includes less and reveals more."

Culture should not be confused with consciousness insofar as culture is a collective phenomenon that cannot exist in a single mind but instead must be shared. In fact, recent work in cultural studies has limited the scope of "culture" to include only the "publicly available symbolic forms through which people experience and express meaning" (Swidler 1986: 273). This is still a slippery definition, but one that encompasses less than earlier attempts. More concretely, Swidler (1986: 273) suggests that "culture consists of such symbolic vehicles of meaning, including beliefs, ritual practices, art forms, and ceremonies, as well as informal cultural practices such as language, gossip, stories, and rituals of daily life."

Swidler (1986: 273) goes on to make an important point regarding culture. She argues that the traditional notion of culture is misleading because "It assumes that culture shapes action by supplying ultimate ends or values toward which action is directed, thus making values the central causal element of culture." In place of this approach, Swidler (1986: 273) persuasively argues for a concept of culture analogous to a " 'tool kit' of symbols, stories, rituals, and world views, which people may use in varying configurations to solve different kinds of problems." Swidler's elaboration of this approach is limited by its overly optimistic description of the helpful characteristics of cultural "tools." There is little discussion of the darker side of cultural power as found in, for example, the work of Foucault. Still, Swidler's approach is helpful in alerting us that people of *differing* cultures may have very *similar* values and aspirations and that people of the *same* culture may have *differing* values and aspirations. These values are not the defining characteristic of a culture. Echoing Bourdieu's notion of "practices," Swidler (1986: 275) contends that culture is "more like a style or a set of skills and habits than a set of preferences or wants."

As an example, Swidler cites the well-known "culture-of-poverty" thesis.

Although much of this argument has centered on whether the very poor value the same things as more secure segments of society, she says this is irrelevant to the issue of culture. Swidler (1986: 275) argues, "lower-class people seem to want secure friendships, stable marriages, steady jobs, and high incomes. But class similarities in aspirations in no way resolve the questions of whether there are class differences in culture. People may share common aspirations, while remaining profoundly different in the way their culture organized their overall pattern of behavior."

Swidler (1986: 275) goes on to comment, "If one asked a slum youth why he did not take steps to pursue a middle-class path to success . . . the answer might well be not 'I don't want that life,' but instead, 'Who, me?' One can hardly pursue success in a world where the accepted skills, style, and informal know-how are unfamiliar. One does better to look for a line of action for which one already has the cultural equipment." This fundamental insight, as I will discuss, goes a long way toward explaining the differences in class participation in politics.

The absence of a firm connection between class culture and aspirations is important in discussing politics because middle-class activists often perceive themselves to be rejecting middle-class values and orientations. While activists may indeed be reorienting their values and aspirations away from traditional middle-class concerns, they are still the beneficiaries of a class culture that has equipped them with tools that are valuable in the political world. As Melucci (1989: 35) puts it: "The propensity of individuals and sub-groups to involve themselves in collective action always depends upon their differential access to resources, such as information, access to networks, and professional or communicative skills . . . . These differences also influence the starting point and the duration of their involvement, the intensity of their participation and the quality of their expectations." Such differentials in resources can be said to be the cultural artifacts of material class conditions.

One of the debates within cultural studies concerns the relative emphasis that should be placed on ideational versus material conceptions of culture. Ideational theories emphasize the meaning people ascribe to the material world and thus see culture as composed of such patterns of ideas and beliefs. Thus, cultures constitute the world in the sense that they impose meaning upon material reality. A purely idealist approach to history, for example, views reality as entirely shaped by human consciousness. Hegel's *Phenomenology of Mind* is the classic statement of this position, and in it Hegel argues that objects that appear to exist in "reality" are in fact only phenomenal expression of consciousness. But classical idealism fails to consider the profoundly different experiences that result from differing material conditions. It ignores the very real impact of the physical world.

A purely materialist notion of history sees culture as the "product" of particular material conditions. This is sometimes how the historical materialism of Engels (developed mostly after Marx's death) is interpreted. The economic "infrastructure," it is argued, produces a "superstructure" of which culture is a part. But if culture is merely the product of material conditions, then it is beyond the ability of humans to change the world. They are merely objects of history. Purely materialist notions of culture emphasize the influence of material constraints on the construction of ideas. Thus, rather than meanings constituting the world, material conditions create cultures. But Engels (1978: 760) himself protested the oversimplification of economic determinism arguing that those who saw the economy as being the *only* determining element of history transformed historical materialism into "a meaningless, abstract, and senseless, phrase."

Clearly neither of these positions is a satisfactory explanation of the relationship between material conditions and culture. A more fruitful approach would suggest that humans make history, *but* their agency is limited by the material conditions under which they labor. In an often-quoted passage, Marx (1978a: 595) argued that "Men make their own history but they do not make it just as they please; they do not make it under circumstances chosen by themselves, but under circumstances directly found, given and transmitted from the past." This general approach recognizes the impact of material conditions while at the same time acknowledging the importance of active agency in the social construction of reality.

The work of Raymond Williams and E. P. Thompson, for example, is in this tradition and it views culture:

> as the set of practices through which men and women actively respond to the conditions of their social existence, creatively fashioning experienced social relationships into diverse and structured patterns of living, thinking and feeling. The emphasis, within this account, is placed on the notion of human agency. It is this that provides the crucial mediation between the determined conditions of a given cultural practice and the outcome of that practice, connecting and yet at the same time separating the two. (Bennett et al. 1981: 10)

By recognizing the necessity of the continuous reproduction of cultural and material forms, neither component is privileged. As Paul Willis (1977: 174) argues:

> cultural forms cannot be reduced or regarded as the mere epiphenomenal expression of basic structural factors. They are not the accidental or open-ended determined variables in the couplet structure/culture. They are part of a necessary circle in which neither term is thinkable alone. It is in the passage through the cultural level that aspects of the real structural relationships of society are transformed into conceptual relationships and back again. The cultural is part of the necessary dialectic of reproduction.

In discussing culture and politics, then, I am not making a simple causal claim regarding the influence of material conditions on political participation. Material conditions, however, *do* influence the development of cultures. And cultural tools can in turn influence patterns of political participation. But neither is mine a purely culturalist argument, for material conditions and historical context have a profound impact on how cultures develop.

The emphasis in this work is on the class base of culture. However, class conflict has no primacy over other conflicts that arise from cleavages along, for example, gender or race lines. Although not primary in any sense, issues of class are important ones to address. However, a worker's relation to the means of production is only one relation that can affect political consciousness. Early socialization, race, gender, and historical climate can all have profound effects as well (Reinarman 1987). Kenneth Roberts (1978: 162) has made the point that "talk of a working class taps a real cleavage in the social structure. At the same time, it should be equally clear that the working class concept can be so inflated as to over-simplify reality and suggest misleading conclusions." I wish to avoid such oversimplification.

Cultural Tools and Political Participation

Critics who argue that there is no working-class culture in the United States are correct to highlight the multiplicity of cultures within the working class that result from, for example, regional, ethnic, gender, and racial variations. Still, as discussed above, workers within these cultures share in some fundamental—though variable—lived experiences.

In considering the relative absence of working people from left social movements, I will argue that working people often have access to a different set of cultural "tools" than those available to middle-class activists and that middle-class cultural tools are more useful and effective in navigating the political world as it is currently structured. Thus, working-class nonparticipation is often not the consequence of different political goals. Instead, it is the consequence of a political world in which, to adapt Swidler's words, "the accepted skills, style, and informal know-how are unfamiliar." As a result, workers, who often experience the political world as a foreign culture, pursue alternative strategies of action for which they are better equipped. The relative absence in the working class of cultural tools appropriate for political participation in the current political environment should be seen as the product of the interaction of structure and culture. The class divide I discuss is not universal and timeless. Instead, it is bound by material and historical conditions.

Political Participation and the SES Model

Even in movements with no obvious links to class issues, we must consider the structural conditions of class and corresponding class culture to understand social-movement dynamics. I turn now to the existing evidence for the impact of class on political participation.

Almost by definition, social-movement activists have a strong sense of political engagement, that is, an interest in and an involvement with politics or social activism. Although this sentiment may wax and wane with the political tides, it is a central part of the identity of activists. Political activism may take a variety of forms. Verba and Nie, for example, classify modes of potential participation as summarized in the chart below (fig. 3.1). Social-movement activists engage primarily in nonelectoral communal actions.[10] However, the relationship between social-movement and electoral politics is a complicated one since most activists vote, many individually contact legislators, and some are involved in electoral campaigning as well (Piven and Cloward 1989: xix–xxv). This participation contrasts sharply with working people in the United States, who are rarely involved in communal action. They generally do not individually contact their representatives and are also unlikely to become involved in electoral campaigns. They even vote at a lower rate than the population as a whole. Reeve Vanneman and Lynn Weber Cannon (1987: 164) observe, "In every election, the main social division in the U.S. electorate is between voters and nonvoters, not between voters for the different parties. The typical working-class response in the United States is to abstain." In fact, significant portions of the working class are what Verba and Nie would call "nonactive."

Observers have long known that a correlation exists between high "socioeconomic status" (SES)—composed of education, income, occupation—and political participation in the United States. One classic statement of the case (Verba and Nie, 1972: 134) summarizes the situation as follows: The higher the socioeconomic status of persons (1) the greater their political interest, (2) the stronger their sense of civic duty, and (3) the more likely they are to believe that they can influence politics (political efficacy). In turn, these "civic orientations" increase the likelihood of political participation. More generally, (Zipp et al. 1982):

It is argued that due to less education, more restricted occupation-related learning experiences, greater social isolation, and higher aliena-

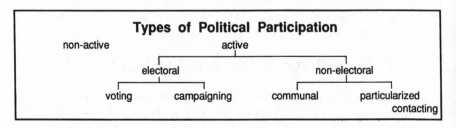

Figure 3.1 Adapted from Verba and Nie (1972: 47)

tion, lower status persons, compared with higher status persons: are less interested in politics; are less aware of the need for or possible benefits of participation; feel less politically efficacious; less often possess those social and political skills (verbal and problem solving skills) which facilitate participation; and have less time, money, and energy to expend in political participation.

Since, compared to members of the professional-middle class, working-class people tend to have lower levels of education, lower income, and thus a lower socioeconomic status, it follows that working-class people are less likely than middle-class counterparts to have an interest in politics, a sense of political efficacy, and a sense of civic duty. Working-class people, then, do not participate in politics as much as middle-class people. In fact, Verba and Nie (1972: 12) note, "Most studies of participation . . . demonstrate that it is just those with higher income, higher education, and higher-status occupation who participate." The observation holds true not only for voting but for all forms of participation. For example, James Q. Wilson (1973: 56) concludes that "the higher a person's social class, as defined by income, education, or occupation, the more likely he is to join a voluntary association." In addition, research suggests that "Social stratification powerfully affects the kinds of persons who can be mobilized and thus the kinds of voluntary associations that will exist."

These well-accepted observations are often taken as simple social facts. As Avey (1989: 7) remarks, "Basically, the contention is that a positive relationship between social status and political participation is a natural or inevitable result of social stratification." But as with all social phenomena, participation rates are the product of a complex interaction of social forces. A closer look reveals that there is nothing inevitable in the impact of SES status on participation. One's education or income does not inevitably correlate to participation. One need only to look at U.S. history to see this.

Paul Kleppner (1982: 143), summarizing his analysis of U.S. voter turnout during the last hundred years, observes, "For the most part, in the nineteenth century there were not the glaring differences in social group participation rates that now mark the electoral universe. Rich and poor, learned and uneducated participated at reasonably similar levels to produce an almost fully mobilized electorate." In fact, Avey (1989: 11) notes that "During the mobilization of the electorate in the last half of the nineteenth century education tended to be related inversely to turnout." In the northern states, Avey (1989: 11) notes, "Until 1940, the poorest persons had the highest turnout. This strongly indicates that systemic factors rather than individual capacities determine SES disparities in turnout." The relative strength of local and state (as opposed to national) politics, the accompanying vibrancy of political parties, and the aligning of parties with existing ethnoreligious cleavages were all contributing factors. The SES model for predicting voter turnout, in fact, applies only to elections since the Eisenhower administration.[11] In addition, the cumulative rise in average years spent in formal education has, in fact, been accompanied by a *decline* in participation rates. Also, some factors, such as age and race, supersede the simple SES model predictions. When Verba and Nie wrote (1972: 157), they noted that African Americans had participated at a higher rate than would be expected, using the SES model.

In addition to this historical evidence, there is cross-cultural evidence (Kleppner 1982: 149) showing that, for example in some European countries, "the presence of working-class parties and associational infrastructures provides a collective boost to participation rates and produces aggregate turnout profiles devoid of strong class and age biases." Avey (1989: 8) concurs: "In most Western liberal democracies, SES does not correlate with turnout. In fact, in Norway, New Zealand, Sweden, France, and Italy, the working class votes at a higher rate than the middle class." The fact that working class citizens are underrepresented in electoral politics, then, needs to be the starting point of inquiry, not the end point of discussion.

Social-Movement Participation

Electoral politics is only one possible vehicle for political engagement. Social movements provide an important alternative to the electoral arena for the carrying out of politics. In fact, it is sometimes suggested (Gamson 1990: 139) that social-movement efforts can be best understood as "simply politics by other means." But it is impossible to acquire thorough data on movement participation rates like that which is available for voting rates. However, as we have seen various studies of so-called new social movements have shown a similar class discrepancy in participation.

Writing about the left tradition, Richard Flacks (1988: 27) summarized the situation this way: "it is not an exaggeration to say that active political involvement in this country tends to be an elitist orientation. It is a propensity reserved primarily for those who have been raised or trained to feel that they can and should exercise authority and show civic responsibility. Such rearing and training occurs primarily among those of relatively high status and education." But, as discussed in the last chapter, social movements have not always been dominated by the middle class. And as with voting behavior, the relative absence of working people from the ranks of contemporary social movements should be taken as a starting point for further investigation. Part Two of this work reports on such an investigation. It examines how workers and activists understand the political world and how this understanding affects their participation.

Class, Culture, and Political Participation

CHAPTER 4

"It's Just Politics"

Politicians and the "System"

It's like this guy I work with, he says, "Hey what do you got when you've got a hundred politicians at the bottom of the ocean?" I says, "I don't know, what?" He says, "A good start."

TOM, thirty-six-year-old telephone lineworker

The relative quiescence of working people in recent years has been an undeniable characteristic of the American political landscape. As always, there are notable exceptions, but for the most part working people have been absent from the most prominent social movements and from political life more generally.

One possible explanation for this absence is that working people are basically satisfied with the political system. As we have seen, political scientists have sometimes suggested that apathy is a sign of relative contentment. Some activists I interviewed also argued that since there seemed to be no widespread opposition to conservative domestic policies and foreign interventions, workers must fundamentally support the status quo. As a result, these activists saw their main task as educating workers about the injustices in the world and the errors in their policy beliefs—a topic explored more fully in Chapter Nine. But in fact workers have a more complex relationship with the political "system," as it is often labeled. Their acquiescence, I suggest, can be more accurately read as a sign of fatalistic resignation than of contentment. This chapter examines how the workers I spoke with view the political system and the most visible agents in that system, politicians.

Belief, Disillusionment, and Resignation

Political historian Edmund Morgan (1988: 13) has written: "Government requires make-believe. Make believe that the king is divine, make believe that he can do no wrong or make believe that the voice of the people is the voice of God. Make believe that the people have a voice or make believe that the representatives of the people are the people. Make believe that governors are the servants of the people. Make believe that all men are equal or make believe that they are not." Part of the American experiment has been making believe that government represents the will of the people. The legitimacy of American government depends upon this liberal belief in representative democracy.

Interestingly, workers and activists share one fundamental orientation. Neither believes that the government lives up to the basic democratic standards it professes to uphold. Neither believes, in other words, that the government is truly representing the will of the people. However, workers and activists have come to this judgment via different routes and have drawn very different conclusions from the existing state of affairs.

Disillusionment is perhaps the single word that best sums up activists' descriptions of their brand of disbelief. Activists discussed having gone through a process of discovery or realization that showed them that the belief they once had, or were taught to hold, in the political process was misplaced. Activists told stories of their having believed the myths of American democracy and of their being dramatically affected by the discovery that reality fell far short of such ideals. However, all activists also expressed a belief in the ability of citizens to change the system. It is ironic then that it was the activists I spoke with—those very people who are the most vocal critics of the political system—who seemed to hold the most faith in the possibility of resuscitating a reformed version of that system.

The shock that activists felt at "discovering" injustice served as a strong catalyst for action. Many of them expected that similar discoveries would serve the same function for others. Karen, a forty-six-year-old peace-and-justice activist is one of them.

KAREN: I think anger is what motivates people. After a while, something happens that really outrages you and you begin to try to figure out why this is happening and what is it all about and it takes a while to get past the bill of goods that we're sold growing up in our school systems in terms of what we are as a nation and what our values are and what we stand on because that really isn't how we play ourselves out in the world.

Having found their own disillusionment to be a source of motivation, many activists have faith in the power of disillusionment to motivate other people to act. In the immediate aftermath of the Gulf War, for example, a twenty-four-year-old peace activist offered this assessment:

JOYCE: I was talking to one of my friends . . . and he said that he was just really depressed. He was really depressed at the way the world is. I see it differently. They probably said that about Vietnam, that people have to see the catastrophe of war. But I really think [the Gulf War is] something that we said we won and look at the catastrophe. I really think that that's a good way to involve people.

Here again, is the belief that seeing the catastrophic truth about an issue, and going through a subsequent process of disillusionment, will motivate political involvement. The applicability of such a belief, at least to working people, was contradicted by the workers with whom I spoke.

Unlike the activists, the working people I worked with and interviewed seem never to have bought the "bill of goods" about democracy that was being sold to them by teachers, politicians, and the media. They want to believe that many things are still "right" with the United States, and they clearly exhibit what can only be called patriotism. But at the same time they are scathingly dismissive of the political system, with one worker summarizing, "I think that for most people the government is a joke. It really has gotten to that point."

While activists and workers share in their disbelief of democratic myths, what never came through in my interaction with workers is the sense of awakening that was characteristic of many activists' political coming-of-age. Many activists say they had once believed in the political myths of their country and are working to make reality more closely resemble those ideals. Workers, in contrast, never seem to have been true believers. They also seem largely resigned to the current state of affairs, not seeing a credible possibility for change. Consequently, for workers, seeing injustice brings with it, not a sense of outrage, but rather a weary fatalism. Peter, a forty-six-year-old postal worker, best sums up the worker response to the political system:

PETER: I think the amazing part is that nothing amazes me anymore, you know? I'm not surprised by anything anymore. Cheating, lying, corruption, bribes, whatever—I'm not surprised. I've come to expect it almost.

Thus, while activists and workers share in their rejection of the political status quo, as I will explore further, they reach far different conclusions about the appropriate response to this situation.

Politicians

Worker cynicism and fatalism toward the political system is often coupled with more specific ridicule and disgust aimed at the system's most visible agents, politicians. Ask working people about their opinion of politicians and you are likely to get a laugh and a response like this one from a fifty-five-year-old factory worker:

BERNICE: Oh, I don't know that I should answer that.

DC: What do you mean?

BERNICE: Well, I'm not sure I should be using that kind of language when I'm being recorded. [laughs]

The tone is almost universal. When I ask Tom, a phone company employee, about politicians his deadpan response is, "I wouldn't want my daughter marrying one." Asking about politicians seems to invite sarcastic responses, but some politician humor is more scathing than others. Ronald, a thirty-eight-year-old forklift operator provides this blunt assessment:

RONALD: [A politician is] someone that will say anything to get elected, you know what I mean? He's scum. No backbone. Greedy. Slimy. "Them goddamn slimy rich bastards," my father used to call them. [laughs] That pretty much sums it up.

For many workers this *does* sum it up. Politicians are seen as self-interested, untrustworthy, and usually "rich" (often by dubious means). Politicians are probably at the receiving end of more deprecating working-class humor than any other group, and the feeling underlying this humor is usually contempt.

Such humor is a symptom of a more profound distaste for those involved in electoral politics. In large measure, workers tend to see politicians as either inept or corrupt. The difference lies in the perceived intentionality of their misdeeds. For some, the politicians and bureaucrats who populate government are in the pockets of those who can afford to buy their favor. For others, politicians are merely inept, though sometimes well intentioned. The pervasiveness of this judgment is such that it has become a folk wisdom. One does not have to know the specifics of political misdeeds to know that when a politician is involved, there is a mess somewhere nearby. As a result, workers who will express scathing critiques of politicians often actually know little about their elected representatives. When asked about their representatives, they commonly answer as Donna, a forty-two-year-old machine operator, did: "To be honest, I don't even know who my elected officials are. I know Bush and [the governor], that's about it."

Survey data confirm the lack of widespread knowledge about elected officials. For example, in 1989 nearly half of all Americans surveyed did not know which party had the most members in the U.S. Senate; more than two-thirds could not identify the congressperson from their district; three-quarters could not identify their two U.S. Senators (Page and Shapiro 1992: 11).

But lack of specific knowledge about politicians does not inhibit generalized condemnation of their behavior. Such criticisms can be grouped under three main headings: (1) politicians are *out of touch* with the issues and concerns of "regular," "average," or "working" people; (2) politicians are concerned almost exclusively with *reelection,* and their actions can be best explained in this light; and (3) politicians are *corrupt,* bowing to the pressures that come with access to money and power. A countercurrent that should be noted, though, acknowledges the good intentions of at least some politicians but sees the workings of the "system" and the vast array of political and social problems as overwhelming the good intentions of the few.

Out of Touch

The most common critique workers make of politicians is that they are out of touch with regular people. This phenomenon seemed more disturbing to older workers who sometimes compare today's officials to those of an earlier era when working people could more readily turn to local politicians for assistance on even mundane issues.

BERNICE: I think people have given up. They throw up their hands. They don't even hope for anything to happen anymore. They've stopped looking for help. When I was young I remember my father calling our [state] senator to help him out with his licensing—he was a plumber—to help him because there was some screw-up in the paperwork. Can you imagine that today? Never. You'd have to make an appointment six months in advance, and then the guy probably wouldn't even show up! [laughs] You'd get a form letter in the mail or something.

Whether the perception is real or imagined, such workers believe that government used to be more responsive than it now is. However, this era of responsiveness is clearly seen as having passed.

Workers understand the nonresponsiveness of politicians as being, in part, the result of the insularity that comes with wealth. Judy, a thirty-three-year-old secretary in an insurance company, puts it this way:

JUDY: I don't think most of them really care. That's how I feel about it. They live in their mansions and their limousines and all that. They don't have to worry about crime or worry about paying the doctor or whatever. They just keep voting themselves raises every year. Why worry when you can just vote yourself a raise? I wish I could do that. I'm overdue for one. [laughs]

Wealth, then, isolates politicians from the everyday concerns of most Americans. Since politicians do not share with working people the concerns of everyday life, they do not understand the needs of regular citizens.

Many workers believe that wealthy politicians are not just isolated from working people but, in fact, actively promote the interests of other wealthy citizens at the expense of workers. Andrea, a young, twenty-three-year-old unwed mother who has been a temporary worker in different settings for several years, volunteers this analysis:

ANDREA: The rich people always benefit, and big business always benefits [from the efforts of politicians]. I think when it comes right down to it, big business is more in control of what's going on than the actual government. And I think a lot of politicians are really highly paid and they forget about the people that are struggling in life. They don't know what it's like to be poor. They have no idea what it's like to struggle through life and wonder where your next dollar's coming from and if you're gonna have a meal tomorrow. They kind of brush that aside. It doesn't seem to be an important issue.

Wealth, then, serves to isolate politicians from regular citizens and at the same time suggests that elected officials have more in common with the leaders of "big business" than with workers.

In addition to wealth and privilege, the insulated world of politics itself also causes politicians to lose sight of the pressing needs of citizens and to pursue misplaced priorities. Diane, a thirty-four-year-old worker who splits her time between operating mailing equipment and maintaining a computerized mailing list, suggests that politicians do not seem to understand the need for programs here at home.

DIANE: I think they get so wrapped up in the fighting and haggling that goes on in, like, Congress that they lose the big picture. Why are they there? What are they supposed to be doing? They lose sight of that. I'd say you've got to be trying to take care of people here first. . . . I don't understand how they can say they don't have money for schools, they don't have money to fix the streets or whatever and then like in Iraq all of a sudden we're gonna send half the army over there. Where does that money come from? Why couldn't we be taking care of our own people with that money?

Thus, opposition to foreign aid and to military incursions abroad is often developed in the context of recognizing unmet social needs at home—a recognition that it is believed politicians have not made.

Reelection

If politicians are not concerned with the everyday issues that affect working people, workers do see them as being concerned—maybe even obsessed—with one issue: reelection.

TOM: [Reelection], that's all these guys care about. They don't really give a damn about crime in the streets or drugs or education. Hell, they're all rich, they live in safe neighborhoods, and their kids go to private schools, so who cares, right? All they have to really worry about is hanging on to their job. And it seems like once you're in there it's almost impossible to get somebody out. They're there till they die. [laughs] Senator-for-life. [laughs]

Workers suggest that this preoccupation with reelection is the motivation for the baseless promises and rhetoric that workers have come to expect from elected officials. Ellen, a twenty-nine-year-old data entry clerk, uses the sentence that several workers repeated almost verbatim, "It just seems like they'll say anything to get elected."

To illustrate their belief that politicians will say anything to get elected, many workers cite what perhaps have become the six most infamous words in the recent history of political rhetoric, "Read my lips. No new taxes." Daniel, a fifty-one-year-old mechanic, is one of them.

DANIEL: I think sometimes that all they're interested in is getting elected. They'll say anything to get into office—like Bush, "Read my lips, read my lips," right? [laughs] "No new taxes, no new taxes." Bang, he's in office and whad'ya know? More taxes! [laughs] . . . It's the same old song and dance. That's their career, you know, their profession. They're there to get elected and stay elected.

Politicians, then, are seen as neither credible nor effective, in part because of this overwhelming concern with reelection.

Workers argue that reelection concerns result not only in broken promises, but in failed policies and lack of political will. John, a forty-eight-year-old factory worker provides this assessment:

JOHN: Yeah, it seems like these politicians are so interested in pleasing every-body so they can get reelected that they're for everything and against nothing, you know? . . . [T]hey'll vote to support anything because then they can turn around and say, "Look I voted to support your program that helped you." And they don't want to be on the record as being against anything so that they don't upset voters who wanted this program or that. . . . They're worried about getting reelected, I think. That's their job, right? They want to get reelected to it.

The shortcomings of politicians, then, are intertwined. Concern with reelection results in concern with doing politically expedient "favors" rather than with staying in touch with the needs of constituents. John uses a metaphor from Hollywood's depiction of organized crime to explain the maneuverings of politicians. He argues that politicians build power and influence by doing each other political favors over the years, and then, "It's like the *Godfather,* you know. [laughs] 'Godfather, I need a favor.' "

Reelection is also tied to money and thus to the interests who have money to donate to campaigns. Workers are very much aware of the role of campaign contributions in influencing election outcomes. They are also aware that in the race for election resources, incumbents have a decided advantage.

TOM: [Incumbents] have all the perks of the office. They can send mail to the voters in their area for free. They get all kinds of media attention because they're the senator or congressman. And they get all the money because all these PACs and things want to make sure they've got access to the office so they make sure they make big contributions to the guy's campaign. I think that's a big one. If you want to stay in office, you've got to have money— big money. Why should somebody—some company or group or something—why should they go with a no-name challenger who's probably gonna lose anyway? They put their money on a winner.

It might be argued that concern with reelection is a healthy aspect of democracy since politicians must be responsive to constituents in order to maintain their office. But such a civics-book picture of the electoral process is undermined by the role of campaign financing.

Campaign financing, according to some workers, serves not only to distract politicians from the work that needs to be done, but the influence of large contributors is also seen as undermining the influence voters might otherwise have with election-conscious politicians.

JOHN: I think politicians are worried about the people who count: the people who have the money. That's how you win elections is to have the money. With advertising and everything they spend a fortune on a campaign now. The important thing is to make sure you can raise the money so that you get voters. . . . Politicians don't care about the little guy, the one vote, they care about the big money. The groups that will bring in money to get thousands of votes. That's what counts to these guys.

Workers believe that the campaign and election process is rigged by the influence of money in such a way as to make their vote mean little or nothing. Money, many workers argue, is how elections are won or lost, and money is what these workers also know they do not have.

As an antidote to electoral dynamics based on money, some workers volunteer their support for term limitations and "none of the above" ballot options.

JOHN: Well, [the "none of the above" option is] a way to tell them that we've had enough, that it's time to get somebody new in there. That and have a limit on how long they can stay. Like the president, right, he can only be there for two terms. Fine, let's have everybody do the same—Congress, everybody. Two terms then you're out. Maybe then we'd have people who were more interested in helping out than making a career of it.

The growing movement for term limitations, which passed in fourteen states in the 1992 election, is one logical result of an electoral process that voters see as being run by monied interests and as being immune from voter control. If politicians are primarily concerned with reelection rather than with the needs of their constituents, then perhaps eliminating the possibility of reelection will help them focus on their work and remove the influence of campaign contributors at the same time.

Corruption

At its extreme, worker criticism of politicians alleges outright, and often widespread, corruption. The issue of corruption is one where the cynicism of workers contrasts starkly with the disillusionment of activists. For example,

Carol, a thirty-four-year-old environmental activist, had been instrumental in working on a citizen petition drive that resulted in revoking a wetlands protection exemption given for a major development project. The effort had been opposed by local real estate developers, and during the campaign Carol became aware of the "relationships" between these developers and the board of aldermen who would ultimately vote on the ordinance. She hesitantly offers this highly tentative critique:

CAROL: We've got a board of aldermen that for the most part have members that have been on that board for ten, twelve, fourteen years and I believe—people get very, very—[pause]—I have never believed, and again maybe I'm still naïve to a certain degree, I believe that there are a lot of loyalties by members of the board to various developers within the community. I am not trying to say that I believe that they are on the take or are on their payroll. But I do believe there is a lot of favor giving in the sense that, "Look, if you get me this rezoning, I'll remember that." That favor might come in the form of a legal contribution for a future campaign [or providing employment for the relative of a board member]. Those are the kinds of favors that are not really vote buying but they do—you can't help but establish some sort of a relationship with anybody that you work with as an elected official.

In contrast to the tentativeness of discussing "loyalties" and "relationships," workers paint a picture of politicians with a broader, starker brush.

PETER: They're all a bunch of crooks, I think. It's sad to say, but it's true. They're either crooks or incompetent, it seems sometimes.

DC: What gives you that sense?

PETER: Well, just look at the news. You see the S and L stuff—what, a hundred billion dollars something like that? It's so incredible we don't—we can't even take it in. A hundred billion dollars! You mean to tell me that nobody saw that coming? Come on. And that's just one case. It seems every few weeks you hear of another case of corruption or greed of some kind. I just think it's everywhere. It's everywhere.

While for many workers politicians' behavior can be best explained by their desire to be reelected, others see the corruption of politics as being an even clearer explanation for their actions. Warren, a fifty-six-year-old salesperson, holds such a view.

WARREN: Basically I think politicians are crooks. . . . They handle issues whichever way they can make the most money out of. That's it. If you want to understand politicians, look at the money. They'll do anything for money.

Joanne, a labor activist, agrees that the rank and file of her union tend to assume the corruption of politicians and that this is a factor in discouraging worker engagement in politics.

JOANNE: I just think that most people think that politics is pretty much corrupt and that there's not a whole lot of reason to get really active in it. . . . For the most part I think that, again, our members are not that different from the rest of the population. They look at the situation and they say, "It's really bad." I think they're right.

Thus, the perceived corruption of politicians is yet another way that workers come to feel that their vote or participation matter little.

I have noted that in speaking of corrupt, or at least inept, politicians, workers paint with a broad brush. But several of them also make room for exceptions to their characterization of politicians. Although they take a clearly minority position, these workers believe that electing different officials could make a difference.

ELLEN: [I]t's pretty clear that a lot of people are crooked who get into politics. I mean, there's a lot of that, I'm sure. But just because some of them do that, it doesn't mean that they're all that way. . . . Well, I guess I'm an optimist. [laughs] I don't know. I think that it's important that we can elect whoever we think is the best person. They may not always do everything they say they're gonna do but still it makes a difference, I think, who you get in there.

The exceptions to the rule, some workers feel, are well-intentioned politicians who enter politics out of a sense of public service. But there is little doubt amongst these workers that such well-intentioned politicians often succumb to various temptations or are overwhelmed by the political system. As Andrea puts it, "I think there are those that are just and good and right when they start out. But I feel that once they get involved, it's all so corrupt, I don't think they can help it."

One temptation cited is simply access to power.

ANDREA: I tend to think that a lot of times when people get into power positions they—how do I explain this—they get caught up in that power thing where they're in control and a lot of time lose sight of what's right and what's good. Because humans tend to feed on power.

Another problem that faces well-intentioned politicians is the need to play by the established rules in order to have any influence inside the system.

BERNICE: I'm sure some people get into it thinking they're gonna change things, but once they get there they find out different. They've got to play the game to get votes and so on. They just can't go in there and do what they want. I think either they change their ideas or they get out.

The importance of identifying the "system," rather than just politicians, as the source of the problem with politics is that it suggests a mere changing of the guard will make no difference. It is generally believed that even the best-intentioned official is likely to succumb to the contaminating influence of the political system. This suggests that calls to change politics by electing someone new are likely to fall on skeptical ears. Instead, most workers envision a more pervasive political "system" that resists such simple attempts at change. Such an analysis also suggests why there is widespread support for term limits that would lead to wholesale turnover of officeholders.

Workers sometimes seem a little surprised at hearing themselves make such pessimistic analyses of the political system. More than one suggested that perhaps they felt so negative because the media highlighted only the sordid side of politics. Cindy, a thirty-five-year-old hospital cafeteria worker, puts it this way:

CINDY: I feel like all you hear from the media are the bad things. We hear about the crooked politicians and the bribes and all the problems, but you never hear about the guy who keeps plugging away at it trying to do the best he can. You never hear about the programs or whatever that do work, that do help people.

So in the midst of cynical resignation some workers continue to believe that there are politicians and government programs that *are* doing a good job. Workers who hold such beliefs, however, are clearly a minority.

Although separated here for the sake of clarity, the three central assumptions that workers made concerning politicians (that they were either out of touch, preoccupied with reelection, or corrupt) are not mutually exclusive and some workers presented two or even all three of these analyses. Whether presented individually or in some combination, however, each of these analyses contributes to a more generalized sense on the part of workers that the political system is fixed in favor of people unlike themselves. As I will explore in more detail in the next chapter, the workers I spoke with unanimously express a feeling of powerlessness to influence the political process. At the same time, they all recognize that there is one universal source of political influence: money.

Money and Politics

In the eyes of most workers, money and politics go hand in hand. Money pervades the system from top to bottom and affects policy from local zoning ordinances to foreign policy. For example, some workers express skepticism about the role money and profits played in the Gulf War, with Helen arguing, "There's got to be something to do with oil companies or whatever at the bottom of this." Money flows, according to workers, both legally through campaign contributions, and illegally, through kickbacks and bribes.

The role of money is most often cited as affecting domestic politics when the rich and powerful buy their influence over the decisions of government. Very often, individual workers cite several different mechanisms through which money influences the process. Workers take it as given that people with money dominate the political process. During the interviews, my regular questions about how things are accomplished in politics were sometimes met with incredulous laughter at my apparent naïveté.

DC: When you say that regular people can't have an effect but that some other people might be able to, what's the difference?

JUDY: Money. [laughs]

DC: Yeah? Is that important, do you think?

JUDY: Oh, sure it is. [laughs] Money talks. I think if you've got money you can do things that regular people can't do. You can get away with things and stuff like that because people know you have money.

Judy goes on to note that the things that people "get away" with include the "bending" of rules from zoning laws and building permits, to differential treatment when the children of the wealthy "get in trouble with the cops." On a larger scale, she argues that it is "big business" that holds the most sway over politicians.

JUDY: I think that business keeps people employed, so the politicians all pay real close attention to them. And there's so much money floating around. Like, I'm in the insurance field and—I don't see any of this stuff myself, I'm just a secretary—but I know that there's millions and millions of dollars that insurance companies have invested in all these different places. So they can go around and say, "OK, we'll invest in this project or that project." That's all legal and everything, but they know that they can get things in return for making investments in certain areas.

DC: What kinds of things do they get?

JUDY: Basically, they can get votes. When something comes up for a vote that affects the insurance industry they can say, "Hey, remember we've got so many millions invested in your state."

Judy's is a sophisticated analysis that goes beyond blatant bribe taking to acknowledge the more subtle and complex ways that corporate money pervades the political system. She is not alone in her assessment. Corporations are the single biggest influence buyers cited by workers.

Some workers see the influence of corporate money coming from the structure of the political process itself, not from illegal corruption. Oscar, a sixty-two-year-old electrician at a defense plant, says the "guys on Wall Street" and the heads of "big corporations" are the ones with enough resources to "pull the strings" that run the country.

DC: How does that work? How do they go about "pulling strings"?

OSCAR: Money. Money and jobs, I think. If you own a big corporation, you can contribute to these candidates when they run for office. I know some of them give money to both of them just so they'll be sure to have a winner. So they finance these campaigns, and when they win they've got their man in there.

Oscar argues that the common perception that corruption in government is increasing is a mistaken one, not because there is not as much corruption as people think, but because there has always been a high level of corruption.

OSCAR: I think people think there's more of it because they see it in the papers whereas in the old days it was everywhere but nobody said anything. In the old days it was business as usual.

As evidence, he cites what he says is a now-defunct local custom of giving voters a ride to the poll, "slipping them five bucks," and saying, "Here you go, now you know who to vote for." Such blatant tactics, Oscar feels, would be quickly reported in the media today.

Workers do not cite only the money behind campaigns as a central influence. A few also suggest the more diffuse impact of money on society's operation. Ronald cites the "system" as the reason social ills are not addressed properly. "If you've got the money, you can get anything done," he says. When I query further about a particular social issue he had cited, crime, Ronald suggests an elaborate hierarchy of corruption that prevents social change.

DC: How does "the system" work to prevent a change in crime—in reducing crime?

RONALD: It's at all different things I think. You've got dope pushers or whatever who are making more money in a day than you or I see in a month. That affects kids growing up in that stuff. What's the way to make money? Not school or work—it's drugs. So you got more and more people getting into it for the money. Then you got cops who'll get their palms greased to look the other way while these kids run their operations—they're looking for the money. The same is probably true of judges and the big guys—the Mafia types. And then the laws in the first place—I mean the criminals got all the rights. These guys, if they ever do get caught, they're out the door in a couple of hours. The lawyers get it, the politicians get it when they're running for election. The money's everywhere, that's what I think. I think a lot of people are naïve about that. It's money that—money makes the world go round, right? I think that's true. It's sad to say, Dave, but I think that's true. That's the real world.

The "real world" seems to be a place where many workers feel they do not stand a chance. The odds are stacked against them, and there is nothing that they can do to change them.

The Intractability of the System

Worker references to "the system" include both the formal government and its processes, and the outside actors that influence government. Thus, references to the system might include the kind of campaign finance issues cited above.

The fundamental point that workers make about the system is that it is intractable. In fact, they often provide an encompassing circularity of argument. Citizens are unable to change the system, it is argued, because the system cannot be changed. Or as Peter puts it, "I guess there's nothing really that I could say that would affect [my elected representatives]. I think those that are honest are already trying to figure things out—what the people want—and those that are crooked wouldn't care anyway." Such reasoning undergirds skepticism about political participation, sometimes even about voting, as a waste of time.

In part because of the corruption of those associated with it, the system is seen to be rife with waste and inefficiency. Interestingly, the two government employees in my interviews are among the strongest critics of government (although both exempt their own particular work from their critique). Roger, a local public-works department employee argues:

ROGER: I think the government is as much a part of the problem as anything now. . . . I think if people saw all the waste and inefficiency that was brought on by the red tape and the bureaucrats, you wouldn't believe it sometimes. It just doesn't make sense. . . . I'm out on the street most of the time. I don't have a desk job. But in my department there are people and secretaries that that's all they do. They push paper all day long.

On the federal level, Peter, a postal-service employee, delivers a similar critique.

PETER: There's so much waste in government work. It's unbelievable some times. . . . At least with the post office you have to interact with the public. If the mail isn't getting out, people know about it pretty quick. But for a lot of the government, people have no idea what's going on because we never see it. We don't know what's happening to all the money that gets spent in these different areas. There's no way to find out. I'm sure a lot of it is wasted. I'm sure.

Not only does the system overwhelm efforts at citizen-initiated reform, but workers believe that even well-intentioned politicians have been overwhelmed by the problems they face. As a result, working people see little hope that significant change will occur any time soon.

ROGER: I don't think politicians right now can do anything about it. They run on these platforms with all these ideas that they're gonna change things but once they get in there they realize there's not much they can do. There's such an entrenched bureaucracy that there's not much they can really get accomplished.

DC: . . . So is there anything that can be done about the political system we have now?

ROGER: It's hard to see what. At some point I think it's just gonna collapse on it's own weight. It's gotten so huge and the deficits are so big that it can't go on forever.

Such a pessimistic view is starkly at odds with the message activists try to communicate regarding the potential agency of citizens organized for political action. Again, it is the issue of potential efficacy that most separates workers and activists.

As noted above, some activists became politically active, in part, because they were startled to learn that the American political system is not what their civics books described. Commenting on the lessons of her involvement with the citizens' wetlands petition, Carol comments:

CAROL: I think that most people are very naïve about how things actually get done and how things really work. I say that now because I think that I was really naïve about thinking that we could do something that was right and fair and then run up against such obstacles that were without merit. It was very frustrating.

It would seem inaccurate to suggest that the workers I spoke with are "naïve about how things actually get done." Workers are more cynical than naïve. They seem to know all too well how politics "really work."

Activists, then, especially those who work in electoral politics, face a dilemma. They are sometimes aware of the contempt most people have for the political system. In their role as activists, however, they are usually trying to get people more involved in some aspect of politics. For example, in working with a progressive electoral coalition of labor and community groups, Phillip sees the coalition's roles as combating the cynicism engendered by politics as usual and promoting candidates who will respond to people's real needs.

PHILLIP: What we want to do is to get people to really stand for issues that are connected to people's lives. You want them to be part of the process. We're inviting them to be part of the process.

But if the "process"—that is, the "system"—is corrupt and bankrupt, why would workers want to become part of it? As we have seen, workers tend to believe that the system is so well entrenched that it subverts even well-intentioned actors.

HELEN: [T]here are some who go in there thinking that they're gonna change things, but they find out quick that to get anything done you have to play by the rules, and playing by the rules means not rocking the boat or trying to change things.

Thus, even if workers are convinced of the sincerity of reform efforts, they generally see such endeavors as doomed to failure.

There are activists, though, who share in workers' frustration with a political system that seems intractable. Some cite their involvement with social movements as a way of addressing social issues without having to get involved in "politics" in the formal, electoral sense. Several activists, for example, distinguished between "politics," which they take to mean electoral politics, and "activism," which they understand to be social-movement participation. In their minds, these are two very different pursuits. Patrick, an environmental activist from a working-class background, notes:

PATRICK: I don't get involved in politics too much. I get too frustrated. Maybe that's the best way to put it. Frustrated that you just can't get anything accomplished. . . . Frustrated by the system. It just seems that when you go back to what politicians are actually supposed to do, represent the people and not special interests—they're always representing special interests no matter what.

But as I shall explore in the next chapter, workers do not make much of a distinction between electoral politics and social-movement politics. The electoral process *and* the external political forces—including social-movement efforts—are conceived as being all part of an intransigent political "system."

"It's Just Politics"

Lack of trust in the political system has led to the identification of politics in general as being an enterprise that should not be taken seriously. The phrase I heard over and over again that best sums up this attitude is, "It's just politics." The expression is an important one that serves multifaceted purposes.

"Politics" is something that workers contrast to "real" work or accomplishments. It is the political equivalent of "paper pushing" in the work place.

RONALD: It's all talk, you know what I mean? I listen to those clowns—come on! [laughs] They're all going on about one thing or another. Naw, it's . . . it's all just politics—lot of stuff that doesn't concern me. I don't have time for that stuff.

After being queried about the meaning of "it's all politics," another worker elaborates:

DIANE: Politics? Well, I guess I meant that you've got these guys talking about some issue like crime or something, and they're up there telling you what ought to be done and what they're gonna do. But really it's all politics. They don't really care about the issue. All they care about it getting elected so they'll say anything they think will make them popular in the polls. They just do it for politics. Like Bush with "No new taxes" and "Read my lips" and all that. I bet he knew all along that he was going to raise taxes once he got in, but he knew that people didn't want that. They wanted someone who would say "no taxes," so he did it. . . . It's like at work when somebody gets a raise or a promotion up front, and they say "it's all politics." It means that the person didn't get it because they were good or qualified or whatever. They got it because they knew somebody or were friends or kissed up to somebody, you know. That kind of stuff, too.

Politics, then, is an activity that is conducted on the basis of something other than merit. Politics is seen as "all talk" because it is about the process of being elected, not of addressing actual issues. In the workplace, promotions can be "all politics" because they are based on personal connections or favoritism, not real merit.

Politics is, in these terms, a sort of sleight of hand, something that distracts, obscures, and serves as a smokescreen for something else that is *really* going on. The phrase, then, is a versatile one that can be appropriately applied in a wide range of contexts, from the workplace politics cited above to the international politics surrounding the Gulf War.

HELEN: I think it's all politics. The U.S. says "Be our friends, and we'll take care of you," and that's how they buy these governments off. Then once we're there, U.S. business comes in and makes money. I think that's really at the bottom of it. I mean, do you think they really care about the people of Kuwait? What happened to them is horrible, but really. They don't even care about what happens to their own people. I don't think they'd be doing all this just to protect the people of Kuwait.

Again, the common thread that holds together the phrase "just politics" in a diverse set of circumstances is the belief that something that is "political" is no longer decided on the basis of merit. Instead, extraneous influences and considerations have an impact on decision making. Those in authority—whether bosses or politicians—will usually work at maintaining the deceptive appearance of a fair and legitimate decision-making process. "Politics," therefore, is being equated with a sort of deception. This contributes to a deep cynicism towards the entire political process. Dorothy, a forty-two-year-old machine operator, says:

DOROTHY: Yeah, you know, all the talk and the bullshit. Sometimes I think that's all [politicians] do is talk—and everybody knows it's crap.

DC: You think so?

DOROTHY: Oh sure. Nobody believes any of those slimy characters anymore.

The harsh judgment of Dorothy's comments is characteristic of workers' cynical dismissal of politicians and the political process. Goldfarb (1991: 13) writes that:

Cynicism, in a certain sense, is an understandable and rational response to our present-day circumstances. Television, our major form of society-wide communication, is saturated with lies and manipulations. Our political leaders are more concerned with reelection than political accomplishment. Social justice . . . is more distant than ever. . . . And pieties about the values of democracy appear quite empty. For those who look closely and critically at the American way of life, there is much about which to be cynical.

The workers I spoke with would concur.

Goldfarb's reference to television as a contributor to growing cynicism is significant. It seems plausible to speculate that the perception of manipulative and deceptive political discourse has been exaggerated by the emergence of mass-media communications. Many political campaigns have relied primarily upon the media, rather than traditional party campaign structures, to communicate their messages. This has significance for voters in that it may nurture the perception that "it's just politics."

The reason is two-fold. First, with the decline of party "machines," with their local ward bosses and precinct captains, voters often do not have direct personal contact with the representatives of political parties. The often-lamented loss of the "personal touch" in politics may indeed be significant in eliminating, for many voters, any sense of immediacy from political life.

Second, such direct contact has often been replaced by political communication that emanates from a core of media-savvy campaign advisers who market their candidates in much the same way as other goods are sold to potential consumers. The slick—and often negative—campaign commercials increasingly relied upon by political candidates may be expedient for them in the short term. However, they may be having a more lasting impact as symbols of a political system that has taken on all of the hucksterism of the commercial marketplace. It should be no surprise, therefore, that voters look upon this political world with great skepticism.

Conclusion

The idea that politics is an endeavor worthy of distrust is not new, nor is it limited to the working class. Over sixty years ago, Lynd and Lynd (1956: 420) noted in their classic study of "Middletown" that "In the minds of many citizens political is identified with fraud." In fact, they noted, "Not the least significant feature of this political corruption is the fact that it is so taken for granted by most citizens and by both parties." The workers in my interviews certainly follow in this tradition.

But political activism requires a certain faith that the political system can be transformed into something other than a corrupt process. Activists must believe in the possibility of positively changing the system. Workers, though, exhibit a near fatalism about the shortcomings of this system.

It takes only a short time of speaking with working people to dismiss any pretense that workers are quiescent because of their satisfaction with the political status quo. As Halle (1984: 201) once noted, "American workers fully subscribe to the ideals of a democratic society while firmly believing that current politics falls hopelessly short of these ideals." When asked directly about the current state of political affairs, their comments are often bitter and hostile, but are usually coupled with resignation. For most workers, understanding political corruption and the role of money in politics is part of being a realist. And, as I shall show in the next chapter, being a realist means understanding that as regular working people, there is nothing they can do to change the situation.

CHAPTER 5

"It Doesn't Make a Difference"
The Absence of Efficacy

[W]hat are you going to do about it? A lot of times I don't like the weather, but I don't wrack my brain trying to think up a way to change it because I know there's nothing I can do about it. If it's raining or whatever, . . . I go inside. I don't try to stop it from raining. I think that's how most people think about the government. There's nothing they can do about it so why bother worrying about it. They just try to get out of the way. There's too many things closer to them that maybe they could do something about.

HELEN, fifty-six-year-old factory worker

Working people recognize that the country faces pressing social and political problems. But regardless of their desire for change, they generally do not feel they have the capacity to produce such change either through voting or through other forms of political action. This sense is part of a larger experience of powerlessness for workers. Managing the worlds of work and home life present formidable challenges for workers; the larger world of politics seems far beyond their influence. Consequently, working people express a somewhat fatalistic belief that they cannot do anything to affect the current state of affairs.

Part of the business of social-movement activists, in contrast, is the promotion of efficacy. Organizers are charged with the task of convincing people that, in fact, they *can* do something about the problems that face them and the rest of society. Thus, the class divide between activists and workers is most apparent with the issue of efficacy.

Inefficacy

Without exception, workers with whom I spoke express a sense of inefficacy in response to the political and social problems that face the nation. They see no role for themselves in addressing the issues that plague the public realm. A major reason for this feeling is that they perceive themselves to be "average" or "regular" people who, almost by definition, are incapable of effecting change.

DIANE: I don't think an average person can do much. They're just one person in a million, you know. I don't really think a person can change the system. Like they say, "You can't fight city hall." I think usually that's true.

This belief often leads to a sense that social and political problems are inevitable and that resignation is the only sane response.

OSCAR: [Y]ou were asking me about all these problems and what can I do about them. The answer, really, is nothing. There's nothing I can do about it so it's pretty hard to get too worked up about it.

Implicit in such comments is the belief that politics is carried out by "other" people better equipped for such tasks. For most workers, this analysis is the logical conclusion of recognizing simple facts of life: as working people they do not have the power to affect political decisions. The resulting feeling of political powerlessness is pervasive, and applies to their roles both as voters and as potential social-movement participants.

Voting and the Electoral Process

The most obvious avenue for potentially effecting political change is through the voting booth. But electoral politics is an arena where workers feel they have no influence.

HELEN: I think just about everyone knows there are problems. I don't know what other people have been telling you, but I think that's pretty clear. Just look at—we were talking about voting. Who bothers to vote any more? Every election they talk about how it was the lowest turnout since whenever. Nobody bothers anymore.

DC: And that's because . . . ?

HELEN: That's because they know it doesn't make a difference.

In theory, representative democracy offers citizens the chance to use their ballots to change the political leadership. Workers, though, are skeptical of the process, and only a few workers I interviewed say they vote regularly. Many more admit to rarely if ever voting. In a chicken or egg conundrum, workers argue that voters have given up because politicians do not change and, in turn, politicians do not change because voters have given up.

DC: Does voting, then, act as a threat to politicians—if they don't do what the people want, they'll get voted out of office?

BERNICE: It should, but I don't think it does. I really don't think it does.

DC: Why is that?

BERNICE: Because I think people have given up. They throw up their hands. They don't even hope for anything to happen anymore.

But some workers, notably older ones, still see voting as a civic duty of every citizen. Some cite their upbringing as the source of their feelings but recognize that such beliefs are no longer commonly held. One worker who has several adult children says:

JOHN: I think it's more something that I grew up with. Again, like with politics, my father's the one that—voting was a big deal. In America, you voted. That was it. It was kind of like a duty, your patriotic duty. I know today they'd laugh at that. Nobody votes anymore. But I guess I got that drilled into me—you're American, you vote.

But when asked if he brought up his children to vote regularly, John admits:

JOHN: No, no, I didn't. They grew up with Nixon and Watergate and Jimmy Carter. I think it's pretty hard to point to all that and say, "See what a good thing voting does?" [laughs]

Some workers, though, were critical of nonvoters. The most common critique was a simple one that Daniel colorfully sums up by saying, "[I]f you don't bother to vote then you ain't got no business bitching." Even some nonvoters agree with this assessment.

KAREN: It's not right to complain about the government if you haven't even bothered to vote. That's the way I feel about it. I didn't vote this time so I really can't say that this or that is wrong or that this candidate shouldn't be in there.

Thus, despite their limited impact, some workers feel the opportunities afforded by electoral politics need to be utilized since they are all that is available to citizens.

HUGH: [Y]ou can't just throw up your hands and say, "Oh, well, there's nothing I can do about it." You've got to at least try and get the guy you think is gonna do the best job—at least the guy who's not as bad as the other guy—you've got to try and get him in there. At least do that.

But even workers who vote are not enthusiastic about the possibility of electoral politics serving as the route to meaningful political change.

Workers seem to think some elections offer more chance for change than others. In a reversal of the belief that all politics are local, workers cite presidential elections as being the most important.

PETER: I vote for the president, I always do that. I don't always get around to voting for—voting in the other elections.

DC: Do you think voting for the president is more important?

PETER: In a way, yes. I mean he sets the tone for the whole country. He can decide a lot of things. And you hear so much more about it. You see it on TV for months and months, especially here with the primary and everything. It kind of gets you out more.

But even such select participation is in the minority amongst the workers with whom I spoke. More often, workers have largely abandoned the idea of meaningful participation in electoral politics.

TOM: I think people have basically given up. They don't trust the people running and so they don't bother to vote. What, now about half the people don't even bother to vote, is that it? . . . I mean, what does that tell you? It tells me that people just don't care anymore. They don't have any faith in the political system.

This lack of faith results in dissatisfaction among voters and high levels of nonvoting among workers.

Nonvoting

Working people do not feel efficacious when it comes to electoral politics, and there are six basic reasons that they give for not participating. First, there is a simple belief held by many workers that their single vote does not really make a difference amongst the millions cast in an election.

Second, workers suggest that voting matters little since, regardless of who wins, elections do not produce significant change.

DC: Do you think who gets elected matters? Does that make a difference?

RONALD: Yeah, I guess so, on the small stuff. I don't think the big things change though. I don't think Dukakis would be doing any better with the economy than Bush is. I mean, look at Massachusetts! [laughs] Would you want the whole country to look like that? . . . I just don't think it really makes a difference, both my vote and who gets in.

Part of why election results seem to make little difference, and a third reason for not voting, is that when workers do vote, they often face what they feel to be a lack of choice between candidates. For example, Donna says she does not vote and gives this explanation:

DONNA: I think they've already made the choice for you by the time you get to vote. I really don't see the difference, like I said earlier, between Bush and Dukakis. I didn't like either one of them. What am I supposed to do, vote for the one I hate less? [laughs] That's what a lot of people do you know. . . . [P]eople vote against the one they hate more so at least they won't get in.

Helen confirms this suspicion.

HELEN: I don't think anybody votes *for* anyone anymore. I think people vote against the person they think will be worse. It's the lesser of two evils. It's the old joke about "Do you want to resign or be fired?" It doesn't leave much room for keeping your job. Voting's the same thing. You're picking the lesser of two evils. Either way, though, you lose. I think people get tired of that. They get tired of not having any real choices.

The limited choice voters feel they have has turned elections into a sort of negative 'democracy. Not only do citizens vote *against* a candidate rather than *for* one, but the primary purpose of voting has become to "throw out" the incumbent.

DC: Do you think voting can be an effective way to change things?

DANIEL: Well, you may not change things but at least you can throw them out, you know? At least they know you got that over them. . . . You can kick 'em out if they don't do the job.

Such a sentiment is the result of frustration with the existing political system and calls into question the fundamental meaning of even limited representative democracy.

A fourth reason people say they do not vote is that the two major parties have become so similar, there is little difference between them. When one party's candidate seems essentially the same as the other party's, it is difficult for workers to develop strong party allegiance.

OSCAR: In the old days, I think, you were a Democrat or you were a Republican and that meant something. The Democrat—in my mind anyway, and that was the way I was brought up—the Democrat was for the working man. The Republican—that was the rich, the businessman, you know? That was the difference. You'd go vote, and even if you didn't know the guy, you knew that if he was a Democrat he was the guy to vote for 'cause he was for the working man. I think it made it a lot easier then. You knew where they stood.

DC: You think that's changed now?

OSCAR: Oh yeah! Now it really doesn't matter—Democrat, Republican, I think it's pretty much the same. I don't think it matters any more. Now I vote for the man not the party. I voted for Bush, I voted for Reagan because I didn't think the Democrats really had anybody that could do the job. I think Dukakis was a joke.

Though Oscar continues to vote, the implication is that strong party identities once made voting "easier." For workers who pay minimal attention to politics, knowing that a vote for one party or the other "means something" helps simplify electoral participation and provides a sense of continuity through various elections. It is a daunting task to assess each candidate in each election because their party affiliations seem to have become largely meaningless.

Fifth, some workers mention that they are less inclined to vote because the outcome of elections has become so predictable.

JOHN: What's the difference? You usually know who's gonna win before the election anyway, right? The polls tell you before you even vote. Why bother?

Relatively accurate polling results, coupled with the media's "horse-race" coverage of elections, seems to create a self-fulfilling prophecy. Election campaigns are fought and won in the media, seemingly without the need for actual voters.

Finally, the sixth reason people cite for not voting is that government doesn't respond to voters, but to the "special interests" who populate the political system. This last issue deserves a closer look.[1]

"Special Interests"

Workers feel that voters are not the driving force behind politics. Instead, they tend to suggest that named or unnamed "special interests" are the real political players. "Special interests," argues one worker, are:

JOHN: [G]roups that are pushing their own agenda. You got GM or something pushing to stop Japanese cars because it hurts their sales, or some oil company fighting to get the right to drill somewhere, or in the old days you had unions pushing for changes in labor laws—women, blacks. Things like that.

Of course business, labor, women, and blacks make up the vast majority of the population. So whereas special-interest groups collectively represent the majority of Americans, the defining characteristic of special-interest groups is that they are concerned exclusively with their own particular membership's interest, and not with the good of the society as a whole, nor with unrepresented segments of society. (Tellingly, nonunion, white, working-class men are notably absent from John's list of special interests.) Workers feel that the influence of special interests can lead to the subversion of democratic politics, thus making voting less attractive.

HUGH: Sometimes I think it's more and more these [special-interest] groups that really run the country. . . . You can vote, and you can get the guy in there that you think will do a good job, but once they're in there, it seems that all these special-interest groups get after him, you know.

Generally speaking, these white working people do not see themselves as constituents in the contests between competing "special interests." This was true for women as well as for men, and it was true despite the fact that some workers have had to temporarily rely on government programs such as unemployment insurance and food stamps. Rather than seeing themselves as a beneficiary "special-interest" group, workers see the tax money taken from their paychecks flowing to the special interests of either the rich or the poor (the latter of whom are sometimes virtually indistinguishable in their minds from urban blacks).

The rich are able to compete in special-interest contests because of their money and influence. The poor compete because they have nothing to lose and because they have influential allies in the liberal establishment. Thomas and Mary Edsall (1991: 8) have argued that the Democratic Party's support for the 1964 Civil Rights Act marked the beginning of a fundamental shift in the party's orientation, leaving the white working class feeling abandoned. "Instead of being seen as advancing the economic well-being of all voters, including white mainstream working and middle-class voters, liberalism and the Democratic party came to be perceived, in key sectors of the electorate, as promoting the establishment of new rights and government guarantees for previously marginalized, stigmatized, or historically disenfranchised groups, often at the expense of traditional constituencies." As reflected by Oscar's comment, cited above, that the Democrats no longer stand for the "working man," workers feel left out and abandoned by politicians who at one time might have been seen as allies for working people.

The fact that these white workers do not consider themselves poor *and* that they often equate the poor with the nation's racial minorities means that the divisions of class and race are inexorably intertwined. There is no doubt, for example, that welfare bashing can be politically expedient because of its double-barreled use of race and class. Working people tend to resent those dependent on government benefits. If those benefit recipients also are disproportionately black, then it makes it all the easier for these white workers to see the poor as different from themselves.

Although labor unions might be said to represent the interests of workers, the workers I spoke with seemed to disagree with that view. Instead, unions are seen as one of the troubling special interests who subvert the political process.

HELEN: Well, you've got all these different interests. You've got business interests who push for their issues and you've got labor unions who push for their side. Things like that.

Labor unions may seem to be an exception to the rule that special-interest battles take place between rich and poor, representing, instead, "average" working people. But in fact, for nonunionized workers, union members are treated as a sort of working-class elite—having nowhere near the power and stature of the nation's "rich and powerful" but still comparatively well-off. Unions, therefore, are caught in a catch-22, shown by Daniel's comments.

DANIEL: Well, I think the American worker got greedy. I mean the unions and everything did good. They helped the average Joe, you know? But they kept pushing and pushing and pushing. Now we can't build anything. The Japanese got all the cars, the TVs and stuff. It costs so much to make anything in the U.S. that nobody can afford it no more. Companies got to go overseas where they can compete. That means jobs gone here. I mean we seen it in New England. The shoes—there used to be a big shoe factory that my wife worked at for ten years. Then one day, bang, they closed up cause of foreign stuff, cheap shoes from Korea and Hong Kong and places like that. I mean they pay them people, what, two bucks a day. It's crazy.

While unions are clearly seen as helpful for some workers, their perceived emphasis on continually higher wages contributes to a sense of greed that undermines support from nonmembers. They become, in this sense, "special interests" interested only in a narrow agenda that benefits their select group of workers.

The four workers among my interviewees who are union members are generally appreciative of union-won benefits and working conditions. However, even they are skeptical about whom unions are really representing.

OSCAR: [U]nions now are big business. That's how I look at it. I say that and I'm in one, right? I pay my dues and all, but I really think unions have become big business now. They're not really interested in the working man—the regular guy on the floor. It's all these union leaders who make hundreds of thousands of dollars a year talking buddy-buddy with the heads of these companies. "I'll scratch your back, if you scratch mine." That's pretty much all it is. I don't think the unions fight for the working man anymore.

Halle (1984: 175) discovered similar relationships between the unionized chemical workers in his study and the unions to which they belong. He writes, "the relation between rank-and-file workers and the union officers is uneasy. Indeed, the general attitude of the former toward their union combines strong suspicion with an equally strong conviction that without the union they would be at the mercy of a potentially arbitrary and capricious management. . . . 'Unions,' they say, 'are a necessary evil.' " The fact that unions are seen by some of their own members as having abandoned working people is an indication of the extent of their skepticism of collective efforts. As we shall see, this skepticism extends beyond unions to include other sorts of movement activity.

In the end, workers do not feel efficacious when it comes to electoral politics. All of the reasons they give for not voting are related to these perceptions that their votes do not significantly impact election outcomes and that elections do not result in significant change. Instead, the electoral process is dominated by special interests.

Collective Efforts

Workers who feel disempowered in the face of an unresponsive electoral system feel similarly about other forms of political activity. All workers I spoke with expressed, at minimum, skepticism about their ability to individually effect change. Most flatly reject the idea, opting instead for an almost fatalistic political vision. A few, though, make a distinction between individual and collective action and feel that in some cases collective efforts can produce results.

DANIEL: Well, you gotta have people together, I guess. One guy can't go and do—you know, "you can't fight city hall," like they say. You need to get together. That's when things can change, when people decide that they're gonna work together.

Some workers are aware of, and appreciative of, successful social movements of the past. One thirty-three-year-old woman cites the "equal rights groups in the sixties" as a source of desirable change for women.

JUDY: I think [the "equal rights groups"] eventually made a difference for the kind of work that women can do—the kind of jobs they can get and stuff. That was a good thing. If a woman can do the work there's no reason why she shouldn't be able to get the job. . . . Now women get equal rights when it comes to jobs but before they didn't.

(The sentiment that the work of social movements struggling for equality is now complete is a common one.) Other workers are skeptical of the effectiveness of political groups but feel their presence is a positive influence.

HUGH: I don't know if it's very helpful. These people go out there and march around all day and stuff but I don't really think anything's changed at the end of the day, you know. . . . [But] they kind of keep an eye on some of the things that big companies do—things like that. So I guess that's good.

While remaining pessimistic, workers see more hope, at least in the abstract, in effecting political change through collective than through individual action. Workers do not, however, see themselves as likely to be part of a social movement.

Social-Movement Support

With a few exceptions (Greenpeace, National Rifle Association, Clamshell Alliance, Ralph Nader), workers are generally unaware of the names of particular movement organizations or activists. But they do have a sense of the issues addressed by such movements and the general purpose of these groups.

The workers I spoke with usually took "social movements" to mean those groups that engage in what William Greider (1992: 161) calls "the politics of rude and crude"—that is, political groups who work outside regular political channels in usually an oppostional manner, often staging dramatic protest actions geared for media consumption. There are workers who express clear support for various social-movement efforts, despite the fact that they do not belong to such movement organizations.

JOHN: I mean some of them are good. Like the Ralph Nader stuff, for consumers. I think most of that is good. You find out about the companies that are trying to rip you off. . . . Some of the protests to stop some of the pollution is good, too. It can get carried too far sometimes, but some of it is good. The stuff that happened around Seabrook [nuclear power plant] was good. That place should never have been built. They were right to protest that. . . . Like I said, some of them have done some real good.

John's comments are by no means universally accepted amongst the workers with whom I spoke. In fact, as we will see below, workers are more often skeptical of the goals, motives, and impact of movements. However, even workers who are skeptical or opposed to social-movement goals are nonetheless universal in their recognition of the right of such organizations to exist and to speak out.

BERNICE: I don't know if it's good that they're around but . . . [pause] I guess it would be bad if they weren't around. You know what I mean? I wouldn't want to be like in Russia where nobody can say anything—what they think. Here you can say what you think. I don't have any interest in this stuff so it doesn't affect me but it's at least they've got the right to say what they think. That's something.

Even Dorothy, whose husband was in a National Guard unit in the Persian Gulf at the time of this interview, affirms the right of antiwar protesters to demonstrate, while simultaneously disagreeing with them.

DC: How have you felt about the people who have demonstrated against U.S. involvement [in the Persian Gulf]?

DOROTHY: They don't have family over there, that's for sure. . . . If they had family over there, they wouldn't be stalling, asking for us to wait and wait. That's what all the guys over there hate the most. They hate the waiting, not knowing how long they're gonna be there. These protesters—they've got the right to speak out, it's a free country—but I think if they talked to the guys there they'd know they're not doing them any good.

In some cases, workers support a surprisingly wide array of political actions in the name of freedom of political expression. One worker notes his support for groups that try to "educate" people about issues.

ROGER: I think you've got the right in this country to speak out and stand up for what you believe in. If you want to have a demonstration or whatever to make your point and try and bring up an issue, that's OK, I think.

When asked if he supports demonstrations or protest actions that include violations of laws that result in arrests—civil disobedience actions—he continues to express some support.

ROGER: It depends. I think if you do something like that as a symbol and you're ready to accept the consequences—you're not trying to get away with something—then that's OK. If you're not gonna pay your taxes on principle and you tell everybody that and go to jail for it, I think that's different than trying to cheat the IRS just to make a little money on the side.

When asked if, overall, such protest groups can be healthy for the political system, Roger says, "Yeah, sure. Sometimes they can be." In fact, all workers support the *idea* of freedom of political expression and saw this as a particularly attractive feature of U.S. political life. However, they are much more skeptical of the practical impact on political life of social movements that exercise their right of expression.

Movements as Ineffective

Most workers feel that social movements are largely ineffective in achieving positive changes. For some workers, the ineffectiveness of such groups is self-apparent. Speaking of social-movement activism and "protest actions," John says, "I think that's probably why you see a lot less of it now. People realized that it usually didn't accomplish anything."

When Tom is challenged with evidence that seems to contradict his statements dismissing the effectiveness of movement efforts, he presents a highly nuanced analysis to defend his position.

DC: Let me play devil's advocate here. Haven't, say, environmental groups had an impact on how people view the environment? Isn't that an example of change?

TOM: I think they may affect how people think about things—like you said, the environment, that's the latest thing now. So people try to recycle and things like that, but I don't see that stuff having any impact on the government or on the companies—the big polluters. Just look at Exxon with that Valdez thing.

DC: So these groups might be educating people but not necessarily changing policy, then?

TOM: Yeah, I think it's two different things. Totally different. On the one hand, you kind of hope that people will see it's in their own interest to save, conserve, things like that. On the other hand, you're telling companies to spend more money to protect the environment and pollute less. It's against their interest in making money. It costs them more, so they're not gonna do it.

Tom's comments are in line with those of a number of workers who suggest that movements should be aimed at getting government and big business to change rather than being aimed at the behaviors of "regular" Americans. Working people see the problems in political and social life as emanating from such powerful elites, not from regular people like themselves.

Workers also make distinctions about the effectiveness of movements depending on the positions such groups advocate. Efforts that resist changes in the status quo, for example, are more likely to be seen as potentially effective since they are considered more realistic and within the "mainstream." In a comment that, as we will see, reflects several of the major doubts workers have about left movements more generally, Steve contrasts the National Rifle Association (NRA) with peace groups.

STEVE: [The NRA is] just saying people should have a right to have guns. They're not trying to change the system or whatever. . . . It is basically saying what I think most people already believe. But these peace protesters are kind of always against the tide, you know. They're always against the U.S. I don't think they can really change things like that. Nobody really wants to hear that stuff. . . . I think you've got to be mainstream. You can't be far out there like some of these people. You've got to be mainstream so that you can get people to belong—or to agree with what you're saying. That way, you get a lot of people and get big. That's the most important thing, I think.

Left movements generally fail to meet the criteria of being "big" and "mainstream."

Social movements are seen as generally ineffective for a variety of reasons. First, workers complain that the fleeting nature of social movements undermines their credibility.

RONALD: They seem to come and go. There's always somebody protesting something or other, but the issue always changes. For a while it's abortion, then it's ecology, then it's dolphins or whales or something.

The apparent transience of movement issues contributes to a distinct sense of jadedness among workers regarding various well-publicized collective efforts for change.

HUGH: The same problems—crime, hunger, poverty, war, whatever—it's the same problems over and over again. Whichever one is worse seems to get our attention for a while. It's like those concerts they have. One year it's starving Africans. The next it's bankrupt farmers, and the next it's the rain forest or something. I'm sure there are still starving Africans and bankrupt farmers, we've just moved on to more interesting things.

In this respect, social movements are seen to mirror the government's own inability to see a problem through to its solution.

DANIEL: Well, [the government] could do a lot more if they wanted. I mean like, take the war on drugs. What ever happened to that? I mean for a while there it was like this was it. This was gonna be the big push. We weren't gonna take it anymore. And that went on for a while and then, bang, it's something new. "War on what?" You know? [laughs]

Workers, then, are bombarded with fleeting and contradictory messages, from both movements and the government, about what is supposed to be the most pressing issue of the day. The fact that these calls appear fleeting and contradictory leads workers to look skeptically towards all such messages.

A second, and related, reason workers see movements as ineffective is due to the sheer number of predictable political actions.

CINDY: [T]here are so many of them that I think people just don't pay attention anymore. . . . It seems like every day there's some kind of demonstration somewhere protesting something. [laughs] I mean, really! I think people just go, "Oh, them again."

Other workers argue that the reason for the limited impact of protest actions is not only the prevalence of such efforts, but the fact that the public has gotten used to seeing them.

PETER: Well, with demonstrators and things, I don't think they're very effective. I don't think that type of thing makes—has an impact. Maybe in the days when nobody did things like that—that was a really unusual thing so everybody paid attention and it was in the news and everything. I think that maybe then it had a sort of impact. Now, though, everybody's got their own cause and their own marches and demonstrations so people kind of expect it.

The predictability of these efforts, then, helps undermine their effectiveness.

A third reason cited by workers for the ineffectiveness of social movements is the belief that such efforts were largely oppositional in nature rather than advancing positive solutions.

CINDY: Sometimes I think [social movements are] kind of like the news, you know. They always focus on the negative. They're against this or they're against that. But they never seem to be *for* anything. [laughs] Why don't they put forward some answers if they're against all these things? I never see them doing positive things like that. It's always negative, negative, negative. I guess that's why I've never really been interested in that kind of thing. I don't think it really helps anything.

Working people, then, see movements as simply pointing out problems and working *against* other groups. Workers, as we've seen, are all too aware of the plethora of troubles that face the society. What they don't see is anyone presenting realistic solutions.

Fourth, the absence of solutions contributes to workers' perceptions that movements are idealistic to a fault.

TOM: I guess [movement participants] are more idealistic than most people. . . . I guess you have to be to a certain degree. You have to think that what you're doing is gonna make a difference, even if it's pretty clear that it isn't doing much.

Furthermore, many workers see social-movement efforts as perhaps well-intentioned but profoundly naïve of political reality.

WARREN: I'm sure there are still some starry-eyed people who think they're gonna change the world out there. There are always those kinds out there finding some crusade to work on. . . . I guess you can't put people down for trying, but really, they're not gonna do anything. Things are not gonna change. There's always some group protesting or doing something, thinking that it's gonna make a big deal but nothing ever really happens, I think.

Such deep pessimism about the prospects for change are common.

Fifth, part of worker pessimism comes from the belief that social-movement and special-interest groups generally fight themselves into a stalemate, thus preventing any real political change. Collective action is seen as being countered by other collective action, reinforcing the image of a vast morass of deadlocked political actors.

RONALD: I don't see anything changing. It seems that things just go back and forth. It's like abortion, right, you mentioned that. It used to be that it was illegal until people protested enough to get it changed and then after a while there were protesters on the other side that started to push to get it back. I think they're just fighting each other. It kind of swings back and forth, but I don't think things change much, no.

Media accounts of demonstrations and other actions, which tend to include a "false balance" (Parenti 1986: 100) in their coverage of demonstrators and counterdemonstrators—regardless of the relative size of the demonstrations—would seem to help fuel such a "deadlock" perspective.

Going "Too Far": Issues

Whereas collective action is seen as largely ineffective, social-movement efforts, ironically, are sometimes seen as being carried "too far." One meaning of "too far" is calling for measures that seem extreme. (In turn, the perceived extremity of movement positions is seen as undermining a movement's effectiveness.) Sometimes this sentiment coexisted with general support for the movement's goals.

SAM: I'm as much for protecting the environment as the next guy. I grew up hunting and fishing and I really love the woods and everything. But a lot of these people—I think they want us to go back to the horse and buggy or something. It just seems like they go too far on some things protecting every little—insect or whatever. They stop all these projects because there's some bug or fish or whatever in the area, you know? I think that gets crazy.

In this case, the perception that protecting insignificant animals sometimes derails construction projects contradicts commonsense beliefs that we cannot return to the days of the "horse and buggy."

The environmental movement is especially likely to be seen as going "too far" in making demands. More than violating common sense, however, the "extremes" of the environmental movement can be perceived as a threat to workers' interests.

HUGH: I think a lot of it is good. It's good that we've become more aware of the garbage and the pollution that we produce—so that's good. I think it can get carried too far sometimes. People want to return to olden times or something, but you just can't do that. You've got to balance protecting against pollution and things with what you get for it. Nobody—well, most people anyway—are not gonna give up their cars even though they cause pollution. The benefits outweigh the problems. So I think you've got to balance the two. Sometimes I think these antipollution groups forget that. They forget that people need to work and have jobs.

Some theorists assert that new social movements such as the environmental movement are "universal" in that they work for goals that benefit everyone, not just a select constituency. Workers, though, clearly disagree.

DC: Would [the environmental movement] be a case where if they succeeded in cleaning up the environment, then everyone would benefit?

JUDY: Not necessarily, because I know a lot of these groups want to shut things down because of pollution. They want to close down factories and things that have been around for years and years. So it might help pollution, but a lot of people would lose jobs.

DC: So there are people who oppose things like that?

JUDY: Yeah, I would think so. I wouldn't want to lose my job. I can understand that.

Perceived "extremism" is a characteristic that haunts social movements. Some workers were careful to distinguish between general support for a movement and opposition to the "extreme" elements in those movements. However, some workers did not make such distinctions, lumping together moderate and more radical groups.

The lumping together of a wide range of social movements contributes to a seemingly contradictory set of beliefs that working people hold about social movements. Whereas workers often dismiss movements for being ineffective, they also see some movements as *too* effective in pursuing demands that go "too far."

DANIEL: If you make life miserable for some politician or other then they give these people money or pass a bill for them or whatever to keep them quiet. So I guess so. Sometimes [it's effective]. But like I said, I think they push too far sometimes. They ask for more, more, more.

Consequently, the very effectiveness of collective efforts can, in the end, be seen as the source of more problems. The budget deficit, for example, is sometimes seen as a result of government being unable to say "no" to organized social-movement pressure (that is, special interests).

DIANE: Well, like my parents, they belong to AARP, it's for retired people. And they get things in the mail about bills and stuff that Congress is considering. So this group can go to Congress and say, "Don't vote for this" or "Vote for this" because they've got all these old people backing them. Politicians know that they can't go against that because when the next election comes they'll lose all those votes from the elderly. So with Social Security, to name one, I think everybody supports that 'cause they know if they don't, there'll be hell to pay from the old folks.

Multiplying this scenario for the plethora of existing movement interest groups goes a long way, for some workers, towards explaining bloated government.

JOHN: [Y]ou get all these special interests that don't represent the people, they represent a certain group, and they push to get their thing passed— whatever that is. And then you've got another group and another group and another group and they're all pushing their own little project so what you end up with is a thousand little projects that add up to big bucks. That's how we get into trouble, I think.

The perception that movements are continually making demands leaves them vulnerable to the critique that they are greedy and self-interested. Warren, for example, suggests that some activists are just "out for themselves."

WARREN: They're trying to get something or get the government to give them something. They want something, basically, that's why they're out there. They're not doing it because they're good people or something. They figure this is how to extort money out of the government.

DC: "Extort money," huh? Do you think that works?

WARREN: Sometimes, I guess. It's like they say, "The squeaky wheel gets the grease," and these people are out there making all kinds of noise and disruption and things. They got the media out there and all that. So sometimes I think the politicians would just rather throw some money at them to make them go away, you know? They don't care, it's not their money they're throwing. It's our money. [laughs] Tax dollars. "Here. Here's some program we'll start" or something like that. "Now go away and leave us alone."

The very fact that movements make demands gave some workers reason for pause. As Daniel puts it, "I mean, they go out to get something, right? They're not doing this out of the goodness of their hearts. [laughs]" The Gulf War provided an immediate example.

NICOLE: A lot of [the antiwar demonstrators] are just scared. I see that on TV. All these middle-class college kids who are scared that there's gonna be a draft, so they come up with all these reasons why we shouldn't be there. Hey, my kid's already there so don't go cutting his legs out because you're scared of a draft. . . . It's just like Vietnam where the kids from working families ended up going over there, fighting for their country, and these rich kids were hiding in college. . . . Who got delays right? It was the college kids. The kids who couldn't afford to go or who didn't have the grades for . . . they—they were shipped out.

Movements, then, face a troublesome dilemma. If they fail to achieve their goals, they can be dismissed as being naïve and ineffective. But if they achieve their demands, they can be seen as subverting the democratic process and contributing to the unseemly influence of special-interest groups. This last point is important because it leads some workers to see social movements as indistinguishable from the "special interests" that are a source of many problems with the political system. Of course, left social movements are very different from the well-financed special-interest groups like AARP. The workers I spoke with, though, often saw them as essentially the same.

Going "Too Far": Tactics

In addition to going "too far" on certain issues, social movements are also perceived as sometimes going "too far" in the tactics they utilize. Part of the problem is that social movements that work outside of regular political channels often stage dramatic protests or events in order to attract media coverage for their cause. The more flamboyant such actions are, the more likely they are to receive the media's attention *and* the more likely they are to be perceived by many as "extreme." Workers feel that demonstrators, for example, should be held accountable to the law and that by violating laws, demonstrators were sometimes imposing their beliefs on others.

NICOLE: I'm not against it. I don't think you can say that its illegal to demonstrate or something. I think if we did that, we'd be no better than the

Russians. If they break the law, though, that's a different story. I think if they block things or whatever, then they ought to be arrested. I don't think they should be treated any different because they do it for a cause of some sort. . . . It's a free country, and you've got the right to say or believe whatever you want. But you don't have the right to try and force other people to believe what you believe. I think a lot of times that's what these groups are doing. They're telling you, "This is what you should believe." That I don't agree with.

Workers are critical of both the Left and the Right for trying to impose their beliefs on others. Nicole, for example, refers to anti-abortion activists this way:

NICOLE: You've got these preachers and things saying you're going to hell for having an abortion. That's crazy. You can believe what you want for yourself, but I don't think you can make others believe something just because you do. I think that's what a lot of these people want. They want you to believe what they believe. They can't win in elections, so they try to force people by blocking things and chaining themselves. That's not the way this country works. We're different here because we believe that you can't tell others what to think.

Workers, then, react negatively to social movements when it is perceived that they are telling people "what to think."

Ironically, the need of social-movement activists to use nonelectoral means to promote their cause seems to undermine people's opinion of them.

NICOLE: No, this is not middle America, that's for sure. I think they demonstrate and do all sorts of crazy stuff to get attention. They don't really have the support of people, so they have to resort to this kind of thing to get on the TV. That's how they make their point.

Thus, there is a generalized sentiment that some movements use disruptive tactics because they have little support.

For example, during the Gulf War, there was clear opposition from my coworkers at MAPS to property destruction as a demonstration tactic. One of the few Gulf War events to receive comment during my field work was the destruction by antiwar demonstrators of a large, street-level window at Boston's JFK Federal Building. The incident was recounted by one person who saw it in the news, and it spread. People remembered it, and it reappeared in later conversations as "violent demonstrations, like those people who smashed windows in Boston." Property destruction, in a sense, can be seen as unfairly imposing beliefs on others.

Workers are also convinced that the activists organized around various issues are, in fact, often the same small clique turning out for a variety of different issues. Their numbers, then, are even smaller than might be suggested by media accounts.

NICOLE: I think a lot of these people are just professional protesters. I really do. It seems like the same crowd that comes out to demonstrate against this, that, and the other thing. They're against Seabrook, they're for these gays and things, they're against nuclear bombs—all that stuff. I think a lot of times it's the same people at all these different things. . . . So on the news it looks like all these different groups and things when really it's just a few people.

This view is at least partially accurate since there is a great deal of overlap in the membership of different issue organizations. Many activists I spoke with, for example, cited their membership, if not active involvement, in a number of political groups *within* an issue area. Others were involved in a wide range of groups working on an equally wide range of issues. Ralph, a forty-four-year-old activist, works on an astonishing variety of projects.

RALPH: I worked for Clamshell for close to sixteen years mostly focused on Seabrook. . . . And I'm working with . . . people in the Ukraine [Green Party] to try to set up a vitamin distribution and food supplement system and then maybe production system to help with the effects of Chernobyl. And I'm working on Middle East peace work by trying to get involved in Israeli-Palestinian dialogue, not so much as an advocate, but more as a peacemaker . . . I've just written a book on [alternative economic systems] . . . I've just signed another book proposal for something [on environmentally sound marketing]. And I'm doing some work with co-ops. . . . I'm also doing some work on presidential campaigns.

Thus, workers' suspicions that the same people are involved in a variety of different groups in some cases can be correct. For workers, this was significant because it was further evidence that social movements do not have broad support.

While workers seem to believe that the effectiveness of social movements is limited by the absence of a broad base of support, they also feel that movements do have one important ally: the media. Workers assert that whatever impact social movements have comes not from their actions, but from the media's coverage of those actions.

DC: What about things like protests or demonstrations? Can that affect politicians too?

HUGH: I don't know if it's so much the demonstrations as the media coverage—the publicity. I think these officials are always concerned about how the media is gonna talk about them so they're always concerned about bad publicity. These demonstrators know that, so they try to embarrass them sometimes. I think that happens.

But Hugh feels that such media tactics are a subversion of democracy.

HUGH: Well, I think these groups just push their own interest. They've got their own agenda, and they don't care who voted for who or what's best for the regular working guy. They're just there—like I said—to embarrass the guy and get him to vote a certain way.

The mainstream news media has come to be seen by many movements as a crucial arena to which they must gain access in order to have a significant impact on the debate at hand. Greider (1992: 205–6) cautions, though, that "Mass-media politics worked powerfully for the civil rights drama, but is a trap for citizens' political aspirations because it defers to someone else's judgment— the news media's—to decide what qualifies as authentic political expression. By depending on stunts and celebrity to attract the press and television, people are essentially surrendering to the media—and sometimes making themselves look clownish in the process."

As Charlotte Ryan's (1991) work points out, there are strategies that activists can use to more effectively gain access to the media on their own terms. But still, Ryan (1991: 9) warns, "In fixating on the value of mainstream media coverage, challengers tend to underestimate the limits of even 'good' expo- sure—coverage may help create a mood, but it will not create an analysis of the issue at hand, nor will it build an organized base of support."

The real danger, as Greider (1992: 206) notes, is when movements neglect fundamental organizing efforts in favor of pandering to the media. He cites J. Hunter O'Dell, one of Martin Luther King's early aides, in making the argu- ment. "O'Dell's point is that the civil rights movement acquired its 'authority' to articulate large political aspirations, not because network television came to Selma or Birmingham, but from the hundreds and even thousands of meetings in black churches, week after week, across the South over many years. The dramatic spectacles that appeared on TV were the product of those mobilizing sermons and dialogues, not the other way around."

Too often in contemporary movements, the groundwork necessary for effective use of media coverage is missing. Greider (1992: 206) says, "Succeed- ing generations of political activists, it often seems, copied the glamorous surfaces of the civil rights legacy—the hot moments of national celebrity that are so well remembered—while skipping over the hard part, the organizational sinew that was underneath." With today's demonstrators, "To be blunt, there is a hollowness behind many of the placards and politicians know it." Part of that hollowness comes from the fact that these movements do not have broad bases of active support that cross class lines.

Workers interpret the theatrical tactics some movements use to gain media coverage as a sign of weakness; a sign that movements cannot generate enough support among the public at large to use conventional politics to promote their cause. The implication, as workers make clear, is that social movements do not represent the interests of the public at large. They are not speaking on behalf of regular people.

Movements and "Regular" People

Workers who feel disempowered by the electoral process find no solace in existing social movements. That is because workers do not see such movements as representing their interests, and they do not see themselves as having a great deal in common with movement participants. Therefore, both the issues addressed by movements and the social location of participants in such movements serve to discourage any potential participation by workers.

Issues

There are social movements that workers do not support because they disagree with the issues promoted by that movement. For example, pro-life workers would disagree with pro-choice organizations, and pro-choice workers would disagree with pro-life groups. But beyond the specifics of issue positions, there is a more fundamental perception that hinders worker support for left social movements. Workers are skeptical of these movements because they do not seem to represent "regular people."

JOHN: I don't think these people represent the average person. I think there are always a few on the extremes who are interested in this kind of stuff and go out there and do these things. But I don't think they're—I don't think they represent most people.

There is an array of reasons why workers feel this way. For example, Ronald expresses skepticism that movements can effect change. When it is pointed out that the civil rights and women's movements seem to have had a significant impact over the years, he responds:

RONALD: Yeah, I guess so, in a way. But it hasn't changed for the average guy. I mean some poor slob's got a woman or a black guy for a boss now instead of a white guy. Is that change? He still gets paid the same. He still does the same shit work day after day. I don't think that's really change, not for *that* guy anyway.

So some movements can be seen as effecting change, but such movements have not been advocating change on behalf of these white workers. Warren agrees with this analysis and laughs at the idea that activists might be representing citizen interests.

DC: Do you think these kinds of citizen groups can be healthy for the political system? Can they help out sometimes?

WARREN: "Citizen groups," I like that. [laughs] I'm a citizen and I'm not in those groups! I always wonder where these people come from. I never hear them asking for things that'll help me out, you know.

Workers, then, feel left out of the agendas pursued by left movements. They do not see how the advancement of movement causes can possibly be of benefit to them.

Participants

Workers do not see social-movement participants as being fundamentally different from the politicians who populate the electoral arena. Both are engaged in "politics" in its most pejorative sense, and both are utterly unlike workers, who sometimes suggest that movement participants are part of a professional political elite who devote their lives to such causes.

HELEN: I think these are people who basically make a career out of politics. It's not running for office like politicians but it's still politics. . . . I think most of these people are people who take an unusual interest in an issue, maybe as part of their job or because they have some personal interest in it. I don't think this is the average person off the street.

Even well-known activists who are cited in a positive light are seen as being clearly different from workers.

DOROTHY: I guess [some groups] may be for the little guy—like that Ralph Nader guy. He fights against big companies and things like that. That's good that he does that, but I don't think that's different.

DC: Different than what?

DOROTHY: I don't think it's different than the politicians because he's doing this as a job too. This is all the guy does, right? I mean, I don't know, maybe he's a lawyer or something, but I bet this is what he does. . . . The regular guy can't really go getting involved in all that stuff 'cause he doesn't know how it all works and all the facts and things, and he doesn't have the time. I guess that's what I'm saying.

Movement participants, then, distinguish themselves from workers by the very process of becoming involved in politics. This distinction is exacerbated when activists pursue political organizing as full-time employment and become, in the minds of many workers, much like full-time politicians.

There is also a sense that movement participants, rather than being an aggrieved group, are in fact privileged. The very fact that they have the time to devote to such efforts is evidence of this privilege.

JOHN: I think there are a lot more kids in these things—college students and the like.

DC: Why do you think that is?

JOHN: Probably because they don't work. [laughs] I mean they work and all but they don't have the regular hours at a regular job that most people do.

That way they can go out to all these things. . . . And I think a lot of them are better off than average.

DC: Why do you say that?

JOHN: Well, [pause] I don't know exactly. I guess if you're going to college these days somebody's got to have money somewhere. I know my kids couldn't afford college. No way. . . . Also it just seems that if you've got the time to be worrying about everybody else, then things at home must be in pretty good shape, you know what I mean?

Such sentiments only reinforce the notion that movements are not concerned with the issues that affect workers.

One especially visible criticism of social movements drew upon this general belief that movement participants are different from regular people. In this case, however, workers discussed activists as "fringe" elements out of touch with mainstream society. Activists are often frustrated at the emphasis the media often puts on the more unusual costumes and appearances of some demonstrators, and they suggest that the "fringe" image of the movements discourages potential participation. Karen, a peace activist, notes:

KAREN: I think one of the things that keeps people from becoming active is . . . that there is a general bias in the media and in the status quo towards portraying anyone that resists as being a real nut. You look at photographs that get in of rallies and things. There can be sixty grandmothers there, and there can be one person with a mohawk, and who's gonna be in the photograph in the newspaper? And the language that's used always expresses it negatively. So I think it's a subtle or intentioned—I'm not sure which—campaign to discredit as being unreliable, as being inconsistent, as being too emotional, as being naïve. . . . [I]t makes it very hard for people to do something because they don't want to be perceived as being outrageous or as being nuts or as being those left-wing kooks, or so on and so forth.

There is considerable truth in this analysis. Often workers equate demonstrators with the more unusual images they remember from media coverage of social movements. The most common label used to imply the "fringe" quality of demonstrators is "hippies."

WARREN: You see them on TV and they're these long-haired hippies—like something that stepped out of the 1960s. [laughs] Really. I don't know where these people have been for the last thirty years, but they seem to show up at all these demonstrations for things.

Another worker says:

JOHN: Well, of course, the first image you think of is long-haired, bearded hippies. [laughs] I guess that comes out of the sixties again but there's some truth to it. I know when the demonstrations were going on at Seabrook that was still the kind of picture you got. It seemed like they were always in the front. I imagine there were other kinds of people there, but that's who you usually saw.

The opponents of social movements have learned that the hippie stereotype can be a powerful one. Gus, an antinuclear activist, noted that a conservative statewide newspaper always portrayed anti-Seabrook activists as "sandaled and long-haired." Gus was indeed what some workers would describe as stereotypically "hippie looking." But he defended his appearance saying, "I wear my hair long because I like it, and not because I need to flaunt it." However, by his own admission, Seabrook officials had tried to take advantage of his stereotypical appearance. He would sometimes debate the "clean-cut, three-piece-suited, public-relations expert from Seabrook station." The Seabrook spokesperson would not debate the more conservative-looking Clamshell members but would readily assent to debating Gus. Clamshell members, including Gus, suspected that, in part, the spokesperson "may have sought to gain some points through mere appearances that he was going to lose through presenting a debate."

Besides "hippies," other labels are used by workers in discrediting movement participants.

DANIEL: I mean who goes out and makes a spectacle of themselves on national TV? [laughs] I mean some of these things . . . jeez! It's like a circus. There are some weird . . . some real weirdos at these things . . . these people who got green hair spiked up and paint up their faces and . . . I mean, some of these people are weird! [laughs] I wouldn't want them in my house. [laughs]

DC: Do you think that these kinds of people are the majority of these groups, or are they just a few in a crowd?

DANIEL: Whenever you see them on the TV, they always seem to be there. I don't know—I mean I don't go to these things, so maybe there are a lot of other people, but it seems like this kind of person is always out there screaming away about something.

The images of "strange" demonstrators clearly undermine the credibility of the movement's message with these workers.

HELEN: They've got these demonstrations where they all dress up like freaks and parade around for the cameras, and then they expect you to believe *them* and not the government. [laughs]

Over and over, workers who dismissed social-movement efforts used the appearance of demonstrators as evidence to justify their conclusions. Steve concluded, "It's pretty flaky stuff."

Activists are aware of such stereotyping and argue that with a few exceptions, such images are false. One environmental activist notes:

PATRICK: We still get a lot of stereotyping from the average person on the street. We're stereotyped into a, you know, long-hair, granola eaters, wearing sandals, and flowers in their hair or something. People really give us a hard time about that—whether they're kidding or not . . . I don't think there's more than two people in our whole group that you could even say are remotely, you know, sixties-ish or something. There's a couple of people with long hair and a couple of people that wear tie-dye stuff, but I mean that's about the extent of it. The rest of us are really the average person.

Most workers do not concur. Movement participants are unlikely to be seen as average. Instead, they are part of the special groups that make up the political system.

Recognizing Inefficacy

Most social-movement activists recognize the seriousness and debilitating effect of inefficacy. One activist from a working-class background explains the nonparticipation of working people by saying:

PATRICK: A lot of it is just the frustration of not thinking they can really do anything. You hear all the time that you really can make a difference. Every commercial on: "You *can* make a difference," but I don't think anybody really believes that.

Activists vary, though, in how they explain inefficacy amongst working people. Some cite a generalized sense of disempowerment and disengagement which, in the end, serves the interests of those in power.

LISA: Well, I think, to some extent, it's the thing that's been happening since the mid-sixties where more and more people just feel disenfranchised. They feel like the government, the political world, doesn't represent them; can't; it won't; why should they vote? Which is at some level just a sort of instinctual reaction, and on another level it's a pretty sophisticated analysis: why spend your energy on something that's not gonna have any impact in changing your life? And yet, the ideal that we're all taught is "Get involved. Vote for your representatives. This country is free," and "democracy," and all that stuff. It seems like on some very basic level it is true that if you don't vote, you certainly will be disenfranchised, and that's exactly what serves the best interest of the ruling class, the ruling elite, or whatever you want to call them. There's that kind of apathy, and maybe that's taught in a lot of ways to people, subtly.

The theme that powerful elites want people to feel disempowered appeared in several activists' comments. Mark is a forty-four-year-old activist whose interests range from Central America to cultural diversity, to homelessness.

MARK: Ultimately, from a radical perspective, [nonparticipation] comes from the fact that that's where the powers that be—I don't see this as a conscious thing, I think that's just the way the system's set up—that's where they want people.

Some activists cited developments in mainstream political culture as having a negative impact on efficacy.

CARLENE: And part of it I think is coming after the whole fiasco with Nixon and the sleeping Reagan years and Kitty Kelly books. I think that people start to feel that they're all crooked and get a little jaded and don't believe anything these people are saying.

The electoral process was also seen as promoting inefficacy and nonparticipation.

ALLAN: Maybe I've been reading too many leftist pundits but I do think [nonparticipation] has to do, in a large measure, with the failure of the two-party system. And with the fact that those people have been abandoned. Their needs are ignored by the Democrats and the Republicans. If there's nobody out there speaking to their condition, then why should they get involved? What's the point? I think that that's a lot of it.

While nearly all activists were sympathetic to the sense of inefficacy on the part of working people, some were impatient. Carlene had little tolerance for what she construed to be "excuses" for not participating and delivered part of the following comments in a mock whining tone of voice:

CARLENE: There are a lot of people that just don't have the self-confidence. "I don't know how to do anything." "I didn't go to college." "I can't type." "Gee, I've never done that." "I don't know where the soup kitchen is."

Occasionally, activists were even less kind in their assessments. In discussing efficacy, Carol stated, "I believe that people are basically quiet because a lot of them don't feel that they can really make a difference," but then she later explained nonparticipation by stating bluntly, "I think essentially most people are lazy." She contended that selfishness was often the real reason for nonparticipation, in this case in environmental issues, concluding, "[T]here is a real strong attitude out there that says, 'It's not gonna happen in my lifetime, so why should I worry about it?' I think that's a very strong feeling among a lot of people, which is unfortunate."

But such attitudes are not common among activists. Instead, activists are generally sympathetic to the feelings of inefficacy that plague working people.

Interestingly, inefficacy is often treated by activists as a *cause* rather than as an effect. That is, activists discuss the fact that people are inactive *because* they feel inefficacious, but activists rarely discuss why people develop this sense of inefficacy in the first place. For most activists, it simply is an undeniable reality. As I will argue, it is impossible to adequately address the issue of inefficacy without examining the causes of this condition.

Cultivating a Sense of Efficacy

Unlike workers, activists generally have a strong sense of efficacy. The waning of this sense of efficacy is often part of the familiar "burnout" syndrome that plagues some overextended activists.

For political organizers there is a clear emphasis on collective efficacy, but most activists also have a strong belief in the ability of individuals to effect change. Sarah, a twenty-six-year-old environmentalist, told me the story of how one person initiated an effort that led to a corporation adopting a major recycling effort. When I questioned the likelihood that individual effort could adequately deal with corporate abuse of the environment she agreed that recycling was just one issue, but she insisted:

SARAH: I really feel that corporations are changed by individuals. . . . Corporations change because one person sticks at it and sticks at it. . . . I don't think it would be a good or fruitful use of energy to question the ability of an individual to make a difference.

Middle-class activists often generalize from their own experience and suggest individual efficacy that is not available to most. An activist who was extensively involved in electoral work observes:

CARLENE: I think when I write a letter about the environment to people like [my congressperson] or Dick Gephardt, there is a face with a name, and they also know that I'm involved with a lot of different areas in this city and that I may be able to impact a certain number of people's opinions, and so maybe a letter from me will have a little bit more weight. Although I think that people underestimate the impact that letters have—particularly if they are writing to their own senators.

Despite the disclaimer, the implication here is that if her letter gets positive response, then everyone's will. Of course, this is simply not true. More generally, activists sometimes seem unaware of how their particular class position may be affecting the political acts in which they engage.

Activists usually have some sense of efficacy that accompanies their involvement with a social movement. But just as activists cite different reasons for the inefficacy of workers, they vary as well in explaining the source of their own sense of efficacy.

Ironically, the most common explanation activists give is the most straightforward: efficacy is cultivated by accomplishing something. The importance of achieving victories in order to maintain commitment is highlighted by one activist. A recent citizens' petition drive had led to the rescinding of a wetlands protection exemption that had been given to a powerful developer. The wetlands protection ordinance was enforced, and the development project was stopped.

PATRICK: That was an unbelievable victory. It just felt so good to actually be able to change something that would have really hurt the city and would have been all for money and nothing for the community. Little things like that help. If we got knocked down on everything we tried to do, I probably would have gotten out of it just from frustration's sake because I don't have a—my temper would take off [laughs]. I would get too mad.

The importance of victories is no surprise, and in fact, emphasis on small victories is a central tenet of the Alinsky (1946, 1971) school of community organizing. This approach, in part, builds upon the sense of efficacy that develops from achieving small goals. This sense of empowerment is then applied to increasingly larger tasks.

CAROL: If you look at the whole picture, sometimes it's just so overwhelming for people that they blow it off completely. If you start on a small level and then start working up, people can see the differences, even in their own households.

Such a belief is implicit in the approach of some activists. This is especially true with environmental activists who seem highly conscious of multiple layers of commitment and involvement. The goal many of them have is to attract people with something small and get them involved in progressively larger projects. Recycling is seen as a perfect vehicle for this process. Especially with curbside pickup, people can take concrete, practical action that requires minimal knowledge or commitment yet often delivers a sense of satisfaction and, as Patrick put it, "it actually makes you feel like you're doing something."

A second observation from some activists is that a sense of efficacy is easier to achieve with some issues than with others. Sarah, for example, contrasts the appeal of recycling with the more daunting task of monitoring toxic waste releases from local businesses.

SARAH: Recycling is very popular and I don't want to profess to know the reasons why it appeals to people, but it's a very hands-on, immediate, and visual type of gratification for environmental improvement. And it also gives the individual a sense of efficacy, that they are actually taking on an action, and they can see the volume reduction immediately. The issue behind toxic chemicals being used is not a very appealing subject for a lot of people. I think people theoretically generally recognize the importance of not releasing emissions and hazardous materials. However, it's chemistry, which is scary. Nobody understands it. And it's something that people feel very powerless to have an effect upon.

Some issues, then, have more general appeal and can more easily lead to a sense of efficacy than other issues. One clear dividing line is that between local and national or even state issues. Patrick contends that with local issues, "you stand a good chance of getting something done yourself . . . . But on a national scale it's just too many different kinds of people, I think." This, of course, presents major difficulties for some groups such as peace organizations, which are usually working with national—or even international—policies.

Conclusion

From the perspective of working people, neither the electoral process nor social movements provide feasible or attractive ways to address problems in the political system. The electoral process is filled with difficulties as workers question the impact of their vote and recognize the important influence of campaign money and special interests. Such critiques are familiar to movement activists, who often concur in this critical assessment of the electoral process. The difference between social-movement activists and working people, though, is that activists see social-movement politics as a viable alternative or supplement to the electoral process. Most workers do not agree.

For most working people, social movements do not seem to be particularly feasible or attractive vehicles to address problems in the political system. But workers have a complex and sometimes contradictory opinion of movement efforts. Helen, for example, gives this assessment.

HELEN: I don't believe in these groups that are out to save the world, you know. I'm not that idealistic. . . .

DC: When you say groups that are "out to save the world," what kinds of things are you thinking of?

HELEN: Well, like some of the environmental groups that want to save everything and stop all building. Maybe there's some truth in what they're saying, but I don't think they're being realistic about needing jobs. And then a lot of antiwar groups—you see a little of that now. Like I said, I agree that we spend too much on war. I don't think we should be in Kuwait. I think that's just stupid. But when I see demonstrators on TV, I don't know. They just seem so naïve sometimes, like if we just loved everybody, everybody would love us back. [laughs] It's like the old hippie thing, you know. They were all against making money because they could get it from their parents for nothing. It seems like there's still some of these people running around who haven't realized it's the 1990s. It's easy to say we should like everybody while you're being protected by the U.S. military.

The contradictory messages in these observations would leave most activists perplexed. Helen expresses support for environmental concerns but feels environmental groups are unrealistic; she supports the antiwar movement's *goals* but thinks movement *participants* are naïve. Finally, she seems resentful of the perceived privileged position of movement participants themselves. The implicit critique here is of hypocrisy: "hippies" could afford to scorn money because they had plenty of it; antiwar activists can afford to condemn the military because they enjoy its protection.

It is too simple, then, to say that working people are universally conservative and therefore reject the messages being promoted by social movements. It is also erroneous to say that working people are eager to become involved in left movements. Neither of these contentions is accurate for the workers with whom I spoke. Instead, in some respects, working people share movement critiques of the status quo, but they simply do not believe that social movements are significantly different from the other actors in the political arena. Movement participants share with politicians, for example, the characteristics of being different from "regular" people, and of not representing the interests of workers. Yet, movement participants can be even less credible than politicians because, not only are they unlike regular people, but they are sometimes seen as stereotypically "fringe" elements of society. As a result of this situation, workers feel unrepresented by both elected officials and social movements.

Activists see themselves as distinctly separate from the "system." Their work is motivated, in part, by the unresponsiveness of politicians and the electoral process. Workers, however, do not make a positive distinction between the system and social movements. They often include movements as part of the "system" in the sense that they are "special-interest" groups whose motivations are not to be trusted. The result is worker skepticism of the entire political system and a resulting disinterest in the whole process.

CHAPTER 6

"People Really Don't Think About It"

Interest and Motivations

I don't think most people have any idea of what's going on [in politics]. . . . They don't follow the news. They don't vote. They live in their own little world and don't give a damn about what goes on outside. . . . What goes on in Washington is a million miles away.

JOHN, forty-eight-year-old factory worker

The absence of working-class participants in left social movements reflects a fundamental difference in orientation between workers and movement activists. Left democratic belief suggests that people should be, and want to be, involved in the history-making chores of political life. It is a largely taken-for-granted notion that democratic participation and general engagement in the political arena is a virtue for which people should and do strive. But in fact, this is often not the case. With some notable exceptions, most working people do not see politics as being particularly relevant to their lives. They do not have a great deal of interest in public affairs nor do they have a clear motivation for becoming involved in politics since they do not see political involvement advancing their interests or making a positive contribution to their existence. Workers also do not feel an especially strong obligation to participate in public life or act on abstract values. Finally, they do not see potential political participation as an intrinsically rewarding activity.

Such observations contrast sharply with the orientations of middle-class activists, who obviously show a great deal of interest in political life. Middle-class activists sometimes look to political action for explicitly self-interested reasons. More often, however, they see political participation as an expression and affirmation of their values. In addition, many activists find politics an interesting and intrinsically rewarding activity that helps constitute a sense of identity.

Examining Disengagement and Nonparticipation

In his study of the transition from the "Old" to the "New" Left, Maurice Isserman (1987: xiii) writes, "Historians are naturally attracted to periods in which the movements they study are at the peak of their influence . . . but there is as much or more to be learned by studying these movements at their nadir." A related point can be made regarding studies of the working class. In an important counter to decades of neglect, the struggles of working people have recently become the subject of numerous studies by a generation of "new historians." But such portraits can be unintentionally misleading. Marxist notions of class suggest that classes are formed as much by their social and political activity as by their objective position within relations of production. As a consequence of this concern with class struggle, "historians and social theorists have characteristically circumscribed the history of the working class by the experience of trade unions and socialist movements" (Aronowitz 1992: 4). The fact is that the admirable working-class struggles of the past, like all social movements, have always been carried out by a minority of working people. The majority of workers have never significantly involved themselves in these efforts. This is in no way intended to denigrate these movements. To the contrary, such efforts are perhaps all the more inspiring, given the odds against which that minority struggled. But with some qualifications, labor unions represent, not working-class interests, but the interests of particular groups of workers, based on their occupations and industries. It is a mistake to equate union and socialist-movement history with working-class history in the United States. If we are to speak of working-class culture, or even more narrowly as I do here, of white, New England, working-class culture, we must look beyond organized labor. More attention needs to be given to the phenomenon of political nonparticipation by working people.

Interest

It should come as no surprise that most workers are disengaged from politics of nearly all forms. Most workers have no cultural context in which to be convinced of the potential benefits of collective efforts, nor do they have structural opportunities to facilitate such action. In the hard light of day it is difficult to see the benefit for most people of pursuing efforts that take time, effort, and resources, and that, in all likelihood, will not provide significant benefits for the participants. There are, of course, nonutilitarian reasons for participation in political life. But here, too, workers are likely to find little reward in a political world that is culturally oriented towards the middle class.

Rather than as a possible arena for collectively addressing problems, workers are more likely to see politics as one of a number of possible "interests" in life.[1] Sam, a thirty-nine-year-old janitor, says about politics:

SAM: I think some people just take an interest in all that stuff, but it's just never really interested me, that's all. I don't really know why.

One consequence of not being interested in politics is that many workers pay little or no attention to the news media.

DC: You seem to disagree that it's important that people keep informed about news and public issues? Why is that?

ANDREA: Well, it could be, but I think that if you don't want to know, then it's not important, that's all. It doesn't have to be important for everybody. It depends what you're interested in.

Workers are sometimes sheepish about not being informed about basic current events, but for the most part, this whole arena of public life is not of much concern to them.

There were many, many hours available for conversations of all types during my stay at MAPS.[2] Conversation, in fact, was the central way workers made the day go by faster. Periods when no one was speaking were often interrupted by calls for someone to come up with something to talk about. Conversations, however, were almost never about politics or public affairs. Instead, family life and entertainment topics, such as sports and movies, were the primary concern. Local events, such as fires and accidents, also received some attention, especially when they affected people who were known to workers. Only one person in the department where I worked (out of about forty workers) brought a newspaper to work, and this was for the sole purpose of surveying the sports pages. Even the Gulf War brought with it only limited conversation about political events.

The reasons for this state of affairs are complex, but one simple source is that workers do not see public affairs as being salient to their lives. As with those quoted above, workers tend to believe that politics, for the most part, do not affect them personally. In fact, even workers who *do* take an interest in politics and follow the news suggest that the information they receive is not especially important to their lives and that the news, in fact, is essentially a diversion or entertainment.

TOM: Most of this stuff [on the news] isn't gonna affect me. . . . I mean I know in the bigger picture it affects the country and the economy and all that, but individual things in the news really doesn't affect me. So I guess I must look at it just out of curiosity. Some people follow their soaps, I read the paper. It's kind of the same thing, "As the World Turns"—global soaps. [laughs]

The media presentation of news, therefore, is clearly not constructed in such a way as to effectively communicate the practical impact of political events. Instead, the evening news serves as an ongoing drama with heroes and villains, but with little apparent concrete consequence for workers.

Influenced by their perception that the political arena is largely irrelevant to their lives, most workers do not take part in politics, nor do they make significant attempts to follow public debate in the news. In some cases, people actively avoid seeing news broadcasts and newspapers.

DONNA: I never watch the news. I see it if [my husband] puts it on, which is rare, but that's it. I don't watch it ever.

DC: Why is that?

DONNA: I guess I just don't want to see it. I know there are all these problems out there but I just don't want to see it every night, that's all. . . . There's nothing I can do about it, so I don't know what watching all this stuff is gonna do. . . . Besides, half the time I don't know what they're talking about anyway.

In the end, for many workers, public affairs are not salient, are confusing, and suggest no viable course of action.

Middle-Class Modeling

Unlike workers, activists attend closely to news and public affairs. They often supplement mass-media information with alternative publications and place a premium on knowing the facts about current policy debates. While movement activists told of a range of political experiences in their homelife during their formative years, for many, attention to public affairs was a standard part of growing up in the middle class. Nearly all activists mentioned their parents' attention to political affairs, and many suggested that there was an "expectation" that they would take an active interest in politics. One environmentalist describes political life in her home when she was growing up by noting that her parents attended to politics. She says, "I think there's a lot of modeling that happens. It's a very natural feeling that you would go and be involved because that's what you expected when you were a kid." A peace activist tells a similar story:

KAREN: My mother always voted. So voting was just something you did. And taking an interest in politics, I guess, was part of the family structure. As I recall, my stepfather had fairly strong political ideas, and so I think discussion of what was going on was part of the family scene and the family dinner table.

A couple of activists even came from left homes. One older labor activist, whose father was a dentist, grew up in a socialist household.

NORMAN: I was very early exposed to political discussions at home and friends of my folks and so on. And I was interested, and many of the things I heard made sense to me, even as a child—eight, nine years old. And I knew about some major things that were going on. I knew about Sacco and Vanzetti when I was a child. I stayed up till after midnight—I was then nine years old—on the night that they were executed, hoping that there'd be a last minute reprieve.

Another labor activist describes her middle-class upbringing this way:

JOANNE: Both my parents went to college. . . . My dad became a professor . . . and he got real active in his union at [the university]. . . . [M]y older sister went to work for [a union]—oh, probably ten years ago, or twelve years ago. She just recently quit. There's always been sort of a tie to labor stuff in my family.

For many activists, then, family members provided clear models of participation. By their actions, they helped to communicate to children in the household that political life was a significant and relevant area of concern. Such an orientation was more likely, though not exclusively, to occur in middle-class homes.

But not all middle-class homes followed this pattern. A couple of activists indicated that politics was never a part of their home life. One of them is Lisa, a twenty-six-year-old activist involved with the feminist and Central America movements.

LISA: I think one of the attractions of [politics] for me was that it could be my area of expertise in my family because no one seemed to be doing that kind of thing. My mom did social work, and there was certainly a tendency toward caring about issues in the world, but certainly nobody read the paper and kept up with politics and what was going on. We didn't have political discussions, ever.

For activists, though, such a tale was the clear exception. Overwhelmingly, activists report that politics was a part of their own upbringing.

Ironically, some activists describe extremely high levels of political involvement in their family, but when compared to their own current level of activism it seems to them that there had been little political involvement in their households. When asked if his family had been politically active, Allan responds "not particularly" but then goes on to describe his family's activities.

ALLAN: Well—my older sister—she's two and a half years older than me—she was a little bit on the periphery of some left-wing countercultural type activities in the late sixties-early seventies. And I had a couple of older cousins who were peripherally involved in SDS [Students for a Democratic Society]. And an aunt and uncle who were more sort of the Beatnik generation than hippies or New Left types. . . . My father ran for city council once . . . maybe before I was born or when I was real little. He lost.

But there was never—I mean, people voted. My parents were both regis-
tered Republicans but not active in party politics. . . . I ran for president of
my senior class and lost. [laughs]

Studies of the New Left student movement revealed the importance of parental
modeling for student activists. Flacks (1972: 248) reported that "students,
through their activism, were for the most part attempting to fulfill and extend an
ideological and cultural tradition already present in their families, rather than
rebelling against the values on which they had been raised." Political orientations
and activities, therefore, were an important ingredient in promoting activism.

. Such a wide range of political activity contrasts sharply with the descriptions workers give of their own upbringing. None of the workers I spoke with
had family members who participated in any form of politics except voting. In
fact, there was typically little or no attention paid to public affairs in the home.

DONNA: I don't remember seeing [my parents] sit down to watch the news. . . .
    [W]e didn't get a paper at the house. My mother would buy the local
    weekly paper sometimes but that was it.

Given the lack of attention to political issues in their childhood homes, it is not
unusual for these workers to continue to ignore current events and the political
world. For all of their lives, workers have seen politics as an alien realm
populated with people unlike themselves. As a consequence, they tend not to
seriously envision themselves as potential political agents.

Voting is the one area where some sense of civic duty lingers on for some
workers—most notably older workers. But most of the time, this sense of duty
seems half-hearted at best. Bernice is a good example.

BERNICE: I try to read a little bit when there's an election so that I'll know
    something before I vote but that's really about it. Like I said, I don't take
    too much of an interest in that.

When we had worked together at MAPS, several months before this interview,
Bernice had mentioned during election week that she had not bothered to vote
since she did not know much about the candidates running for office.

The idea that they might be active political agents is largely unimaginable
to most workers. Even the line of questioning I pursued in these interviews was
clearly foreign to their experiences. After Peter said he felt powerless to
influence political issues, I asked if this situation bothered him.

PETER: [laughs] It probably should, more. When you sit down and talk about it
    like this it sounds pretty crazy, but I don't think people usually do this.

DC: You mean, talk about politics?

PETER: Yeah, people bitch and moan about taxes and things, but they don't
    really sit down with their neighbors or whatever and say, "OK what's
    wrong here and what can we do?" I don't think people do that.

Workers, then, relate to the political world as spectators, not potential agents. Such a relationship may be frustrating for them under some circumstances, but for most, this position of powerlessness has been internalized as an almost "natural" arrangement. Judy summarizes the situation well:

JUDY: I don't know if people think about it very much. I mean when you sit here and ask me how I think things are going, I know there are big problems, and things just seem to be getting worse. But most of the time, I guess, I don't really think about it. I sort of accept that that's the way things are. You wish it was different—I think everybody does that. You wish you didn't have to pay as many taxes and didn't have as much crime and stuff like that. But most of the time, I think, people really don't think about it—until, like now, someone asks them about it, or they see something on TV about an issue.

Without thinking about it then, most workers accept their position of relative powerlessness in political affairs. Similarly, without much need for thought, middle-class activists have learned that political activity is, in fact, an appropriate pursuit.

There is an irony in inquiring about issues in which people have little interest. Pollsters and interviewers may obtain statistically precise data by asking working people about their relative agreement or disagreement with a whole variety of issues—including their level of interest in political issues. What is lost in the accumulation of such data, however, is the sense of distance that most people feel from virtually all of those issues. Public affairs and politics are simply not a significant concern to most working people. It is background noise to the real stuff of daily life, a daily life, as I will explore in Chapter Ten, based on work and home.

Flacks (1988: 51) observes that "Americans do not simply avoid politics; their avoidance tends to be a feature of their political consciousness. People on the average believe that they are politically inactive, that history is being made by actors other than themselves; and they are prone to accept and even welcome this situation." Such was the case with most of the workers with whom I spoke. At most, workers feel some vague need to occasionally monitor current events in case some issue should threaten to impact their lives. If the business of daily life is likened to driving a car, the extent of most working people's political activity is limited to occasional glances at the rear-view mirror in an effort to check on what is going on "out there." There is not much drivers can do to stop somebody from rear-ending them, but they would like to know if it is about to happen so they can brace themselves.

Maintaining the Distance

Abandoning the public sphere in favor of a strategy based on work and home life can lead to a startling level of isolationism. Oscar, a unionized electrician, firmly summarizes his philosophy this way:

OSCAR: I pay my taxes, don't break the law, and leave me alone. I really don't care what goes on in Congress or in city hall or up in [the state capital]. As long as it doesn't affect me, *I don't care.*

This is not a reckless call for abandoned self-interest. There is a simple but important social contract implied in such a statement. Oscar is careful to preface his strong dismissal of political participation with an agreement to hold up his end of the contract. He agrees to pay taxes and abide by the laws of the land in exchange for liberty—freedom from further government constraint. As I will show later, this social vision, which generally rejects the relevance of public life, is often coupled with a belief in the importance of caring for the private realm from which government is excluded, especially the family.

The ability to maintain such a distance from public affairs requires a sense of relative independence from government influence, an independence that workers sometimes assert.

DC: Do you feel like you're someone on whom government has a great deal of impact?

ANDREA: No, they definitely don't at all. [laughs] I do what I want. This is America. It's free. [laughs] That's how I feel.

The notion that the United States is a "free" country comes up repeatedly in conversations with workers. The meaning of "free" in this context is relatively consistent: if one abides by most basic laws, one may live in this country with relatively little direct government constraint.[3]

HELEN: I don't think people are happy, that's for sure, but then again they don't worry about it either. People complain all the time about taxes and government and rates on things like car registration or whatever, but I don't think they really lose sleep over it.

DC: Is that a contradiction? I mean, why do you think they don't worry about it if it's so bad?

HELEN: I don't think they can do anything about it.

DC: Is that it then?

HELEN: Well, that and the fact that while they don't want to pay taxes and they don't want a lot of these things, they still can basically go on with their business. They live in a free country.

Being able to go about one's business without overwhelming government intervention, it seems, is the best that can be expected from the political system. Thus, workers are able to hold what otherwise might seem to be contradictory beliefs. On the one hand, they admit to being powerless to influence public policies with which they clearly disagree, while on the other hand, they assert that the United States is a "free country." This combination of beliefs allows workers to maintain a distinct distance from the political arena.

In addition to having a sense of "freedom," workers must have a basic level of material well-being in order to successfully maintain a distance from politics. A perceived threat to this well-being—a well-being that can, in fact, be very modest—can stir resentment and anger (as was evident in the 1992 presidential election). This is especially true if the government—which is supposed to stay out of people's lives—is seen as the source of the economic threat. But an economy that can still, at some level, hold out the promise of "delivering the goods" is a powerful insurance against citizen rebellion. After a worker had made a reference to the changes in Eastern Europe, I asked why citizens in the United States were not also demanding changes from their government.

PETER: I think our politicians aren't that stupid. In the communist countries they can't even feed people right. People stand in line for bread, stand in line for fresh meat, or whatever. So people have to deal with this every day, every day, just for the basic things to live on. Here, we don't have that. You walk in to the supermarket and you've got a thousand different things you can buy. You go to [a department store] and you can buy a big color TV, a big stereo, anything you want. So I think people think, "Well, as long as they leave me alone . . . ." I think that's what they think. They're free, and they can feed their families so let's leave it at that.

The point here is not whether or not workers could afford to buy "anything you want"; obviously, they could not. The point is that workers experience the realm of consumption as one that successfully provides them with choices.

The reference to communist countries was not surprising given the fact that these interviews were taking place during dramatic changes in Eastern Europe. Workers here, however, did not believe that the actions of Eastern European citizens were especially relevant for the American political context. In an analysis uncannily similar to the one just quoted, Warren provides a strictly materialist analysis for the fall of communism:

WARREN: [I]n communist countries they didn't do all that because they wanted to be free or something. They got rid of those guys cause they wanted to eat. They didn't have meat. They had to eat rotting vegetables, things like that. That's how those people lived over there. They're all packed into little apartments with twenty people in them, things like that. That's why they got fed up.

Once again, the perceived limitations of the communist economy serve as a foil against which to compare the apparent abundance of American consumer culture.

WARREN: But here though, most people can feed their families decent. They have a nice house or a decent apartment. Maybe it's hard to make ends meet, but it's nothing like they have over there. Here, we complain because we don't have enough money, but that's because we've got two cars and a new TV and a VCR and Nintendo for the kids and all this stuff we *have* to have. In those communist countries they can't even think of getting stuff like that. That's just for the party bosses or whatever. They're the only ones who can get things like that. As long as people can feed their families and live decent lives, then I don't think they really care what the politicians do.

Thus, to the disappointment of many activists who might hope otherwise, the fall of state communism is not seen by American workers as a product of collective citizen action. (Nor, to the disappointment of conservative jingoists, is it seen as a victory for the forces of United States–sponsored "democracy.") Instead, workers see it as the product of the economic ineptitude of government. If anything, the lesson American working people learned from the collapse of the Soviet Union may be a reinforced belief that government bureaucracy is incompetent and unworkable.

Without basic material well-being, the ability to maintain a belief that government is irrelevant falters. Being unemployed, for example, brings workers into direct contact with government agencies and bureaucrats in order to obtain unemployment benefits. During my stay at MAPS there were several cases of workers who told stories about the difficulty they had in obtaining such benefits. Thus, the less economically secure strata of the working class are more likely to feel the immediate presence of government and politics. But even with very modest material conditions it is possible for workers to feel they are escaping the direct influence of government. For these workers, politics is a decidedly distant affair.

The Distance Bridged: The Gulf War

The distance that workers generally maintain from politics can be bridged by particular events or issues. Some events can be quite mundane, as in this case of car theft reported by Judy.

JUDY: I think—like with crime—you don't really think about it until it happens to you. Like I told you, my girlfriend got her car stolen last fall. I never really thought about crime until that happened. I really didn't. I saw things on TV and all and hear about things, but it was always something that happened to other people. But then there was this incident that happened to someone I know. That made a big difference to me. I think that's true for other things too. You don't really think about things until they affect you.

Politics can be seen as the defensive actions citizens must take to protect their interests. In this sense, politics is something that intrudes upon one's daily life but is still not something one actively pursues. One worker mentioned that politics concerned those who were "involved," and when I asked who he meant by this he responded:

KRISTEN: [P]eople who are affected by things. If there's going to be a toxic dump someplace, the people who live around there are going to be affected. I guess I mean those kinds of people. The people who are involved with an issue.

Thus, people who are generally not "affected by things" can find themselves in the middle of a political issue—a decidedly unenviable position. But participation is only stimulated in order to regain control over immediate spheres of life and thereby facilitate a return to private life. But some events that intrude upon workers lives are more far-reaching. One unexpected example developed dramatically during the fieldwork portion of this study.

During my stay at MAPS, the United States became involved in Operation Desert Shield and then Desert Storm in the Middle East. I was laid off from MAPS just before the brief ground offensive was launched, but I was present during the build-up and air bombardment phases of the war.

For some workers, the Gulf War posed a threat to loved ones who served, or might be called to serve, in the military. Peter, who was the father of an eighteen-year-old son commented, "The world is getting smaller, like they say. What happens in Kuwait can really affect you, like what's going on now." His son was not in the military but, as he put it, "when you see all this happening you can't help but think, you know, he's just at that age. It makes you think."

Nicole, a forty-seven-year-old worker in the mail-processing department at MAPS, faced an even more immediate threat from the development of events thousands of miles away from home. Her son was serving in the Persian Gulf during the war with Iraq.

NICOLE: [W]hen you've got a son there it really brings it all home. We get letters from him now and then, but really it's the news, that's how you find out what's going to happen. So I watch CNN at night and see what happened and look at it in the morning before I go in [to work] to see if anything happened at night. Things like that. So now it's a big part of my life. . . . I used to look at [the news] sometimes but it wasn't a part . . . of my routine every day the way it is now. It was much more casual.

Wars bring with them special significance for working people since it is members of the working class and poor who disproportionately make up the military troops. In addition to Nicole, there was another worker at MAPS who had a family member in the Gulf; this worker's husband was in a National Guard unit that was sent to Saudi Arabia.

The Gulf War's impact on family members of soldiers sent to the region was undeniable. What I was not prepared for, however, was how quickly the war, and preparations for it, became, once again, political background noise for nearly all the other workers at MAPS. After an initial flurry of interest in the air war, workers quickly acclimated to the new reality of the nation at war, and the war faded in importance within a week. Within two weeks it was almost never mentioned.

In the weeks and days leading up to the war virtually no reference was made to events in the Middle East. There was no discussion, for example, of the wisdom of sending troops versus pursuing a boycott. The only exception occurred when announcements began regarding the National Guard units that would be called up. Since many workers had family and friends in the National Guard, information—news, and sometimes just rumors—about the fate of call-ups was regularly shared. Again, though, this was not accompanied by any discussion of the wisdom of such a move. Instead, it was simply treated as a fait accompli.

When the air war started, there was a good deal of interest in the immediate developments. Television, especially CNN, seemed to be the major source for news. This interest lasted only about a week and a half however. The war quickly receded as a topic of conversation. This quick routinization of the conflict was absolutely remarkable to me. While at work, I had to keep reminding myself that this was a country at war. It would not be an overstatement to say that the early days of the war felt like some huge, shared miniseries that people tuned in to every night. It was completely a spectator sport with a gloss of unreality about it.

My field notes summarizing events during this period exhibit the confusion I was feeling about this state of affairs:

> The [air] attack on Iraq began at 7:00 on the 16th [of January]. Apparently the night shift stopped working at 9:00 so they could listen to Bush's speech, which was piped in over the intercom. On the morning of the 17th, everyone looked haggard as they came in, since they had been up late watching the news. There was no sense of jubilation even though early reports showed that the bombing was very effective with minimal casualties. Instead the mood seemed to be: "Well, I had my doubts about this whole thing, but maybe Bush was right since it seems to be going well." This kind of sentiment was expressed by a number of people.

The intense interest in the war, though, was remarkably short-lived. My notes summarize this development.

> [During the] first couple of days, there was a fair amount of attention to what was going on. Many people knew the number of SCUDs that had been launched the night before. Many people knew the details of what had happened. Many people had seen the live coverage and talked about seeing reporters and Israelis who had to put gas masks on, etc. Several things were clear at this point. One, people were riveted to the coverage. Two, they were concerned about it. They talked about it being "scary." Would there be terrorist attacks in the U.S.? etc. Clearly, there was serious consideration of the event going on.
> This continued to a certain degree, but by the fifth or sixth day,

discussion of the events dropped off enormously. People were no longer talking about what the news coverage had been the previous night, etc. There was almost a "ho-hum" attitude developing. "Nothing much happened" they'd say after a night of a couple thousand bombing runs and a few SCUDs being fired. It settled into a quiet lull. There's very little discussion.

After the initial flurry of interest, people stopped watching the news again. In its place, a daily routine developed to share basic information. Again, an excerpt from my field notes summarizes the situation.

Basically there developed a morning ritual whereby people who didn't watch the news would inquire about any major developments in the war the night before. This would take place at the [break] table before work when people were having coffee. Someone would ask, [and] someone who had watched the news would give a quick comment . . . summarizing the events. For example, a report might come as: "Three SCUDS; two at Israel, one at Saudi. One at Israel landed in the middle of nowhere. The other two were shot down by Patriots. No planes lost." People would nod in assent and the topic of the war was over for the day. The entire interaction would usually take less than a minute or so. After the first few days of the war, this was the extent of war discussion.

The lesson for me was driven home poignantly. Even in the midst of war—a war which involved the sons and husbands of coworkers—political news was very quickly routinized and was only a peripheral part of people's daily lives.

The Distance Bridged: Taxes

Although government and political affairs are generally perceived as distant and irrelevant matters, Kristen, a thirty-two-year-old mail-processing worker, makes clear that care needs to be taken not to overgeneralize this point.

DC: I'm curious about how you said that politics doesn't affect you—or something like that. Do you—

KRISTEN: —Well, it affects me. Oh yeah, it affects me. I see it every week when I take out that paycheck. Sometimes it seems like it doesn't pay to work, you know what I mean? The more you work, the more they take from you. That really gets me. It's like they don't want you to work. They don't want the average guy to make a decent living. That's not right. That shouldn't be that way.

Other workers also cite taxes as exempt from their general belief that government doesn't affect them.

SAM: If they're gonna raise taxes, then that concerns me. [laughs] But other than that, most of the stuff don't. I don't even know what they do most of the time. I really don't.

Overwhelmingly, people are most conscious of the effect of government through their paychecks. In a manner unparalleled in politics, the government's impact on workers is clearly and unambiguously quantified in dollars and cents on every week's pay stub. When asked about government impact on their lives, workers most often mention taxes. In fact, they are often the only way that workers see the government impacting their lives.

JOHN: These guys are up there making the big bucks doing jack while the rest of us are busting our butts off everyday to pay their salaries. For what? You look at the taxes they take out of you and it makes you sick, you know? It just makes you sick. And what do you get back for that? Roads, OK. Garbage. That's about all I ever see.

Workers feel that they are stuck in the middle, making too much money to be exempt from taxes or to benefit from government programs but not making enough to be among the wealthy, who can hire lawyers and accountants to get out of paying their fair share in taxes. (Consequently, the workers I spoke with seem to support the notion of a flat tax with essentially no exemptions.) There is very strong support for using government funds to help those in need—those who "really" need it—but there is equally strong resentment of those, both rich and poor, who try to subvert the system for their own gain.

RONALD: You've got rich people who sit on their ass all day and make piles of money and don't pay taxes, and then you've got the welfare bums who sit on their ass and get their government checks. It's crazy. It's the working stiffs like us who get screwed coming and going.

When the Right promotes images of "welfare queens" and the Left critiques corporate "fat cats," they are both tapping into this same stream of resentment.
Sometimes, as with African Americans (and to a lesser degree with women) and affirmative action, the gains of some groups appear to these white workers to be unfairly achieved at the expense of the working people caught in the middle.

DANIEL: Well, like blacks, right? I mean you had the civil rights groups that were marching and asking for stuff. I mean, they were right. They weren't being treated equal so they went out. But that kind of thing continues, you know. . . . They keep pushing for more and more.

DC: Do you think that's fair? You sound a little unsure?

DANIEL: Well, yeah, it's—I mean, they were right. It wasn't fair. But now, you know, the tables turn, and they're asking for what's not fair the other way, you know, to help them. *That's* not fair.

But similar logic is used to condemn bailouts of the the wealthy as well.

ROGER: I don't think the government should be bailing these [bankers]. That's one thing. I'm against using our tax money to step in and save these guys that made bad business decisions. I don't think that's right. . . . You let them go down. If some of these banks were too busy chasing the almighty dollar to see that they were making all these bad loans, too bad. That's their problem. I don't think the government should get involved.

Workers can clearly see how much government is taking away from them—money that they could better use to pay rent or mortgages, make car payments, meet grocery bills, or do house repairs. But there is absolutely no equivalent sense of where this money goes.

KRISTEN: Well, I pay taxes! [laughs] So that affects me. If they're going to be spending more and more on welfare, then it's going to take a bite out of my check. You can see that every week. But that's really it. I pay for it—I don't know what "it" is exactly. [laughs]

Not knowing what "it" is on which the government seems to spend incomprehensible amounts of money is a central component of the entire tax issue, and it generates a good deal of hostility towards politicians. There are generalized feelings that tax dollars are wasted on everything from military spending to foreign aid to "welfare" to "bureaucracy."[4] Interestingly, workers whose employment puts them in direct contact with government agencies were among the harshest in their criticism. Oscar, a defense worker, complained:

OSCAR: They spend billions and billions on things people don't even know about. People don't know where their money goes. You just pay it out and never see it again. . . . I see it at work. [I]n a place like that with all the money coming in from the government it's amazing how much is wasted. [F]irst you've got the paperwork. It seems like half the people in that place fill out forms to show how the other half spent the money. [laughs] Really, though, there's so many people, that's all they do, paperwork. And then the money they spend on prototypes and test projects that just end up nowhere, you know. They put millions into different projects, and then they decide that it isn't going to work so it just gets dropped. Where did that money go? Who pays for it? *You* do that's who. . . . That's the way bureaucracy works. The money never gets down to where it's supposed to be going.

For many workers then, government is something that takes away, wastes, and gives little, if anything, in return. Workers simply do not see themselves as the beneficiaries of government programs.

DC: What about in other areas besides taxes. Do you think that what goes on in politics affects you?

RONALD: No, not really. It affects the . . . the very bottom . . . those that get money or food stamps or whatever from the government. It affects them. But for the average working guy, the only thing we see is taxes. We pay, pay, pay. But all that other stuff doesn't affect us because us poor slobs are out there paying our own way.

Activists see workers as being isolated and restricted from political participation due to their meager material resources. Workers, though, are more likely to see themselves as having the political world foisted upon them through the ever increasing burden of taxes. In other words, activists essentially argue that workers want to get involved in the political world but cannot, whereas workers say they do not want to be involved but have to be. This involvement, however, is strictly limited to their role as taxpayer. Rather than see themselves as without resources, workers tend to see themselves as being the primary providers of the resources that keep the country going: taxes.

The recipients of this tax money are seen to be people unlike themselves, either the rich or the poor. Workers clearly feel abandoned by a political system that seems to them to address the needs of those two groups while ignoring the needs of those not poor enough to be on government relief but not wealthy enough to take advantage of political loopholes. Although such a predicament might suggest strong motivation for political involvement, workers see their situation as merely further evidence of the system's intransigence.

Motivations: Interests, Values, and Intrinsic Rewards

Working-class nonparticipation is, in part, the result of a lack of motivation for political involvement. Political participation is largely motivated by one or more of three factors: the pursuit of self-interest, strongly held principles, or the intrinsic rewards of participation.[5]

Interests

First, there may be some material interest or instrumental reason to become politically involved. That is, participation may begin in order to achieve a particular goal that will benefit the participant in some direct or indirect way. Examples of this type of motivation may include housing activism, NIMBY campaigns, or the antinuclear movement, where the reasons for involvement are the protection of existing circumstances and opposition to a perceived threat. Other recent efforts such as antitax campaigns can also have this defensive characteristic. Other social movements, such as the women's and civil rights movements also work, in part, on promoting some interest of group members, though these are not necessarily defensive efforts.

Workers, though, generally see no instrumental reason to enter the political arena or support left-movement projects. Often, left movements are not addressing political issues that carry significant salience for workers. Consequently, the potential success of the Left is not seen as a likely source of aid for them in their daily lives. In fact, some left movements—especially environmental movements—can be seen to pose a threat to the interests and well-being of some workers.

Although none of the workers I interviewed were directly involved in the debates between environmental activists and workers, most were clear about where their sympathies lay. As one worker put it, "If you don't have to kill whales or whatever, then I guess you shouldn't, but for some people I think this is their livelihood. That's the only thing I'd be concerned about. Like fishermen, what are they gonna do?" The notion that environmentalists sometimes cared more about animals than they did about workers was a sentiment that often coexisted with genuine concern for the destructive effects of pollutants and waste.

The bottom line is that left movements generally are not seen as a mechanism to protect workers' interests. In fact, workers are sometimes mobilized to oppose left efforts in order to protect jobs and other features of daily life. The battle over New Hampshire's Seabrook nuclear power plant was one such effort that was familiar to many of the workers and to almost all of the activists I spoke with.

Gus, an antinuclear activist, noted that from the beginning the plant was portrayed by promoters—falsely as it turned out—as an economic boom for a struggling community.

GUS: The town of Seabrook was offered incredible incentives including a fire station, a police station, a community center, the promise of [a stronger] tax base was certainly made. . . . [But] the town is still just as hard pressed as it ever was, which is the reason [the promoters] chose the town in the first place was because it was economically disadvantaged and therefore vulnerable to these kinds of arguments.

But the economic arguments made on behalf of the Seabrook plant appealed to some union members, and a confrontation was set up that pitted union members, who saw jobs as their central priority, against environmentalists and other progressives who were concerned with the environmental impact, safety, and other issues. Efforts to bridge the gap between activists and workers were largely unsuccessful. This process is described by Rob, an activist who had ties to both the labor and the antinuclear movements.

ROB: I sensed a need to organize in the workplace in order to reach working people who are part of this also. . . . People got to eat. If you're not careful about that, you'll wind up doing some not-so-great things. I thought the people who have control are the people who work there, so we had this labor committee. I remember, right after they announced that there was gonna be a license and there was gonna be this demonstration, putting together this little flyer and going down by myself in the morning as the guys were going into work and handing this out and explaining what was going on and trying hard not to get the dynamics set up of the granola gang versus the hardhats. I was trying not to let this antagonism play out. And also part of it was lessons taken from the Vietnam War when they were playing off the hardhats against the peace people. So that's what I was trying to do. . . . I had to work on how to build those bridges. It wasn't really successful really. Not as successful as we should have been. But also part of it has to do with—a lot of the dynamic of what was going on—it was a lack of class consciousness, to some extent, within the antinuclear movement. But there was also, within the leadership of labor there were just people who didn't understand where the labor movement was going.

The collision between workers, especially the more conservative elements of organized labor, and left activists resulted in a continuing legacy of antagonism.

The clash between material interests and larger ideological ideals sometimes takes place *within* a movement. Stuart, a thirty-eight-year-old Central America activist, told the story of having recently attended a meeting of New England activists where such a dramatic confrontation occurred. One woman at the meeting represented a newly forming local group made up overwhelmingly, as Stuart put it, of "blue-collar" Hondurans—an unusual contrast to the mostly middle-class, white Americans involved in the movement. This new group was trying to develop a strategy to reach American working people. The different class base of this group resulted in a markedly different approach with which the rest of the middle-class Central America activists were uncomfortable.

STUART: The issue that [the new group] had identified was U.S. military bases and talking to people here about "Hey they're closing military bases, it's costing you jobs and housing and medical services in your home town, but did you know that there's twenty-six of them operating in Honduras and they're not closing any of them down?" And immediately people . . . almost literally jumped up and said, "We have a major problem with this. That's no solution to the problem, keeping military bases open here. What kind of argument is that to make?" . . . Here's a woman talking bread-and-butter-issues: jobs, job security, housing, medical care. That's it, right there. And here are these wealthy, white progressives telling her that her issue is full of shit.

Thus, left social movements sometimes find themselves mobilizing efforts that confront the interests of some working people. Sometimes, as we've seen above, activism threatens the livelihood of workers in particular industries. At other times, the advancement of some social groups is perceived by white, often male, workers as a threat. Women's organizations and civil rights groups, for example, clearly pursue goals with the potential to directly benefit their constituency, most notably through affirmative action programs. What appears simply to be a call for justice against, for example, sexist and racist hiring practices can be interpreted by white workers as a threat to their livelihood.[6]

The environmental movement is similarly fragmented. Greider (1992) relates the story of bridge-building efforts by Lois Gibbs of the Citizen's Clearinghouse for Hazardous Wastes. Gibbs invited about thirty grassroots community activists and lawyers and lobbyists from the so-called Big Ten leading national environmental groups to a series of roundtable discussions. " 'It was hilarious,' Gibbs said. 'People from the grassroots were at one end of the room, drinking Budweiser and smoking, while the environmentalists were at the other end of the room eating yogurt. We wanted to talk about victim compensation. They wanted to talk about ten parts per billion benzene and scientific uncertainty. A couple of times it was almost war' " (in Greider 1992: 214).

Values

Values or principles constitute a second type of motivation for political involvement insofar as they comprise a moral or ideological connection to political issues. Whether or not they are religiously based, moral or ideological principles can provide motivation and sustenance for continued involvement, even in efforts where the odds are foreseeably insurmountable. Moral or ideological principles can also foster empathy with oppressed groups and may motivate involvement in activities where the actor has no immediate interest. Such was the case for many activists, for example, who opposed South Africa's apartheid policies or the United States' intervention in Central America.

The *Golden Rule* was a small boat that sailed into a nuclear testing area in the Pacific ocean in 1958. Its captain was Albert Bigelow, the product of a Boston patrician family. Martin Oppenheimer (in Isserman 1987: 127–28) wrote of the *Golden Rule*'s journey:

> If, as they admit, their effort may bring no real change, why do it at all? . . . They did it because they could do no other, because no one else did it for them, because politics failed to do it, because the hour was late and because they had to. Effectiveness had little to do with it. This was the individual act undertaken against a state and a condition which seemed omnipotent; above all this was propaganda of the deed, one's physical body thrown into a void where no other bridge seemed to exist.

This is the epitome of acting out of a moral imperative from a politics based largely on values. (Of course, the opposition to atmospheric nuclear tests might be said to represent partially a politics of self-interest, though at a rather abstracted level.) Pacifists have often taken the lead in performing such acts. This strategy can be an attractive one, in part, because it allows for political action without needing to organize large numbers of participants. These actions are sometimes dramatic, such as those of Buddhist monks who immolated themselves to protest the Vietnam War, or "Ploughshare" activists who broke into U.S. military bases in the 1980s to pour blood upon and to pound upon nuclear-weapons components with hammers. The image of protesters attacking nuclear weapons with hammers is a fitting encapsulation of the futility often associated with such acts. Clearly, they serve as a symbolic call for action, not as pragmatic politics in the usual sense.

But more mundane political acts, too, are often motivated by values rather than interests. Many left activists will admit that their efforts have produced little that can be truly called success when measured in purely instrumental terms. Still, they feel their efforts are worthwhile and right. They too, can do no other. But strict appeals to values do not seem to resonate with most working people. This is not to say that workers do not have a sense of justice or fairness, but when it comes to the issues addressed by most middle-class movements, workers have neither the guilt nor the sense of responsibility that seems to be associated with many middle-class-value-based actions.

For example, appeals from the peace or Central America anti-intervention movements have often played on the idea that citizens must stop actions that are carried out in their name. (In fact, "Not in Our Name" was actually the title of one such national anti-intervention project.) That is, people are asked to take responsibility for their government's actions. But such an orientation is largely foreign to most workers. Since they often do not vote and since they see themselves as having virtually no input into government decision making, most workers find rather incomprehensible the suggestion that they are responsible for the actions of their government—a theme often sounded by middle-class activists. In addition, some middle-class movements clearly have more than a kernel of guilt associated with them. This approach, too, needs a sense of privilege in order to be effective. Once again, most workers simply do not identify themselves as being in such positions of privilege.

When activists use values as the basis of their politics, they can justify their political actions despite their inability to connect with a broader citizenry. For example, Gus described his political life as entailing "Living a life of simplicity in order to be effective as an organizer." At the same time, however, he recognized that his rejection of mainstream values and adoption of a lifestyle based on alternative values put him at odds with most Americans. He had once worked in an inner-city urban program, for example, and he noted that his lifestyle was not a model "for economically disadvantaged blacks that we were working with . . . who wanted to aspire out of their poverty, not take on voluntary poverty." Still, he argued that his value orientation resulted in "interesting dynamics that were maybe a counterpoint to [the people] we were working with as much as they were facilitating a movement." As we saw in the last chapter, the value-based politics of some middle-class activists do not seem to resonate with the workers I interviewed. Most see such cultural and political "counterpoints" as expressions of fringe elements who can be readily dismissed, and they see those engaging in futile political acts as privileged and naïve actors.

Intrinsic Rewards

The third motivation for involvement does not directly concern the political *issue* being addressed, but rather, it relates to the rewards intrinsic to the *process* of political participation. Some activists clearly find social rewards in their political activities, through making friends and sharing social and cultural interests, in addition to political concerns. The world of politics can sometimes be an exciting one, with dramatic demonstrations and confrontations, and shows of solidarity. Validation of activist actions is sometimes received from press coverage, and the mutual support activists give one another can be a very strong positive reinforcement. Some activists pursue their involvement, in part, as a sort of hobby or form of entertainment. Others also enjoy the process because it gives them a chance to cultivate and practice various skills such as writing, public speaking, graphic arts, or program development. Such rewards of self-expression and fulfillment should not be seen as trivializing people's involvement or commitment to the issues under consideration. They are simply a separate realm of motivations for involvement which, to some, are very important and sustaining. Clearly, most activists who enjoy the process of politics are also motivated by either interest or values.

The fact that left social movements feature a distinctly middle-class culture suggests that the intrinsic rewards of the political process often are less accessible to working people. The reasons for this are simple. The middle-class culture that predominates in most left movements is a relatively alien one for workers. Rather than encourage participation, the process involved with becoming active in a political organization is more likely to prove decidedly uninviting. As we have seen, workers in this study certainly did not see political action as an attractive source of self-fulfillment. Instead, they considered the political arena to be a sordid realm populated by people very much unlike themselves.

Electoral politics can bring activists into frequent contact with powerful public figures. Carlene, an environmental activist, calmly told an extraordinary tale of her "dabbling" in presidential politics. During the 1988 presidential primaries she worked for the Gephardt campaign and, among other things, provided food and housing at various times for forty-two different campaign workers. She recalls a campaign-season ritual:

CARLENE: My husband, he always does Sunday morning breakfast, he does these outstanding breakfasts—and he would just send one of the kids downstairs and have them count heads, "Tell me how many I'm cooking for," and we'd feed whoever was here.

Political campaigns, Carlene learned from the experience, were "tremendous fun." Participation of this sort—which clearly requires substantial resources—

can help people feel connected and a part of the political process, and consequently serve as its own reward.

CARLENE: It's really fulfilling on a personal basis. I really, really do enjoy [it]. . . . [W]ith the political campaigns the people we had in here were incredible. We had attorneys from the West Coast. We had a woman who was the transportation director for the city of Los Angeles. We had a guy who spent three years conducting orchestras in Germany who came back here, didn't have a home, and decided to join up with a campaign and travel from place to place. So you meet some incredible people that you might not otherwise meet.

But as a byproduct, Carlene also found there were other rewards from her involvement.

CARLENE: It's been helpful to know people in different people's offices in Washington that may or may not have been here during the campaign. That was fun. I got involved at a level that I hadn't really expected. . . . I wound up a delegate to the New Hampshire convention in Concord. And Gephardt still writes to me and sends me clippings. That was very interesting.

For some activists, then, an important part of political action is that it is "fulfilling," "interesting," and just plain "fun."

In left-movement circles, political activists also tend to have strong movement cultures in which people share cultural and political interests that are clearly fun. Political folk music and progressive music, vegetarian cooking, even political T-shirts, posters, and buttons are all common artifacts of left, middle-class, social-movement communities. These cultural ties are reinforced in the often tight-knit friendship circles that politically active people share. Working people, then, who do not share in the cultural background, skills, lifestyles, or material resources of middle-class activists are unlikely to find middle-class social movements a comfortable or rewarding environment for self-expression or self-fulfillment.

In part, the reason for this is that middle-class social movements have identity formation as part of their agenda. Melucci (1989: 208), for example, suggests that new social movements "invest much time and energy in constructing norms of organization which are not considered instrumental for the achievement of social and political goals, but are viewed primarily as a way of experiencing collective action itself." He argues that these movements operate as "signs" within "complex" societies communicating the importance of diversity and that such movements are prefigurative in the sense that actors are practicing in the present the future social changes they seek. In the tradition of McLuhan, Melucci argues that, in effect, "the movement is the message."

The intrinsic rewards involved in political participation, especially the importance of solidarity and identity formation, are an interesting twist on

Olson's (1965) notions of the need for selective incentives to overcome the classic "free rider" problem. In Melucci's analysis, individuals are afforded an identity as a result of their participation in social movements. Although this may be an individual "benefit," it is inextricably linked to the group. Thus, in developing a sense of identity through movement political culture, the differentiation between individual and collective incentives is obscured. A key "individual benefit" is the acquisition of a collective identity, thus closing the circuit between individual and collective. This is different from Fireman and Gamson's (1979) argument that preexisting feelings of solidarity affect individual decision making. In the case of new social movements, Melucci argues that solidarity does not precede participation, but rather it is a product of participation and is therefore important for the ongoing maintenance of movement organizations. Unlike classical theories, however, this formulation recognizes that the initial involvement of an individual is largely a political decision and not based merely on psychological needs.

The Consequences of Motivations

Working people and middle-class activists tend to judge the value of political actions on different terms. The former speak of politics in largely utilitarian terms, complaining, as we have seen, that social-movement efforts seem not to accomplish anything. Workers see, therefore, little reason to make political life a priority. Working-class participation tends to be limited to defensive actions aimed at concretely protecting the existing conditions of daily life. Even the labor movement has shown a propensity to become most active when it is defending workers against the onslaught of capital's concessionary demands. The motivation for working-class action is usually the protection of interests.

Middle-class activists may also pursue actions that have clear interests involved. Successful campaigns for civil rights or environmental protection help to foster a sense of utility for collective action. But whereas many activists may often acknowledge the failures of their movements to achieve substantial concrete successes, such as in the peace movement, they look to other criteria to judge the value of their involvement. Even if it appears to accomplish nothing, acting on a sense of values can bring with it its own rewards.

The downside of a politics based on values is arrogance. At various times in history, sections of the Left—middle class *and* working class—have been oblivious to the concerns of fellow citizens because they were blinded by the apparent primacy of *their* issue. Working-class movements often dismissed the important cleavages of race and gender in their focus on white, male workers. Parts of the 1950s peace movement regarded the civil rights movement as a distraction, arguing, as one activist put it at the time (in Isserman 1987: 159), it would not matter "whether we blew up integrated or segregated." Similar remarks about the primacy of the nuclear issues were a notorious feature of the nuclear-freeze movement, and equivalent attitudes are part of some aspects of the contemporary environmental movement.

Finally, for middle-class activists there are rewards that are intrinsic to the process of political participation, regardless of the effectiveness of the campaign or movement. This produces another problematic dynamic. To put it bluntly, much of middle-class politics is comfortable. That is, since participation brings its own rewards and middle-class activists generally are not working for their own immediate interests, it often makes little difference whether such movements succeed or fail. Measured on the scale of intrinsic rewards, these movements are always a success for those who choose to participate. To outsiders like the workers I interviewed, however, continued pursuit of apparently futile efforts can seem baffling. Not participating in social movements is similar to not voting. It is, in part, the realization that such activities will not provide benefits. It is also, implicitly, a critique of social movements and of the political system.

CHAPTER 7

"People Have Got Their Hands Full"

Material Resources and Constraint

I think that being oppressed can lead to activism out of self-preservation. In my experience though, the people that I've found working in the peace movement are pretty well educated, pretty well . . . self-sufficient financially or choosing to be poor because they have enough money so that they can do that.

PERRY, forty-four-year-old Central America activist

When social-movement activists talk about why their organizations have little or no working-class participation, they are less likely to mention issues of efficacy, interest, or motivation than they are to cite material constraint. The implicit assumption in many activists' analysis is that working people want to involve themselves in politics and would be more likely to participate if they had more material resources and more free time. The material-constraint argument does have some explanatory power. Workers do experience a relative paucity of material resources that makes political participation more difficult. However, there is another dynamic at work that makes the material constraint argument less useful than activists suggest. The first half of this chapter presents the material-constraint argument, whereas the second half explores some of the limitations of this argument.

Activists and the Notion of Material Constraint

There is a dilemma surrounding the issue of material resources and constraint. On the one hand, being materially *secure* can lead to political complacency that is shaken only by changing events. The student antiwar movement of the 1960s is a classic example.

STUART: The opposition to Vietnam came to life when the existence of middle-class and upper-class kids was shaken by the draft. . . . They were ignorant, and they were complacent, but they became educated, and they were given a reason to get out in the street, and they did in huge numbers. That's what it takes—the existence of a large group of people to become rattled. I think that's a real key element.

On the other hand, being materially *insecure* may result in priorities being placed on meeting immediate material needs rather than on larger political goals.

Regardless of how activists think (or do not think) about class as an issue, they generally recognize that there are differences in material conditions between the working and middle classes and that material resources and constraints are an important element in understanding political participation. Some believe that working people have abandoned political life as they have become more materially secure, what in social science is referred to as the "thesis of embourgeoisement" (Goldthorpe et al. 1969). But most activists cite the *lack* of material security as the key factor in explaining working-class disengagement. In fact, activists cite material constraint more than any other reason to explain the lack of working-class participation in politics.

Some suggest that economic pressures contribute to a more generalized abdication of political responsibility. One activist talked of the appeal of Reagan-like leadership.

GUS: I think that people are more inclined to look to paternal images, to hand over responsibility than to make those decisions [. . . when] they're looking to free up more time for economic livelihood in strapped times.

Describing conditions that in fact do not apply to most working people, another activist argues:

CARLENE: [Y]ou do at least have to have the basic necessities of life taken care of for you. And if you are coming from a family that isn't sure that they're gonna have a roof over their heads tomorrow or are not sure where their next meal is coming from, it takes a pretty incredibly strong person to be able to think about reaching out to other people.

But most activists do not think middle-class people participate more because they have more money. Instead, the importance of economic differences is primarily related to the issue of discretionary time. The general material-constraint argument made by many activists is essentially this: Working people labor at lower-paying jobs than do middle-class people. As a result, working-class people must spend significantly longer hours on the job in order to make ends meet. This is done by either working overtime or taking on a second (or even third) job. Both partners of working-class couples are seen as more likely to hold jobs outside the home. One consequence of this situation is that working people have less free time and are therefore unable to take part in political activities. Thus, while all Americans may be experiencing less leisure time, it is the working class that is hardest hit and thus has the least amount of time for political activity.

Activists have plenty of evidence to support this general argument. First, of course, is the relative absence of working-class people from their groups. Second is the clear material advantages that some members possess. Several activists noted that the volunteers who were most active in their organizations did not work full time. Volunteer leadership positions, especially, are apt to be filled by people with limited or at least flexible work hours. Activists know well the time demands that political participation makes on their lives. Referring to a recently won citizen's initiative, Carol commented, "It was a really big project. It was time consuming. It consumed everybody's life for six months or so. It's all most of us did. There's a level of dedication there that isn't available to everybody." Since several full-time campaign volunteers were financially supported by their spouses, there was also a level of material resources that is certainly unavailable to most.

Stuart summarizes well this argument, applying it to his own movement:

STUART: I think the Central America movement in the United States is purely a middle- to upper-middle-class movement. My personal view is—I have the time. I don't have to work two jobs to put oil in my tank and food on my table. I either have the money to go on a trip to Central America, or I have the time to devote to raising money for a group that I'm part of to go. And that is very much a class thing.

The other thing is my feeling that if a really working-class person or a very poor person is gonna be politically active, my guess is it's probably gonna be on a bread-and-butter issue. It's probably going to be improving their neighborhood. It's probably going to be improving their schools. It's probably going to be labor type activity. Mainly because that's what's in their face and that's what they have to deal with. Those of us who are fortunate enough to not have that kind of stuff in our face have the luxury of being more outward looking. So, coming full circle, I see the Central America movement here as predominantly middle class, and that's my guess as to why.[1]

This approach is consistent with the arguments of Maslow (1962, 1964), who postulated a "hierarchy of needs" and contended that to pursue goals of self-fulfillment and altruism, more immediate material needs must first be met.

Activists' observations are clearly grounded in reality. Middle-class activists do have material resources that facilitate participation at their disposal. As Kahn (1986: 171) writes, many left political activities are supported by a middle-class "economy that allows individuals to disdain materialism because they have their own informal social safety net. Should the need for money arise, members of the middle-class economy can draw on their background and experience, education and savvy, and a lifetime of social connections to gain access to the requisite resources."

Workers themselves sometimes cite the lack of time as a reason for not participating in politics.

BERNICE: Who's got time? People are too busy with work and with kids and everything. Especially today with both parents working all the time and the kids at daycare. Who's got time to go to board of aldermen meetings or whatever? It's just unrealistic.

The motivating pressure for all of this work is the need to pay bills. But the seductive pay of overtime work is also an important factor. Several of my coworkers mentioned that overtime was their "play money," with which they bought consumer goods, went on short trips, completed household improvement projects, or pursued hobbies (one woman had an expensive fascination with tropical fish that tended to die shortly after she bought them). For others, overtime pay is more basic.

RONALD: I'm at [MAPS] my regular shift and then I try to get in some overtime every week. That's where you make some money. You can't really get a decent paycheck without doing some overtime. And then on weekends, sometimes, I work for my brother-in-law. He's got his own little business— he's a contractor . . . so on weekends a lot of times I work with him for a day. . . . You've got to pay the bills somehow. Car payments, rent, child support—that all adds up.

In addition, several single mothers at MAPS were stuck in an endless cycle of working as much overtime as possible in order to pay for child care so they could work more.

Some workers see a relationship between long work hours and disengagement from a wide variety of social institutions.

KRISTEN: I have an aunt who teaches sixth grade, and she talks about how she can't see the parents because everyone works and nobody has time to come and talk to a teacher anymore. I mean, if parents can't even get to see their children's teachers, then they're not going to do much about other things either.

Lack of time can also cut into leisure pursuits. When asked about reading the newspaper, one worker lamented that he did not follow sports anymore because he did not have the time. Another worker said that despite the fact that she came to work with a book almost every day, she never had time to read. "I get a book . . . from the library and it takes me two months to read it. [laughs] I have to keep going back to renew it." So the case for the constraint of material commitments on political participation seems strong. Activists seem to believe it, and workers sometimes cite it.

The case can be strengthened even further by considering the all-important realm of unpaid labor in the home. Activists generally believe in an inverse relationship between family commitments and involvement in politics. Work is work; whether it is paid or unpaid, inside or outside the home, it still takes up time that might be devoted to other pursuits. One major difference about work in the home, though, is that it is disproportionately carried out by women. Activists see this as another barrier to women's participation. One pointed out that "Men are more likely, if they work full time, to be able to volunteer than women, if there are children involved, because the women wind up with a lot of the parenting." Some organizations try to facilitate the participation of parents by providing child care at meetings and events. However, such efforts are unlikely to overcome the difficulties presented by the presence of children.

Workers, too, recognize the time-consuming nature of families, especially those with children. Kristen cites this as a reason for limited participation.

KRISTEN: Take the people at work. Most of them have children. They go to work—both parents work—they get home and they have the kids to take care of. They don't really have a chance to get involved in much.

For nearly all of the married workers I interviewed, both partners *did* work outside the home. Of the ten married male workers, eight had spouses who worked outside the home. All of the eight married female workers had spouses who worked.

Nicole describes her life in terms that make clear the double duty often faced by women.

NICOLE: You've got your day so full of things to do, I think, that sometimes it's hard to make room for reading a paper or something like that. Especially if you're a parent—you're driving kids here and getting dinner going and bringing that one to practice or whatever. You never really stop. I think most people have got their hands full dealing with getting done what has to get done.

For many workers, what needs to get done is divided largely along gender lines, with women dealing with cooking and most child-care responsibilities while men tend to work more overtime and pick up car and home maintenance.

As with longer work hours outside the home, middle-class people also feel the pinch of family commitments in the home. But middle-class people also have more resources to cushion the impact of such demands by buying time-saving services. For example, middle-class people are more likely than working-class people to have available money for paid child care, for eating out, or for hiring people to service cars, do home repairs, and provide other services. In fact, it is exactly these sorts of service jobs that are among those performed by members of the working class.

An interesting perspective on the issue of family commitment was provided by Carlene, an environmental activist who had originally come from a working-class family in Pittsburgh but who became politically active after having married a professional-middle-class man. She believed that family ties are stronger in working-class families than in middle-class ones, in part because middle-class people are more willing to change location to advance their careers.

CARLENE: In many cases, not all cases, but some of the women that I know and a few of the men that I know that are very active have moved away from their families, which is interesting. And I think, very honestly, that I couldn't put this much time into these things if I were living in Pittsburgh because of large extended family and there's always somebody's shower or birthday or somebody's sick or needs something. So you tend to spend a lot of time helping family members or working with family members. When you're as far away as we are, that time is available to you. Where there, there are people who have a lot more demands put on them as far as maybe taking care of elderly parents or grandparents or nieces and nephews, that kind of thing. So I guess there's a time element involved.

Thus, on the one hand, such relationships may be time consuming and can divert energies that might otherwise be available for political causes. But on the other hand, such relationships also form the basis for important community ties, especially among working-class women. Women's traditional role as family caregiver can put them in a social network of family and friends who share in the events of both good and bad times. From an activist's perspective the obligations of private life may be interpreted as interfering with potential participation. For workers, though, such community may be an important social support meeting the needs of daily life.

So there is reason to believe that activists are correct when they argue that economic constraints—especially as experienced in a lack of discretionary time—are a primary reason why working people are not involved in politics. There is a basic need for free time in order to participate in politics. Longer work hours, child-care responsibilities, and other commitments to daily life can severely limit the amount of time available for political pursuits. For working people especially, tight finances may necessitate working overtime or a second job in order to make ends meet. The result is little or no working-class participation in social-movement activities. But as with all simple explanations, there is more to this story.

Contradictions in the Material Constraint Argument

Despite the seductive neatness of the material-constraint argument, there is actually significant evidence to suggest that it is incomplete. For example, strong family commitment may not be as bad for political participation as suggested above. In fact, having children may contribute to a heightened interest in politics.

DC: Do you think having kids affects how you look at these things?

DIANE: Oh yeah, definitely. You hear things and you think about how it might affect your kids, you know. I never did that before. I know I pay attention more to stuff that might affect [my daughter]—school budget stuff, things like that. Definitely, you pay more attention. If it's gonna affect you, you know, you think about it more.

Another worker also admits she has taken more of an interest in politics since having children.

DC: [W]hat kinds of issues interest you most?

ELLEN: Well, I guess things that can affect my kids—what's going on in the schools. I've got one that's in the second grade now and one that's in kindergarten, so you like to know what's happening in the schools and what they're gonna have by the time they get there.

Local issues such as schools naturally top the list of concerns for parents. But as we have seen with the Gulf War, the relevance of other issues can also seem heightened by the presence of children. This can also include a more generalized concern for the impact of issues in "the long run."

HUGH: Yeah, sometimes if I'm watching the news with my wife, we'll talk a little about things going on, you know. Or sometimes with school things— we get like a little newspaper from the school telling you what's going on and so forth. We had to talk quite a bit about schools when we were thinking of moving. . . .

DC: So these are things that really do affect you then?

HUGH: Yeah, I think so. Maybe they don't affect us now—like the deficit or something—but in the long run I think they could. They could have a big impact on us—on the whole country really.

Family, then, plays more of a mixed role than might at first be apparent. Having children can make parents more concerned and attentive to political issues, especially local ones such as schooling.

Left social movements have sometimes tried to tap into parental concerns in mobilizing people. The anti-atmospheric testing movement of the 1950s drew upon concerns that strontium 90 was making its way into milk that children drank. Helen Caldicott, a pediatrician, came to public prominence in the nuclear-freeze movement in the 1980s and often called upon parents to act to protect the interests of their children. Parts of the environmental movement have also drawn heavily on parental imagery to promote their message of care for "Mother Earth" and its future. However, it is unlikely that appeals to parenthood, in and of themselves, will be enough to elicit participation from those who have not been previously involved. The extent of parental activity mentioned above was limited to what is now a familiar pattern: the passive "monitoring" of news for signs of potential threats.

Although the legacy of family commitment may be more complicated than at first glance, it does not invalidate the basic point that lack of time is a key barrier to participation. It also does not address the argument that long work hours outside the home are the most significant component of the barrier.[2]

Perhaps the strongest supporter of the idea that economic concerns were an important barrier to participation is Patrick, an activist from the working class who mentioned an earlier period of his life when he was politically "uninvolved." After I inquired further he explained that this was a period when he was financially insecure. He makes a direct equation between his obtaining a higher-paying and more secure job and the growth in his involvement. He concludes, "When you stop spending half your time worrying about money you realize you've got time for lots of other things."

This is the central point of the material-constraint argument. Activists assume that politics would be among the "other things" workers would be taking up if they were more financially secure. The evidence for this, though, is mixed.

A Different Dynamic

There is a bigger problem with the material-constraint argument. The assumption in this analysis is that working people would be more likely to participate in politics if they had more material resources and more free time.[3] This assumption shifts attention away from attempts to make political participation more appealing and meaningful, and toward an interest in addressing issues of material constraint. From this assumption there are three logical actions activists can pursue. First, they can work to improve the economic status of workers, thereby creating more discretionary time for political participation. Second, they can make participation in politics less time consuming. Third, they can conclude that politics is a pursuit available primarily to the middle class (rather than to the working class), and it is therefore the responsibility of the middle class to look out for the interests of working people.

Since the first route is—to say the least—a rather daunting task that would probably require an already mobilized working class, activists generally rely upon the latter strategies. They sometimes try to make participation convenient and less time consuming. For example, one peace group, for which two of the activists I interviewed work, has an effort called the "20/20" program, which asks people who are too busy for most politics to donate twenty dollars and to commit twenty minutes a month to a political action such as writing a letter to their newspaper. Although not specifically aimed at encouraging the participation of working-class people, the implicit assumption in this type of program is that it is lack of time that is the primary barrier to participation. The results were predictable. As one of the organization's staffpeople told me, the program was adopted by some middle-class people who otherwise would not have time to take part. Working-class people were still nowhere to be found.

More common is the belief among middle-class activists that their efforts are all the more important because workers and other groups facing constraints are unable to participate in politics. Thus, activists take on the role of working on behalf of those locked out of the political arena by material constraints.

But, in fact, economic constraints are not the central key to the problem. For some working-class people, harsh economic realities *do* discourage participation. But for most people, merely changing the amount of free time they have would make no difference in their level of participation. That is because the mechanisms of nonparticipation are much more complex and subtle than can be described by simple material reductionism.

The material-constraint argument is incomplete, in part, because activists tend to see material conditions as *preventing* people from becoming politically involved. Ironically, given that activists spend their lives promoting human agency, this view relegates people to the status of objects of history. For some middle-class activists, the resulting image of workers as victims of material constraints may be a comforting (and paternalistic) one. The image of worker-as-victim allows activists to explain the absence of working-class participation by blaming neither themselves (for not having organized effectively) nor workers (for being conservative or indifferent). At the same time, activists can reinforce the belief that their efforts are all the more important because they are working on behalf of others less fortunate than they. Thus, the absence of workers is explained away while the belief that the movement is working for supraclass issues remains intact.[4]

A belief in the importance of material constraint, when coupled with a sense of value-based politics, can provide a comforting explanation for why some left movements are made up almost exclusively of middle-class activists but still claim to speak for all of society. In a comment reminiscent of ones I had heard from freeze activists in the 1980s, one environmentalist told me:

CARLENE: I have this feeling that if we don't take care of the environmental issues, there won't *be* any other issues. This is something that if you can make a change even in a small area in terms of air quality and water quality and those kinds of things, you are helping even those people who are, let's say, in the ghetto or that are having problems in different areas. Indirectly—or directly I guess—you're helping those people too because that's not something they will ever be able to fight for for themselves because they're struggling with other issues.

Thus, the absence of working people and the poor is neatly explained while current efforts are reaffirmed as being important precisely because of the inability of others to engage in them.

In reality, a different dynamic is being played out. Workers see material conditions of home and family as demanding their immediate attention *and* see that the political arena does not provide relevant solutions to their immediate concerns. Work life, however unpleasant, *can* provide some immediate, though incomplete, relief.

Workers do not believe that the problems they face in daily life will be addressed in the political arena. Steve, a twenty-nine-year-old factory worker, observes:

STEVE: Well, people complain. You hear it at work all the time. People are having trouble with their kids or making payments—things like that. But that's not stuff that politicians are gonna fix, you know? They don't go, "Hey George [Bush], my kid's really been a brat lately. What're you gonna do about it?" [laughs] It's not those kinds of problems that bother people, I don't think.

What is fundamentally different here from the activists' vision of economic constraint is the relative absence of desire or motivation for political participation on the part of working people. Such a desire is implied by the activists' vision of economic constraint, which posits that working people are being *prevented* from participating by the material conditions in which they find themselves. Only one activist I interviewed explicitly contradicted this belief. Interestingly, it was Ruth, a feminist activist who also conducts workshops on classism.

RUTH: I think there's a huge ignorance about why people aren't politically involved. First of all, there's the expectation that they must *want* to get involved. Why should they? That's all part of the middle-class myth.

One worker summarizes the situation this way:

HELEN: There's nothing they can do about [political issues] so why bother worrying about it. They just try to get out of the way. There's too many things closer to them that maybe they could do something about.

DC: Like what?

HELEN: Work harder or more overtime or whatever to make paying the bills easier. Things like that. Things that have solid results.

Working people, then, have learned to see their own individual and family efforts as being the only ways to address the difficulties of daily life. Politics is seen as something "out there" that has little direct impact on their lives and that certainly cannot be seen as a potential source of solutions to their problems. As I will argue later, this perceived absence of power is an important reason why workers abandon the political sphere as a source of potential solutions, relying instead on the arenas where their efforts can have more direct and immediate results, especially in the home.

Conclusion

Richard Flacks (1988: 50) has commented on the strategies citizens pursue in dealing with material constraints:

> American work and family life embody a variety of conditions that are alienating and unfree. The prevailing way of responding to such conditions is to try not to change the social structures that produce them but to expand the time, space, and resources available in the personal sphere for personal expression and fulfillment. The moral foundation of the search for personal solutions lies in the American ideal of liberty—that every person has the right and the responsibility to live his or her own life.

Such an analysis clearly holds true for the workers with whom I spoke. Activists often make the faulty assumption (or at least wishfully suppose) that if given the chance, working people would be more politically active. Instead, workers largely reject the political world as a source of solutions, seeing it instead as a source of material obstruction through the burden of taxes. Such taxes, though, are grudgingly paid as part of a social contract that offers liberty in exchange. Workers, in effect, are paying for the privilege of *not* having to deal with the political world. The resulting concern with private life is, in itself, a political stand.

Finally, it is important to realize that, as Flacks (1988: 246) notes, "The popular return to everyday life is also a critique of the left. For when the left insists that history takes precedence over life, it is (like the ruling elites) pushing people to sacrifice their lives in the name of goals that go beyond their experienced needs. Isn't it perilous for leftists to label as 'false consciousness' the desire of people to make their own lives rather than submit to the historical projects of the powerful?"

In summarizing the various approaches that are used to explain why women take various pathways to job and motherhood, Gerson (1985: 37) highlights theories emphasizing external structural constraints and childhood-socialization theories based in psychoanalytic theories. She argues, however, "We can ignore neither the subtle ways that childhood experiences influence later life choices nor the structural constraints on women's options. But neither is enough. A complete theory of women's behavior must include how women themselves, as actors who respond to the social conditions they inherit, construct their lives out of the available raw materials." Something similar can be said about explaining the choices workers make about politics. It is important to recognize the material constraints that affect the potential choices of workers. However, by itself, this explanation is incomplete.

CHAPTER 8

"They're Speaking the Same Language"

Cultural Resources

Who are these people? Do they have jobs or what? Is this what they do for a living?

DANIEL, fifty-one-year-old mechanic

Although material constraint is most often cited as a reason why working people are not involved in left social movements, a lack of efficacy is sometimes cited by activists as another *cause* of nonparticipation. But I will argue here that a sense of inefficacy must also be understood as an *effect* of structural conditions. In particular, I will suggest that differentially available cultural resources—based on class status—help to facilitate or hinder the development of a sense of efficacy. If we are to better understand the dynamics of nonparticipation, we need to look beyond just material resources and consider the impact of class on the availability of cultural resources. We must also be aware of how differing class cultures may affect the reception of movement messages.

Cultural Resources

It is individuals who do or do not experience a sense of efficacy. But efficacy, like all social phenomena, is shaped by social structures and varies in individuals according to social status. It is all too easy to emphasize an individual's sense of efficacy and overlook the collective context within which it was developed. When examining efficacy, class is one such structural variable that must be considered.

Class is a structural phenomenon, but it is experienced by individuals through class cultures. Differing cultural resources, based on class, encourage different perspectives on political life and, most important, different senses of efficacy. I will briefly consider some of these cultural "tools" and examine how class affects their development.

137

Vision

Activists possess what several of them referred to as the ability to envision alternatives. One said that in order to be seriously involved in social-movement politics, activists need "a real strong vision of how things could be different; how society could be organized in a different way that would meet people's needs better than the way society's organized now." For this peace and justice activist, such a vision came early in life.

ALLAN: I loved reading utopian novels when I was in high school—Thomas Moore. And anti-utopian novels, too—*1984* and *Brave New World* and stuff like that. I was just really into that stuff. I don't know what else was there, but somehow I had this idea that the way society was organized was not the way society had to be organized, that there were alternative ways that were better. . . . So when the opportunities came to realize that there was something that I could do to bring that about, I just went for it.

Such a sense of possibility is undoubtedly influenced by socialization into a class where other goals in life seem accessible and possible. If material security and personal self-fulfillment are reasonable and attainable goals—as they often are for the middle class—then envisioning broader changes can seem possible as well.

Working people, as we have seen, are socialized into a very different worldview in which it is largely unimaginable to be considering the very reorganization of society. Such issues—the making of history—are recognized by working people to be the work of others, not of people like themselves.

Most of the workers with whom I spoke fall into a category of citizens whose patterns of beliefs Jennifer Hochschild (1981: 278) has labeled as "acquiescence." Her description of people's beliefs regarding redistributive justice can be broadened and apply quite well to most workers in this study.

> Most people do not seek downward redistribution because *they cannot imagine it* or *do not believe in its possibility.* Those who acquiesce do not endorse the dominant pattern of beliefs in American society. They do not believe that capitalist differentiation will improve their own lives or the lives of their children and the deeply poor. They are painfully aware of the disjunction between economy and polity. But *they perceive no other set of beliefs available to them* and no way to resolve their disjunction; therefore they passively concur in the norms with which they were raised and which everyone else apparently holds. They are deeply ambivalent about their own beliefs and often deeply unhappy about the actual distributions they see. But people who acquiesce *do not know what to do,* and *they do not feel politically effective;* therefore they simply accept their lot and hope that some-how, someday, something will change. (emphasis added)

This is exactly the sort of sentiment expressed by workers who recognize problems, hope for change, but cannot really imagine either participating in or achieving such change.

DANIEL: I think things—some things anyway—have gotten out of hand. We don't really know what to do about all this stuff. What can you do? It's everywhere. What can you do? You hope, you know. You hope people will come to their senses. But really, what can you do?

A sense of possibility is perhaps more important than any other cultural resource. History is filled with tales of those who have struggled against apparently insurmountable odds to achieve beloved goals. Belief in possibility opens the door for the recognition and development of skills and resources that have previously lain dormant or have been overlooked.

Jason, a thirty-six-year-old community-housing activist, makes this important point. In talking to tenants about cooperatively buying their building or trailer park, he says,

JASON: First thing [that's needed], I think, is the sense that it's possible. People don't realize that it's even possible. . . . It's like, "I can hardly get a car loan, and you're talking about me working with others to buy this park or this apartment. You've got to be crazy."

He goes on to elaborate that this lack of efficacy is a cultural product. "Let's just face it. I don't think there's a lot of positive validation of low-income people's abilities in this society." Consequently, "I think that that truly is one of the obstacles, either an internal sense of lack of confidence and also lack of confidence of others around you." However, he points out that, ideally, an activist's role is to work with people in helping them discover their own abilities.

JASON: My experience tells me that it doesn't require professional skills to do this kind of thing. People's life experiences that they've developed over the years are sufficient and are quite substantial. But that's not always recognized by the people nor by the neighbors of those people. In fact, we've got a video, and that was one of the comments that one of the members of the first cooperative started was that one of the benefits of this was that she has come to learn that she—through her life experiences—had developed skills that she didn't know she had. Forming a cooperative provided her with the opportunity to realize that.

Such developments, however, are all too rare. The pragmatic material concerns of such housing struggles are foreign to most middle-class social movements that do not focus on such "bread-and-butter" issues. Developing a sense of efficacy in the face of more amorphous and sometimes global issues is less likely for workers, who already express a fatalistic sense of inefficacy and inevitability, than for middle-class activists.

Skills

The role of formal schooling, especially college education, in establishing a sense of efficacy, is one important difference between the middle and working classes. The benefits of formal schooling are primarily cultural in nature, training students in how to develop and use information. Schooling also provides important social skills that can be helpful in future political endeavors. Interacting with and learning about the middle class, from which the bulk of political actors are drawn, is an important benefit of higher education. Being able to interact, socialize, and work comfortably with members of the middle class is a skill that may be taken for granted by those raised in such a culture but can pose formidable obstacles to those for whom middle-class expectations and assumptions seem foreign.

Work life also fosters different skills for middle- and working-class people. This issue will be explored in Chapter Ten. Along with specialized education, work tasks can train middle-class people in skills that are useful for political participation.

Activists have differing levels of recognition for the difficulty of the work they do. On the one hand, a belief in democratic principles suggests that "anyone" can become involved in the political arena. As Carol put it, "If you really believe in what you are doing and that what you are doing is right, then that is 50 percent of the battle." But on the other hand, when asked about concrete needs of their organization, activists readily cite the need for people with particular skills. In a typical response, Karen says her group needs people with "interpersonal skills, followed by computer skills, writing, speaking, clerical." These communication skills, along with a generalized ability to be "well organized," are highly valued by activists.

The heavy emphasis on communication skills means that middle-class people are usually better prepared to enter and to participate actively in politics because their education and employment often stress these very same skills. Most working people, by contrast, are less likely to be called upon in their work to exercise such public communication skills. As a consequence, working people may feel intimidated by the prospect of working in largely middle-class groups, or they may feel that they have nothing to contribute to the political process, given their lack of specialized education and training. Although everyone may be welcome into an organization, people with skills that are in demand may more readily find a comfortable niche within the group.

Socialization and Entitlement

Robert Coles (1977: 54) has written that being socialized in relative affluence affects how children perceive the external political world. He argues that for such children, "the newspapers, the radio, the television offer news not merely about 'others' but about neighbors, friends, acquaintances of ones' parents— or about issues one's parents take seriously, talk about, sometimes get quite involved in. These are children who have discovered that the 'news' may well be affected, if not crucially molded, by their parents as individuals or as members of a particular segment of society." Coles (1977: 54) argues that the final result of being socialized in relative affluence is the development of a sense of entitlement. He writes, "There is, I think, a message that virtually all quite well-off American families transmit to their children—an emotional expression of those familiar, classbound prerogatives, money and power. I use the word 'entitlement' to describe that message." A similar, though more limited, socialization occurs in the professional-middle class.

Coles (1977: 55) argues that parents teach children what they have a right to expect from life because of who they are. "The child has much, but wants and expects more, all assumed to be his or hers by right—at once a psychological and material inheritance that the world will provide." This sense of entitlement is important in political work. Activists tend to express anger at the fact that things are not the way they should be. They believe that people have a right to clean environment, equal rights, peace, and so on.

Workers, by contrast, often have not developed such a sense of entitlement. Part of growing up in the working class is learning that workers are the people who get "screwed" by the wealthy and powerful. Instead of entitlement, workers often develop a sense of fatalism about this state of affairs. They learn to expect things to be unjust and are usually not surprised to hear of systemic injustices or corruption. This perspective can lead to some profoundly pessimistic evaluations of the political system. As Warren says about the government, "I think people have stopped expecting anything." This contrasts starkly with many in the middle class who may be disgusted by the government precisely *because* they still have expectations for it.

Activists from the middle class, argues Mark Kahn (1986: 280), "are strengthened by the attributes that come with being members of a privileged class." They are well equipped both materially and culturally to pursue politics. "They have known relative success from birth and have the skills and confidence that produce more success. Theirs is the optimism that you can fight city hall and win. Furthermore, they usually have little to lose by engaging in grassroots politics. Their occupations and lifestyles provide opportunity for part-time political engagement." The feelings of entitlement of middle-class activists can be passed on to their children as well. Kahn (1986: 279) says that middle-class activists:

> encourage their children, by example and instruction, to develop the sense of middle-class efficacy that builds self-confidence and the experimental attitude toward learning and living that facilitates movement toward the cutting edge of culture and technology. The children of the affluent have the advantage of middle-class social security, of knowing that family and friends can help out financially when it comes to putting a mortgage together or riding out hard times. They also have

the educational credentials and social contacts that open the doors to a broad range of occupations. And they generally have the optimism and sense of unlimited choice that can be the basis for self-fulfilling prophecies.

Political participation is more likely when one not only sees a problem but also envisions an alternative, has a sense of entitlement about change, and possesses the skills to work for change. Efficacy is the product of having such cultural resources.

Identity and Cultural Resonance

In evaluating political action, workers place a high premium on effectiveness.

DC: Would you ever consider joining a group like this that was working on an issue that you thought was important?

TOM: I suppose if I thought it would make a difference, I might. But I'd really have to see how it would work—how it was gonna change things. I'm not one to go out and do things just to make myself feel better, you know. I need to see some results. With what I know about these kinds of things, they usually just kind of fade away. Nothing really gets changed.

Activists generally believe that their efforts *can* achieve results. But as we have seen, while they are sincere in their desire for change, some activists also value political participation as an end in itself. Receiving the rewards of identity,[1] community, and self-fulfillment can often be a strong motivation for continued involvement in movements that have not had significant or immediate impact. This aspect of movement culture is significant as well.

Ron Eyerman and Andrew Jamison (1991: 2) suggest that social movements are "forms of activity by which individuals create new kinds of social identity." This sense of identity is vitally important. It encourages activists to continue to labor despite often formidable odds and despite lack of success because it offers rewards that are inherent in the process. One key reward is association with other similarly minded activists.

CARLENE: It's almost addictive at times. You enjoy being involved. It's a way to meet people who have common interests, and at times you find yourself socializing with those people you work on causes with. It's a way of extending yourself to different people.

When politics are conceived in terms of identity, it is possible to seek political rewards from the structuring of one's own life. Frequently, activists place a good deal of value on living their politics.

KAREN: The people I find that I admire the most are maybe people that are able to live out their values in their personal way of life as well as what they do politically. It becomes a real spiritual kind of thing too, I think. I'm a Unitarian, and a lot of that religious background deals with, for me, living your religion in a daily way. I don't see how you can say you revere life and support the war in the Persian Gulf. To me they are diametrically opposed, and I don't understand how so many people can do it and not have a real sense of interior conflict. Maybe they do, and they're not aware of it.

The environmental movement has most clearly encouraged the belief that ecologically sound politics can be promoted by changing one's own lifestyle.

The structuring of lifestyles around political and social values, coupled with the nurturing of activist identities in a collective context, results in the development of distinct political subcultures. William Gamson (1988) writes that political culture "refers to the meaning systems that are culturally available for talking, writing, and thinking about political objects: the myths and metaphors, the language and idea elements, the frames, ideologies, values and condensing symbols." The arena of contesting packages and frames "is the battleground for forming and activating mobilization potentials" (Gamson 1988: 220), or what Bert Klandermans (1986) calls consensus mobilization. Gamson further notes that "Certain packages have a natural advantage because their ideas and language resonate with larger cultural themes. Resonances increase the appeal of a package; they make it appear natural and familiar." The availability of such meaning systems is affected by class status, and the salience of issue frames is likely to differ by class.

Along lines that are similar to Gamson's work, David A. Snow and Robert D. Benford (1988: 210) argue that some framings "resonate with cultural narrations, that is with the stories, myths, and folk tales that are part and parcel of one's cultural heritage." They also write (1988: 205) that "if the values or beliefs the movement seeks to promote or defend are of low hierarchical salience within the larger belief system, the mobilizing potential is weakened considerably and the task of political education or consciousness raising becomes more central but difficult."

For example, Snow and Benford (1988: 206) suggest that values promoted by the peace movement:

> such as sanctity of human life, preservation of the species, and peaceful coexistence, are those with which most citizens would agree, but the questions of how intensely they feel about the values and of how salient they are in relation to other values are problematic. We suspect that the mobilization difficulties encountered by peace activists in the United States are due in part to the relatively low hierarchical salience of the issues and values promoted by the movement. This hypothetical disjuncture was clearly recognized by the former national coordinator of the Freeze Campaign following the 1984 election: "The important message [of the election] is that the American people are in favor of a

freeze but they don't feel the freeze is an urgent necessity. To them it's not more important than short-term economics or personalities."

Although not explicit, there are certainly issues of class involved in such an analysis. Certain strains of the peace movement are notorious for blindly arguing for the "primacy" of the peace issue since nuclear war would mean the destruction of us all. Such callous disregard for the day-to-day struggles of working and poor people ("short-term economics" to the freeze activist quoted above) is clearly alienating to people dealing with less hypothetical and more immediate threats.

Differing class experiences can affect "resonance" with a movement message in another way. Snow and Benford (1988: 208–9) describe the concept of "interpretive screens" through which "evidence" for a political cause is filtered. They write that:

> One such important screening mechanism is the personal experience of the targets of mobilization. Does the framing have what we call experiential commensurability? Does it suggest answers and solutions to troublesome events and situations which harmonize with the ways in which these conditions have been or are currently experienced? Or is the framing too abstract and distant from the everyday experiences of potential participants?
>
> We think this variable of experiential commensurability is perhaps one of the most important determinants of individual and cross-cultural variations in the mobilizing potency of peace movement framing efforts.

If Snow and Benford are correct in their analysis, the differing life experiences of middle- and working-class people would clearly affect their responses to the political messages and agendas of social movements. In addition, the conscious attempt by some middle-class social movements to eschew traditional cultural discourse in favor of creating "alternative" or "oppositional" cultures contains the danger of isolating these movements from broader segments of society, including the working class.

The cultural component of left politics that contributes to the development of alternative identities can seem foreign to those not part of this subculture. The stronger the subcultural identity, the more likely it is to isolate itself from mainstream society. For many working people, then, the cultural accoutrements of the Left may obscure the political message being delivered. As we have seen, workers often cite the "bizarre" appearance of social-movement participants as one reason they feel such participants are different from themselves. Norman, a labor activist I interviewed, was disappointed that in making a presentation to his labor group, a local Central America organization used someone with a "hippie kind of presentation" to act as spokesperson for their group. Despite the fact that this person was "a wonderful guy and very witty and smart," Norman wished another choice had been made. Not only was the countercultural appearance likely to be foreign to the workers being addressed, but Norman also felt the speaker made inaccurate assumptions about people's political orientation.

NORMAN: [H]e kind of assumed certain attitudes of identification with the Nicaraguan revolution or with the guerillas in El Salvador. They can't assume that, when they're talking to . . . working people. So when I talk about Nicaragua or El Salvador, as I have, with labor people, I talk about working people and trade unions, and I talk about these revolutionary and guerrilla movements as movements that arose in reaction to the oppression and exploitation by the rich oligarchs who control the economy of the nation and the government. But I do it in a way and in a language that people who are listening, they can understand it.

This kind of problem, felt Norman, was indicative of a more generalized gap between left movements and workers.

NORMAN: Much of the antiwar movement and much of the feminist movement has developed not out of working-class people, primarily—although always there's some working-class people that have been very involved. So they've sort of written off the labor movement and regard them as Archie Bunker, redneck kind of people. That's been a problem.

In the end, he felt that progressive movements needed to alter their approach to working people and make their message resonate culturally.

NORMAN: So in their thinking, in their attitudes, in their welcoming to working people, their language, their style of approach, they need to be sensitive to try to understand working people, to make compromises to make some changes in the way they present themselves and their issues so that their message can be better received by working people.[2]

The cultures of working people and the professional-middle class in general differ substantially. In their study of professionals, Derber, Schwartz, and Magrass (1990: 158) write that:

Professionals feel farthest removed from working people. A lawyer says that "advanced educated people are attracted to each other and don't spend their time in blue-collar bars drinking and swearing about what happened on the baseball diamond." This crude view of the culture of workers and references to their limited horizons is common. One scientist observes that workers cannot understand his job, and he is not much intrigued by theirs: "I'm not particularly interested in how they loaded the railroad car that day." A lawyer says that if he were to meet a truck driver, he doubts "whether we would have much to talk about." A doctor remembers living briefly in a working-class suburb and being bored by discussions of children and domestic matters. Many emphasize that these are simply cultural differences and do not imply superiority or inferiority, but others are basically elitists.

Most political activists have rejected such middle-class cultural biases, and they are unlikely to verbalize an elitist position in relation to workers. Some are truly committed to trying to break down class barriers. Still, most would readily admit that cultural differences between middle-class activists and workers are abundant and significant.

In speaking of the difficulty in generating diverse class participation, Adam, a Central America activist notes:

ADAM: One thing we learned in trying to work with labor was that it's a lot easier to work with labor leaders than it is to work with the rank and file.

DC: Why was that?

ADAM: Well, some of it was very practical. It's easier to get three or four leaders in a room for a meeting than it is to turn out forty or fifty rank-and-file members. . . . The other thing was that organizers tend to think alike. Union organizers and Central America activists can talk the same language. They may not agree all the time, but they're speaking the same language.

The "language" of activism is a crucial component of movement culture. The only working people with whom PMC activists tend to discuss political issues are representatives from progressive unions—who often are college-educated and who are not typical members of the working class. They are activists who have come to share many of the cultural resources that are available to new-social-movement activists. Ironically, the process of becoming labor activists often results in a sense of alienation from rank-and-file members. Labor lawyer Thomas Geoghegan (1991: 173) puts it colorfully:

> While I have no special bond with the rank and file, I do sometimes have one with the officers. Or put it this way: the rank and file, when they run for union office, become . . . well, like me. They stop working nine to five. As officers, they become bohemians, artists, they can hang out in coffeehouses: now, at last, we become brothers and sisters. Nobody can find us. We set our own hours. All of us in organized labor, we sit on the rim of the world, the rim of the GNP, and watch the other people, the "members," go to work.

The labor activists I interviewed lamented how union activists were "out of touch" with the rank and file and in fact now had more in common with other progressive activists than they did with their own union's membership.

Research suggests that cultural differences between activists and working people are important, in part, because they affect the ability of social movements to communicate effectively and engage citizens. Cultural symbols are an important communication consideration in how a social movement "frames" its issues and itself. Ideally, movement messages are developed with potential audiences in mind.[3] Thus, communicating to a working-class audience is facilitated by drawing upon cultural imagery that resonates with that class's experiences. However, NSMs, which are dominated by the middle class, are likely to cloak their messages in cultural imagery that is based in the middle class and that "resonates" with middle-class experience. Such framings are unlikely to be salient to the working class, who experience very different daily lives and resulting cultural symbols.

Conclusion

Culture plays a dual role in limiting the likely participation of working people in new social movements. First, working people are unlikely to share in the cultural resources or "tools" that activists possess. They are unlikely to have the sense of entitlement, vision of achievable change, and specialized skills that result in a sense of efficacy and that facilitate movement participation. Second, working people are unlikely to respond favorably to movement images and messages that are grounded in middle-class reality. One key element of this class-based reality is knowledge and its role in politics, the topic of the next chapter.

CHAPTER 9

"It Takes a Special Kind of Person"

Knowledge

> *Politics is very, very complex. Even though things look*
> *straightforward, they're not. . . . The less educated you are,*
> *the more likely you will be just too frustrated for this.*
>
> PATRICK, twenty-eight-year-old environmental activist

Knowledge is the "property" controlled by the professional middle class. Elaborate processes of education and training help to establish members of the middle class as credentialed agents in society. Middle-class social-movement activists are the product of this socialization. At the same time, though, such activists often think of themselves as opposing the influence of specialized knowledge professionals. They position themselves as "counterexperts" trying to make the political process more open and accessible to all. This positioning, however, usually does not succeed in encouraging working-class participation.

Knowledge is a necessary ingredient of political action. However, there are different kinds of political knowledge that receive varying degrees of emphasis from workers and activists. These different types of knowledge must be disentangled to make sense of the impact of class on political culture. A distinction must be made between the *awareness* and understanding workers often possess and the *information* and expertise that activists often promote. The relative emphasis placed on different kinds of knowledge can have a significant impact on potential political participation.

Awareness

An awareness of the existence of an issue or problem is necessary for citizens to become politically involved. This need not be awareness of a particularized policy question in the narrow sense. It may be a generalized sense of a signi-

ficant issue area. There are several different possible sources of initial awareness of a problem or issue.

Most important, life experience can be a very powerful source of awareness. The existence of crime, poor air quality, sexism, racism, and so on can be
experienced on a firsthand basis in a way that some issues, such as foreign
interventions (geographic distance) or the budget deficit (social distance) generally cannot. Activists who work on foreign policy or national military issues
expressed the most concern about making the significance of their issues "real"
for people. They see this hurdle as a central challenge of their work.

However, people can be made aware of issues that cannot be experienced
firsthand. The firsthand experiences of family, friends, coworkers, and other
acquaintances can be communicated to an individual and have a significant impact on awareness of issues. Social-movement organizations recognize the power
of secondhand experiences, and they sometimes utilize speakers who are directly
affected by the issue at hand in order to convey a sense of immediacy. Anti-
intervention activists, for example, host visiting Central American labor representatives as a device to communicate Central America issues to labor audiences who
they feel would be otherwise unaware and uninterested. Such presentations are
valued by anti-intervention activists, not so much for the particular information
presented in such talks, but for the speakers' ability to trigger a generalized sense
of awareness about the existence of relevant political issues in Central America.
Workers speaking to workers are able to make unique connections.

More generalized awareness of political issues can be achieved in a number
of settings. Schooling is a site of socialization regarding political and social
issues. The length and type of schooling can be expected to produce different levels of awareness of political issues. Activists are keenly aware of the
"captive-audience" character of schools and often try to gain access to class-
rooms. Environmental activists, especially, credit schools with serving as a
conduit for information on recycling, conservation, and other basic environmentally related topics. Repeatedly, activists discussed how children are teach-
ing their parents about environmental issues. The "older" generations, they
believe, are the least attuned to environmental messages, while children are the
most receptive and enthusiastic supporters. Increasingly, environmental clubs
are becoming a common part of many high-school activities.

The media is another important mechanism for generating awareness of
issues and problems. All media (television, newspapers, radio, books, videos,
music recordings) and all forms of programming (news, entertainment) potentially play a role in heightening awareness of issues. Although they require
significant engagement as a precondition, community associations, such as
church groups and parent-teacher associations, can also serve as mechanisms
for expanding an individual's awareness of issues. Finally, political groups can
do public outreach in an effort to raise awareness of issues. Often this outreach
entails the generation of media coverage, but it can also take more direct forms
of leafleting, phone banking, or canvassing door-to-door.

Workers can readily recite a litany of social and political problems that face our society. Most immediately, they are aware of the struggle that faces them in daily life. Economic and family demands are frequently cited as troublesome areas. But beyond issues of immediate experience, workers are also aware of a wide variety of social problems. In fact, one theme that workers often invoke is that of a society whose problems are out of control.

BERNICE: So you see all this trouble all the time and you think to yourself, "This can't go on like this. Something's got to change." It just seems crazy. People are killing each other at the drop of a hat. Teenage pregnancies are skyrocketing. Drugs. All of that has just gotten out of hand.

For the workers in these interviews, awareness of broader social problems comes almost exclusively from the mass media. The workers' belief that society's problems are out of control is largely the cumulative effect of "negative" news stories.

DANIEL: I mean, just turn on the TV. Every night. Every night it's the same thing: somebody's killed somebody, somebody's crooked, somebody's telling us about the Japanese or the Russians or whatever. It just seems like it never ends. . . . I mean you look at the TV, and there it is. Killing, murder, rape, that's where we're going. I mean, it seems that way. Every day. It don't make sense no more. It's crazy. It seems like we've gone crazy.

Kristen says of the news, "It's always so bad. It's the last thing I want to see at the end of the day." Diane, who says she doesn't pay attention to the news, says, "I just find it too depressing. You turn on the TV and all it is is murders and crime and disasters and plane crashes, [laughs] you know? I mean it's pretty depressing day after day."

The importance of the media's role in communicating an awareness of social and political problems is highlighted by the fact that workers often do not see such problems as affecting themselves, their families, or their friends personally. Almost invariably, workers admitted that the host of problems they saw on the news actually had little impact on their own lives. The worker cited above, who saw "killing, murder, rape" as "where we're going," was asked:

DC: Is crime a real problem around here?

DANIEL: No, not really. I mean, not in [this city].

DC: Do you worry about crime affecting yourself or your family personally?

DANIEL: No, not me personally. But just look at the news, you see it everywhere, a lot of people are scared.

Another example is the worker who was quoted above as seeing crime and other problems as having gotten "out of hand." When asked if crime had any impact on her life or those of her family and friends, she responds, "No, we've been lucky."

Feeling "lucky," ironically, may be one of the most important effects of seeing so many news stories about problems in the world.

STEVE: I think most people—if they have a job and can pay the bills—are basically happy. Everybody bitches and moans about all kinds of things, but I think they know they're basically well-off. . . . You look at the news, like we were talking about, and you see countries with civil wars and people starving and terrorism and stuff. I mean, compared to that, I think people know they're pretty good.

For these white workers in a small city, the chaos of international affairs and the stereotypes of urban crime may well represent a frightening foil against which they measure their own lives. The result is that they are able to hold what at first seem to be contradictory views: society as a whole is disintegrating, but the quality of their own lives—although not necessarily improving—is *comparatively* good. When workers speak of their own lives in isolation they cite many difficulties, but when they change their frame of reference and put their lives in the perspective of broader society, they see their position as one of relative security.

Workers, then, are aware of the existence of significant social and political problems and issues. They know government does not represent their interests. They see poor and working Americans struggling to meet health care costs and to work for a decent home while billions are spent on military ventures and foreign aid. They see the sharp inequities in our tax structure and the resulting benefits for corporations and the wealthy. They see the inequities in access to higher education that will help ensure that the next generation of working-class kids will have to continue to struggle. Social-movement activists, however, often do not fully recognize this awareness on the part of workers because activists are more interested in a different kind of knowledge: information and expertise.

Information and Expertise

Simple awareness of the existence of an issue can be supplemented by more detailed information about the issue. The sources for such information are very similar to those associated with awareness: direct experience, acquaintances, schooling, media, interested groups, and so on.

The amount of information that workers have about current political issues is very slight. Through the years, surveys have repeatedly shown that many Americans do not have even the most basic information about political issues. They do not, in any sense, have expertise on such issues.

Activists tend to be aware of this generalized level of ignorance. Further, they believe that this lack of information is an important reason why so many people are politically inactive. As a result, they see "education" about political issues as perhaps their single most important task. This view is not surprising, given the importance of knowledge and informational skills to the middle class.

But most activists mistakenly equate awareness with information and expertise. Karen notes, for example, "If you're really gonna understand [the issues], you've got to read a lot of alternative sources." But this is not necessarily true. Workers have a good grasp of major issue areas and recognize the need for change in the political sphere. For example, most workers would not be able to give even a ballpark figure of our national debt, nor would they have much of an analysis of the many different factors that have contributed to the current situation. However, they do have an understanding of the fundamental dynamic: government is spending more than it is taking in. That is really all anyone needs to know to understand the perilousness of the situation. The irresponsibility of government just does not make sense to people. You do not write checks that you cannot cover. Period.

Activists, by contrast, are hell-bent on educating people about how and why we got into this situation, usually laying blame on the part of government spending with which they disagree. For most people, though, it is not runaway military spending, or even welfare spending, that is at the heart of the issue, it is the irresponsibility of politicians.

But activists tend to overlook such basic awareness of issues and skepticism of government.

LYNN: I think that the public is deluded, essentially, by the administration. . . . [T]here's nothing more important to do almost than to help the public get a clearer picture of what is really happening and how they're really being treated and how they're really being screwed. So that's what I see, that [my organization] has a very important role to shed light on these issues and to try and shed that light as far and as wide as they can.

Lenin argued that socialist consciousness had to be introduced to the working class from without by an intellectual vanguard. These activists would shudder at being labeled Leninists, but their approach is not very different from Lenin's. The ideology they promote is no longer socialist, and their target population is not defined in class terms; but the role of a "vanguard" is maintained.

The assumption behind the strategy of educating a "deluded" public is that "if people only knew" about an issue, they would act. As a result, activists often see themselves as educators providing information that will "raise consciousness" about an issue or that exposes what is "really" going on, especially in the government and corporate sectors. The flood of activity that results from this analysis includes the creation of newsletters, magazines, informational brochures, reports, leaflets, films, slide shows, educational forums, conferences, seminars, speaker bureaus, and a host of other educational projects. Indeed, for a surprisingly large percentage of groups, these educational efforts are the *only* activities in which they engage. For workers, the relevance of most of these efforts is questionable.

The emphasis on education is perpetuated by volunteers who are often said to have significant levels of "expertise" on particular issue areas and to see education as a prime motivating factor for their involvement.

SARAH: People come into the group having read a lot of environmental books, having read magazines like *Garbage Magazine* or *E Magazine*. . . . That consciousness has already been opened to them to some extent. I think the reason you'd want to join a group like this is that you want to educate others about the changes that you've learned and made in your life. You sort of want to spread the knowledge.

One way middle-class activists differ from middle-class nonactivists is in this belief in "spreading the knowledge." They are, in effect, "counterexperts" who symbolize "a democratic ideal, a sharing of knowledge" (Eyerman and Jamison 1991: 105).

The goals of education efforts are to make people aware of the issues and of the need to act. However, this orientation reflects the conflation of two types of knowledge: awareness and information. That is, activists are correct in suggesting that working people do not have much *information* or *expertise* about contemporary issues. As I will show, working people themselves often readily admit they do not have the same type of expertise that is available to those who are more active in politics. However, activists are incorrect in concluding that this lack of information means people are *unaware* of problems and issues. If anything, workers say they are overwhelmed by the range of problems that face society.

Some activists I interviewed did not seem to fully grasp the level of skepticism about the current state of affairs that permeates working-class political culture. One explains her analysis this way:

KAREN: I don't know enough about the data in terms of who votes and who doesn't vote. My impression would be that you have a huge under class that does not vote; that if they understood the issues that they would certainly be with us. But it seems to me that . . . we live in wonderland. It's like Alice in Wonderland. Your government says one thing, but if you are able to read it and analyze it, you realize that that is complete, opposite to what they're doing. But it's real painful to recognize that. We all need to feel there are leaders we can trust. I think that's really a human need—heroes we can trust. And I think that the last couple of decades have eroded that so badly—and I think it's really so painful for people that they don't want to look at it. They don't want to acknowledge that that's the way things are.

There is, of course, an internal contradiction in this line of argument. People are said to need leaders and not to want to acknowledge the existence of problems *because* their level of trust has eroded so badly. In fact, it is activists who often seem to be unaware of the deep level of working-class skepticism about all things political. Instead of recognizing this fact, this activist sees the problem as being people's unwillingness to admit the extent of the nation's problems.

KAREN: I feel like denial is maybe what is really taking hold here. And either people recognize it and don't want to get involved, so they say they can't do anything about it, or are in a state of denial about what's really happening. I mean I really do think that basically people are good and that people want to be proud of what their government does and what their country does and want to be associated with things that feel good. But the reality, if that's not the case, is maybe too hard to [acknowledge].

Another activist makes a similar observation, claiming that mobilization will come about when people learn the truth about the current situation.

GUS: I think that there still is a sleeping giant. I wouldn't be here in this work if I didn't believe that there was power still in the people. The old saying goes, "Bad news is good news for organizers." We're still counting on the fact that the people will eventually arrive at a time where they recognize that you can't trust the current administration.

The emphasis in this analysis seems to be misplaced. I would be hard-pressed to suggest a single worker from my interviews who could be said to "trust the current administration."

The emphasis on information is problematic in another respect. Greider (1992) has argued that information-driven politics can be as manipulative and unfruitful as politics based on money. The reason is simple. Greider (1992: 46) says that:

Middle class and liberal-minded reformers, trying to free government decisions from the crude embrace of the powerful, emphasized a politics based on facts and analysis as their goal. They assumed that forcing "substance" into the political debate, supported by disinterested policy analysis, would help overcome the natural advantages of wealth and entrenched power. But information is never neutral and, in time, every interest recognized the usefulness of buying or producing its own facts.

Think tanks and public relations firms on the payroll of monied interest can overwhelm reformers with their own facts and figures. Meanwhile, ordinary citizens are left out of the battle of experts. As Greider puts it, "The reality is that information-driven politics, by its nature, cannot produce a satisfying democracy because it inevitably fosters its own hierarchy of influence, based on class and money." In addition, the emphasis on knowledge and expertise excludes many citizens simply because they cannot gain access to the debate. Again, Greider (53) writes that the "most dreadful consequence" of information-driven politics "is the way in which ordinary citizens are silenced and demoralized—made to feel dumb—by the content of information politics."

Formal Education

Middle-class activists do not see daily life experiences of workers as an adequate source of information about politics. Instead, they tend to emphasize formal schooling as a central site for political education.

CAROL: I would say to a very large degree the better the education, the much greater chance that, not only are they aware already of what the problems are, but they're also more perceptive and responsive to solutions.

A college education, felt one activist, provided people with a "worldview" that widened their scope of identification.

LISA: [T]he tendency is that people who have had the opportunity to go to a university are more likely to have that kind of a worldview [that sees the connection between foreign policy and economics] and therefore see how . . . political work connects to their life. So it is an issue of class. I mean education and economics are certainly class issues.

However, such positive references are almost always to *college* education—a sphere more readily accessible to middle-class students. Most activists believed that elementary and high schools tend to promote compliance and complacency because they do not teach critical thinking skills.

LUCY: People have been taught not to take initiative. People have been taught to read distorted versions of history and take them as fact and memorize them and regurgitate them on tests and never question what they say. People have been taught to watch TV news or read *USA Today* and take that as gospel and not to question. And unfortunately, in this country the poorest people are also the least educated, generally, and it seems like . . . if you don't have the benefit of at least teachers, if not your folks, cultivating that kind of questioning ability in you, it's real easy to accept the party line, accept the government's line.

Since the education system provides the credentialing mechanism that reinforces a mental/manual divide in the workplace, there is often a substantial gap between the education received by children of the middle class and that given to children of the working class, even before getting to college.

Other shortcomings of the education system were also cited by activists as contributing to the decline in political participation. One suggested that people were intimidated by environmentalism because it involved science, and she complained:

SARAH: [S]cience is considered or taught as if it's a discipline for the few and that the mainstream people aren't gonna like it and won't understand it. I think that in our school, science is taught as a snobby geek club. [laughs]

Between you and me that's how I feel a lot of teachers approach science. "You're all gonna fail." . . . That's just something that sticks with people the rest of their lives. "Oh, science is not for me. Chemistry? No." And they don't want to touch it.

Some of the negative impact of schools is seen as resulting from their structure.

CARLENE: Whether or not kids have a say in school, I think, has a lot to do with it. There are some schools that are absolutely dictatorial that make the kids believe that the system's gonna run the way the system wants to run anyway, and it doesn't make any difference, no matter what I do.

But here activists reveal a tendency to generalize middle-class experience. The effective socialization of students into a role of compliance is perhaps best achieved with middle-class students, who identify with teachers and authority figures and learn to play the system effectively to reap its rewards.

Studies suggest that working-class students may not be as affected by such socialization—at least not in the way middle-class kids are. For example, Willis's (1977) ethnographic work on "how working-class kids get working-class jobs" finds that it is through their active *resistance* to middle-class socialization in schools that working-class kids disqualify themselves for a middle-class future. Rather than being passive recipients of the school's disciplinary curriculum, working-class kids often refuse to submit to middle-class expectations and end up reproducing themselves as "uneducated" workers. This pattern of interaction between working- and middle-class people continues throughout the life cycle. Working people experience the middle class as "authority" figures: teachers, bosses, "experts" (doctors, lawyers, politicians, activists, etc.). Even while rejecting the lessons of such "experts," workers often learn to internalize a sense of inadequacy regarding these areas of social life.

Feeling Inadequate

Activists seem to underestimate greatly working people's recognition of the extent of the problems that face this country. But if workers are aware of problems, why are they quiescent? The following exchange—which was repeated with a number of workers—suggests part of an answer. I posed the argument, presented by some activists, that the relative lack of participation on the part of workers suggests that people see no need for change. This worker responds:

TOM: That's crap. It really is. Just listen to people—just go out and ask them—like what you're doing. I imagine you don't get too many happy people. You don't get people who are happy with the government and what it's doing, right?

DC: Not too many, no.

TOM: See. I mean anybody who talks to people knows that people are not happy. They're fed up with taxes going up every year—year after year. They're tired of paying more and getting less. That's basically it.

DC: If people are fed up—I'm not disagreeing—but if people are fed up, why isn't there more action to try and change things?

TOM: . . . I think people have given up on trying to change things. It's so overwhelming that they don't see how anything's gonna ever change. Where do you start? I think that's a big problem. People can't do anything about the government or whatever so they just ignore it. They just go on with their own lives and try and make things better there.

Comparing the comments of activists and workers suggests that the role of education and information in motivating people to become politically active is overemphasized. Explaining disengagement primarily as the result of lack of information diverts attention from the explanation most often given by workers: a lack of political efficacy.

Workers have learned to internalize doubts about their own abilities. They learn from the media and in the workplace that their ideas are not valued and that in these arenas action is carried out and authority is held by people who are unlike themselves. Workers are aware of social and political problems and believe that government is largely incompetent, but the political system is usually only a distant concern for workers. As Steve put it, "Usually, I don't think about it. It doesn't really affect me. It doesn't really matter to me whether or not politicians listen to me. I'm not sure what I would be saying to them anyway."

The phrase "I'm not sure what I would be saying to them anyway" is an important one that reflects a deep-seated sense of doubt and inadequacy which many workers share.

DC: Does that bother you that you don't have an impact on policies?

DIANE: I don't think about it. Maybe I should, but I really don't. I guess it doesn't [bother me] because I don't know all about the issues, you know? There's a lot of technical stuff that I just don't know about. On some of this stuff I think there are a lot of people who know a lot more about this than I do. I can only hope that they do the right thing.

This type of resignation is common. Some workers use self-deprecating humor to make the point.

SAM: We always have some problems so I guess that's not going to go away overnight. . . . There are smart people who study all these kinds of things and it looks like they can't really come up with what to do. So I guess I'm not gonna solve it either. [laughs]

A perceived lack of knowledge and expertise can inhibit even the most fundamental engagement with issues.

JUDY: Well, I don't think we are really interested in politics, I guess. I mean you probably study this stuff and everything, but when you don't really know what's going on it's kind of hard to try and follow it, you know. I mean I hear "Bush said this" or "Bush said that" or some other things like around the Middle East but—I don't know—maybe it's just me but it's pretty confusing to me. . . . I don't even know sometimes—I hear about this country or—like Jordan or Syria or something—I mean I don't know—I don't even know if they're on our side or what. [laughs] I'm serious though. It gets really confusing. I think that's another reason I just don't watch it. If I was more interested in that kind of thing and understood it a little better, maybe I'd watch more of it I think. But really it's not something that I bother with too much.

Such a hesitancy to engage in public affairs reflects a more generalized sense of unease about lack of education. For example, Halle (1984: 48–49) found that even for the well-paid chemical workers he studied, the lack of a college education often led "to a certain defensiveness and to some feeling of unease and inadequacy when faced with highly educated persons and with school personnel. Most workers are sensitive about their lack of formal education."

Workers make the connection between their lack of formal education and their inability to understand the political system. This lack of understanding can lead workers to conclude that political activity is beyond their capacity.

SAM: You've really got to be read up on all the different things that they do there. I don't think most people really know enough about all of that to do much. . . . You've really got to know how to go about doing whatever you want there. There are all these rules and committees and things. I don't think the average guy is gonna go in for that.

So while workers are quick to make disparaging remarks regarding the ineptitude of politicians and the flaws of the political system, they also acknowledge their own limitations regarding the amount and type of expertise they have about the business of running government. They often blame themselves for this situation.

CINDY: I was never interested in all that [political] stuff in school so I didn't really learn much about it. But now, when I see things on TV I wish that I had paid more attention in school. I wish that I understood it more now.

Sennett and Cobb (1973) have written that because of the appearance of a permeable class structure, workers tend to internalize shortcomings or difficulties. They blame themselves for not having studied or worked hard enough. They tend not to dwell upon the collective nature of their situation. This kind of thinking has serious implications for political mobilization by undermining any sense of efficacy. If workers find it difficult to get better jobs, buy a house, or care for their family, then they certainly do not feel capable of influencing political systems.

Activists, too, sometimes blame people for their lack of attention to public affairs. While being critical of media messages, one activist noted:

PATRICK: I think it's the people. The media can only do so much. They have a lot of things affecting them. They may be able to do it better but I don't think it's all their fault. I think it's more the people themselves. They just don't want to—for whatever reasons—they don't want to get involved.

But as Avey (1989: 23) notes, apathy "has a circular relationship with information. People do not listen because they are not being addressed; this makes it difficult for those who wish to reach them." Workers do not find news media coverage to be particularly useful or accessible, and as a result they tend not to pay much attention.

Such worker sentiments may simply reinforce activists' belief that they need to be educating the public to become active in political life. But I believe such a conclusion is misleading. Instead, the emphasis placed by both politicians and movement activists on the centrality of information for political participation may have the unintended consequence of suggesting that political involvement requires a level of expertise and sophistication that is not generally available to the working-class public. Often, workers are explicit in making references to "experts," as seen on television, as evidence of their own lack of understanding. By serving as "counterexperts" and entering the battlefield of experts and pundits, activists may simply be reinforcing for working people a sense of inadequacy—often inhibiting the expression of very sound, commonsense understanding of the issues.

The role of common sense is probably undervalued by those who have been subjected to the influences of "higher" education. In her study of working-class women's ways of knowing, Luttrell (1989) challenges contentions by some feminists that all women share a single or universal way of knowing. Instead, she argues that race and class also influence how these women view learning and knowing. Luttrell (1989: 38) observes that the working-class women in her study "thought that although schoolwise intelligence can enhance one's life, it can also interfere with one's ability to meet the demands of working-class existence: they suggest that the *more* schooling one has, the *less* common sense she is likely to have." A similar dynamic is present around political issues. The possession of expertise on a topic does not necessarily correspond to sound common sense.

Rather than affirming people's life experiences, activists emphasize information and education and thus communicate the message that "you, too, can become a well-educated (read: middle-class) citizen just like me." Workers, though, recognize that they are worlds apart from middle-class movement activists, and they do not see the possibility of ever becoming sufficiently educated about the issues to challenge the expertise of officials or activists. Although they may affirm the value of their commonsense understanding of events, workers see the emphasis on expertise in the political realm as another reason why they do not see themselves as ever being active political agents.

Political Agents: "It Takes a Special Kind of Person . . . ."

Feelings of inadequacy in dealing with political issues mean that, for many workers, the Left's belief in broad democratic participation is a foreign one. It is simply a taken-for-granted fact of life among working people that politics is carried out by people who are not like themselves. Speaking of political involvement, Helen says:

HELEN: It takes a special kind of person to get involved in that kind of thing.

DC: What's the "special" part? What's the difference?

HELEN: I think, first of all, that these people study the issue a lot more. I'm sure they've all been to college or whatever and have their field of expertise. I think that makes a big difference.

Even in cases when workers personally know people involved in politics, they can still see a difference between themselves and the "type" of people who get involved in politics. One case is a worker whose brother-in-law was involved in a citizen effort to resist a proposed wood-burning incinerator.

DC: What do you mean when you refer to "the type" that will do something like that? What makes up this "type"?

PETER: Well, like [my brother-in-law], he's interested in all of this so he knows everybody. He knows his alderman or whatever they have in [his city]. He knows people in government because he's a lawyer so he's really involved in that. He's used to speaking out and making arguments and talking to people. I think that's important too. . . . He does all this in his job, you know. He's got his degrees, and he knows where you go to get certain kinds of information and how you go about doing things. Most people, I don't think, would even know where to start on something like that. It's very, very complicated. And he's his own boss, so he can do things while he's at work, and he can make phone calls or whatever. Most people can't do that, either. They've got their job, and that's what they do. They don't have their own office and their own secretary and all that.

Thus, the point made earlier that workers often do not feel that they have the specialized knowledge necessary for politics is coupled with this belief that there are some people who possess at least some of this knowledge and expertise.[1] The belief that participation requires specialized knowledge can easily foster disengagement by suggesting, then, that it is experts who should rightfully run the affairs of government. Such a belief often tempers any resentment workers might feel about not being efficacious.

DC: Do you think that that's bad, I mean, that people don't have much input into what the government does?

SAM: I guess it can be if you want to get something done and you can't do it. But I think most people—maybe it's just me, I don't know. I'm just not interested in that stuff. I think that if you are then maybe you can learn about it and take an interest in that. . . . I think, if you want, you can vote and put people in there that you hope will do what's right. But there's no way that you can know everything that's going on. You've got to leave that to the people who study things like that. It's like in the trades, you know, you get an electrician to do the wiring and a plumber to do the pipes. Politics is for the politicians. That's the way I see it. I'm no politician.

The analogy is a useful one. We all rely on the expertise of others to function in our society. Most of us do not know how to repair an automobile, for example, even though many of us are dependent on cars for transportation. We try to find a decent mechanic whom we feel we can trust and hope for the best. We don't, however, feel compelled to study auto-repair techniques in order to be able to challenge the mechanic's diagnosis—even if it does seem expensive. At best, workers view political life in a similar vein: try to find a politician you feel comfortable about and hope for the best. Many activists would cringe at comparing democracy to auto repair, but that is because they see "making history" as taking priority over making daily life, a judgment with which most workers do not agree.

A belief in rule by experts is apparently held by the experts as well. In the study by Derber, Schwartz, and Magrass (1990: 172), professionals "proposed time and time again that experts should be the leading planners of political life." Three-quarters of them believed that "in any industrial society it will always be necessary to have a division between those experts who make the decisions and people who carry out those decisions." One doctor in the study observed, "Experts are becoming more influential, and that's inevitable as a result of the complexity of our society. . . . The cost of that complexity is that decision making is concentrated in fewer hands. I think that's a problem because it alienates people who do not make decisions, but it's unavoidable and not much can be done about it." Such fatalism is shared by the workers I interviewed. They saw little or no possibility that they could be involved in shaping a political alternative.

There is little evidence to contradict the belief in rule by experts. It is clear to most workers that the political actors featured on their evening news broadcasts are not people like themselves.

DOROTHY: You don't see workers involved in [politics], at least on the news.

DC: Who is involved then?

DOROTHY: . . . It's people who specialize in that: politicians and lawyers, people like that. . . . That's their jobs. That's what they do for a living.

Studies of the news media confirm the observation that working people and labor representatives are underrepresented in media coverage (Croteau and Hoynes 1994; Hoynes and Croteau 1991; Puette 1992).

Derber, Schwartz, and Magrass (1990: 208) have remarked that reliance on political experts can disenfranchise a supposedly unqualified citizenry. "When the war in Vietnam heated up, mandarins in Lyndon Johnson's administration—many of them holdovers from the Kennedy era—repeatedly told the media that the people in the antiwar movement could not be taken seriously because they did not have all the facts." Not only is such expertise used to discredit protesters, but it can be valuable in preventing dissent in the first place. Opposition to the Gulf War was stunted, in part, by the media blitz of pundits and analysts who populated television news programs. One worker says:

HELEN: I think a lot of people push down their doubts about [the Gulf War] because they think that all these experts you see on TV must know more about it than they do. "Who am I to question this?" I think that's a lot of people's attitude. They hope that they know what they're doing.

Activists sometimes recognize—and are frustrated by—this situation.

LISA: There's that kind of apathy and maybe that's taught in a lot of ways to people, subtly. . . . I think that people just get the idea that they should just leave it to the politicians and that the issues are really complex, and it takes someone who's studied it and does it full time and all that stuff to really understand it. I just don't believe that that's true.

Activists, however, do not extrapolate from this insight. That is, they usually do not see that, in the eyes of working people, political activists are part of the special "type" that gets involved. Instead, they try to educate people to become one of those special "types."

Theorists, too, sometimes underestimate the gap between activists and others. Eyerman and Jamison (1991: 114) argue that the gap between intellectual vanguard and movement members has greatly diminished because "[c]ontemporary social movements, measured in terms of the years of formal education of activists, are largely movements of intellectuals." But this ignores the gap, then, that exists between movement "intellectuals" and working people; a gap that leads workers to see activists as *part* of the political elite, not as outsiders fighting the system. The observation that working people are not among the political actors applies not only to professional politicians and "expert" bureaucrats but to social-movement participants as well.

RONALD: If you're gonna go protesting all this stuff then you've got to know a little bit what you're talking about. These people go do research and look into those things. You've got to know how to do all that. Hey, I drive forklifts, right? What do I know about nuclear power or whatever. [laughs] I *do* know that I don't want it in my fucking city! I know that! [laughs]

Stymied by a political system and social movements that are made up of people unlike themselves, workers often turn—as I explore in the next chapter—to the only arena where they do have influence and control, home and family.

The Professionalization of Political Life

We live in a society where "expertise" has become a powerful influence in all realms of life. The purview of professionals now covers everything from intimate personal troubles to global social issues. It is a "credential" society, as Randall Collins (1977) calls it. It is a society, as Derber and his colleagues (1990) argue, where professionals make up a "new mandarin order." Along with a range of activities that used to be performed by family, informal social networks, and citizen organizations, political participation has also become the realm of professionals. Derber, Schwartz, and Magrass (1990: 6) argue "increasingly, experts also take over public affairs as their own province, creating a technical discourse about such issues as nuclear war or industrial policy that is impenetrable to the uninitiated; many citizens increasingly withdraw from politics as an alien realm."

Certainly, the realm of electoral politics has been at the forefront of professionalization. Routinely, modern politics is now thought of as an arena for professionals where specialized knowledge is required. Eyerman and Jamison (1991: 148) observe, "Indeed, in modern society politics has become a career, an occupation one can choose to enter, even at an early age, just as one can choose to be a doctor or automobile mechanic." Talking about electoral politics, one labor activist argued:

JOANNE: I think there's a real reluctance in this country to talk about class. I think there's a lot of gut-level understanding about class, but I think that it plays itself out in some ways that are not helpful to working people. The state is run by upper-class people, and it's really obvious, I think, to most people that that's the way it's run. Working people cannot run for the legislature. . . . The access to political power is quite limited.

Even "radical middle-class" electoral efforts like the one documented by Kahn (1986: 102) run into the problem of access versus expertise. "The range of participants who might become movement leaders was constricted considerably when [the campaign] instituted the computer technology and sophisticated campaign techniques that lend themselves to special expertise." The apparent importance of expertise to the political realm has often led to the conclusion that

"Workers are more likely to feel the stings of the market's sharp edges. But privileged experts might have, if not greater motive, more opportunities and weapons for subverting capitalism" (Derber, Schwartz, and Magrass 1990: 167).

Social movements, too, have increasingly professionalized their efforts. They are likely to have a leadership that devotes full time to organizing efforts while having a limited or inactive membership base, and they try to impart the image of speaking on behalf of a particular constituency (McCarthy and Zald 1987: 375).[2]

The professional-middle class is based on the control of knowledge. It should come as no surprise, then, that social movements made up primarily of members of the middle class are preoccupied with the issue of information, knowledge, and expertise. Some theorists have even argued that new social movements were created in part to advance the interests of a "knowledge" class (Goulder 1979; Konrad and Szelenyi 1979), providing them with a space to unite technical expertise with humanistic orientations.

At its extreme, some parts of middle-class social movements have come to look more and more like professional associations. For example, Eyerman and Jamison (1991: 106) observe:

> As the environmental movement grew to prominence, . . . particularly in the struggles against nuclear energy, many of these movement intellectuals tended to become ever more professional, at the same time as new types of professional consultants, publicists, and debaters entered the scene to "take over" from the movement organizations. This tendency towards professionalization has perhaps been especially strong in environmentalist movements where science and technology play such a central role. . . . Trade unions and the labor movement face different but related problems in their need to hire professionals to help with complicated collective bargaining agreements, internal education, and political lobbying.

Although this description certainly does not apply to all new social movements, the issue of expertise within organizations is an important one, affecting, especially, national organizations.

But even activists who are involved in local groups can feel intimidated by the role of knowledge and expertise in politics. Patrick, an environmental activist from a working-class background, comments:

PATRICK: The less educated you are, the more likely you will be just too frustrated for this. I graduated from high school, took a year of college, and that was it for me. So I'm not to the point where I can go and sit and discuss very complex things with, like, a politician or lobby and things like that. I would love to do that, but I can't do that. I think if I had quit school at eighth grade, I would shy away from anything that was complex. Politics is very, very complex. Even though things look straightforward, they're not.

A peace activist who was a college graduate makes similar remarks regarding members in her organization.

JOYCE: I feel really weird at [my organization] sometimes. I feel [like a] young, know-nothing kind of person sometimes. There are some major people involved in that organization. Some real good scholars and I guess I think of like [another member], who just blows me away with what she knows . . . . I think I feel like I must not know what I'm talking about, whereas when I was in college I thought I was kind of an "expert" on this stuff. [laughs]

Even "counterexperts" then, can be disempowering, intimidating existing members and discouraging nonparticipants from ever becoming involved.

No Answers, No Alternatives

Workers' recognition of their lack of information, coupled with their grudging admission that some "experts" seem to know more, often results in deference when it comes to offering political alternatives. When asked what they would say to their elected officials if their opinion were solicited, one worker admits,

KRISTEN: Like I said, I don't follow the news enough to really be well-informed. I don't know what I could tell them. . . . I'm sure anything I had to say they would have heard already. I don't think I could really convince them of anything. Why would they listen to me?

Workers, then, do not need to be told there are problems. They already know that. What they do not seem to have is any sense of viable alternatives or a way to implement them. If workers had a clear sense of what changes they wanted, then their disgust with politicians and politics might more readily translate into action for change. Instead, their disgust is coupled with a lack of confidence about knowing what needs to be done and how to do it. The stage is set, then, for disengagement from politics.

DANIEL: I mean there's nothing a little guy like me can do about this stuff. I mean this is big stuff. I wouldn't know where to begin, you know? I can complain, you know, everybody bitches about this and that and the other thing. But I don't know, I mean, what would I do? It's too big. I don't have the—well, me, personally—I don't have the kind of education it takes to understand this stuff. When you're talking economics and jobs and trade and the savings and loans and all that stuff—I mean, it makes your head spin, you know? I don't think I really understand that all well enough. I'm a mechanic, right? I fix machines. [laughs] I leave all that big stuff to the big boys. [laughs] I got a hard enough time balancing my checkbook! [laughs]

Workers do not necessarily feel they have the "answers" to solve the difficult problems that face society. However, they also feel that those who "should" know—the experts and politicians—have also lost any ability to deal with the vast array of problems that face us. For many workers, the most immediate and pressing issue during the period of these interviews was the economy. Kristen comments, "From what I see and hear it seems like they don't really know what to do. You look at unemployment now, at the economy in New England. I don't think the politicians have any idea what to do about it."

This worker perhaps states the case most completely:

DIANE: You listen to all these "experts" on TV, and they can never agree on anything. [laughs] I mean sometimes you think you don't have the answers 'cause you don't know enough about it, but then these people don't seem to know what to do either. At least they can't *agree* on anything. So it seems sometimes that they just end up fighting each other about what should be done. The Democrats fight the Republicans and the Republicans fight the Democrats. That's what a lot of it seems to be. And then nothing gets done. The problems are still there.

The negativism of politicians is complemented by the negativism of media accounts and by what many workers see as the negative emphasis of social movements that protest developments but do not provide viable alternatives. No wonder, then, that political issues can seem so overwhelming and are so easily dismissed as "just politics."

Conclusion

A certain amount of information and expertise is, of course, necessary for social-movement efforts. But it is problematic to make the dissemination of information the primary focus of political action.

First, the middle-class emphasis on political information is akin to what workers often refer to as "book learning." That is, it is highly abstract intellectual knowledge that may very well be true but that is not particularly useful in navigating through daily life in the real world. The information that activists offer often appears to be of little use to workers, since it explains problems but usually does not offer practical or realistic solutions. Workers not only already recognize problems in the political system, but they sometimes feel social-movement activists are naïve for their belief in the possibility of change.

Second, the emphasis on education—no matter how well intentioned— ends up contributing to workers' perception that they are not qualified to take part in public life. This emphasis, in effect, reinforces the message that political involvement is for the "educated."

Third, through their emphasis on information, activists undervalue the kind of understanding that arises from daily life. Workers have as much to teach activists about the realities of this country's social and political life as activists have to teach workers.

Fourth, social movements *do* need information in their work. Boyte (1989: 5) argues that "Effective citizen action in our times is possible if—and only if—citizens develop the abilities to gain access to information of all kinds (from the roads and sewers to educational, environmental, and economic patterns) and the skills to put such information to effective use." However, there is an important distinction here between information and the skills needed to access and use that information. Activists tend to emphasize the former and largely ignore the latter. They give facts and figures about issues intending to "enlighten" citizens, but what workers really could use are the cultural resources—the skills—that allow for the *use* of information. Good education, for example, does not provide information as much as the skills to *use* information.

Offe (1985: 850–51) offers the theory that:

> Two factors may contribute to the direct correlation between levels of education and unconventional forms of political participation. One is that a high level of formal schooling leads to some (perceived) competence to make judgments about complicated and abstract "systemic" matters in the fields of economic, military, legal, technical, and environmental affairs. The other is that higher education increases the capacity to think (and conceivably even to act) independently, and the preparedness to critically question received interpretations and theories about the world.

Thus, again, it is not necessarily the information that a student takes away from school that is of vital importance, but rather the skills and cultural tools derived from such an experience.

Education, particularly college education, becomes a shorthand symbol for the possession of skills that facilitate political engagement. Flacks (1988: 26) has noted that "In this country . . . differences in political participation are very much related to differences in the amount of formal education people have acquired." In fact, he argues (1988: 27) that "it is not an exaggeration to say that active political involvement in this country tends to be an elitist orientation. It is a propensity reserved primarily for those who have been raised or trained to feel that they can and should exercise authority and show civic responsibility. Such rearing and training occurs primarily among those of relatively high status and education."

But there are mitigating factors that can undermine the significance of educational differentials. The issue is not so much access to more information as it is the presence of skills that lead to a sense of adequacy in making political judgments, and a political environment that facilities participation by nonexperts.

Some activists have long ago recognized the importance of coupling information with opportunities for action. One peace-and-justice activist tells this story:

ALLAN: I spent four and a half months as a canvasser for [a] Citizen Action Group in '77 and '78. We were working on utility rates and returnable-bottle legislation and agricultural-land preservation. I forget what some of them were. These were not radical issues, but they also weren't—they were definitely issues. The organization itself was an advocacy group. It was a progressive group. And I learned that it was possible to articulate those issues to people and that most people would agree with what we were saying if it was put to them in the right words in a way that they could understand it. And if they were given something that they could do about it, . . . they would do it. That was a really important lesson for me. . . . If you are able to articulate the issues to people and give them an opportunity to make a choice or decision to participate in some way, then people will participate, and they will take positions more or less like the ones that we think they should—the true or correct or right or better.

But, more often, the Left has not learned such lessons.

The right wing, in some ways, has empowered people to reclaim territory given up to professionals. "Traditional values" and a reemphasis on family are two issues that give legitimacy and value to commonsense notions of the world. They also dovetail nicely with common perceptions that "taking care of your family" is a highly valued notion. Activists on the Left could learn a lesson in valuing workers' life experiences.

CHAPTER 10

*"You Do Your Work, You Pay
Your Bills . . . You Hope It
All Turns Out Okay"*

Politics, Work, and the Private Citizen

*What am I gonna do about the economy, right? What am I
gonna do about drugs? I make sure my kids don't do that
stuff. That's about it. There's nothing else I can really do.*

DONNA, forty-two-year-old factory worker

A left political analysis, as I have argued, is fundamentally based on the notion
of expanding democratic participation. But there is in fact little belief among
working people that the political realm is meaningful to their lives. Consequently, there is little interest in pursuing the Left's vision of expanded democracy. Instead, workers place enormous value on carving out private spaces of
autonomy. The privatized vision of workers is, in part, the result of a lack of
efficacy. Workers do not experience power and control in most areas of their
lives. First, workers see political life as outside of their influence. Therefore,
they tend to avoid politics and resent government intrusions into private life.
Second, work life is also largely out of their control. Here, too, workers pursue
resistance strategies that attempt to develop autonomous spaces. It is only in the
private sphere of family and home that workers feel some degree of control. It is
this sphere, then, that workers value most.

Political and Social Life

The political culture of workers is fundamentally different from that of social-
movement activists. Spend any time with activists, and they will discuss the
government, corporations, U.S. interventions abroad: the world of power

politics "out there." Spend any time with working people, and they will tell you of unemployment, family hassles, the spectre of bills and taxes: the endless struggles of "regular" people to "get by." Activists, by definition, "do" politics. For most working people, politics is either irrelevant or it is something that is done to them. Activists engage in politics; working people survive it. The differences are vitally important.

For most workers, democratic participation is seen as impossible or ineffective. There is little reason, therefore, to expect that those who feel excluded and powerless will highly value political participation. Instead of democracy, such workers tend to value the ideal of liberty. Essentially, many workers conclude that if you cannot influence the system, then the next best thing is to limit the system's influence on you.

Pursuing liberty entails the creation of free—and usually private—spaces that are sheltered from regulation. Such spaces are found especially in the home, but the workplace can also be the site of resistance strategies aimed at carving out areas of relative autonomy. Liberty also implies the development of self-sufficiency, and workers' orientations in the political realm can be best understood in this light.

Workers appreciate the political system's ability to accommodate free spaces of autonomy. This, as we have seen, is the essence of what workers mean by a "free country."

DC: What do you see as being *right* with the political system?

JOHN: I think basically the biggest thing is that you've got your freedom, right? Say what else you will about it, at least here you don't have to worry about the military taking over or whatever. You can do what you want. You can move where you want. You can work in whatever kind of job you can get. Those aren't little things. There are a lot of places that would love to have that. You've got to balance the pros and cons. There are still some good things. . . . You do your work, pay your taxes, and the government leaves you alone. That's democracy. That's the good part of the system.

While, in fact, this is *not* what is generally implied by "democracy," it *is* the essence of liberty, and it forms the core of working-class political culture.

As I have argued, disengagement from political life is a central feature of working-class culture. There is a clear recognition of the problems facing society. But such a recognition is coupled with a sense of profound inefficacy.

DC: If there's so many things wrong, then why aren't people out there demanding change?

DANIEL: [laughs] Good question! I don't know. I mean, what are you gonna do, try and change the world? [laughs] You just try . . . the average guy, I think, just looks at it all, and it don't make sense. I mean, he ends up trying to keep his own head afloat, you know? You can't change this stuff. It's always been here, and it will always be here.

This sense of inefficacy extends beyond individual ineffectiveness to include most collective efforts. Change on a societal level seems impossible to these workers. Such realms are out of their control. What they *can* have an influence over, however, is the personal, private sphere. It is here, then, that their energies are focused.

STEVE: I think you can change your own life. You can change—you can improve yourself and stuff, but I don't think you can do much about these big issues—the economy and things.

Central to this approach is a vision of the private, responsible citizen.

The civic orientation of workers is not simply a negative one, rejecting participation in mainstream politics. There is implicit, and sometimes explicit, belief in being a responsible citizen. But this vision of citizenship is highly privatized, emphasizing commitment to one's family. Thus, a strong sense of immediate community, in the form of family, often coexists with a privatized notion of citizenship.

RONALD: I think the average guy is just working, feeding his family, and paying the bills. He doesn't want to get all wrapped up with this political stuff going on in Washington or someplace else. It's just too much. Who can make sense of it? You do your work, you pay your bills, maybe—if you're interested in that stuff—you vote, and you hope and pray for the best. You hope it all turns out okay. There's nothing much you can do about it, so there's no point getting yourself all riled up about it. Standing on a corner with a protest sign isn't gonna change the world. You do what you have to do. That's it, I guess.

Thus, a profound sense of resignation permeates this vision. Workers are left doing "what they have to do" in order to take care of their loved ones as best as they can while the political world "outside" develops without them.

The only contact most workers have with the political realm is through the news media. The news media, especially television news, acts as a keyhole on the political world towards which workers may occasionally glance. There are two important aspects of this use of the news media. First, as Herbert Gans (1988: 71) puts it, news is used "primarily for surveillance reasons." As one worker commented, "You want to keep an eye open for anything that might be coming down the road." Thus, news is largely background noise that is occasionally monitored in the unlikely event that some development—usually negative—may impact workers.

A second feature of news watching is that it reinforces the role of workers as spectators of political and social events. As noted, concern for public affairs is simply seen as one of several possible "interests" in life. For some workers, watching the news is not very different from watching entertainment media since, usually, neither has any concrete impact on their lives.

Curtis Gans (1984: 314) has argued that:

> It is probably no coincidence that voter participation has been going down since television became the primary staple of American communications and the primary method of political campaigning. For what television has done more than anything else is to send the majority of the public home to watch the tube rather than continue to participate in community or political activities. As a result, the individual citizen has become a consumer of politics rather than an involved participant.

Unlike political rallies or conventions, the spectacle of politics as transmitted through the media is a one-way form of communication that is experienced by privatized citizens. As Boyte (1989: 153) summarizes, "In a glitzy, high-tech age of media consultants and airbrushed personalities, public life usually seems to most citizens a far-distant spectacle. We watch others on the political stage—making decisions, deliberating current events."

Civic "Duty"

Workers have generally accepted their spectator role in public affairs. Little is asked of them regarding political involvement, and they are generally comfortable with their nonparticipation. But despite their belief that government issues are largely remote from their lives, and that they can have little impact on these issues, some workers show a mild sense of guilt about not being well informed about current affairs.

KRISTEN: There's nothing I can do about most of this. I know I should know more and follow it and everything, but I can't seem to find the time. Maybe I'm not really interested, I don't know.

There is a great deal of ambivalence on this point. On the one hand, politics is viewed as a vast wasteland of corrupt and ineffectual actors, and workers have no sense that they can affect the system. On the other hand, despite all, some workers still feel a sense of guilt for not having "kept up" with events. They have internalized a sense that it is their civic "duty" to be informed and to take part in politics, at least to the extent of voting. Thus, for many, voting is the civic act that absolves what little guilt there is over disengagement. In fact, it is virtually the only form of participation that seems within reach of workers. Workers' references to "protesting" or "demonstrating" usually arise in the context of pointing out the extremity and implausibility of such actions.

But with the occasional exception of parents encouraging their children to vote, the sense of civic duty does not usually come from fellow working-class members. Instead, workers most often cited middle-class teachers as the source of such feelings of "duty."

DC: You said you weren't really concerned [about the unfairness of the political system], but you knew you "should be." What makes you think you "should be"?

STEVE: Well, all the stuff they teach you in school, I guess. You've got freedom, and you're supposed to take responsibility and stuff. Vote and all that.

DC: What does "taking responsibility for freedom" mean? What do you think that means?

STEVE: [laughs] I don't know really. I mean it's what you hear, you know. I guess, vote. Voting is what you're supposed to do.

Another worker says:

SAM: As long as it don't bother me, I'm not really interested. Maybe that's wrong but that's the truth.

DC: What makes you say "maybe that's wrong"? . . .

SAM: I don't know. I guess you're always told that you should—you know— you should, follow the news, get involved, things like that—like you were saying. But really I don't think many people really do that. I don't.

DC: Why do you think—first, who do you think is saying you should follow the news and things like that? Where did you pick that up?

SAM: I know in school the teachers would always say that. They'd try to get you interested in current events and things like that. Educate yourself on what's going on and all of that.

DC: But you don't really agree with that?

SAM: Well, I think it's fine, like I said, if you're interested in that kind of thing. But that's not for everyone, that's all.

The difficulty for the Left, of course, is that it is preaching a message that argues just this point: politics *is* for everyone. Many working people, though, have other ideas.

Ironically, the one area in political life where workers do have some sense of belonging is the realm of international politics. Workers see themselves as Americans, and patriotism plays a part in their political identity because it is virtually the only type of identification available to workers that is seen in a positive and effective light. In their role as working people in the context of U.S. politics, they have little or no influence. In their role as Americans on the global stage, they can see themselves as part of American leadership. More concretely, military service by working-class youth is perhaps the only other civic "duty"— besides voting—regularly performed. This intense service is associated with the international sphere and thus transcends the divisions of domestic politics. Military service is often seen as a positive experience both in pragmatic terms of employment, training, and adventure and in terms of contributing something worthwhile to the nation.

Despite their criticisms of American politics, workers value the liberty afforded by the present system, especially when compared to the perceived chaos of other countries.

NICOLE: I think people complain, that's for sure. People complain about everything. But then again you don't see them going to Russia or some other country, do you? There still may be problems in this country, I'm not denying that, but it's still a heck of a lot better than anyplace else. You don't see immigrants heading into these other places like you do here. People know that America's where there's the best chance. That's why everyone wants to live here.

This sometimes fierce pride in country can be effectively manipulated in international conflicts. But care needs to be taken in overgeneralizing from the apparent displays of patriotism that seem to erupt during times of international conflict. As I discussed earlier, many workers were at least skeptical of the entire Gulf War effort. Others were outright critics.

ANDREA: I think the idea of patriotism has really become demented. To me patriotism is "Yeah, this is America. [gestures to trees, and landscape] It's beautiful. I love it." That's patriotism to me. Not, "Yeah, let's go over and kill the Iraqis."

The conservatism that is characteristic of segments of the working class is real. However, "working-class conservatism" can become a shorthand that blinds observers to more complex dynamics.[1]

Responsibility and Social Programs

Although it does not necessarily foster a consistent conservative philosophy, working-class political culture is marked by a strong valuation of individual responsibility. Social issues such as teen pregnancy, drug use, and crime are all seen by workers as issues of individual responsibility.

KRISTEN: [W]ith crime I'd say it's more how people are raised; what kind of values they got and things along those lines. . . . The fact that the family seems to have fallen apart is very sad. I don't think kids get the kind of education at home that they used to. There's a lot less guidance—a lot more permissiveness there. That makes a difference, I would imagine.

This is the context for "family values" that was so well exploited by conservatives in the 1980s. Workers do believe that the family is the central site of socialization and that the family's breakdown has been the source of many social ills. Thus, even in discussing social and political issues, workers return to the family as the site for action.

Caring for the family is a principal concern for working people. Workers see the family as the most appropriate place to respond to the difficulties and injustices of society. When asked if there was anything they could do to contribute to addressing social ills, workers most often cited actions within their own families.

ELLEN: A lot of things, I think, start with the family. How the family raises up their kids can really affect how those kids turn out, you know. You've got all these kids who get into drugs and crime and stuff like that. I think that's got a lot to do with how they were brought up. . . . I think it all starts in the family—how you are brought up. That makes a big difference.

Another worker responds this way.

DC: Is there anything that regular folks can do, even if it's just small?

DANIEL: Yeah, I mean, you can work and take care of your family, your kids, you know? You do the best for them so that maybe they've got a better chance than you did.

Working people, though, recognize that social issues can penetrate even the strongest families. The poor economy during this study was an area of intense concern for workers. All workers I spoke with knew of someone who had been recently out of work. Thus, workers were well aware of the fact that people could become victims of structural factors. As a result, there was strong support for government programs intended to help the unemployed. This support, though, was clearly contingent on the recipients making every effort to find employment. (There was little sympathy, for example, for single mothers who say they cannot work because of child-care responsibilities.)

There was also very strong support for private efforts to help those who were trying to help themselves. A wide variety of private programs were approvingly cited by workers. These included food banks, holiday toy drives, donations to private social-service groups, crime watches, and other volunteer efforts:

NICOLE: Some people really do a lot in helping out with the needy and things like that. . . . I know my sister is active in her church, and they have a food collection—a food bank, I guess. They take in can goods and things like that, and they give it to needy people. It may not seem like much but for these people that can make a big difference—especially now with so many people out of work.

However, the workers I interviewed were vehemently opposed to ongoing dependence on government programs. They felt the government was too often assumed to be responsible for caring for social ills. The long excerpt below is a good example of how a worker can coherently combine disengagement from politics with support for those in need, an antitax/antigovernment sentiment, and a critique of the Republicans.

ROGER: I don't think it's up to the government. . . . I think, really, that's part of the problem we have. Whenever something's wrong we always assume the government's the one that's got to do something about it. . . . [T]he government has become this huge middleman. It takes the money from us in taxes. Then it skims off half of it to pay for these big salaries for politicians and advisors and studies, commissions—all that stuff. So all we end up getting for our money is half of what we could have got if this big bureaucracy wasn't there. . . . I think, eventually, that people have to solve their own problems and stop relying on the government for everything. . . . I think we've gotten out of the habit of doing things for ourselves because the government does everything. That's got to change. People have to realize that they should take care of their own. You've got to work at the local level and take care of your own. . . .

DC: So you're talking about things like voluntary groups—groups that try to help with particular issues?

ROGER: Yeah. I think it's a lot more effective.

DC: Is that what George Bush means when he's talking about "a thousand points of light" and so on? Is he talking about that sort of voluntary spirit?

ROGER: I guess so, but at the same time he's heading the biggest bank bailout in history. So I think Bush can talk out of both sides of his mouth.

In the political sphere, then, workers bring strong concerns for private life and family. They see individual responsibility as a key element of their philosophy. But included in this vision of responsibility is a belief in responsibility for those in need. Thus, unlike the individualism that has come to be associated with middle-class life (Bellah et al. 1985; Gans 1988), privatized, working-class orientation tends to be tempered with notions of responsibility to family and to those who are in need due to forces outside of their control.

Work Life

If the political sphere teaches workers that they are powerless, the workplace offers more of the same. The democratic vision of an active citizenry is antithetical to the workplace experiences of most working people. Regimentation and the division between mental and manual labor are perhaps the most important elements of workplace dynamics.

Regimentation and Conformity

The factory shop floor is perhaps the most dramatic example of a work environment where worker autonomy is restricted and paternalistic dependence is fostered. But the regimentation of clerical and office work has also become highly developed. Service work, too, brings unique demands that result from "working with the public." Whatever its form, regimentation can be significant for political participation. As Reinarman (1987: 187) points out, "A substantial body of research shows that the necessity for conformity to managerial expectations and supervisorial rules at work makes for conformity outside of work. Similarly, workers granted autonomy and discretion at work are likely to have, for example, higher self-esteem and confidence in their critical judgments in all spheres." My fieldwork at MAPS was in a light industrial, factory environment, and I will limit my examples to this kind of work, but many kinds of working-class jobs include dynamics similar to the ones I describe below.[2]

The absence of autonomy in a factory can seem suffocating to someone unaccustomed to it. Most workers, though, are taught well about the paternalistic routines of factory life; it is a central feature of their formal schooling. I had worked in factories before this fieldwork, but returning to this environment reminded me of how easy it is to forget the incredible regimentation workers experience. The most fundamental form of regimentation is the strict organization of time.

MAPS does not use timeclocks, but the mechanism of time regimentation remains. There is extensive use of bells piped in through the intercom to signal the beginning and ending of work, breaks, and lunch. I wrote in my field notes, "The memory of high school came flooding back as I sat there waiting for the bell to ring so I could go to lunch. It makes you feel like a child." The time bells are strictly enforced: workers cannot leave the building to go to lunch, to break, or home until the bell rings. My flagrant violation of this rule brought a memo from a manager to the department and a verbal reminder from the supervisor. Clearly, I, and a couple of other people, were the culprits. Pressured into submission, I quickly learned to dutifully wait with the others for the bell to ring.

The strict regimentation of time had a powerful impact on me. I found myself staring at the clock, longing for my ten-minute break when I could dart to the front cafeteria, grab a coffee and donut, dart back to my department, and wolf them down. This break became the highlight of the day. I stood there all day thinking about how much time there was until the next break. There was a running gag among workers that plays upon the fact that workers felt one should not look at the clock because it just makes the time seem to go by more slowly. Workers would very casually mention that there was "only an hour and a half (or whatever) to lunch!" thus telling the time to the person who had struggled not to look at the clock, forcing him or her to think about it, and making the time go by more slowly. The key to success was in the deadpan delivery to the unsuspecting worker, a skill coworkers felt I quickly mastered.

Time is a constant feature of the day. Workers have to get to work on time. They are constantly checking their production rate against the clock to see how they are doing. Workers are always thinking about how long it is until the next break.

I found myself playing little games to make the time go by faster. One game simply involves estimating the amount of time needed to finish an order: "So whad'ya think, get it done in an hour?" "Naw, no way. Hour and a half." After such an exchange you have entertainment for the next hour as you check the progress of the order (which is marked by large electronic counters on all the machines) against the passage of time.

Another game I played was in "offloading," which entailed gathering up printed material being cut and folded on a machine (baum) and placing the material on wheeled racks of shelves to be pushed to the next step in the production process. Basically, the game involved guessing how many shelves would be needed for the order. You filled one shelf, checked the counter to see how many you had on there, and then divided that amount into the total order to come up with an estimate. I got a sense of pride and accomplishment by being able to pick just the right rack with just the right amount of space for the order. As I wrote in my field notes, "Boredom makes you do funny things."

This single control mechanism of time and lack of control over it profoundly affects the entire work process. Other forms of regimentation are discussed below.

Mental and Manual Division

The "rationalization" of work in the last century has formally divided work into mental and manual components. The rise of the professional managerial strata of society is directly related to the de-skilling of workers. It is here, within the radical division of mental and manual labor, that workers are most clearly commanded *not* to exercise authority.

Research has shown that "manual" workers control important information about how to perform their jobs successfully (e.g., Buroway 1985; Halle 1984; Howard 1985; Kusterer 1977). Even the originator of scientific management principles, Frederick Taylor, acknowledged: "[The] foremen and superintendents knew, better than anyone else, that their own knowledge and personal skill fell far short of the combined knowledge and dexterity of all the workers under them' " (in Derber, Schwartz, and Magrass 1990: 123). However, many workplaces adhere to a formal division of mental and manual labor, and manual workers quickly learn that they are not supposed to perform much, if any, mental labor. Or, as one MAPS worker put it, "They want you to check your brain at the door."

Workers have, for the most part, resigned themselves to the existence of this division. Workers whose knowledge is unrecognized and unrewarded by management learn to abdicate responsibility for decision making. Workers at MAPS who were faced with some snag in production turned to management for solutions even when the workers knew how to solve the problem. The reason for this was summed up in a commonly used phrase, "They don't pay me enough to think."

One example summarized from my MAPS field notes will suffice to illustrate this process. I was working on a machine that stuffs catalogs into large envelopes with cutout windows for the computerized address label to be stuck on. We were stuffing a new catalog, and the usual way of handling them resulted in the mailing labels being stuck on the side of the catalog that had type on it, making it difficult to read the address on the label. We quickly realized it would be a simple matter to turn the catalogs upside down so a solid color would show through the window, thereby solving the type problem. Instead of doing this, however, the machine operator muttered the often repeated phrase "They don't pay me enough to think" and left to find the supervisor to ask him what to do. After about ten minutes, the operator returned with the supervisor and explained the whole situation. The supervisor looked at the catalogs and told the operator to run them upside down.

The incident prompted this comment in my field notes:

There's an interesting process going on here which reminds me of Willis's [1977] *Learning to Labor* [in which he describes how in rejecting teachers' authority, British working-class "lads" help pave the way to getting working-class jobs]. Workers know they are doing relatively mindless work. This somewhat demeaning position results in a defensive reaction which basically says, "OK, you think I'm not smart enough to think so I won't." This is the workers' "last laugh" so to speak. Just as the "lads" of Willis's book think they're making out but in reality are fitting in perfectly to the system that oppresses them, so too these workers believe they are getting away with something by not having to put the effort into figuring problems out. Managers' belief in the mental/manual division, in turn, is reinforced by the apparent inability of workers to "think" when a problem arises.

Abdicating responsibility for developing solutions to shop-floor problems reinforces the belief in the minds of management that workers are unable to make such decisions. Thus, in thumbing their noses at management, workers can further entrench themselves in their position of relative powerlessness.

The division between mental and manual workers within the factory brings profound differences in how work is experienced and the status afforded to each kind of labor. There were several features of the physical plant and the organization of work that relate directly to the mental-and-manual divide.

Space and Turf.   There was a clear and relatively rigid division of space between mental and manual workers. Mental workers received much more pleasant, comfortable surroundings than manual workers. The offices of supervisors, for example, were constructed to cut off managers very dramatically from workers. But even the low-level office workers such as secretaries worked in a much more pleasant environment than most workers: the lighting was better, the noise was lower, there was no smell, the heat was better regulated, and it was cleaner.

The issue of space is also one of turf. Bosses sometimes wandered back to the floor. This was expected. They came and talked with floor supervisors and other personnel. When workers needed to go to the front offices, however, they seemed to do so quite sheepishly. It was clear in such situations where the power lay. People in work clothes with dirty hands simply looked out of place in a neatly carpeted, muzaked office. The bottom line, then, was that mental workers could venture relatively comfortably onto the manual worker's turf, but manual workers could not easily wander into mental workers' turf. There was a good deal of resentment about turf infringement, however. Everyone got a little edgy when they knew bosses were walking around. The horseplay stopped, and everyone kept an eye out, often warning other workers through gestures of the impending approach of a boss.

Noise. Workers who operated machinery were constantly subject to the noise of that machinery. In addition to the physical impact of that noise (there was a faint buzzing in my head for the first few days) there was a social impact on workers. Workers in a noisy environment cannot easily talk to one another. In order to communicate, they must, at least, speak in unusually loud voices.[3] This necessity discourages casual or prolonged exchanges. Instead, people's conversation tended to be either directly about the work at hand or quick joking references. Again, this work atmosphere was different for mental workers, who were in much quieter surroundings. (It was also different from that where the work was done manually, rather than by machine. It was in doing manual work that I was able to converse freely with workers.)

Structure of Work. People who worked on particular machinery were largely tied to that machinery during their working hours, and communication between workers on the same machine was limited because of noise and the distance between work stations.

Dirt. There is a basic reality about manual labor that can easily get overlooked. People get dirty. Workers dress differently anticipating this fact. There is no point getting neatly dressed if you are only going to get grease or ink on your clothes. I quickly joined my fellow workers in wearing only "work clothes," a miniwardrobe of old T-shirts and stained or torn pants. The result is a clear distinction between manual and mental workers on the basis of sheer appearance. It was easy to tell immediately upon seeing someone whether he or she worked on the floor or in an office.

The mental/manual division, therefore, is a profoundly important part of the workplace. Such issues as space and turf segregation can be the source of intense resentment. One MAPS worker told me this poignant story.

RONALD: I remember about two weeks ago I had to go talk to [the personnel director] about insurance stuff. So I went up there [to the office section of the plant], and I was sitting in the little hall there waiting to see her and all these bosses in suits and ties and the secretaries in their nice clothes are going back and forth, you know. Nobody says "Hi" to me. Everybody kind of looks away. That's how it felt anyway. There I am—working stiff—in my boots and jeans and T-shirt, you know. It's kind of like a little protected world up there—carpeting and music and all that. It reminds me of school.

DC: School?

RONALD: Yeah, you know, "Be quiet, be polite, dress neat." All that shit. That's what it reminds me of. All these people kissing up to bosses. Fuck that. "Get me out of here!" That's all I kept thinking. I was getting really nervous.

Workers, however, do fight the mental/manual division. Manual labor and service positions often help foster ingenious skills at avoiding, subverting, ignoring, or surviving workplace supervisory systems. Cultures of resistance develop in these contested terrains. But such skills are largely inapplicable to the needs of participatory democracy. Rather than confronting and directly engaging authority systems, workers are often socialized into quietly struggling for "free spaces."[4] In a parallel to the larger liberty/democracy dichotomy, workers on the work floor learn to value the absence of constraint rather than active involvement in decision making. In addition, the process of outwitting low-level managers can often foster resentment of these overeducated professionals.

Conversely, in their employment, middle-class professionals are often rewarded for a certain amount of independent thinking and for verbal and written communication skills, all of which are useful in engaging in political action. Such skills are rarely nurtured in manual-labor and service-sector positions.

The separation of mental and manual labor can result in significant tensions in the workplace. During my stay at MAPS, for example, such tensions were clearly evident. But managerial techniques were employed that had the effect of isolating workers and making them competitive with each other, rather than with bosses. For example, workers were not paid on a quota basis per se, but production output was closely regulated, and output was a key factor in semiannual performance reviews. (In the envelope with their paychecks, workers were given a computer printout showing their day-by-day production and the corresponding expected standard.) I found it surprising how often workers would complain to supervisors about a coworker's inferior work that had made its way from one part of the plant to another. This was especially true when the inferior work caused downtime for operators and thus affected production numbers. Such managerial techniques, therefore, helped to undermine any collective sense of solidarity amongst workers.

But workers clearly resented what they saw as the ineptness of managers. This was most apparent when it came to the planning of work—supposedly an area of expertise for managers. That is, there was a fair amount of resentment about how little managers knew about how work was "really" done and about how much production could be reasonably expected.[5] There was also resentment that managers did not know what could and could not be expected from the equipment that was available. Workers often thought that managers did not realize how badly things ran—both how bad the equipment was and how bad certain materials ran on the machines.

The resentment workers hold for management sometimes leads to the withholding of information about the production process. The withholding of information can sometimes reach comic proportions. From my field notes:

> On the day before Thanksgiving, inventory was done in the plant. I was sitting at the table with several other workers while other people did inventory. This inventory was structured in two waves. The first wave was the regular people that usually work on the machines. They were putting tags on all the boxes and marking how many there were of each kind of item (samples, flyers, etc.). The second wave was management people who would come around and check the work of the first wave to see if it was accurate.
>
> Between the first wave, when all the samples had been counted, and the second wave, when the bosses checked the count, we at the table—who were still inserting—had to use up a couple of boxes of samples. When the bosses came by to check the count they were a couple of boxes short. They were only about 10 feet away from the table, and we could overhear their conversation. They were discussing why the count appeared to be wrong. . . . There was a mild debate going on between the bosses as to whether the counters had made an error or whether the boxes ought to be somewhere.
>
> We were all sitting there, knowing perfectly well that we had used the boxes and torn them down, like we always do, and they lay in a pile of used cardboard just a few feet away waiting to get picked up for recycling. We knew exactly what was going on, but it quickly became clear that no one was going to say anything. At one point, [one worker] leans over to me and says, "So, I wonder how long it's gonna take 'em to figure it out." We, of course, all laughed at this point. Clearly the unspoken culture here was: these were stupid bosses who didn't know

what they were doing, and if they weren't gonna ask the workers for help, we weren't gonna give it.

The bosses continued to talk about it. One thought a mistake had been made, another said that no, that couldn't be it. . . . Finally after at least 15 or 20 minutes of discussion they came over to us and asked, "Hey, do you know anything about this sample?" Of course we said, "Yeah, the empty boxes are right there. We used them up."

The point of all this is that bosses just don't ask workers—the people who know most. The other point is that the workers know this and tacitly withhold information out of resentment.

The mental/manual divide is important for another reason. It helps to form a key dividing line between what working people see as "us," that is, workers, and "them," those who do not work. Much has been made of whether or not working-class people see and identify themselves as working class. Halle (1984: 204), for example, argues that the male chemical workers he studied referred to themselves as "working men," largely reserving reference to "class" for lifestyle issues outside of the workplace. The workers I spoke with used a variety of labels to refer to themselves, but the mental/manual distinction was an important element of almost all self-descriptions. "Working," "regular," or "average" people were almost always identified as those who had to work for a living and did not have family wealth. But "working" for a living was usually confined to either manual or service work. There was little tolerance for "paper pushers" of any kind. After some hesitation, workers usually acknowledged that secretaries—despite their office perks and nice clothes—were essentially in "the same boat" as shop-floor workers.

The mental/manual divide is also important because of its political ramifications. Middle-class activists tend not to fully understand how their class position is different from that of the working class. The middle class benefits from the oppression of the working class through the rigid division of mental/ manual labor and the resulting difference in expertise. Understanding this dynamic goes a long way toward explaining the resentment of the working class toward professionals and intellectuals.

The professional-middle class has served as a buffer between labor and capital. Workers can see benefits they get from capital, namely jobs, and they do not see capitalist exploitation very clearly (unless a factory closes). Working people see managers and professionals enforcing the mental/manual divide but do not see benefits coming from this professional-middle class. Thus, working-class resentment and anger—at least in the short run—gets channeled towards the PMC. The Right has effectively capitalized on this resentment.

The pursuit of a career, which characterizes the professional-middle class, signals and helps to reinforce a sense of control over one's destiny. Employment is no longer a random series of jobs. Instead, it results from long-term planning and follows a logical progression. Things do not just happen to a professional—the professional, as much as possible, plans and prepares to make things happen to improve his or her lot in life.

Workers do not share in the security and control that comes with the pursuit of "careers." Working people earn their living by working at the best job available. In speaking to workers about their employment history, one quickly gets a sense of the randomness of employment developments. A fortuitous contact is made, a relative hears of an opening, an ad is seen, or an employment office reference is pursued, and a new job begins. Workers, then, feel a lack of control not only over the work process itself but over the process of obtaining work as well. They understand that their position—especially in nonunion jobs—is often precarious, and a layoff or firing could result in their returning to square one. Unlike professionals, they do not possess credentials to help open doors. They are at the mercy of the market.

Derber, Schwartz, and Magrass (1990: 158) observe that "A professional's career, perhaps more than anything else, defines his or her identity. It is likely to be the first thing a professional mentions when meeting someone at a party." This is much less true for working people. Work is an important aspect of their lives, and it takes up the largest single block of time, but it does not usually have the same identity-defining characteristic as a professional's career does.

Workers are usually much more constrained in their choice of work than professionals are. In her study of how women make choices about work and family, Gerson (1985: 84) notes that "For working-class respondents, the range of job options was limited and the freedom to choose among them circumscribed. They were, therefore, far more dependent than their college-educated counterparts on the structure of the workplace itself for both the discovery of new insights and access to work that could nourish and support developing capacities." This dependence on an existing workplace means that often workers try to find fulfillment in their existing jobs and take pride in the quality of the work they do.

Making the best of the situation includes getting along with coworkers. This is a crucially important aspect of the workplace. Workers know that very often they are partially dependent on the goodwill and cooperation of their coworkers to accomplish the jobs for which they are responsible. In addition, a pleasant working relationship with coworkers often makes a bad situation at least tolerable. Workers constantly look to one another for entertainment and humor to make the day go by faster. An important unwritten rule, then, is to keep the conversation light. Political discussions potentially threaten the important relationship that workers have built up—often over a long period of time.

DC: But you and the other secretaries don't really talk about politics or what's in the news?

JUDY: No, not really. I don't think any of us are that interested really. We talk about movies and all kinds of other things but not really politics. I think some people don't like to talk about it because they don't know what other people will think, you know. Will people disagree or whatever. They don't want to bring up anything controversial or nothing.

DC: What do you mean "anything controversial"?

JUDY: Well, I think sometimes if you know someone thinks something about an issue, you just kind of avoid it, you know, so you won't start an argument or anything.

Fantasia (1988: 80) makes similar observations about the workers in his study. He notes that there was an apparent harmony between workers, but that "harmony seems to have been maintained by what workers did *not* talk and laugh about as much as it was by the things they shared. Potentially divisive social, political, and religious issues were rarely discussed." This general pattern was certainly true for my coworkers at MAPS. Two to ten workers would do manual work stuffing envelopes while seated at a long table relatively isolated from the heavy machinery. These were ideal conditions for long conversations. In fact, this work almost demanded conversation for people (me, anyway) to stay awake. The boring, repetitive work invites some sort of diversion. It is easy to talk with people and still get the work done. During my stay there was a running joke about coming up with topics of conversation to make the time go by faster.

Since people ran out of things to talk about, everyone who worked at the table was assigned the task of coming in the next day with a topic of conversation to introduce. More often than not, this turned out to be retelling the plot of one of the more popular television programs (e.g., *Rescue 911, Unsolved Mysteries*) or the previous evening's movie rental. Political topics were virtually nonexistent. The closest people would come to them were topics from talk-shows (e.g., those of Oprah Winfrey and Phil Donahue), which were very popular and which some people would record and watch at night.[6] The major topics of conversation, instead, were: families (children, pregnancies, schooling, and illnesses were most prominent); gossip about coworkers (homelife scandals, sex, productivity, quality of work, how they were to work with); gossip about neighbors and mutual acquaintances (crime, affairs, divorces, home life, pregnancies); immediate workplace (the kind of orders people were processing, how the machines were running); media (especially television and movie rentals—a major topic that was often used intentionally to "make the time go by faster"); home life (stories of and advice about house and car repairs, also hobbies); sports (an exclusively male pursuit especially popular with the thirty-five-and-younger crowd, seemingly much less popular with men older than that). It is difficult to quantify which topics were most often discussed because some were discussed at length but only occasionally, whereas others came up consistently but only briefly.

Workers at MAPS spent hours talking about entertainment media, especially television and movies. The television programs that were discussed most frequently were not the sitcoms of prime time. Instead, they were the "reality" programs such as *Rescue 911* and *America's Most Wanted*. The poignant stories of disaster and crime portrayed in these programs were retold by workers the next day. It was almost ritualistic that the people who watched these shows religiously would retell the stories to coworkers who had not seen them. A typical scene might occur while tabling, where one person would ask, "Hey, did you see the story about that little kid on *911* last night?" Those who had would vouch for the quality of the story: "Oh yeah, that was wild. That poor kid. I couldn't believe it." By this point, those who had not seen the story were asking that it be retold, and someone would begin. The telling of the tale was a group effort. Although there was a main narrator, others would chime in with additions and corrections they deemed appropriate. They seemed to relish the telling of gruesome details of decapitations, accidents, and grisly crimes. These were often met with cries of "Oh, gross!" that were in no way meant to stop the proceedings. (There was a definite gender bias here in that men tended to tell the more gruesome stories, with women protesting the grisly details. There seemed to be a delight taken in this ritual, which reminded me of mythical stories of schoolyard boys showing frogs or spiders to squeamish girls.)

Another favorite program was *Unsolved Mysteries,* which reflected a strong interest in the occult, supernatural, and spiritual. These tales would often spark debates about the existence of ghosts, supernatural powers, ESP, and the like.

Movies were another source of seemingly endless storytelling. People would recount the plots of movies they had gone to see or, more often, rented. Nearly always, a critic's summary would come with a recommendation as to whether this particular movie was worth renting. A pan by one critic seemed to mean instant death for a film, whereas a rave review almost always meant the movie would make a return engagement in a future discussion after someone else had seen it. Popular movies during this period included *Pretty Woman, Ghost, Die Hard 2,* and *The Hunt for Red October.* The interest in genres broke down stereotypically along gender lines: women professed a liking for romantic love stories whereas men liked "action" adventures. This was clearly an item of contention between couples, and it apparently was often resolved by renting two movies, one of each genre.

The viewing of these rental movies appears to have been a very private affair. Viewings were either done alone, couples only, or couples with their kids, if appropriate. I never heard of someone going over to somebody else's house to watch. Perhaps this was a consequence of the near-universal possession of VCRs and the inexpensive cost of tape rentals, combined with the spontaneous nature of many viewings.[7]

The communal or shared nature of these viewings came after the fact. It was in the retelling of plot lines that people shared their experiences. People would compare likes and dislikes about films. These seemed to be along predictable lines. First, people were concerned with actors. They debated how good a job the actors did in this film and compared these performances to their other work. Second, plots were discussed and evaluated on whether there were interesting "twists" and whether they had happy or sad endings. Third, a variety of miscellaneous concerns were consistently raised: What was the level of violence? Were there good sex scenes? Were there notable special effects?

The point here is that the movies were taken as entertainment, pure and simple. There was virtually no discussion of social issues that may have come up in the films (although most of the films favored by workers would steer clear of such things in the first place). There was clearly no interest in "heavy" films that examined social issues. My rave reviews of *Roger and Me*—the documentary about the GM president and the layoff of GM workers—were quickly undermined by a coworker's later review of it as "boring," with little story line. His review made no mention of the politics or issues brought up in the film—striking, given the rash of layoffs and the general economic downturn in the area. As far as I know, no one else bothered to see it after that. It was interesting to find out later that it was unclear to this worker that this film was based on a "true" story, and that he took it instead for some sort of reenactment and fictionalization.

Mass-communicated entertainment media, then, seems to have this double effect. Relaxation time is spent in the home with immediate family and is not shared with others. However, this isolated experience is then the basis for shared conversations at work.

Engagement with mass media was almost exclusively—on the basis of conversation anyway—around entertainment issues: sports, prime-time television, and more than anything, VCR movie rentals. This definitely was a core common culture to which just about everybody related.

For workers, both the political and work realms offer little in the way of control, stability, or reward. It is not surprising that workers turn much of their attention to home life.

Home Life

Working-class culture was an urban by-product of industrialization. The gathering of workers in industrial centers facilitated their organization into unions. It also fostered vibrant cultures that grew out of the strong ethnic communities that made up working-class neighborhoods. Aronowitz (1992: 40) writes of one aspect of this culture: "The socialist or labor party political club was mainly a male social center, providing library facilities, rehearsal rooms for music and drama groups, Sunday schools, and, especially, space for card games and games of chess. Saturday nights were times for youth or adult dances, concerts, sings, and other social activities involving the whole family. Electoral activity arose 'organically' from these social and cultural activities."

Urban culture nurtured such public spaces, which included cafes, churches, social clubs, and the stereotypical working-class bar.

But the rise of suburbia and the subsequent de-industrialization of America have undermined urban working-class communities as workers—especially white workers—move to the greener pastures of suburban life. A quarter of Americans lived in the suburbs in 1950, a third in 1960, and nearly half in 1990 (Schneider 1992: 33). Although working-class identities are strongly felt in the workplace, such identities become more malleable in residential communities that feature a variety of occupations and professions. Such communities, however, are not necessarily diverse. Instead, they are characterized by what Bellah et al. (1985: 72) call "lifestyle enclaves," which celebrate "the narcissism of similarity."

The weakening of working-class communities contributed to the Left's abandonment of the working class as political agent. Isserman (1987: xviii) writes that: "The dilution of ethnic working-class cultures brought about by Hollywood, television, and *Life* magazine, the dispersal of ethnic working-class neighborhoods brought about by suburbanization, VA mortgages, and the interstate highway system, left radicals bereft of the old reliable constituencies and issues. . . ."

The decline of working-class culture is also a part of the decline of community in America. Increasingly, workers have left communal lifestyles in favor of the isolated retreat of suburban dwellings. One worker noted with dismay:

BERNICE: I don't think neighborhoods are what they used to be. It used to be that neighbors were there to help each other. They looked out for each other and so on. Now—like my son, my oldest son lives in [a nearby city]. He got his own house two years ago and he still doesn't know the names of his neighbors. Can you believe that? . . . People just don't talk to each other anymore. . . . I think TV really changed people. They don't visit anymore. They don't play cards together or spend time together. They're all watching TV. . . . I think that has hurt neighborhoods a lot.

Isolated residential environments discourage collective support networks. Often, what has been lost is the kind of mutual aid that once characterized working-class communities.

The support networks that once existed for many workers should not be romanticized. As Halle (1984: 46) reminds us:

A primary foundation of the solidarity so characteristic of working-class culture in the past was a common economic insecurity. Ties of friendship and kinship were critical in an era without government unemployment insurance, Social Security, or medical insurance, and with limited or nonexistent pensions, medical insurance, or job security from the company. Such ties provided a degree of protection against the numerous economic catastrophes to which everyone was vulnerable.

Of course, we should not overstate the effectiveness and reach of these government programs. But they have contributed to a reduced need for the kind of networks that were once the only source of support for many workers.

More and more, workers—like all Americans—look not to each other but to corporate-controlled mass media to gain an understanding of themselves and the world around them. Boyte (1989: 45) writes that in the increasingly fragmented society of the 1950s:

> older republican themes of active citizenship and public life became radically weakened. The citizen was now reinvented as the oxymoron "private citizen." Home ownership, seen by community activists like Mary Follett earlier in the twentieth century as analogous to Jeffersonian small freeholds, foundations for involvement in the public life of the community, had dramatically changed in meaning. The house was a refuge, a private retreat, a fortress from the world "out there." A "man's home" was "his castle," while for women the "feminine mystique" bore an eerie resemblance to the concept of the feudal, helpless lady. The ideal became isolated nuclear families tied together by the consumer culture of the suburbs.

The isolated retreat of the privatized citizen represents something else for workers. It represents the only area in life where they can feel security and a sense of influence and control.

One of the primary manifestations of the privatized citizen is the importance of consumer culture. Some activists argue against the more common position that material constraint is the primary hurdle to working-class participation. Instead, they suggest that it is material *abundance* and its pursuit that is at the root of the problem of political apathy. Interestingly, it is an activist from a working-class background who comments:

PATRICK: You have more toys than you ever did. They take up your time. People own all kinds of recreational things and they go a lot more places, I think, than they ever have. I think they're busy doing their own thing, trying to get whatever they can into their own life rather than trying to affect society. I think it's more of a me, me, me thing rather than helping.

There is another—perhaps more subtle—analysis of consumerism that does not focus on the castigation of working people for being greedy. Instead, there is a cultural critique of consumerism that is applicable to the middle class as well.

ALLAN: I would say that the mass consumer culture is a factor. That people sort of don't learn how to be participants in their own lives. That we relate to the rest of the world as consumers rather than as participants, and I think that's a process that's moving, things are getting worse in that direction.

And that mainstream politics is also becoming more and more something that happens on television, and that therefore it just becomes part of that same consumerism where it's something almost that you buy rather than something that you do.

Consumer culture is sometimes linked to a more generalized sense of personal inability to confront the outside world.

CAROL: Maybe sometimes—for a while they were talking about Americans getting this homing mentality. It's kind of like, "I'm gonna take my wife and my kids. I'm gonna close up my house, and we're gonna stay here, and I'm gonna protect them, and let the rest of the world take care of itself." I guess that's a real part of it too. Almost being afraid of what's out there and who's out there.

Privatized citizenry are dependent on the media for communication with the outside world. In addition to the news media, entertainment media, too, are a central part of workers lives and serve as the most visible common cultural experience among workers.

Conclusion

In response to political and work environments that seem uninviting, working people develop strategies of coping that emphasize the value of private life. Such a strategy is also based on family-centered self-reliance to try to secure a lifestyle that is acceptable to workers. Such an approach is a stark contrast to the Left's assumption of the need for collective action to achieve necessary change. As such, that strategy presents a formidable challenge to those who would convince workers of the utility of political action.

CHAPTER 11

Class Diversity and the Future of Social Movements

See, you ask these questions and if the answers were clear and right there, then we'd have this all done already. It's not clear, but it's important that we keep asking the questions.

ROB, forty-four-year-old antinuclear activist

The promise of democracy continues to elude us. In the United States today, broadening disenchantment with politics and politicians is being accompanied as much by declining voter turnout and diminished public participation as by calls for change. The "middle class" that has traditionally been seen as the backbone of American public life is now beginning to exhibit signs of a disengagement that has long been a characteristic of the working class and poor.

Meanwhile, the political nonparticipation of the working class has become virtually accepted as an inevitability and has generally raised little serious concern.[1] But it *should* raise concern for those on the left. Despite the difficulties that exist, the issue of working-class participation in progressive social movements and in electoral politics remains a crucial one. The left vision of democracy is incomplete as long as working people are largely absent from the political arena.

With this in mind, this chapter focuses on several summary issues—in necessarily brief form. First, I look at what activists think about the limited class base of their movements and suggest some consequences of this homogeneity. Second, I explain my understanding of how some left movements get to be middle class, examining factors both within social movements and beyond them, larger external social and political forces that affect movement development. Third, I suggest some lessons that might be learned from this study for the future participation of working people in left social movements.

The Absence of Working-Class Participation

The class composition of social movements is a difficult issue to explore in part because of the nature of class identity. One Central America activist notes:

ADAM: I've spent most of my life working on racism and sexism and homophobia, but somehow class is often left out. It's invisible—at least to many middle-class activists. . . . You can *see* race, you can *see* gender. Class, though, is harder to identify. I think that's one reason why it often gets overlooked. . . . I mean you're either white or you're not, you're female or you're male, but class is often a lot murkier than that.

One consequence of the invisibility of class is that the issue of class diversity can easily take a back seat to other, more obvious concerns.

The absence of working people in many middle-class movements also means that there is usually no one present to pursue the point. The result can be an "out of sight, out of mind" mentality. One activist, who sometimes led workshops on classism, put it this way:

RUTH: [Middle-class activists often expect] someone from a targeted group to teach them. "If this is really so bad why aren't they coming to us? If they're not coming to us then there's not a problem." . . . [I]t's somebody's classism that is continuing to help them to believe "Here I sit and I want them to come to me." That's such a thing of privilege.

The fact that working people are not confronting middle-class activists with this issue means that it can be easily ignored. In some groups, class is simply not addressed as a salient issue.

Another type of activist response is facilitated by the "murky" nature of class: well-intentioned activists sometimes overestimate the class diversity in their own movements. One story will illustrate the point. An environmental activist I interviewed said that volunteers for her organization came "from a variety of class and education backgrounds." She noted that the group had "a lot of people who are blue-collar who have never attended college. . . . It's not just all college-educated, white-collar workers, like you might expect." When I asked for names of working-class members whom I could interview, she told me of a married couple who, indeed, were from such a background. (In a subsequent interview, another member of this group volunteered the names of the same couple as evidence of the group's class diversity.) In interviewing them, however, I learned that, as far as they knew, they were the *only* people in the group—not counting high-school-age volunteers—who were not college-educated and middle class. This, they felt, was a problem in the organization, and they were sometimes troubled by the middle-class assumptions and styles of work. One noted, "I think sometimes people's education gets grandstanded. You know, I mean, they get up, and they make a point of knowing more than other people, and that kind of makes some conflicts." Thus, token working-class participation can be generalized by activists to suggest broader class diversity in a group than in fact exists, and assumptions of existing class diversity can easily go unchallenged.

Some activists, though, are acutely aware of the class homogeneity of their membership. One Central America activist acknowledged:

ADAM: Of course lack of diversity is an issue for the Left—in the Central America movement and elsewhere. We've got lots of white, middle-class, college-educated supporters. Some of them have tried over the years to reject their background, and they don't live a lifestyle that we stereotypically think of as being "middle class," but still, they're a product of that background, and it's an issue.

Lack of class diversity is an issue because it can hurt the effectiveness of middle-class movements.

The Consequences of Homogeneity

Limited class diversity holds several basic negative consequences for left social movements. First, the gap between the democratic ideal and social-movement reality is a troubling one since it clearly contradicts the Left's more general belief in the empowerment of all and in broad participation from all sectors of society. The legitimacy of the left democratic project is brought into question by the absence of working-class participation. Without such participation, the Left cannot be said to truly represent more than a relatively narrow slice of society.

Second, more than just a violation of the spirit of democracy, limited class diversity has serious political ramifications. Linda Stout, founder of North Carolina's Piedmont Peace Project, is a rural-based, peace-and-justice activist from a working-class background who has made leaping class, race, and gender boundaries an integral part of her work. Stout (1993: 1) says, "Until low-income people can join hands with middle-class and wealthy people to fight for economic justice, it will just continue to be a dream. And until the peace and environmental groups and the women's movement learn to include the majority constituency that's most impacted by the things they are fighting for, they will never have enough power to win, either."

Too often, middle-class movements that represent the "public" interest in fact have relatively inactive membership made up of a small segment of U.S. society. Their claims to represent a broad public are often not taken seriously by those in power or by the uninvolved public. Thus, their potential impact is reduced.

Third, a narrow range of participation means that social movements can easily become as "out of touch" as many politicians with the views and interests of working people. The isolation of movements that results from their middle-class membership is compounded by the fact that activists—especially those who are employed full-time in political positions—spend a good deal of time with other activists, limiting their contact to already converted members of the middle class. Allan, a full-time peace-and-justice activist observes:

ALLAN: I don't talk to real people very much. I don't spend time in a factory talking to people and finding out what people think. I spend my time relating to other activists, which is really bizarre. I think it's possible for somebody in my position to go way off in some sort of strange direction where you think that you're on the cutting edge of social change and what you're actually doing is relating to this tiny little fringe group. It's sort of a sub-subculture which is totally detached and totally irrelevant to most of the community.

This situation is exacerbated by class difference, since as Allan put it, "We tend to live, work, and socialize with people like ourselves."

This is no different for activists than for the rest of society. In a largely class-segregated society, middle-class activists—like most middle-class people—tend to regularly interact with people from a similar class background. One consequence of their constant interaction with politically active people is that activists sometimes vastly overestimate the amount of political participation that takes place amongst "regular people."[2]

Some activists acknowledge that movements "miss out" by not hearing the perspectives of people from other classes.

ALLAN: [I]f we're gonna work on economic issues or class issues, if the group is homogeneous in terms of being middle- and upper-middle-class, college-educated professionals, we're really not gonna have a clue as to how to work on issues that relate to people whose experiences are different—the people who are struggling to meet their rent checks.

As a result, left movements are often isolated, lack broad support, and are powerless to effect significant change.

But those activists who are aware of the importance of working-class participation tend to talk about the significance of class primarily—or sometimes only—in relation to economic issues. If working people are missed by movement activists, it is likely to occur when talking about bread-and-butter topics. Little attention seems to be paid to their importance on *any* issue the Left addresses. There is an assumption that, for workers, only narrowly defined economic issues are proximate, that is, only such issues have direct and immediate consequences. This assumption ignores the plethora of issues that relate to health, family well-being, and quality of life that are of central concern to working people.[3]

Fourth, isolated movements tend to lose their ability to communicate effectively with those outside of their small circle. All of the cultural attributes that characterize middle-class life can act as barriers to effective communication with those outside of this culture. Stout (1993: 2, 3) says that such barriers "include everything from language, to how one defines a leader, to how meetings are held and facilitated, to how organizational priorities and budgets are decided." On the issue of language, for example, she argues that "the groups working on national issues—peace, environment, the women's movement . . . tend to target a narrow constituency," in part because "all of their newsletters and educational materials are written at college level, automatically excluding most low-income people." Stout (1993: 2) cites her own experience as a working-class person in the women's movement: "At first I was excited and thought I had a lot to offer. I very quickly began to feel discouraged and bad about myself and my abilities. I constantly experienced attitudes and comments that made me question my own worth. I became painfully aware of my lack of a college degree, my 'different' way of speaking, and my 'lack of knowledge' about important events and people, etcetera. For the first time in my life I really felt stupid." The kind of cultural resources that middle-class activists tend to have—and tend to take for granted—can seem to be a formidable obstacle for potential working-class participants. At the same time, middle-class activists may not appreciate the unique and valuable resources that working people might bring to their organization. For example, working people may bring to middle-class organizations different ways of knowing and communicating, coupled with access to different communities—invaluable resources for organizations trying to communicate to a broad audience.

Fifth, if the Left does not facilitate and accommodate participation by workers and strive towards the empowerment of working people, it leaves open the possibility that the political right will draw upon workers to support *its* agenda. Certainly the rise of the Reagan era must be considered in the context of a Left that failed to speak to the needs of working people. In some cases, the Right managed to exploit the cultural conservatism (and sometimes racism) of the white working class along with their resentment of liberal elites who were said to be engineering social and political life from the vast bureaucracies of government.

The ability of the Right to mobilize working people, though, should not be overstated. Working-class disenchantment with the political system is more likely to translate into withdrawal from political life than a turn towards conservative movements. The reason is that while the Right often may be more culturally resonant among workers, its economic policies contradict working-class realities. Research has shown that the professional-middle class tends to be liberal on civil rights and civil liberties issues, but relatively conservative on economic policy issues (Brint 1985). Inversely, as Page and Shapiro (1992: 300) note, compared to those of higher incomes, working people of more modest means tend to support "social welfare spending programs that promise to help them with jobs, schooling, medical care, and related assistance, particularly when there is an explicit element of redistribution of income or wealth."

There is indeed a class divide along economic and social or cultural issues. As Hart (1993: 29) summarizes: "The strongest factor predicting economic opinions is income: people with more income tend to be economically conservative. Views on cultural issues, on the other hand, are predicted by education, with the more educated tending toward liberalism. Since people with higher incomes have usually had more schooling, the different aspects of their privileged status incline them in opposite directions on economic and cultural issues." Middle-class activists who focus on cultural and social issues rather than economic ones, therefore, tend to recognize working-class conservatism on cultural issues but miss the relative liberalism on economic issues.

How Does the Left Get to Be Middle Class?

Traditionally, the class differential in political participation has usually been explained by highlighting the "deficiencies" in working-class political culture. Working people are less likely to participate, such a perspective argues, because compared to people of higher status, workers do not have enough awareness, skills, or resources. There *are* features of working-class culture and daily life that make political participation particularly difficult in the contemporary political context. However, it is more useful to understand activist and worker cultures in terms of differences rather than deficiencies. There is nothing inherent or absolute in the "tools" provided by different class cultures that encourages or discourages political participation. Instead, it is the interaction of agent and structure—or the "fit" between person and environment—that shapes likely behavior.

Therefore, to get a fuller picture of the dynamics that affect political participation, it is necessary to consider both people and their environment. For our purposes, this environment includes movement mobilization efforts and the broader political and social context in which movements operate.

Movement Mobilization

In order to examine movement mobilization efforts, it is useful to disentangle two elements that in the real world are inextricably intertwined: form and content. The *form* of mobilization efforts involves how movements try to communicate their message and contact potential supporters. The *content* of mobilization efforts involves what issues movements are addressing and what they are saying about those issues.

Mobilization Content

Messages. In developing political communication, Snow et al. (1986) suggest that movement organizations face three core framing tasks. First, they must present a diagnosis of some aspect of society as problematic and in need of alteration. Second, they must propose a solution to the diagnosed problem that specifies what needs to be done. Third, they must present a call to arms or rationale for engaging in ameliorative or corrective action. As movements struggle to accomplish these three tasks, they tend to lose working people as potential participants. Focusing on movement actions, this section explores some possible explanations for this phenomenon.

"Education."   Social movements often focus their attention on the first task facing movements, diagnosing a problem that needs attention. They do this by promoting "education" efforts aimed at convincing the public of the need for change. Often, the assumption is that "if people only knew" about the problems being raised, then they would be more likely to act. At the very least, educating potential supporters is seen as the first step toward potential mobilization.

Part of the reason for this emphasis is a belief that the public in general, and working people in particular, are unaware of particular social problems and the need to address them. This may be true when addressing issues that are remote from the daily lives of working people, such as opposing U.S. involvement in some regional conflicts. In such cases, movements do face the need to inform the public about the existence of their issue and the need for change. However, the promotion of such new issues sometimes is a symptom of the different social location of activists and working people.

This situation was evident in the politics of privilege that characterized much of the New Left. Flacks (1988: 230), himself active in the New Left, observes:

> The trouble was that the New Left principles were to a considerable extent derived from what was often called "post-scarcity consciousness." They were most salient for those who were freed from preoccupation with fundamental issues of economic survival and security, and most applicable to a society in which minimally adequate standards of living were promised by the official social charter. . . . Such views presented a political problem that New Leftists only gradually took cognizance of. They prevented those influenced by the New Left from finding common ground with traditional working-class constituencies—i.e., with those who had less reason to believe that economic scarcity and insecurity were no longer problems.

This lack of common ground continues in many left social movements today.

One especially important gap is that between unions and other left social movements. By moving away from a broader vision of social change, unions often have turned a blind eye to the political context of their work and to the social consequences of the goods their members produce. As a result, many left activists no longer see unions as prospective allies. Indeed, sometimes progressive activists have to face unions as impediments to social change. At the same time, middle-class social movements have often been insensitive to the importance of jobs for working people. The result is too often a lack of communication that reinforces the middle-class nature of many left movements. Paula Rayman (1983: 197) notes, for example, "It was not uncommon during the anti–Vietnam War actions for young, college-age students, fresh from the suburbs, filled with passionate critiques of the War to label workers in the defense plants as 'pigs,' 'war-monsters' and 'baby-killers.' In turn, some workers responded by wearing hard hats and taunting the students with shouts of 'pinkos' and 'go to Russia.' "

Sometimes the absence of communication is between middle-class left movements and even the organized sectors of the working class. The story of the Seabrook nuclear power station in New Hampshire's seacoast region is an example of this problem. Unions fought for good-paying construction jobs; antinuclear activists opposed Seabrook's construction on safety and environmental grounds. The standoff pitted workers against largely middle-class environmental activists. In the end a scaled-down version of the project was built and brought on-line, but the lengthy conflict brought to a halt the expansion of the nuclear industry in the United States.

The ongoing conflict between workers and antinuclear activists was often confrontational. One activist I interviewed was closely involved with the Seabrook issue. He described the conflict this way:

ROB: Well, it was this whole thing about "Go get another job" and this thing about construction workers must hate their babies, otherwise they wouldn't work in a nuke. A lot of people just didn't get the fact that they just don't have that option. There was definitely this class privilege there. The same thing, like, the antinuke movement was just flower power that wanted people to freeze in the dark, didn't want people to have houses and running water, wanted people to live in teepees. Those were the two stereotypes.

The stereotypes were manipulated and exploited by the supporters of Seabrook. They were often effective because the unions involved had narrowed their focus to the jobs issue.

ROB: This was the time when the blinders had been put on the labor movement and the only thing you were supposed to look at was wages, hours, working conditions. You get constricted by what the NLRB says your purpose was and you no longer thought of yourself as being part of a social movement or being a social movement or being involved in those things. The other analogy that's made is they would build the chambers and produce the Krylon-B if you wanted them—to kill your own members.

The clash between left ideals and workers' material interests did not originate with the environmental movement, nor even with the Vietnam War. Difficulties emerged in the 1950s. But prior to that time, the middle-class Left's relationship with organized labor was much more cooperative. Isserman (1987: 163) tells this story, which illustrates the evolution of the Left-labor relationship:

In 1946 the Committee for Non-Violent Revolution had canceled a planned demonstration at the atomic weapons plant at Oak Ridge, Tennessee, because CIO officials feared the effects such a demonstration might have on the workers they were trying to sign up as union members. "Despite this disagreement," Jim Peck had written at the time to the local CIO organizer, "our committee wishes you the best of luck in your campaign to organize the South." In 1960 CNVA, a lineal descendant of the Committee for Non-Violent Revolution, thought in very different terms about its own political priorities. . . . As far as the pacifists were concerned . . . workers were accomplices to murder as long as they contributed their labor to building missile bases and submarines. Most of the pacifists came from better-educated and more prosperous backgrounds than the workers they were trying to reach, even if many of them now proudly lived lives of "voluntary poverty." They made no effort to understand why a high-paying union job was not something that workers . . . were likely to quit on the advice of high-minded middle-class strangers.

Isserman (1987: 157) notes that at one 1958 demonstration at the Cheyenne, Wyoming nuclear missile site, peace movement demonstrators handed out leaflets that asked, " 'How do you feel about helping to build a base for weapons that can kill millions of people? . . . No man really believes that a few quick dollars are more important than the future of the human race.' " Some of the town's residents turned out to taunt and assault the demonstrators.

Middle-class insensitivity to the economic realities of workers continued to be a mark of the predominantly middle-class New Left. The classic Port Huron Statement of the student Left, made little mention of economic concerns. Kahn (1986: 61) notes:

When the Port Huron Statement did address economic issues, it did so half-heartedly. It envisioned an economy founded on the principle "that work should involved incentives worthier than money or survival" and gave precedence to the middle-class desire for "meaningful" careers over the lower classes' demands for jobs, decent wages, better working conditions. Thus, the document stated, "the serious poet burns for a place, any place, to work; the once-serious and never-serious poets work at the advertising agencies." The idea that intellectual careers may have been of little immediate interest to Americans in uncertain economic straits received little consideration beyond "a new left cannot rely only on aching stomachs to be the engine force of social reform."

The result has been a perpetual gap in how middle-class left movements and workers see issues.

Activists, however, tend to be unaware of the class basis for working-class resentment of them and their issues. Rejection of left messages by large segments of working people are often ascribed to a deeply embedded working-class conservatism that can be overcome, if at all, only by "education." What is often ignored are the material structural reasons workers have for being skeptical of the messages from the middle class. Kahn (1986: 282) writes of middle class radicals that they

> tend to forget about their interdependence with the larger society. They often ignore the fact that their own affluence and education were not simply the result of individual efforts but were subsidized by privileged parents. And, in many instances, those privileges derived from businessmen who made their livings by employing the cheap labor of semiskilled and unskilled workers, minorities, and women or from professionals who earned healthy incomes by working for big businesses and bureaucracies that administered and constricted people's choices.

Workers relate to this reality by suspecting that left and liberal politics are politics of privilege. The clashes between workers and environmentalists are perhaps the most obvious examples. The issue of most salience for materially secure, middle-class environmentalists is the preservation of natural beauty and resources. Workers are concerned about the environment, but such concern is more likely to take a back seat to more directly salient issues such as the economy and jobs. Such a tension between left forces and workers is more generalized. There is, in fact, sometimes a mismatch between the primary issue interests of activists and those of working people.

Over the years, the environmental movement has developed a deep chasm between two distinct wings of the movement. First, what essentially has been the white, middle-class movement, symbolized by the "Big Ten" Washington-based, environmental organizations, has focused on more traditional issues of conservation and environmental protection. Second, an emerging array of local and regional "environmental justice" groups have developed much greater diversity in membership—including more working people and people of color—and have focused on environmental issues that more directly affect these communities, such as toxic waste disposal sites and workplace environmental hazards. Thus, the participation of a more diverse range of people was facilitated, not by convincing people of the importance of the middle-class movement's analysis of the environment, but rather by developing new organizations that addressed the issues directly facing working people and people of color, thus creating new and more accessible means of participation.

So one reason that some movements become middle class is that they emphasize issues that, relatively speaking, are not especially salient to working people or that even contradict some interests of working people. The Left, then, sets itself up with the task of educating workers on why particular issues should be of importance, rather than addressing issues that workers already identify as significant.

However, I believe that such little-known issues are a minority on the left agenda and that many middle-class social movements are trying to address issues that already concern working people. In fact, as I have argued, working people are all too aware of the existence of a wide range of problems and the need for change. In reality, it is with the second and third framing tasks—presenting solutions and calling for action—that left social movements most often fail.

Proposing Solutions.   If many social movements address issues that working people already recognize as problematic and important, then why do such movements lack working-class participation? One reason is that while working people are aware of a wide range of existing problems, they are less certain of the existence of adequate solutions, the second framing task movements face. There are two reasons for this. First, more than middle-class citizens, workers perceive the world of politics to be a complex maze that requires more education and expertise than they possess. They have little basis, therefore, for evaluating proposed solutions to problems. Since most political and social problems have a range of advocates proposing different solutions, working people are left uncertain about the viability of any particular solution. Since working people have come to see the political system as corrupt and political actors as suspect, they are usually doubtful of all proposed solutions. Instead, they fully expect political and social difficulties to continue, and they do not trust the various actors proposing solutions.

Second, workers are suspicious of proposed solutions because history has taught them that solutions often mask more difficulties. The "boom" of the Reagan years has left a legacy of debt. The social programs of earlier decades have left a welfare system that is often seen as bloated, ineffective, and fraud-ridden. The "war on drugs" has done nothing to stem their devastating effect on cities. Union advances have led to a greedy working-class elite that has contributed to the uncompetitiveness of U.S. industry. At least from the perspective of many workers, "solutions" often turn out to bring more problems. Social movements, then, largely fail to convince working people that they have realistic solutions to the host of undeniable problems that face our society.

Many social movements are distinctly middle class because they have also failed to convince workers of the need for and utility of collective action, the third task facing movements. There are several factors that contribute to this phenomenon. I wish to examine briefly here the issues of recruitment, movement culture, and, most importantly, efficacy.

Mobilization Form

Recruitment.   Class diversity is usually discussed by activists in terms of how to get working people involved in what are now middle-class organizations, rather than how middle-class activists could support working people with *their* issues and organizations.[4] Thus, the issue of recruiting working people is of some concern.

Snow, Zurcher, and Ekland-Olson (1980: 792) make the proposition that "Those outsiders who are linked to one or more movement members through preexisting extramovement networks will have a greater probability of being contacted and recruited into that particular movement than will those individuals who are outside of members' extramovement networks." Since social barriers exist along class lines, this has significant implications for social movements. Essentially, working-class people are generally not part of what Kriesi (1988) calls movement "subcultures" from which organizations develop their themes and recruit their supporters. As Klandermans and Oegema (1987: 520) put it, "Networks condition whether people become targets of mobilization attempts." Working people are largely outside of such middle-class networks. Thus, working people are not part of some social movements because no one ever asks them.

For example, in a unique study of the mobilization for an anti–cruise missile demonstration in the Netherlands, Klandermans and Oegema (1987) found that agreement regarding the goals of the demonstration existed across class lines but that actual participation in the demonstration was dominated by young, educated professionals. They suggest that the discrepancy can be partially accounted for by looking at recruitment networks. Klandermans and Oegema (1987: 526) conclude that "It is not that more highly educated individuals who are sensitive to political or economic developments create new mobilization potentials but that these individuals are more connected with the social networks engaged in recruitment." More importantly, in this case,

> informal networks restricted themselves to a large extent to the small leftist parties. The composition of the peace platform reproduced itself in the composition of the group reached by mobilization attempts. As a consequence, the subset of the mobilization potential reached by mobilization attempts was biased to the more highly educated, radical left, a make-up much more characteristic for new social movements than the mobilization potential, demonstrating that network factors were responsible for this typical make-up of the constituency rather than factors generating mobilization potentials.

Some of these findings are particular to the European context, but it is quite easy to imagine a similar dynamic occurring in U.S. recruitment efforts. For example, in the U.S. context, McAdam (1988) has shown that personal affiliations with movement participants are important in encouraging individuals to participate in high-risk action. Once again, such affiliations with middle-class activists are less likely to exist for working-class people.

Conversation with activists about their organization's recruitment efforts quickly reveals the processes described above. When asked how they go about recruiting new members activists mention the use of newsletters, flyers, mailings to other organizations' membership lists, ads in newspapers, public events such as "coffeehouses" or lectures, newspaper and local television coverage, and most important, word of mouth. One activist says her group targets influential people.

CARLENE: Teachers, that's one big group. People who are educated; who have influence over others, who come in contact with a lot of different people. Professionals of different types who can influence others. They're the ones we need to target. Community leaders, things like that.

Not surprisingly, such efforts reach a largely middle-class population.

Sometimes even small differences in recruitment techniques can have significant results. Groups that address working-class issues can provide a clue. One middle-class housing activist who worked with a working-class constituency told a story of how he learned such a lesson. His early attempts to generate attendance at informational meetings were failures because he relied upon ads in the local paper. Since, as he later realized, many of the working people he was trying to reach do not read the paper regularly, such ads were ineffective. After several trial-and-error attempts, his group learned that one good way to reach workers was to leaflet at grocery stores in working-class neighborhoods. This simple change in approach achieved positive results for the group. The organization also adopted other strategies to reach out to working and poor constituencies. These include asking for time to do short presentations at meetings of organizations that have working-class membership, and putting together a video featuring some of the working people who belong to the organization. The video is used in house meetings and public presentations.

For the most part, though, middle-class movement activists live and work in isolation from members of the working class. Consequently, their reliance on word-of-mouth communication and on the media to recruit new members does not overcome the class divide.

The problem, noted one activist, is that organizers do not see the class bias in their recruiting techniques. For example, the failures of the freeze movement were cited by several activists as illustrative of the pitfalls associated with a movement whose class base and focus was too narrow. Allan noted that in the aftermath of the freeze's collapse, many local freeze groups became "peace" groups or even "peace-and-justice" groups, signifying the intent, at least, of expanding their focus and reaching out to a more diverse class base. The irony, he noted, is that these groups then went out and organized in exactly the same way that they had for the freeze, thus failing completely in their attempts to diversify. In the end, Allan says, "groups haven't been successful in diversifying because they haven't tried." He argued that the political will simply is not there to actually make changes and explore new possibilities.

The will for change may not be there because movements already spend a surprising amount of their time trying to mobilize their own membership. Groups that are supposed to have members with high interest in political issues often find that, in reality, their own membership is largely inactive. They are, in fact, organizations on paper, holding meetings, producing newsletters and informational leaflets ("education" work, as it is usually called) but actually engaging in very little, if any, political action. Instead, the groups serve largely as an informal social network—a network that often has a distinctly middle-class culture.

Culture.   The problem of class homogeneity in left social movements would not be solved by simply recruiting working people more actively. There are broader issues that discourage working-class participation. One of these is the fact that many social movements have developed distinctly middle-class cultures. Such movement cultures are likely to appear alien to workers and reinforce the notion that political action is pursued by people unlike themselves.

Most activists I spoke with did not see their organization's informal culture as a barrier to class diversity. One who did, however, was an activist who worked for a feminist group that provided "oppression awareness" workshops for the community, exploring issues such as racism, sexism, homophobia, and classism. She told a story describing the period during which the organization's staff seriously examined their *own* practices. To their dismay, they found a whole range of issues that related to class bias.

RUTH: What we found—and I think this is not only our organization—is that we buy into classist myths to some extent—the middle-class myth and all that. We have certain standards that we expect everyone to conform to. . . . It is a middle-class based kind of standard, and it is not affirming of diversity. [This standard includes . . .] ways of talking. There's an expectation that people will kind of use the same lingo, jargon. That somebody who talks a different way, uses different words doesn't really fit in and is expected to conform. . . . Expectations around ways of dressing, around clothing. . . . [T]hat kind of stuff. . . . It's very easy, for example, to expect and assume that everyone's going to assimilate, and if they don't assimilate, they can actually be asked to leave. Or they'll feel that they don't fit in to such a great extent that they'll choose to leave.

Some of these issues are relatively minor, but the total package of middle-class cultural bias adds up to what can be a foreign, if not hostile, environment for anyone but members of the middle class. In fact, the production of collective "identity" associated with NSMs is often an identity that is distinctly alien to working people.

But what may appear to be alien and uncomfortable for working people can seem familiar and reassuring for activists from the middle class. One activist describes her early political experiences this way:

KAREN: [T]he group that I began, the Central America study group, were a group of people in my church, mostly, that I'd known for a long time, felt very good about as human beings, knew that they were people that I respected and liked. The other people who came as part of the group were also people that share the same set of values I shared in terms of life and behavior and all this kind of thing. So as a group it was easier for us. It wouldn't have been easy if it had been a group of people that were from a different class or from a different social background. You need to feel comfortable with the people that feel like-minded. You need to feel a sense of them sharing your values and your set of behaviors, the kinds of behaviors that feel comfortable.

Adam, a Central America activist, agreed, conceding, "When you get right down to it, it's hard to work with people who are different from you. It's a lot easier to support people who are different if they live a couple of thousand miles away in Central America or South Africa or somewhere." Thus, the very cultural characteristics that may make an organization a comfortable "home" for middle-class activists may serve to alienate potential working-class supporters. This sense of insularity has of course been noted in relation to race and gender issues. It should also be recognized in terms of class.

Rather than class, the cultural diversity issue most cited by activists in my interviews might be described as the debate between the "straights" and "radicals"—both contingents firmly rooted in the middle class. A "straight" approach is described as presenting an organization as a middle-class, mainstream group in an attempt to appeal to a broader spectrum of moderate citizens. The "radical" approach is to simply acknowledge the progressive nature of an organization and its politics and to accept the often "countercultural" aspect of its middle-class members whose appearance and politics may be outside of the mainstream.[5] The latter strategy has the advantage of providing a comfortable cultural home for middle-class members who are challenging mainstream political and cultural conventions. At the same time, though, it carries the danger of exacerbating the Left's isolation from the more mainstream middle class and from many working people.

Some of the activists I interviewed cited the nuclear freeze campaign as an example of an organization that had tried hard to appeal to "straight" mainstream citizens. By contrast, the antinuclear Clamshell Alliance was often portrayed as the classic radical, countercultural group. During the campaign against Seabrook, the conservative *Manchester Union Leader,* New Hampshire's only statewide daily newspaper, had often portrayed Clamshell members in its editorial cartoons as long-haired, hippie throwbacks to the '60s. But activists who were central to the organization contest this perception.

GUS: [Clamshell was] a broad-based movement. I mean we're talking about being able to sit in on meetings with middle class *and* upper class. When you're talking about endangering our seacoast, everybody's at stake. I think that Seabrook has borne out that we weren't just "back to the cave" types.

The consideration of diversity, then, is too often limited to discussing diversity *within* the middle class or, in the case above, apparently equating the middle and upper class with "everybody." Debates on political strategies and cultural appearances fuel the perception that there are significant differences amongst the people involved. Often, however, the differences are more slight than might first appear.

Earlier in my discussion of issue salience, I alluded to another part of movement culture that contributes to the Left's isolation from workers—that many left social movements are perceived to be pursuing a politics of privilege. In "rejecting" their middle-class backgrounds, committed activists often give up the possibility of substantial material affluence (though few embrace truly modest lifestyles and nearly all maintain a "safety net" of associations with family and friends who have middle-class means).[6] What they do not—and indeed cannot—renounce, however, is the cultural heritage of their middle-class status. The education, cultural skills, and expectations of middle-class life are a legacy that cannot simply be denied at will. These are the benchmarks that make activists forever middle class, even in the midst of voluntary material modesty.

The rejection of the material component of middle-class life, coupled with the retention of the cultural elements (often with a middle-class "counter-cultural" slant), puts activists at double odds with workers. First, activists often do not recognize the cultural/knowledge gap of which workers are painfully aware, and second, activists sometimes reject the material comforts for which most workers are adamantly striving. The positioning of middle-class activists who are critical of their class background, then, seems very peculiar indeed from the perspective of many workers.

Efficacy. Finally, some social movements that address issues of salience to working people still end up as middle-class movements because they are unable to overcome the sense of political inefficacy that pervades working-class culture. The inefficacy experienced by workers has two key dimensions. First, as noted above, working people are skeptical of the possibility of realistic solutions, and they are distrustful of the various actors promoting change. Working people tend to believe that the problems that face our society are intractable and that current efforts by politicians and social movements are incapable of achieving change. Thus, they see the efforts of others as inefficacious.

Second, and more significant, working people do not have a sense that *they* can take meaningful part in efforts for change. Instead, they follow an individualized strategy of cultivating private life in an effort to protect their interests. In my opinion, much of this sense of inefficacy on the part of working people comes from a relatively accurate reading of the contemporary social and political context. This broader environment is one that is largely devoid of strong social and political institutions based in the working class. Consequently, it is one in which the voices and interests of working people are often unheard. It is to this larger environment to which I now turn my attention.

The Social and Political Environment

It cannot be convincingly argued that workers are quiescent solely because they lack adequate education, resources, or skills—a sort of "blaming the victim" approach. Such an argument flies in the face of a history filled with examples of working people actively engaging in politics. Indeed, one of the lessons to be learned from the historical evolution of social movements in the United States is that there is no inherent connection between someone's class position and the level of his or her political participation. For a long time, the Left's social vision was carried forward to a large degree by movements based in the working class, whereas more recently, middle-class movements have moved to center stage.

The accuracy of "blaming" working people is also contradicted by the existence of more vibrant working-class political cultures in other countries, pointing instead to the significance of the political and social environment in influencing political participation.

Understanding the forces that help shape middle-class social movements in the United States and that discourage working-class political participation requires looking beyond these movements to the broader social and political environment. Some relevant issues in this environment include electoral politics, the labor movement, the state of working-class institutions, and the impact of race. These are issues that extend well beyond the scope of my limited study, but I will take the liberty here of making some speculative observations regarding the future of political participation.

Electoral Politics

Working people see the political environment as being, at best, indifferent to their concerns. They often feel that, beyond taxes, what passes as "politics" in this country has very little impact on their lives. They know that although politicians *talk* about key issues such as jobs, health care, taxes, welfare reform, education, and crime, in the end—regardless of who is elected—very little ever seems to change fundamentally. As a result, the workers I spoke with show decided skepticism and a lack of interest toward the mainstream political world. The political realm does not speak to them, and they see no role for themselves in this arena. For many working people, nothing seems to be gained by their voting, and nothing seems to be lost by their staying home.

The traditional SES model of electoral participation must be tempered by the recognition that it is not socioeconomic status per se that influences participation, but rather the response of members of a socioeconomic class to the political arena *as currently constituted*. For example, in summarizing his findings of voter turnout, Avey (1989: 22) argues: "[T]he most useful way to conceptualize the relationship between SES and turnout is: (1) parties and social movements mobilize mostly high SES; (2) government responds to high SES; (3) those with high SES have more reason to participate; (4) SES belief systems expect government to have a bias in favor of high SES; (5) therefore there is SES bias in turnout." Such an analysis recognizes nonparticipation as a sane response to a system that does not meet the needs of workers. Gans (1988: 155), too, suggests that those interested in liberal politics need to recognize the rational choice being made by Americans who avoid politics.

> People who lack reasonable control over their environment and power over their employers and the holders of political office, and who doubt that they could change society even if they could organize, calculate that relying on their own efforts and the people they trust may get them close to what they want. Unable to risk the failure of collective action, unwilling to be dependent on organizers and political leaders who may ask them to rearrange their routines of living, conform to the organizational needs of the group, and consider new political values, they choose self-reliance with all its faults. In terms of their own, middle American values, their calculus is rational more often than not!

This rational response reflects some unique features of U.S. political culture and not some inevitable connection between socioeconomic status and political participation. In contrast, Flacks (1988: 27) notes that "working-class members can be highly motivated to political responsibility and activism is more evident in European countries where parties and traditions of working-class politics have developed over more than a century."

One of the unusual aspects of U.S. electoral politics is the absence of a working-class-based party. Some would argue that the Democratic Party once served a largely working-class constituency. But even the Democratic Party has now distanced itself from its former working-class and organized labor base. The result has left working people with no serious electoral options to two business-dominated parties. It should come as no surprise, then, that U.S. workers have a difficult time mustering enthusiasm for elections and tend to stay away from these periodic rituals.

Verba and Nie (1972: 340–41) suggest, "If there were more class-based ideologies, more class-based organizations, more explicit class-based appeal by political parties, the participation disparity between upper- and lower-status citizens would very likely be less." In fact, summarizing existing work on voter turnout, Zipp, Landerman, and Luebke (1982: 1140) note that "for most of Western Europe, working-class voting levels are as high or higher than those of the middle class, and this often is explained by the fact that political parties and organizations mobilize the working class."

In the United States, party voting is less closely associated with class membership than in other democracies. In other countries, class divisions are revealed by *which party* citizens vote for. Compared to the pattern in other countries, the U.S. pattern reveals relatively little class difference between Republican and Democratic voters. Instead, in the U.S. context, class divisions are revealed by *whether or not* citizens vote. Summarizing the argument of Walter Dean Burnham, Vanneman and Cannon (1987: 11) conclude, "precisely that type of voter who in Europe votes for socialist and Social Democratic parties, is the one who, in the United States, doesn't vote at all." With little to command their loyalty, workers tend to stay home on election day. This pattern is understood by the established parties who know they can ignore working-class concerns with relative impunity, thus reinforcing workers' perceptions that the electoral arena is unresponsive.

The result is an electoral climate of relative indifference towards working people. Workers often do not see their views and interests well represented and conclude that political participation is of little benefit. In turn, by their nonparticipation, working people help to reproduce a self-fulfilling prophecy.

The Left has been divided on what should be done in the unusual climate of U.S. electoral politics. Some activists have focused on strategies that operate completely outside of electoral politics. Skeptical of working in the "system," they have instead concentrated their energies on pursuing efforts that operate largely independently of the electoral sphere. Some grassroots strategies, for example, rely on the organization of people to work in civil society and sometimes to influence those in power, but their aim is not to elect new representatives. The electoral arena is often seen as "tainted" with compromise, requiring the moderation of political views for success. It is also seen as an unproductive place for the use of limited resources.

Other activists have made electoral politics at least a part of their activism. While often not entirely trusting the electoral system, these activists have seen the potential impact of key electoral victories and do incorporate electoral politics into their action repertoire. Even these activists, though, vary in their relationships with the electoral arena.

The most straightforward involvement by progressives in electoral politics is through supporting individual candidates who run in one of the two major parties. This candidate-driven approach is perhaps the simplest, since it can utilize existing party structures (though often with resistance from the party establishment). This approach also has the advantage of implementation on the local level, where the chance of success may well be highest. However, such an approach is piecemeal at best and unlikely to yield long-term results. Changing select officeholders does nothing to change the larger balance of power in society, nor does it necessarily nurture more active citizen organization.

Some activists argue that the existing parties will never serve as an adequate home for progressive politics and thus should be bypassed. They argue instead for the development of a new, third party, often envisioned as representing the broad interests of middle-class progressives, working people, and people of color. A number of such efforts have been attempted in recent decades, and this strategy continues to be pursued today. (Some small, third-party efforts are intended more as a way to raise issues rather than as serious attempts to gain election.) Although there is clearly truth in the argument that the politics of the two major parties are largely bankrupt, the establishment of a serious third-party effort is likely to require more resources and a more broad-based, engaged constituency than currently exists. This approach is putting the party cart before the organizational horse.

Finally, the strategy most likely to yield benefits is that of developing, within the existing two-party structure, progressive coalitions based in community organizations and the labor movement. Such coalitions would help organize and support the major-party campaigns of progressives from member organizations and are already underway in a number of states (Shapiro 1990). However, *the success of this approach is dependent on the strength of the coalition members as social-movement organizations independent of their electoral role.* The influence such an electoral coalition may have is based, not on the traditional source of party power—money, but rather in the old-fashioned source of democratic power: the ability to organize and mobilize people.

The use of separate member organizations in coalition may facilitate the participation of a more diverse constituency than a single-party effort. The utilization of existing party structures will inevitably create frustrations but will provide advantages by reducing the need for re-creating existing structures. But electoral politics cannot be the sole focus of these coalitions. Instead, they need to function as a way to channel the electoral concerns of organizations that have a larger social agenda. However, the long-term benefits of electoral cooperation may well spill over into the other work in which these groups engage, and, if successful, may serve as the framework for launching a third party in the future.

The absence of responsive political parties might seem to put social movements in a strong position to recruit disaffected workers. But instead, when social movements attempt to convince working people of the utility of political participation, they usually face the daunting task of overcoming the legacy of skepticism fostered by an indifferent electoral arena.

The Labor Movement and Working-Class Organizations   •

If the electoral arena is unresponsive to working-class interests, and middle-class social movements seem unable to reach out effectively to working people, one might suspect that the labor movement would serve as a natural home for working-class politics. For some Americans it does. But more often, the labor movement has failed to be an effective vehicle for progressive working-class politics both because unions have too often abandoned their larger social vision and, more generally, because unions have been struggling for their very survival in an unfavorable political and economic climate.

As discussed in Chapter Two, labor unions in the United States have been decimated in recent decades. The reasons cited for drastically declining membership are many (Cornfield 1991: 29). The movement of mobile capital to nonunion states and foreign countries is one contributing factor. So is the more general shift in the U.S. economy away from manufacturing, where unions were strongest, to service and "knowledge-based" employment. More active "union busting" by employees has been aided by a conservative, pro-business political climate and a hostile National Labor Relations Board. Workers have expressed skepticism about the utility of joining unions. Unions themselves have been criticized for being, among other things, rigid, bureaucratic, and undemocratic. Finally, the diversity of the U.S. working class—encompassing many different racial and ethnic groups—has been seen as a hurdle to successful organizing efforts.

Whatever the reasons for labor's decline, the fact is that unions that once could have been a working-class alternative to middle-class social movements have largely abandoned their role as true "social movements" in favor of more limited service to their members on issues of wages and working conditions. This limitation has had a profound effect on the political landscape.

But employment remains a common experience for working people, and the workplace continues to offer great opportunity as a site for organization and mobilization. Progressive organizations that represent the interest of workers are simply a necessity in capitalist societies.[7] Aronowitz (1984: 267) summarizes:

> there is little chance that a new politics will be born . . . until labor becomes a "movement" again. That is, the chance for reconstituting the progressive coalition depends on whether millions of workers can be brought into unions from the new, growing sectors and, having been unionized, are subject to a coherent progressive ideology and program that, at least, provides an alternative to the dominant conservative economic and social discourse. No other force in society can provide the counterweight to the finances, the command over media and the sheer economic and ideological power of giant corporations and neoconservative institutions. The illusion of the Sixties that strong feminist, minority and antiwar coalitions could displace the "labor bureaucracy" as the core of a new politics has been definitively shattered in the wake of the progressive defeats of the last decade.

The revitalization of labor unions, therefore, must be seen as a key component of a left strategy for encouraging working-class empowerment.

Strengthening unions will require that they become democratic organizations open to the needs and desires of the rank and file—not an easy task given the entrenched and unelected bureaucracies of many unions. It will also require labor law reforms such as making scabs (so-called permanent replacement workers) illegal, removing Taft-Hartley restrictions on sympathy strikes and boycotts, and most important, protecting the rights of workers to organize without reprisal from their employers. Geoghegan (1991: 276) puts it well: "I can think of nothing, no law, no civil rights act, that would radicalize this country more, democratize it more, and also revive the Democratic Party, than to make this one tiny change in the law: to let people join unions if they like, freely and without coercion, without threat of being fired, just as people are permitted to do in Europe and Canada."

Although there is much discussion about the best form for revitalized worker organizations, it is clear that unions must become bridges to political action rather than just servicing agencies. In other countries, organized labor has used a two-prong approach to organizing, relying on unions to organize workers in the workplace but also using labor-based political parties to pursue a broader political and social agenda. Lacking a labor-based party or a labor movement actively pursuing such goals, workers in the United States have depended almost exclusively on union contracts to secure better wages and working conditions. This single-approach strategy, which fails to codify their rights in the political realm, has not only left out the majority of workers not covered by union contracts (thus fostering working-class resentment of a privileged union sector), but in recent years it has also left unionized workers at the mercy of corporate and political attacks.

The current crisis in health care is an example of the pitfalls of struggling for benefits on a workplace-by-workplace basis rather than striving for politically guaranteed national rights for workers. Unions negotiated health-care coverage for their workers on a workplace-by-workplace basis, leaving unorganized workers at the mercy of the their employers—and resentful of union benefits. When the economic and political climate turned against organized labor's arrangements, employers were able—one by one—to gain concessions and givebacks from weakened unions.

Pursuing labor politics in the political arena provides the opportunity for more coalition efforts that can bring together middle- and working-class organizations. The primary reliance on workplace contracts has made it difficult for sympathetic middle-class organizations to provide much in the way of support for working-class struggles. The exceptions have been strategies such as "corporate campaigns" and other community-labor alliances that have attempted to reach out to community organizations for support of labor struggles (Brecher and Costello 1990).

One labor activist who works with a labor-community coalition offers a strategic analysis of the reasons for union involvement in such efforts. He thinks that unions believe their enemies are out to destroy them totally. As a result,

DOUG: I think the more progressive people have decided to try and do something about it and are more willing to reach out. Sometimes I think the mainline union people are just trying to mark time and hope that it will go away or else that they'll retire and they won't have to worry about it anymore. Some of them just don't know what to do about it. But that's only one part. There's massive changes, I perceive, in society, the economy, and all that kind of stuff. I think that labor's got to change. But I don't know if that's got to do with [coalition efforts]. This is just a tool for us to be able to gain some strength right now. To be able to gain some strength so that we can achieve our goals.

But, *by themselves,* coalition efforts are unlikely to revitalize working-class political life. For one reason, working-class participation already tends to be limited to union members, and it is a mistake to equate the working-class with existing unions.

What is also needed in the long run is attention to the invigoration of both democratic unions and broader working-class political and community organizations. Such organizations would pursue cultural as well as economic and political goals. This holistic approach is more likely to sustain movements through political droughts and make full use of workers' abilities. Rather than a single organization, strength and diversity are more likely to arise from a confederation of local organizations. This confederation would allow for recruitment and membership in various subcultures including communities of color and white ethnic communities.

As part of an affirmative politics, working-class organizations should help nurture the positive values and culture of working people. Such a task may involve what appear to be decidedly nonpolitical endeavors including social events, church, and school functions. It is crucial, though, that we broaden our conception of what is "political" and recognize the importance of developing community as an intermediate political goal.

Indigenous Institutions

Workers who find no hope in either the electoral system, left movements, or the labor movement have little to give them comfort in other social or political institutions. The de-industrialization of America coupled with increased suburbanization and the proliferation of mass-media entertainment has struck a devastating blow to what used to be vibrant working-class communities.

The dispersal of white workers into suburbia has meant more isolated, privatized lives for those who leave the city and has contributed to more extreme and desperate lives for those who remain to deal with declining local economies and rising crime. The loss of good-paying, blue-collar industrial jobs has been accompanied by the rise of lower-paying, service-sector jobs and by the increasing prevalence of single-parent families, or families where both parents work outside the home. Such conditions cut into the availability of time for volunteering with school, church, and other community groups.

Finally, the proliferation of mass media, especially television and VCRs, has facilitated privatized entertainment and leisure and contributed to the corresponding loss of public forms of socializing and entertainment.

The loss of community institutions is a devastating development for social movements since successful movements often tap into existing social networks for recruits and resources. The labor movement, for example, drew upon the institutions of ethnic enclaves for support. Workers were usually organized on the basis of such ethnic identities rather than on purely class lines. Aronowitz (1992: 37) observes: "Social clubs, civic associations, and political organizations were frequently organized along subcultural rather than overtly class lines, even if their composition was delineated by class membership. . . . The local branch of Polish, Ukranian, or Russian-based national 'home,' equipped with a bar, dance hall, and meeting rooms, provided the gathering place within which politics as well as friendships were forged." The absence of such vibrant institutions often has left the white working class adrift and without strong institutional supports.

Research has shown that indigenous institutions play a crucial role in engaging citizens in political action. Such affiliations are important in bridging the class gap in participation. With electoral participation, Verba and Nie (1972: 203) note that organization affiliation "works in the direction of lowering the participation gap between upper- and lower-status citizens. If a lower-status citizen becomes an active organization member he is much more like a comparable upper-status citizen in terms of participation than if he is a nonmember."

A similar phenomenon affects social-movement efforts. Drawing heavily on resource mobilization theory, Aldon Morris (1984) argues for an "indigenous perspective" to understand social movements by dominated groups.[8] Morris (282) argues that sustained social movements within a particular dominated community are dependent on "(1) certain basic resources, (2) social activists with strong ties to mass-based indigenous institutions, and (3) tactics and strategies that can be effectively employed against a system of domination."

The role of existing institutions, in this perspective, is vital (Morris 1984: 282): "The basic resources enabling a dominated group to engage in sustained protest are well-developed internal social institutions and organizations that provide the community with encompassing communication networks, organized groups, experienced leaders, and social resources, including money, labor, and charisma, that can be mobilized to attain collective goals." The absence of such strong institutions in most working-class communities makes the development of working-class movements very difficult. Not only do indigenous institutions provide the resources cited above but they also serve as a base from which activists can work. Morris (1984: 283) suggests that "In order for activists to mobilize indigenous resources they must have access to them. Therefore, activists who have strong ties to mass-based indigenous institutions are in an advantageous position to mobilize a community for collective protest." As working people have become increasingly isolated from such institutions, they have become more difficult to reach.

The relative absence of organizations that speak to the needs of working people and the lessons of movement history do not bode well for the mobilization of workers in the near future. Certainly, there are community organizations that are able to serve as vehicles of empowerment for a limited number of working people. Too often though, such organizations have used members as little more than pocketbooks and foot soldiers.

Gans (1988: 77–78), for example, notes that with the largest national federations of community organizations, ACORN and Citizen Action, "their main strengths are their professional organizers" who "make the plans and decisions, so that often the elected leaders are little more than figureheads. The memberships function largely as an infantry. . . . Their achievements are in many ways impressive, but they too have not persuaded many middle Americans to stop practicing political avoidance." Although there are important lessons to be learned from such organizations, they are unlikely to be the future of politics for the white working class.

The absence of a clear institutional base for mobilization suggests two bleak possibilities. First, it may well be that we are entering a time of postmodern politics where citizens will no longer be organized through their physical interaction but rather through their interface with communication networks. Conservatives in the United States have effectively utilized, for example, direct-mail databases to target, solicit, and mobilize citizens, bypassing institutional structures. Perhaps such tactics are just the beginning. It may be that in the not-too-distant future, electronic town halls, cable-access programming, and computer-based networking will be the only remnant of democratic political discourse left in this country. The days of political meetings and rallies may become a quaint artifact of history. But such a politics is unlikely to fulfill the mandate of a truly democratic politics. Instead, electronic balloting, media polling, and television-town meetings are more likely to trivialize politics and further transform citizens into consumers of centrally developed ideas. It is difficult to imagine a truly interactive communication system that can stand in for the give-and-take of face-to-face encounters. It is even more difficult to imagine working people competing on an even footing with the middle class in gaining access to and utilizing such a communications network.

There is a second and darker possibility for a postmodern politics that has been addressed by Jean Baudrillard (1983). Although fraught with many conceptual difficulties, Baudrillard's thesis suggests the possibility of only further alienation and silence on the part of the "masses" leading to the "absorption and implosion" of the social. Extrapolating for my own purposes, I would argue that Baudrillard's notions suggest, in effect, that if political and social systems cannot be changed through participation, they may simply collapse as a result of silence and refusal—a kind of politics undreamed of by movement activists. The loss of legitimacy resulting from escalating levels of electoral nonparticipation, for example, may ironically be the impetus for change. Although a legitimation crisis arising from nonparticipation is certainly a possibility, the direction of resulting change is unpredictable. A romanticized notion of silence and refusal may, in effect, underestimate fascistic possibilities. Certainly, this vision of the future should be of no comfort for those interested in revitalizing democracy.

The Role of Race

Race relations in the United States are another element of the social and political environment that must be noted. Since my focus has been on the relationship between white workers and the largely white, middle-class Left, the relationship between workers of color and whites has not been a central theme. But being white *is,* in and of itself, a racial issue in the United States, and race and class issues have become deeply intertwined.

For much of the white working class, race is one more characteristic that designates "others"—people unlike themselves—creating a distance that separates working people who otherwise might have a great deal in common. When looking at the political scene, people of color (and their middle-class, liberal allies) seem to have a civil rights agenda that, once again, does not represent the needs or interests of white workers.

Thomas and Mary Edsall (1991) contend that the Democratic Party has lost white, working-class voters because it has been seen as the party of blacks and special interests.[9] Republicans have used race effectively to split the New Deal economic base (working/lower middle class) of the Democratic Party.

The use of race as a divisive tactic has been successful for several reasons. First, there is a long and not easily transformed history of racism that has plagued American society in general and undermined working-class solidarity in particular. Opponents of working people have fueled the fires of this racism.

Second, affirmative action decisions tend to threaten jobs and opportunities of working-class whites, not the white liberal elites who are seen as promoting such programs. The most extensive race-based workplace affirmative action efforts have occurred with traditionally working-class jobs such as police officers and firefighters. Well-reasoned intellectual arguments about the legacy of white oppression and the biased nature of civil service exams are small comfort for white workers who see some of their few secure employment opportunities endangered. The fact that relatively few white workers are actually affected by such policies does not diminish the symbolic importance of such programs. Many working people interpret affirmative action as giving preference to minorities because of the color of their skin—a direct contradiction of the "color-blind" society most workers would say they support. One need not be an opponent of affirmative action in principle to see the difficulties in practice it raises for some white workers. Simply dismissing such criticisms as racism does not do justice to the complexity of the issue.[10]

Third, working-class resentment of increasing taxes is often directed towards government spending aimed at the poor (read: black and Hispanic) as much as it is at giveaways for the rich. Resentment of the poor is in many ways easier to conceptualize. Some able-bodied people do not work and are supported by taxpayer money. Corporate giveaways, tax breaks for the wealthy, and middle-class mortgage allowances account for vastly greater transfers of tax dollars, but these tend to be shrouded in the fine print of tax codes and legislative initiatives. I suspect that if we lived in a single-race society, welfare recipients would still be resented by those who see themselves as struggling hard for a living. The complication of racism occurs when people of color are assumed to be poor, and vice versa. Here, too, the issue of race has been used to fan the fires of what in many ways is a resentment based on class.

The history of working-class organizations has too often been tainted by racism. When white workers have organized they have sometimes consolidated their security at the expense of workers of color (and women). The racist practices of some unions have left a legacy of mistrust and division between workers of color and whites. Those in positions of power have often exploited these divisions at the expense of working-class solidarity. The class divide, then, is profoundly affected by race, and the racial divide carries overtones of class.

Conclusion

Those concerned with the future of democratic politics should not ignore the impact of class status on how people tend to view and relate to political life. Some of these effects are materially based. Political participation can be facilitated or impeded depending upon such factors as the amount of available money and free time, access to formal education, and location in particular social networks (which is relevant to recruitment).

However, the cultural heritage of class status that is developed from these material differences is at least as important. Middle-class activists tend to focus either on material explanations for the absence of working-class participation, or on working-class conservatism. They tend to underemphasize the importance of cultural differences.

The cultural "tools" developed in different classes are more or less helpful in navigating and influencing the political world. Middle-class forms of knowledge, communication, and sense of efficacy tend to be a better "fit" with the social and political environment as it is currently constructed. The skills and resources working people bring have a more difficult time finding a home in the contemporary political landscape.

At first glance, the political orientations prevalent amongst working people do not suggest likely participation. Working people tend to: (1) be critical of politicians and the political system; (2) show little interest in politics; (3) be fatalistic about the possibility of effecting change either by themselves or by others—including social movements.

But in large measure these characteristics are a response to a political environment that: (1) does not meet the needs of working people and is often perceived as unfair; (2) is full of deceptive rhetoric and does not offer meaningful opportunity for participation; and (3) seems impervious to successful attempts at change.

Too often, the attempt to create a better "fit" between working people and the political environment has been pursued by trying to transform working people into the image of middle-class activists via "education" efforts and other means. Instead, there is a need to nurture a more hospitable environment of social and political organizations that speak more directly to the needs of working people, in a style accessible to them, and that are composed in large measure of working people like themselves. Ideally, such organizations can serve as a home for working people to exercise the skills, knowledge, and insights they already have. This sort of environment does not, of course, preclude the need for continuing education and the development of socially useful skills, but it does not make the possession of middle-class skills the necessary ticket of admission to social movements either.

Working people cannot be expected to use "new" social movements as a base for their political activity. Middle-class efforts to diversify their groups by trying to bring working people into existing organizations are misdirected. Some of the issues that such movements address and the cultural overtones of these middle-class groups are simply not salient to workers. The peace, anti-intervention, and much of the environmental movement, for example, are likely to continue to be the realm of middle-class politics.

The political mobilization of working people is more likely to take place utilizing existing networks and institutions. The dearth of vibrant working-class institutions suggests that the workplace will continue to be the site of most opportunity. Consequently, the reconstruction of labor unions into democratic social movements remains a key item on the Left's agenda. Unions must shed their "business union" limitations and move towards coordinating their protection of workers in the workplace with a broader vision for social change that is carried out in the political arena. The importance, therefore, of issues such as labor law reform, the democratization of union structures, and the broadening of organizing efforts in response to the changing economy has potential reverberations that reach well beyond the labor community.

With the pressures brought on by mobile capital in a global economy, labor can no longer expect to go it alone successfully in the political world. It must recognize the importance of reaching out to other progressive social-movement organizations, many of which are based in the middle class.

Middle-class movements similarly need to recognize the importance of reaching out beyond their currently narrow constituency. Their issue focus and style of organizing are, and will continue to be, largely alien to working people. However, they need to incorporate into their work a greater consciousness of the repercussions of their efforts for working people. More concretely, they need to build bridges with labor and other working-class-based movements, most likely in coalition efforts. In the current political and economic climate, coalition efforts of working-class and middle-class movements—rather than the development of a single multiclass organization—offer the most likelihood of success.

There needs to be eventual development, however, of coalition efforts that go beyond local, regional, and state projects. The economic environment is increasingly determined by international treaties and organizations. As long as capital is global, and many policy directives federal, the Left cannot remain local. The coordination of national and even international efforts, therefore, must be on the Left's long-term agenda.

The reality of the global economic and political climate, coupled with the reality of the constraints facing working people, means that organization building must be seen as having two distinct though interrelated components. First, there is a need for the development of accessible local and regional organizations whose task is to organize and mobilize people directly. Second, though, there is also a need for the development of democratically accountable organizational structures that will represent the interests of working people in the larger national and international arena. Thus, the ultimate goal is a political structure that serves both mobilizing and mediation functions.

It has been a long time since the labor movement has led the Left, and too often, stereotypes of a monolithic, conservative, white working class populate our political landscape. These working-class stereotypes—like all stereotypes— do not hold up to scrutiny, but their influence comes from providing observers with powerful and widely recognized shorthand symbols. Little else needs to be said when referring to white working people as Archie Bunkers, rednecks, or hard hats. These dismissive terms—used at times by the most "progressive" of leftists—imply an inevitable quality about the conservative elements in white working-class culture. Such a belief, however, is mistaken.

There are substantial areas of potential overlap between the Left's promotion of democracy and the needs and interests of working people. Working people are aware of a wide range of social and political problems in this country that need to be addressed. They are not happy with the status quo. But workers must be convinced that meaningful change is possible and that they can be part of it. The deep distrust and skepticism about government and all things political that characterizes working-class culture is a problem for activists trying to encourage political participation. But it also suggests that there is a well-established recognition of the need for change—and thus fertile ground for potential activism.

Progressive politics are not an end but rather a means to achieving substantial results that help to protect and enhance the quality of daily life for people. Jobs and the economy are high on the list of worker concerns, but so are health care, taxes, child care, welfare, education, affordable housing, and crime. It is these sorts of issues that are likely to be of most salience to workers and that offer the most promising opportunity for progressive movements.

The Left cannot succeed by promoting an oppositional politics that merely points out the faults of the status quo and opposes existing policy. Working people are already all too aware of the shortcomings of the existing political system. Instead, a left politics must become a politics of affirmation; a politics that affirms basic values of justice and fairness *in practice* and pursues constructive programs for change that enhance the quality of daily life at work, at home, and in the community.

Activists who recognize the problem with the narrow class membership of the Left generally are not optimistic about changing the situation. One peace activist told me that faced with the daunting task of mobilizing their existing middle-class constituency, her organization never got to the point of reaching out to new people or working with groups that had a different constituency. She admitted, "Something else always seems to get priority." But if the Left is to develop a democratic movement for political and economic justice that reaches beyond the middle class, efforts that support the empowerment of working people must once again become a priority.

The conditions under which individuals labor and live are now largely determined by forces that are national and international in scope. If the Left is to succeed in responding to such large-scale forces, it cannot do so as a movement divided by the fractures that plague our society—including that of class. Progressive democratic politics can succeed in building a more just society only if social movements begin to reach across the class divide.

Class: Structure and Collective Action

My discussion in Chapter One of the relationship between class and politics draws upon existing class theory. This appendix examines some of these theories in more detail.

The Concept of Class

Class is perhaps one of the most "successful" sociological concepts in terms of its adoption in popular discourse. However, it is often unclear precisely what is meant when someone uses the term "class." The ambiguity that popularly accompanies the term is understandable, given the diverse and sometimes vague interpretations class has received within academic disciplines.

Perhaps we should not be surprised at the uncertainty associated with "class" since the appearance of the term itself, argues Lewis Coser (1973: 441), resulted from a sense of growing ambiguity about social divisions. "Class" is a less definite and more fluid term than "rank" or "order," and the use of this less specific term subtly indicates the erosion since the Industrial Revolution of the earlier clear-cut hierarchical rank order that used to govern English social structure and a shifting of focus from social status to economic criteria. Despite this shift of focus, however, "class" continues to be used in different perspectives to mean either or both a position in social hierarchy (e.g., "middle class") or a relationship to the means of production (e.g., "working class").[1] Different notions regarding the relative importance of social versus economic criteria are often what lie behind different perspectives on the concept of class.

There are four major approaches to understanding class (Wright 1979). First, some argue that class is merely a functional differentiation of positions within a society (Davis and Moore 1945; Parsons 1975). This perspective suggests that, as Davis and Moore (244) put it, "Social inequality is . . . an unconsciously evolved device by which societies ensure that the most important positions are conscientiously filled by the most qualified persons." Although differences are acknowledged to exist in the various societal strata, there does not necessarily exist a sense of injustice or conflict resulting from these differences. The many difficulties with this orientation, including its assumption of the universality of a definite system of societal ranks, its assumption of the unambiguous nature of "most important positions" and "most qualified persons," and its overemphasis on individuals rather than group phenomena, have been elaborated upon elsewhere (Tumin 1953) and need not detain me here.

A second approach to class recognizes an element of contention in social divisions. Adherents of this perspective describe classes as conflict groups unified by their common position in a hierarchy of power or authority. For example, writing in the late nineteenth century, Pareto (1966) argued for a form of social division based on power and comprised of "governing elites" and nonelites. Such a vision of relatively undifferentiated masses, who were unfit to govern themselves, left a good deal to be desired. Dahrendorf's (1959) conflict theory, by contrast, saw authority attached to *positions,* rather than people, and argued that this was the key to understanding the development of dichotomous interests and conflict within any association. But this approach has been critiqued for, among other things, its deficient adaptation of Marxist principles—despite its claims to the contrary (Hazelrigg 1972), its overreliance on discredited structural functionalist precepts (Weingart 1969), and its tendency to equalize all types of associations and their resulting conflict.

A third approach to understanding classes comes from the work of Weber (1946), who argued that classes are groups with different market capacities which result in different "life-chances." Although capital is one source of market capacity, Weber argues that skill and education are another. Weber proposed a four-class social system (propertied, intelligentsia, petty bourgeoisie, working) and suggested that class conflict is common and is most likely to occur between groups with immediately opposed interests.

Finally, a fourth approach to understanding class is that of Marxists who argue that classes are defined by a shared location in the social organization of production and that class relations are inherently antagonistic (Wright 1980, 1985). Wright says (1989b: 269), "At the core of Marxian class analysis is the claim that class is a fundamental determinant of social conflict and social change." Capitalist societies, according to traditional Marxism, are characterized by two antagonistic classes; those that own the means of production (capitalists) and those that do not (proletariat).

The distinctions between these perspectives are not insignificant for the work of social movements. A perspective that treats class differences as simple gradations in social strata may suggest a neutral and functional differentiation devoid of conflict or exploitation. Thus, a gradational view of class is not likely to engender a mobilizing frame. However, when the meaning of "class" goes beyond mere differentiation and suggests a hierarchical, value-laden system based on inequality, notions of injustice and collective grievances may be fostered. These notions may form the basis for social-movement mobilization.

For example, while describing class structure with the popular and suggestively dispassionate term "stratification," Davis and Moore (1945: 242) are able to argue that no society is unstratified and that one can use "functional terms" to explain "the universal necessity which calls forth stratification in any social system."

In contrast, Davis and Moore's faceless "universal necessity" is replaced in Marx's work by a vivid portrait of an insatiable capitalist class described as "werewolves" and "vampires" in *Capital* (1977). By revealing the exploitative nature of class relations, Marx and Engels (1978: 473–74) were able to argue that "[t]he history of all hitherto society is the history of class struggles" and to contend that capitalism has merely "established new classes, new conditions of oppression, new forms of struggle in place of the old ones." Although Marx also used a more complex scheme of class analysis in his less rhetorical work, his emphasis on the exploitive nature of class relations remained constant.

Therefore, for the history of social movements the differences in the conceptualization of class are not mere semantics. They carry profound implications for notions of social justice and for movement mobilization.

Marx and Class Theory

Although I will be departing significantly from its "orthodox" form and will adopt ideas associated more often with Weber, I base my discussion of class primarily in the Marxist tradition. It is important, therefore, to elaborate on this perspective.

For Marx (1978b: 179), "separate individuals form a class only insofar as they have to carry on a common battle against another class; otherwise they are on hostile terms with each other as competitors." This is his concept of a class "for itself," which was his paramount concern since he was primarily interested in the *development* of classes and in their role in bringing about social and political change. However, in much of my analysis I am referring to what Marx would have labeled a class "in itself," that is, a class based on objective economic criteria. This distinction should be kept in mind.

Despite the fact that it was a central concept in his analysis of history, Marx never fully developed a theory of class. What he meant by the term has to be inferred from his many writings on related issues, especially production.

Production

Inequality in societies, argued Marx, arises from the social organization of production. The "mode of production" refers generally to the manner in which a society organizes its productive activities. The mode of production can be broken down into its two components, the "forces of production" and the "relations of production." The forces of production refers to the machinery and instruments of technology that are used in the production process. The relations of production refers to the social arrangements established to produce and distribute goods. These relations are malleable and are influenced by the forces of production prevalent in an historical era. Thus, the rise of industrial technology necessitated capital investment and wage laborers instead of the peasants and nobility that marked earlier, feudal production.

The key to identifying classes, for Marx, is ownership of the means of production. In feudal society, it was largely nobility who owned the land that the peasants worked, though nobility drew upon extra-economic sources of authority. The serfs, though, often retained ownership of the meager implements of their work and sometimes even owned small pieces of farmland. In a capitalist system, however, capitalists own the machinery, factories, and all other materials necessary for the production of goods and services. Wage laborers "own" only their labor power. Workers are paid a fixed wage that allows them to survive and raise a new generation of workers. But workers create more value than they are compensated for, and the "surplus value" of their labor is appropriated by their employer. This forms the basic exploitative class relation in capitalism.

Perhaps the most significant contribution of the Marxist perspective is the recognition of the social nature of production. Individuals involved in production inevitably take part in social relationships with other participants in the production process. Giddens (1971: 35) writes that, for Marxists, "the conception of the 'isolated individual' is a construction of the bourgeois philosophy of individualism, and serves to conceal the social character which production always manifests." The social nature of production is at the foundation of a Marxist conceptualization of class.

Class

The Marxist concept of class structure has at least three broad tenets (Wright 1979).

First, class is a relational phenomenon. Most stratification theory sees class in terms of gradations where "lower classes are simply defined as having less of something that upper classes have more of—income, wealth, education, status. . . ." In contrast to this approach, Marxism conceptualizes classes in terms of their social relation to other classes. "[T]he working class is defined by its qualitative location within a social relation that simultaneously defines the capitalist class" (Wright 1979: 6–7).

Second, class relations are exploitative in nature. Unlike other notions of class, the Marxist perspective insists on the presence of exploitation within class relations. An exploitative class relation, within Marxist theory, is one in which the dominant class is able to appropriate the surplus labor of those within the subordinate class. Thus, capitalists are able to live off of the labor of others while at the same time enjoying the social and political power that accrues by controlling the surplus product. Workers, in contrast, are paid less than the value their labor produces.

Third, class exploitation is based in production. In the Marxist tradition, classes are not income or status groups. The basis of class identity is unequivocally rooted in one's relation to the means of production. Correspondingly, class exploitation is based in production, not consumption. More recently, there have been attempts to understand the potential for exploitation that exist in the consumptive and reproductive arenas, for example, through the re-appropriation of wages through individual and collective consumption and through state taxation and monetary policy (Yago and Blee 1982). Still, these are supplemental to the primary milieu of exploitation, production.

The result of this line of thinking is a picture of capitalist class structure that is divided into two major groups, capitalist and proletariat.

Weber and Marx

Although Weber agreed that economic forces were the most important factor in determining social inequality, he also argued for the relative importance of cultural considerations. Weber (1946) highlights three realms of significance in assessing social inequality. In addition to economics (class) and power (or party), he argues that status (or social honor) is also an important considera-tion. Although these three domains often overlap in the real world, it is nonetheless important to keep them analytically separate.

Whereas Marx divided classes according to their relations to the means of production, Weber did so according to economic differences of market capacity which resulted in different "life-chances." Whereas capital was one source of market capacity, Weber argued that skill and education were another. Thus, traditional Marxists would probably argue that any recognition of a third class based on knowledge is more Weberian than Marxist.

Weber's notions are valuable in sensitizing us to the fact that social inequality is more complex than a simple dichotomous economic division. However, it is Marx's understanding that classes arise from a society's mode of production—that is, the organization of both productive technology and the social relations of production—that provides us with the clearest tool to differentiate between class power and other forms of power. Maintaining the integrity of "class" in this way proves invaluable in assessing competing analyses of a "new class."

Although the simple traditional Marxist perspective has much to offer, its dichotomous conceptualization of class runs headlong into what appears to be a contradictory reality. The problem lies in what Wright (1989a: 3) has called the "embarrassment" of the middle class. Marxist thinking suggests that capitalist development should lead to the polarization of the two primary class groupings: capitalists and proletariat. Marx and Engels (1978: 474) write, "Our epoch, the epoch of the bourgeoisie, possesses, however, this distinctive feature: it has simplified the class antagonisms: Society as a whole is more and more splitting up into two great hostile camps, into two great classes directly facing each other: Bourgeoisie and Proletariat." History, however, has told a different tale as capitalist societies have adapted and showed a resiliency unanticipated in Marx's day. The rise of the welfare state, corporate-labor accommodation, and other developments are phenomena unexplainable in simple Marxist terms. Most damning, however, has been the rise of a middle class. It is a phenomenon that has supported a cottage industry of theory development.

Explaining the Middle Class

The idea of a three-class system to explain social division dates back at least to Aristotle (1979: 180–81) who argued that "In all states there may be distinguished three parts, or classes, of the citizen-body—the very rich; the very poor; and the middle class which forms the mean." There are some who would argue that in the twenty-three hundred years since his death, class theory has advanced little. Aristotle was not the only person to conceive of social division in a trichotomous way. The concept has reappeared throughout history. The medieval church saw the world in terms of three estates that roughly conformed to clergy, soldiers, and workers. In France, until the eighteenth century, the "three estates" referred to clergy, nobility, and commoners. The rise of capitalism did not undermine the notion of tripartite societal divisions. In his influential *Wealth of Nations,* Adam Smith argued for the existence of landowners, stockholders, and laborers as the basis of fundamental social divisions, though he uses the term "order" not "class" in his descriptions (Coser 1973).[2]

The existence in advanced capitalist societies of a more complex social division than the one Marx fully envisioned has become apparent. It is difficult to imagine placing a surgeon employed at a prestigious hospital in the same class with someone flipping hamburgers at a fast-food restaurant. The explanatory power of a conceptual system that places two such positions in the same class is, to say the least, limited. But are these two wage laborers part of separate classes, or do they merely represent different strata within a single, highly differentiated class? These sorts of questions have fueled competing explanations of the nature of a "middle class."

There have been four general approaches to the issue (Wright 1985). First, an adherence to traditional Marxism suggests that "the class structure of advanced capitalist societies really is polarized; the 'middle class' is strictly an ideological illusion" (Wright 1989a: 3). Such a position is empirically untenable and theoretically unfruitful.

A second approach argues that the middle class is not a class at all but instead is actually a *segment* of some other class. This approach was first used by those arguing that the middle class was really part of a "new working class" (Aronowitz 1992; Gorz 1964; Mallet 1963; Touraine 1971). This approach suggested that knowledge professionals shared with workers a common antagonism to capital. As Gorz (1964: 104) argued, technicians, engineers, students, and researchers "are ruled by the law of capital not only in their work but in all spheres of their life because those who hold power over big industry also hold power over the State, the society, the region, the city, the university—over each individual's future."

But the fall of the New Left suggested that the gap between the traditional working class and the "new" working class was greater than some had hoped. The "new working class" approach was subsequently criticized for ignoring the lack of worker control over and understanding of new production processes (Gallie 1978), for lumping together in a single category a group of workers with widely diverse skills and characteristics, and for misrepresenting this "new working class" as potentially more militant than the old working class (Blauner 1964; Wright 1979). The "new working class" theory was also seen by some (Horton 1977) as a self-serving attempt on the part of intellectuals to portray themselves as part of a "new working class" vanguard. Even Gorz (1972) largely abandoned his earlier analysis. On the whole then, these approaches have proved to be inadequate.

Theorists such as Poulantzas (1975) argued that the middle class is really a "new petty bourgeoisie" and argued for the distinction between productive labor involved in making commodities and reproductive labor involved in perpetuating capitalist social relations. Under this scheme, workers in the "ideological apparatuses" of the state, schools, media, and so on are in a different class than production workers. But as Gorz (1972) pointed out, it was not just "ideological" workers who served to reproduce capitalist relations. Technical and scientific workers were often also a vital element. Poulantzas's formulation was too narrow.

Third, another approach which denies that the middle class is truly a class suggests instead that positions within this middle realm should be viewed as locations that are simultaneously in more than one class. That is, they are in contradictory class locations. Thus, a certain occupation may feature elements characteristic of both capitalist and proletariat positions. For example, a management position may not involve ownership of the means of production, but it might include a good deal of autonomy and authority over other workers. Wright (1978) once made an influential argument for such an analysis. However, this formulation, as Wright (1989b) himself later acknowledged, is fraught with difficulty.

Finally, the most productive approach has necessitated the furthest deviation from the traditional Marxist two-class structure. This perspective recognizes that the middle class is indeed a distinct class in its own right, thus resulting in a three-class system. However, this general perspective is by no means monolithic in its details nor in its compatibility with the fundamental Marxist precepts examined above. Consequently, the competing notions of "new class" theory deserve to be examined more closely.

The Varieties of New Class Theory

There have been several attempts to conceptualize a solution to the "middle-class" dilemma in recent years. Although there has been some useful work, it is clear that a comprehensive resolution has not yet been developed. In this section, I will briefly examine some competing claims, look at how they conceptualize the basis for a "new class," and look at how they envision new class relations with other classes.

Wright

Marxists generally have been reluctant to adopt the notion of a third class. Wright (1989b) calls the promise of a coherent class theory based on three classes the "Weberian temptation" and suggests that such an approach is inconsistent with a Marxist analysis. The inconsistencies, he argues, are three-fold. First, Weberian analysis does not link class structure to an abstract concept of "mode of production." Second, "while the Weberian concept of class is relational . . . , it is not based on an abstract model of polarized relations" (1989b: 316). Thus, unlike Marxists, Weberians are not constrained by the need to produce concepts of class that reflect the underlying conflictual logic of class relations based on exploitation. Third, the Weberian tradition contains a "lower level of aspiration of conceptual and theoretical integration" resulting in a "rather pragmatic, empirical attitude towards the introduction of specific distinctions in a class structure analysis without worrying too much about the implications for a larger theoretical structure" (1989b: 316).

Despite these concerns, Wright acknowledges the need to refine traditional Marxist notions of class structure and suggests a formulation that departs significantly from the two-class Marxist model. He revises his earlier notion of "contradictory class locations," using the concept of "multiple exploitations" to emphasize more clearly exploitative class relations rather than mere domination. This revision also helps to better account for the role of the state. In this interpretation (1989b: 305–6) he argues that "different 'modes of production' are based on distinctive mechanisms of exploitation which can be differentiated on the basis of the kind of productive asset the unequal ownership (or control) of which enables the exploiting class to appropriate part of the socially produced surplus."

This new formulation identifies four types of assets, the "unequal owner-ship or control of which constitute[s] the basis of distinct forms of exploitation." These assets are "labor power assets (feudal exploitation), capital assets (capitalist exploitation), organization assets (statist exploitation), and skill or credential assets (socialist exploitation)" (1989b: 306). Thus, Wright accounts for historical variation in the nature of class exploitation. Within capitalist society, capital still reigns as the primary form of exploitation, although it sometimes faces challenges from controllers of other productive assets.

Wright is suggesting, then, that "skill" is a "productive asset" that can be used to gain economic advantage. However, because of the hesitations noted above regarding the "Weberian temptation," he does not go so far as to suggest that skill is the basis for a new class. He argues that the differences between professionals and the working class are not so much differences in material interests—which in a Marxist framework would suggest distinctly separate classes—but rather they are differences of lived experience, a different level of analysis. He writes (1989b: 337):

> the lived experience associated with professional employment is relatively nonproletarianized. First, by virtue of viable self-employment alternatives, the labor market has a less coercive aspect for professionals than for most other categories of employees. Second, within the employment relation professionals and experts exert much more control over their own work. And third, because of their career roles in corporations and bureaucracies, professionals are typically much more involved in decisions over the allocation and use of resources than are workers . . . . With respect to each of these aspects of lived experience, professionals and experts can be thought to be less alienated than fully proletarianized workers, and in this sense they are in the "middle class."

It can be inferred then that the antagonistic relations between professionals and workers are likely to be based on these differences in lived experience.

As I will argue below when discussing the work of Derber, Wright's analysis does not see the privatization of knowledge as the basis of the "middle class" and thus does not foresee the conflicting material interests—and thus separate class identity—that result from this need for privatization.

Gouldner

Alvin Gouldner (1979) suggests a simpler and more distinct break between a "new" middle class and workers. He argues that a new social class has developed that is composed of "intellectuals and technical intelligentsia." These professionals actively seek power through the benefits provided by their education and skills. For Gouldner, these professionals constitute a new class because they command the scientific discourse on which advanced societies depend. In his terms, they possess "cultural capital."

Gouldner believes that professionals wield cultural "capital" in a literal sense. He (1979: 19) argues that "The special culture of the New Class *is* a stock of capital that generates a stream of income." Consequently, capital theory needs to be broadened to include a notion of stocks of culture.

Gouldner envisions this new class's relationship with the capital class as an uneasy and often antagonistic one. He argues that New Class members share a culture of critical discourse. So, although professionals use their skill and education to obtain power, in terms of social change Gouldner sees this class as perhaps "the best card that history has presently given us to play." Thus, for Gouldner, professionals are largely antagonistic to capitalist interests.

By returning to the fundamental notion that class power is relational in nature, we can see a potential shortcoming in Gouldner's work. Capitalists, as Marx argues, can exist and profit only through the exploitation of workers. By definition this is the relation between propertied and nonpropertied classes.

Attending to this fact, we see that similarly, a professional knowledge class can exist only if there is a relation of exploitation between it and the working class. That is, the value of their knowledge and skill comes from the fact that others do not have it. This is different, it should be noted, from a "pure" exploitation model based on the appropriation of surplus. Discussing exploitation in terms of the relationship between professionals and workers is a problem that has not yet been fully developed (Wright 1989b). Wright recognizes the essential importance of exploitation in class analysis, but Gouldner, in not seeing the basis for antagonism between a professional class and workers, seems to ignore this facet of class relations.

Barbara and John Ehrenreich (1979) have pointed out most clearly the existence of an antagonistic relation between professionals and workers. They argue (1979: 9–10) that "salaried mental workers," including cultural workers, managers, engineers, and scientists, form a separate "Professional-Managerial Class ('PMC')" and that this class "exists in an objectively antagonistic rela-tionship to another class of wage earners." The Ehrenreichs (1979: 10, 12) argue that this class is "specific to the monopoly stage of capitalism" and its major function is "the reproduction of capitalist culture and capitalist class relations." But as Derber, Schwartz, and Magrass (1990) point out, this argument misses the more enduring aspects of a knowledge class. Still, the Ehrenreichs' work was extremely helpful in identifying the kinds of conflicts that were likely to occur between workers and professionals, especially in attempted political coalitions.[3]

Martin and Szelenyi (1987) criticize Gouldner on another front. They suggest that in arguing for a literal interpretation of "cultural capital," Gould-ner's horizons are limited by his implicit economism. They argue that a distinction needs to be made between practical and symbolic mastery and that the power of the "new class" comes from their "symbolic domination." Their criticism draws from the work of another theorist, Pierre Bourdieu.

Bourdieu

Bourdieu's work can be loosely characterized as falling primarily within the Weberian tradition. However, for Bourdieu this does not imply a wholesale rejection of Marxist principles. He argues (Brubaker 1985: 748) that Weber, "far from countering Marx's theory, as is commonly thought, with a spiritual-ist theory of history, carried the materialist mode of thinking into domains which Marxist materialism in effect abandons to spiritualism." What Bourdieu is arguing for is a broader conception of "interest" that sees all practices as aimed at increasing material or symbolic profit.

Bourdieu sees the condition of all practices as being material in nature. Thus, he writes (Brubaker 1985: 772, n. 20):

> Against the typical regression of Marxism towards economism, which knows only the economy in the narrow sense of the capitalist economy

and which explains everything by the economy thus defined, Max Weber extends economic analysis (in the generalized sense) to regions ordinarily abandoned by economics, such as religion. Thus, he characterized the Church . . . as monopolizing the control of the goods of salvation. He suggests a radical materialism that would investigate economic determinants (in the broadest sense) in regions such as art or religion where an ideology of "disinterestedness" reigns.

What interests Bourdieu, however, is primarily the realm of lived experience. His analysis of class is based on the concepts of "capital" and "habitus."

In conceptualizing capital, Bourdieu suggests that economic capital and symbolic capital are distinct forms of power, although on occasion they are mutually convertible. By utilizing both concepts of capital, he can claim a sort of metaclass analysis that is conceptualized in the field of generalized social relations, not in relations of production and is thus a universal explanatory principle. For Bourdieu (Brubaker 1985: 762), "social class (in itself) is inseparably a class of identical or similar conditions of existence and conditionings and a class of biological individuals endowed with the same habitus, understood as a system of dispositions shared by all individuals who are products of the same conditionings." As Brubaker (1985: 762) notes, "This definition envisions the perfect coincidence of divisions established by differences in external conditions of existence and divisions established by differences in internalized dispositions." Bourdieu argues that in contemporary society classes have been increasingly taking the form of status groups rather than traditional economic classes. Instead of conflict around power and privilege, competition and emulation between status groups is based on the perception of the social worth of different lifestyles. Unfortunately, the totalizing nature of this attempt at metatheory renders it impractical for any kind of productive class analysis. One fundamental problem is that it strips "class" of the distinct meaning it holds in Marxist analysis and transforms it into a much broader concept that covers more and explains less.

A more useful aspect of Bourdieu's theory is his concept of habitus. A class habitus can be identified by a set of common "conditions" of everyday life which produce common "conditionings" (roughly, what I have called lived experience). In turn, these conditionings generate a common set of internalized "dispositions" to act in certain ways. These dispositions range from tastes (Bourdieu 1984) to receptivities to particular ideological appeals and calls to action. In Bourdieu's analysis, a class habitus is not simply constituted within the workplace, but in community, schools, families, and other institutions as well. These institutional settings generate lived experiences (conditionings) over the life cycle that reinforce certain modes of thought and action and undermine others.

Bourdieu's theory is suggestive of a way to explore the evolution of a class "in itself" to a class "for itself." He (1985: 723) sharply criticizes Marxists for never adequately dealing with "the mysterious alchemy whereby a 'group in struggle,' a personalized collective, a historical agent assigning itself its own ends, arises from the objective economic conditions." Instead, Bourdieu argues, Marxists have either presented a purely determinist or a purely voluntarist explanation of this transition. In the former case the change is seen as a "logical, mechanical, or organic necessity" that is an inevitable effect of the " 'maturing of the objective conditions.' " In the latter case, the transition is seen as the result of an "awakening of consciousness" usually catalyzed by an enlightened party (1985: 726–27). While Bourdieu appears to oversimplify Marxist analysis to make his point, he does identify an important concern in utilizing class theory, namely, the need to more plausibly account for the interaction of objective conditions and subjective interpretations.

Class and Collective Action

Although there is clearly no complete agreement on how to analyze class structure in such a way as to account for the complexity of social division, there are central themes that emerge from theories of class that have implications for understanding the political world.

First, in one form or another, a professional middle class exists in capitalist society. Although Wright acknowledges differences in the lived experiences of professionals and workers, he denies fundamental differences in their material interests. However, Derber, Schwartz, and Magrass (1990) suggest a way of understanding the basis for a "knowledge" class that leads to a contradiction of Wright's perspective.

Derber and his colleagues have argued that the professional middle class is not "new" at all but instead represents a basic element of all productive societies. Martin and Szelenyi (1987: 28) have criticized Gouldner for "his failure to show that cultural capital is as much a necessary precondition for production as economic capital." This is where Derber's work proves valuable. He does not adopt Gouldner's notion of cultural capital per se. Instead, he shows that throughout history, power has resulted from knowledge, and he argues that "Knowledge, capital, and labor are the three basic factors of production. Each is essential to produce *all* goods and services in *all* societies and eras (1990: 12)." The power of the "new" class arises from its "ownership" of special knowledge.

Social arrangements can result in different groups controlling different resources (see fig. App. 1.1).[4] Some craft workers of the Middle Ages (Type 1) owned their tools and materials (capital), conceived their own plans (knowledge), and performed the labor necessary to carry out these plans (labor). Contemporary high-technology firms (Type 2) are often owned (capital) by scientists who bring needed expertise (knowledge) to production processes that

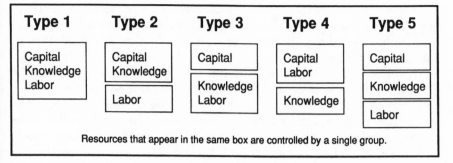

Fig. App. 1.1. Adapted from Derber et al. (1990: 13)

are carried out or supported by other workers (labor). Nineteenth-century industrialism (Type 3) often featured skilled craft workers who conceived (knowledge) and carried out (labor) production that was largely financed (capital) by owners. Spain's Mondragon cooperatives (Type 4) feature worker ownership (capital and labor) coupled with the utilization of professional managerial and engineering expertise (knowledge). Likewise, state socialism may feature socialized capital, but experts and technocrats who control the knowledge of organizing production and distribution may have a separate base of power (Konrad and Szelenyi 1979). Finally, contemporary capitalist societies (Type 5) feature the control of capital, knowledge, and labor by three separate classes—capitalists, the professional-middle class, and workers.

Building from this schema, we can see how production entails the coordination of capital, knowledge, and labor, each component of which is associated with a class position based on the "ownership" of this resource. Capitalists own capital and derive power from their ability to direct the form and nature of investment in production. They attempt to maximize profit and undermine the power of other classes through the manipulation of their capital.

Workers, on the other extreme, "own" only their own labor power. The only resource they have in influencing other classes is through the withholding of labor power (e.g., through strikes). Capitalists pursue different strategies to minimize the likelihood of such an event and the impact it has if it does occur. For example, the presence of a "surplus" of labor helps ensure the cooperation of workers. In times of abundance, corporate-labor pacts and managerial strategies help to stabilize the labor market.

In capitalist societies, the professional class is in the "middle" in its ability to exert power. Ultimately it is controlled by capitalists who own, fund, or heavily influence the universities, research institutions, government agencies, and firms that employ professionals. For their part, professionals attempt to establish different criteria, based on specialized knowledge, for the decisions made in society, thus attempting to undermine capitalist power. More effectively, professionals control access to higher education and professional membership, thus discrediting and undermining workers' influence in the workplace and in broader society.

A "new class" of professionals can thus be said to exist within the fundamental framework of Marxist class analysis because professionals have—with varying degrees of success—consolidated "ownership" of knowledge, especially as it relates to production. This class is not monolithic, however. The members of the class more closely aligned with the capitalist class are those with more "practical" mastery skills that are fundamental to production efforts. Those professionals with more "symbolic" mastery are less likely to benefit significantly from the advancement of a capitalist agenda and may thus be freer to examine that agenda with a critical eye. In the end, however, even such "critical" professionals are dependent upon the capitalist class.

Derber's recognition of the importance of treating knowledge as property through the control of access to it has important political implications. Both factions of the professional class have an interest in excluding working-class participation in their knowledge specialties. The socialization of knowledge would undermine the basis for professional-class power just as the socialization of capital would undermine the basis for capitalist power.

The first fundamental political insight that class theory affords us, then, is that there exists a noncapitalist class distinct from the working class, and the interests of this class are ultimately different from those of workers. This insight occurs at the level of what Bourdieu calls "classes on paper." It is a macrolevel analysis of the collective condition of social cleavages.

However, by adapting Bourdieu's notion of habitus, we can extend our understanding of the implication of these differing classes. Even Wright, who does not accept the premise of a totally separate "middle class," admits that workers and professionals have distinctly different lived experiences. Bourdieu, however, is careful to argue that we should not privilege the workplace in looking at the common conditions of everyday life that make up a habitus. Instead schools, families, and other insittituions need to be examined. But although these institutions may serve important functions in mitigating the effect of workplace experiences, they cannot be conceptualized as being independent of class position. Family structure and home life, access to educational and cultural opportunities, all are related to class position. The different lived experiences (conditionings) of professionals and workers, therefore, has a profound impact on their respective worldviews and on the likelihood that they will act in certain ways (dispositions).

The political significance of these observations is made apparent when we remember that "new social movements" are made up primarily of members of the middle class. At the very least, the lived experiences of new-social-movement activists are fundamentally different from those of workers.

Conclusion

It is important to understand these collective dynamics between the three classes if we are to understand the significance of new class domination of "new social movements." As explored in Part Two, knowledge is not only a weapon to be wielded by professionals in the economic sphere. It is also a crucial ingredient to participation and success in the social and political realm. By disempowering workers in the productive world, professionals have contributed to the disempowerment of workers in the political world.

The Concept
of Culture

There are very few concepts that can match the vagueness, complexity, and provocative implications associated with "class"; "culture" is one of them. Theorists examining culture sometimes speak of different phenomena using the same term or of the same phenomenon using different terms. Sorting through these many definitions and meanings can—and has—taken up entire volumes. Here, however, I merely wish to outline some of the major traditions associated with work on "culture" and suggest some of their strengths and weaknesses.

Consciousness, Ideology, and Culture

The difficulty in specifying the nature of culture is compounded by the presence of the related and sometimes overlapping concepts of consciousness and ideology. Before proceeding to discuss culture, it would be helpful to distinguish it from these other terms.

First, despite the fact that—as I will argue below—it is sometimes conceptualized in an idealist fashion, culture is *not* consciousness. Without entering the scrap over the definition of consciousness, let me cite Wright's (1985: 244) helpful observation that "to study 'consciousness' is to study a particular aspect of the mental life of individuals, namely, those elements of a person's subjectivity which are *discursively accessible to the individual's own awareness.*" Culture is a much broader concept than this. It incorporates more than what is discursively accessible to an individual by including unconscious or unrecognized patterns of thought and behavior. In some formulations, it also includes the material artifacts of culture. In addition, despite the common usage of terms such as "class consciousness," we cannot legitimately speak of any form of "collective consciousness." That is, "supra-individual entities, and in particular 'classes,' do not have consciousness in the literal sense, since they are not the kind of entities which have minds, which think, weigh alternatives, have preferences, etc." (Wright 1985: 243). Culture, it can be argued, exists at precisely this shared, collective level. Culture, by most definitions, cannot exist in a single mind the way consciousness can. This constitutes a fundamental difference between the terms.

The concept of culture has more in common with some formulations of "ideology." Therborn (1980: 2) defines ideology as:

> the medium through which . . . consciousness and meaningfulness is formed. . . . Thus the conception of ideology . . . deliberately includes both everyday notions and "experience" and elaborate intellectual doctrines, both the "consciousness" of social actors and the institutionalized thought-synthesis and discourses of a given society. But to study these as ideology means to look at them from a particular perspective: not as bodies of thought or structures of discourse per se, but as manifestations of a particular being-in-the-world of conscious actors, human subjects. In other words, to conceive of a text or an utterance as ideology is to focus on the way it operates in the formation and transformation of human subjectivity.

In the structuralist tradition, the term "ideology" is preferred over "culture" and refers to related, though not identical, sets of issues. Hebdige (1979: 11) distinguishes ideology from consciousness by noting that "Ideology by definition thrives *beneath* consciousness. It is here, at the level of 'normal common sense,' that ideological frames of reference are most firmly sedimented and most effective, because it is here that their ideological nature is most effectively concealed." Though "ideology," thought of in such terms, overlaps many definitions of "culture," I will privilege the latter term over the former.

The difficulty with the term "culture" also stems from the long and varied history of its usage.[1] The work of recent cultural theorists has been to narrow the concept of culture. The need for this narrowing process is the consequence of early definitions that were overly broad and nearly all-encompassing. In 1871, Edward Tylor (1958) defined culture as "that complex whole which includes knowledge, belief, art, morals, law, custom, and any other capabilities and habits acquired by man as a member of society." Kroeber and Kluckhohn (1963: 181) produced an entire volume based on the review of several hundred definitions of culture and arrived at a summary formulation that they suggested would be acceptable to most social scientists:

> Culture consists of patterns, explicit and implicit, of and for behavior acquired and transmitted by symbols, constituting the distinctive achievement of human groups, including their embodiments in artifacts; the essential core of culture consists of traditional (i.e., historically derived and selected) ideas and especially their attached values; culture systems may, on the one hand, be considered as products of action, on the other as conditioning elements of further action.

Unfortunately, such a distilled definition reflects a particular approach to culture (as the "distinctive achievement of a people") that has long since been superseded by more fruitful formulations.

Theories of Culture

Reviews of cultural studies often mention two traditions, neither of which is by any means monolithic.[2] The specific boundaries and particular labels used to describe these traditions vary: Hall (1980) refers to them as the "culturalist" strand and the "structuralist" approach; Williams uses the terms "idealist" and "materialist" to draw boundaries; in the anthropological tradition, Keesing writes of cultures as either "ideational systems" or "adaptive systems," the latter of which emphasizes the relation of humans to their ecological setting.

I will examine these traditions, using the idealist and materialist labels, with an eye towards their relative emphasis on either human *agency* in the making of culture or on the *constraint* upon action that results from material or structural sources.[3] After assessing some of the problems with each approach, I will examine the integration of both agency and constraint in a single concept of culture based on the idea of *practice*.

Over the years, the concept of culture has gone through various configurations and emphases. Williams (1981: 10) summarizes:

> Beginning as a noun of *process*—the culture (cultivation) of crops or (rearing and breeding) of animals, and by extension the culture (active cultivation) of the human mind—it became in the late eighteenth century, especially in German and English, a noun of *configuration* or *generalization* of the "spirit" which informed the "whole way of life" of a distinct people. Herder . . . first used the significant plural, "cultures," in deliberate distinction from any singular or, as we would now say, unilinear sense of "civilization." The broad pluralist term was then especially important in the nineteenth-century development of comparative anthropology, where it has continued to designate a whole and distinctive way of life.

But the recognition of a diverse set of "cultures" then presents the researcher with two options. First, one can attempt to describe, *understand,* and interpret differing cultures, looking for the "meaning" in symbols, rituals, language, and so on. This is the approach that is associated with Weber's and Mead's concern for subjective meaning in social life. Second, one can attempt to *explain* the existence of different cultures, looking at the relationship between cultural elements and other features of the social structure. This distinction forms another important axis of division within cultural studies. My examination, however, will focus on the axis that divides the idealist from the materialist tradition.

Idealist Tradition

The idealist tradition, broadly speaking, sees culture as a result of mental processes. This tradition can be seen, for example, in the phenomonological approaches that take Hegelian concerns for being and knowing as their basis.

As a result, the idealist tradition is usually characterized by attempts to understand cultural differences, rather than to explain their origins. The reason for the idealist concern with the mind can perhaps be best summarized by the famous invocation from W. I. Thomas and Dorothy Swain Thomas (1928: 572) that "If men define a situation as real, they are real in their consequences." How humans define, understand, and organize reality, then, becomes the stuff of cultural studies.

As Williams notes, Dilthey (1976) distinguishes between the "natural sciences" and the "cultural sciences," the latter of which has humanly made "objects of study." The significance of this distinction is the recognition that an individual studying humanly made objects and processes is examining something unique in which the researcher necessarily participates. Consequently, different methods of study must be employed to adequately gauge this realm. Dilthey suggests a methodological approach using *verstehen* or "sympathetic understanding" as the most appropriate method. Although this approach is most associated with the work of Weber, it is characteristic of an entire tradition of cultural studies that takes as its goal the understanding of cultures from the perspective of its participants.

Cognitive anthropology follows this emphasis on understanding by locating culture in the minds of a society's members. Culture is everything an individual has to know in order to participate in an acceptable manner in a particular society. Culture is not made up of things, behaviors, or emotions. Instead, it is an organization of these things. As Ward Goodenough (Keesing 1974: 77) suggests, culture "is the form of things that people have in mind, their models for perceiving, relating, and otherwise interpreting them." Also, culture "consists of standards for deciding what is, . . . for deciding what can be, . . . for deciding what one feels about, . . . for deciding what to do about it, and . . . for deciding how to go about doing it." As Keesing (1974: 77) points out, when cultures are conceived of in this manner, they are "epistemologically in the same realm as language (Saussure's *langue* or Chomsky's competence), as inferred ideational codes lying behind the realm of observable events." Goodenough argues that these concepts and models people use in interpreting the world must exist in the mind of the individual for that individual to have access to them. Thus, all culture is fundamentally "private culture" and is more real than any notion of "public culture."

An important counterstrand to the cognitive anthropological tradition is the semiotic work of Clifford Geertz. Geertz (1973: 448) sees culture as shared codes of meaning where culture can be seen as "an assemblage of texts." In this sense, culture does *not* exist in people's heads as Goodenough claims. Instead, culture can exist only in the *social* realm of shared meaning. The goal of anthropological studies, then, becomes interpreting these texts through the use of "thick description" (3–30). As Geertz (452) puts it, "The culture of a people is an ensemble of texts, themselves ensembles, which the anthropologist strains to read over the shoulders of those to whom they properly belong."

In sociology proper, Berger and Luckmann's (1966) work on the "social construction of reality" shares with Geertz an emphasis on the ideational nature of culture and on its social character. Berger and Luckmann argue that people socially construct the reality that they perceive, within the limits of natural environmental and biological constraints. But the introduction of socially based differentiation presages the discussion below of material approaches to culture.

Significantly, Geertz (1973: 453) emphasizes studying the "substance" of cultures rather than developing "reductive formulas professing to account for them." He warns against such neat formulas imposing a supposed internal consistency on complex cultures that are in fact disconnected and contradictory. Such criticisms were aimed at Lévi-Strauss and others who attempted to "de-code" cultures by revealing their structural composition (e.g., Geertz 1973: 345–59). Geertz (fn., 449) writes of Lévi-Strauss, "He does not seek to understand symbolic forms in terms of how they function in concrete situations to organize perceptions (meanings, emotions, concepts, attitudes); he seeks to understand them entirely in terms of their internal structure, *independent de tout sujet, de tout objet, et de toute contexte.*"

Lévi-Strauss is part of a line of thinking that can be labeled "structuralist" in orientation. However, it should be noted that along with Lévi-Strauss in anthropology, the other key "structuralist" figures—Foucault in history, Lacan in psychoanalysis, and Barthes in literary criticism—have each repudiated the label. Despite their objections, we can think of these theorists as being related insofar as they draw upon Saussure's work on linguistic structures.

Structuralists base their analysis on the existence of irreducible signifying practices that play a constitutive role in determining the subject-self and reality. So, for example, although Lévi-Strauss, like Geertz, writes of cultures as shared symbolic systems, he sees these systems as *creations of mind*. He views cultural studies, then, as the attempt to discover in the structuring of cultural terrains— myth, art, kinship, language—the principles of mind upon which cultural elaborations depend. Lévi-Strauss, then, can be loosely discussed within the idealist tradition only after noting that the task he set for himself was more *explanatory* than interpretive, with the mind as cultural product rather than as agent, thus contesting the tradition's more predominant trend.

Structuralists see material conditions of life as imposing constraints on lived-in worlds. But external material factors do not explain these phenomena. Instead, the mind imposes its own order upon a continuously changing material world. Cultural themes, such as Lévi-Strauss's emphasis on binary contrasts, helps bring perceived order to this otherwise chaotic world. The very process of cultural ordering creates an important divisional axis between the realm of human-made order (culture) and the material world (nature) (Keesing 1974: 78–79).

Structuralism is thus anti-humanist insofar as it identifies human thoughts and actions as the product of cultural determinants. In this perspective, lived experience is not the source of culture but instead is the effect of culture.

The Materialist Tradition

The materialist tradition is that which sees culture in the broader context of a "whole social order" and emphasizes the constraints placed on cultural development by other factors in the social order. Within the anthropological tradition, materialist concerns are addressed by what Keesing (1974: 75) calls the "cultural adaptationists," who argue that "cultures are systems (of socially transmitted behavior patterns) that serve to relate human communities to their ecological settings." This tradition, as articulated by Harris (1964; 1968) and others, highlights differing types of production, the role of settlement patterns, modes of social grouping and political organization, and religious beliefs and practices, among other factors. Unlike Marxism, it downplays the role of conflict and contradiction in generating and guiding social and cultural change in favor of an "adaptive" approach similar to that of "natural selection."

But clearly, the materialist tradition is most associated with Marx. However, his unfortunate use of a "base-superstructure" metaphor left a legacy of confusion about just what was being claimed for culture in a Marxist framework. In its traditional form, Marxism seemed to suggest that culture was a mere epiphenomenon that was determined by an economic base. There was little or no room for suggestions that culture, in turn, could have an impact upon material conditions.

This reductionist contention, of course, has been dramatically reformulated by neo-Marxists. The Althusserian notion of the "relative autonomy" of cultural and political processes has, in one form or another, permeated contemporary Marxist thinking. The base/superstructure metaphor has been reformulated (Hall 1977; Williams 1977: 75–82). The emphasis in this materialist tradition, then, has shifted from the *determination* of culture by material conditions to the examination of cultural *practices* as they interact with economic and political processes.

Problems With Each Tradition

The difficulties associated with purely idealist or purely materialist traditions in some respects mirror one another. At the most basic level, the idealist approach can be criticized for subsuming the "social" under the label of "cultural," while the materialist tradition can be castigated for underestimating the autonomy of culture by conceptualizing it as secondary to other social processes. But other significant critiques of each tradition deserve attention as well.

Researchers working in the idealist tradition have difficulty in defending how they can "prove" what people "really" think. This approach is often criticized as being too subjective and of ignoring the role of the unconscious. As a result, it is difficult to assess the relative merits of differing interpretations of the same culture.

A second criticism of the idealist approach—and one that may become more influential in the future—is that, with the exception of its structuralist strand, it cannot account for the possible existence of cultural "universals" that have been theoretically proposed in the study of language structures. As Keesing (1974: 87) cautions, "it has been revolutions in science (evolution, relativity, quantum theory, cybernetics, molecular biology, linguistics) that have progressively transformed modern philosophy, not the reverse. A revolutionary advance in our understanding of the organization of intelligence—in a broad cybernetic sense that includes coding at a genetic, cellular, organismic and ecosystemic level as well as in mind and brain—is now in its early stages." If one admits the possibility of such universal ordering of thinking processes, then most ideational theory must be reconsidered.

Finally, idealist approaches do not adequately deal with parallels in cultural and social differentiation. For a more complete understanding of such differences we must incorporate a materialist approach.

But the purely materialist tradition suffers from its own shortcomings. Most notably, social structures are first created, shaped, and constrained by individual minds and brains. "What forms cultures take depend on what individual humans can think, imagine, and learn as well as on what collective behaviors shape and sustain viable patters of life in ecosystems. Cultures must be thinkable and learnable as well as livable" (Keesing 1974: 86).

Second, as Geertz has pointed out, treating culture as transcending individual understanding can lead to false assumptions about the coherence and consistency of cultures. Theorizing a false integration of divergent cultural practices may result in a failure to identify important cultural cleavages and potential avenues of cultural and other change. A recognition of the importance of social structural considerations, then, must be accompanied by a recognition of social—and relatedly, cultural—differentiation.

A "Culturalist" Alternative

Both the idealist and materialist notions of culture have something to offer in generating a better understanding of the relation between human agency and cultural constraints. The most promising school of thought along these lines has come from a radical reworking of the materialist perspective. At the center of this development is the reworking of the base/superstructure distinction which grants culture at least "relative autonomy" from the determination of an economic base. The work of Raymond Williams and E. P. Thompson forms the basis for such a "culturalist" tradition. This tradition views culture, as Bennett (1981: 10) summarizes it, as the set of practices through which men and women actively respond to the conditions of their social existence, creatively fashioning experienced social relationships into diverse and structured patterns of living, thinking and feeling. The emphasis, within this account, is placed on the notion of human agency. It is this that provides the crucial mediation between the determined conditions of a given cultural practice and the outcome of that practice, connecting and yet at the same time separating the two. The transition between the conditions of cultural practice and its outcome is never automatic, never guaranteed in advance; how the one is translated into the other depends on how the gap between them is filled by the operations of human agency. In short, within this tradition . . . the stress is placed on the making of culture rather than on its determined conditions.

By recognizing the necessity of the continuous reproduction of cultural and structural forms, we privilege neither component. As Paul Willis (1977: 174) argues:

cultural forms cannot be reduced or regarded as the mere epiphenomenal expression of basic structural factors. They are not the accidental or open-ended determined variables in the couplet structure/culture. They are part of a necessary circle in which neither term is thinkable alone. It is in the passage through the cultural level that aspects of the real structural relationships of society are transformed into conceptual relationships and back again. The cultural is part of the necessary dialectic of reproduction.

Distilling the Essence of Culture

In the end, I use culture in the following sense:

(1) Culture itself is ideational, not material. It is the "meaning" that people bring to cultural artifacts that is the essence of the culture, not the artifacts themselves.

(2) Culture is social. Meaning is cultural only insofar as it is shared. An understanding of reality that does not have shared meaning is a type of psychosis. Thus, culture is social.

(3) Culture is constitutive. Language and other components of culture help us to order and make meaning of a plethora of "facts." In the process, culture actually constitutes our world. The concept of gender, for example, is cultural and in fact orders behavior along sex-lines. It helps to create the self (Weedon 1987). Culture "frames" the world by drawing our attention to some things and suggesting it is acceptable to ignore others.

(4) Culture is constrained by material conditions. Although the material "base" does not "create" a cultural superstructure, it does suggest affinities.

Material conditions are like trails through the woods shared by many cultural hikers. Hikers can always wander through the woods and start new trails or stumble onto different ones. However, this trailbreaking is likely to cause cultural and cognitive dissonance. It is easier for cultures to stay on the trails suggested by material conditions.

(5) Culture enables. Experiencing "culture shock" is, in part, the experience of confronting a society in which we do not have access to the culture necessary to conduct our affairs. Culture gives access to a particular social life and enables us to participate. It is, in Swidler's (1986) analogy, a "tool kit."

Methods

This appendix presents some additional details on the methodology used for this study. I describe the fieldwork setting and interviews and conclude with some comments on the use of the self in social science.

Fieldwork

The participant-observation portion of this work was carried out in a printing plant and mailing house which I refer to as Mail and Printing Services (MAPS). I was hired by MAPS through a temporary employment agency. MAPS is a business products company. It produces and sells hundreds of different kinds of invoices, tags, forms, and stickers, mostly to small businesses. It markets largely through direct-mail advertising, though it also services dealers of business forms. It has several manufacturing locations across the country, with its major headquarters located in New England.

The plant at which I worked employed approximately 250 workers, split among different shifts. Nearly all the workers are white. Roughly 40 percent are women; 60 percent, men. MAPS pays its starting manual workers $6.50 per hour. Mail-processing-machine operators earn a top wage of about $10.00 per hour. Printers make considerably more—up to the $15.00 per hour range, but there are few of these. There are benefits that include health insurance (70/30 split) and profit sharing (which, during the last few years, amounted to a nearly 10 percent annual bonus). People make their money, though, by working overtime. Approximately half of the workers regularly work the equivalent of one full day of overtime a week. Some work more. Overtime includes coming in early, leaving late, and working on days off. Over and over, I heard people say something to the effect that overtime was "the only way to get a decent paycheck." Men were more likely than women to work overtime, with women more likely to be responsible for child care and cooking duties.

The shift structure changed during my stay at MAPS. Originally there were two shifts, days (7:00 A.M. to 3:30 P.M.) and nights (3:30 P.M. to 12:00 A.M.), both Monday through Friday. This structure changed, however, when a third weekend shift was added. The new day schedule was 6:00 A.M. to 4:30 P.M., Monday through Thursday. The new night schedule was 4:30 P.M. to 3:00 A.M., Monday through Thursday, and the weekend schedule was 6:00 A.M. to 6:30

P.M. Friday through Sunday. (This weekend shift was extremely unpopular and was populated primarily by singles with no family responsibilities.)

Since many people traveled thirty to forty-five minutes to get to work, on the earlier shift, people left home at, say, 5:30 A.M. and did not get back until 5:00 P.M. Add in basic time to get up, eat, shower, get home, cook dinner, and so on, and the workday easily lasts from 4:30 A.M. to 6:30 P.M. If people want to get seven hours of sleep (eight hours is a luxury), then they would have to go to bed at 9:30 P.M. This is clearly inhibiting to any kind of outside activity. Even the more modest five-day schedule results in a 5:30 A.M. to 5:30 P.M. schedule with bedtime at 10:30 P.M..

The time structure of the day, therefore, makes it very difficult for people to do anything besides go to work during the week. (Given the amount of overtime worked on weekends, this schedule often extended to six and sometimes even seven days a week.) This is a basic, fundamental reality that, I believe, often gets overlooked.

The Plant

The plant layout is quite traditional (see fig. App. 3.1). The main doors open onto a carpeted reception area that features what looks like a life-size reproduction of a Guttenberg press. There were two secretaries/receptionists working at this station when I first reported.

The "employees only" entrance opens onto a short hallway that leads past a cafeteria to the shop floor. To the right there is the "service/prep" room. This is a large room with perhaps a dozen layout tables where design of forms and advertising material is done. There are also several desks where customers are met and orders taken. The graphic artists that work in this area do not seem to have much, if any, interaction with the rest of the crew in the factory.

The factory floor is essentially one vast room. The various printing presses and related equipment are to the front right. At the back, where the presses end, there are piles of paper in large rolls and the shipping and receiving area. Behind that are the loading-dock doors. In the center third of the building there are the stock racks—huge, heavy shelving housing the inventory on pallets or skids. Towards the back are the mail bins where outgoing mail awaits shipping. The left third of the building is made up of the various folding and mailing equipment. At three separate locations on the floor there are built-in offices, one each for the various supervisors of printing, mail processing, and shipping/receiving. Forklifts and clamp trucks are constantly buzzing up and down the aisles, horns tooting, moving stock. In many parts of the plant, the roar of the presses and mailing machinery make it necessary to speak very loudly— just below a shout—to be heard. The smell of ink and chemicals is heavy in the air.

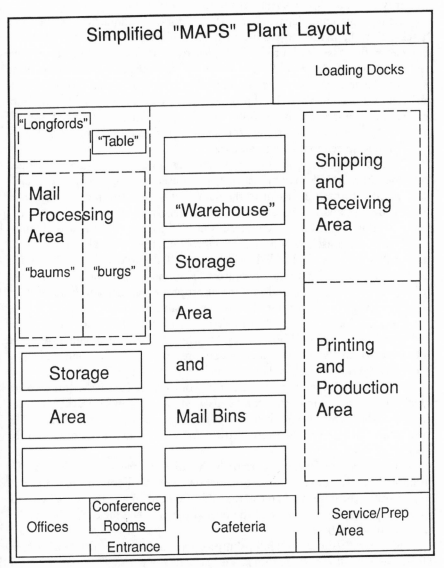

Fig. App. 3.1

The Work Process

The work that is done in the mail-processing section of the plant—where I primarily worked—follows roughly the following routine.

The mail-planning department at the corporate headquarters decides on a "package" to be mailed to a particular list. For example, they may decide to send eleven flyers (six with product samples) to thirty-four hundred automotive dealers. This package would likely contain a mix of generic and specialized products. Generic products include sales slips and other items used by a wide variety of businesses. Specialized products, in this case, might include automotive repair estimate forms or other products specifically designed for the automotive industry. All of these products are produced in the printing area of the plant and stored in the "warehouse."

Once the package is decided upon and a mailing list is either developed from the larger MAPS mailing list or is purchased for use from some outside vendor, the information is sent to the manufacturing plant under a particular "mail code" number. Here, a work order is generated specifying the requirements for this order. First, the materials needed for the package are obtained from the "warehouse" section of the plant. Next, the materials are left in the mail-processing area for the "baum" (short for "Baumfolders"—machines that cut and fold printed material) operators. The baum operators get the work order, find their material, and fold the appropriate number and kind of flyer. There are a variety of baums with differing capabilities.

The folded materials are "offloaded" onto large wooden or metal racks that resemble two-sided bookshelves on wheels. Cardboard signs are made indicating which flyers and which orders are on each rack, along with who folded the flyers. The rack is then rolled out onto the floor.

The Longford operator next gets the work order. He or she looks to see which flyers need samples that can be inserted on the Longfords, then gets the samples and the appropriate flyers, loads them up, and does the "nesting." The flyers with samples are then returned to racks and rolled back out onto the floor.

If there are samples that cannot be handled by the Longfords—usually because they are too tiny or are somehow awkward for the machines to handle—then the order will go to "the table," where "manual nesters" will get the appropriate sample and stuff the flyers by hand. The racks are then rolled back out onto the floor.

The "burg" (short for Phillipsburg) operators next get the work order. They assemble all the needed racks and lay out the packages' contents in the twelve-station machine, adding a business-reply envelope (BRE) and a special outside envelope. Here, it is the stacker's job to keep the stations filled with the appropriate flyers. The operator makes numerous adjustments to insure the feeding and operation of the machine goes reasonably well. The burg grabs one of each flyer and stuffs it into an envelope. The envelope travels down a conveyor belt and reaches the label head where a label is cut off from the computer printout and glued onto the envelope. The envelope continues into a "stacker," which usually reads for an asterisk indicating the end of a bundle and "breaks" the pile. The pile of (usually six to twenty-five) envelopes drops down the stacker onto another conveyor belt, and the utility worker picks up the bundle, ties it with string on the tying machine, and (reading off of a computer printout) puts it in the appropriate canvas mailbag that has been prepared with mail tags. When full, the bag is put on a "bin" that, when the order is over, is wheeled via palette jack to an area where a forklift will weigh it and place it in the appropriate storage area to await mailing.

The cycle has its variations, but this is the general routine. There are more specialized jobs in mail processing, such as handling first-class mail composed of responses to specific customer requests for catalogs, but most of the work is as described above.

The Job

The job opening I took, I later learned, arose because of a major shift in the company's marketing strategy. The company has moved away from large mailing lists (twenty to forty thousand or more) toward "micromarketing," which targets very small lists of companies. Individualized direct-mail packages are then sent to these smaller lists. For example, pet store owners might make up a list of two thousand names. They would receive a package of eight to twelve flyers featuring products that would be of interest to them. The envelope used for this mailing would have a special graphic and message such as "Good news for pet shop owners," supposedly to pique customer interest.

The consequence of shifting to these smaller mailing lists is that there is much less "run time" on the mail-processing machines because the runs are so much smaller. The baums, Longfords (nesters), and burgs (inserters) all have to be adjusted for each order. This can take a fair amount of time. For some very small orders it sometimes takes longer to set up and adjust the machinery than it does to actually run the order. Also, finding the orders on the racks, getting envelopes, getting samples, and getting the "tape" (the mailing label computer printout) all take time and coordination. Thus, with the new marketing strategy, management was finding that they were falling behind in processing the mail. Productivity had dropped dramatically due to the increase in "down time." A new weekend shift was added to the already existing day and evening shift. The shifting of personnel resulted in a need for temporary workers until they got it all straightened out.

My primary job was doing "manual nesting"—which, because of the mindless nature of the position, was jokingly referred to as the "MNT" job, for "manual nesting technician." Basically, I sat at a table and stuffed samples into flyers for hours on end. The work was extremely boring, monotonous, and repetitious. The only possible way to get through it was to talk to people.

In the past, there had been no real "manual nesting" job in and of itself. Instead, the work was done by people during "down time" on their machines. Thus, there was an ever changing group of workers who sat at the nesting table for varying periods of time. Regular workers continued to do manual nesting, however; with the recent changes there had developed a backlog of work. Thus, temporary workers were brought in to help out, and I was assigned the job of manual nesting. The situation was ideal for me. I was able to sit at the nesting table and talk with a wide variety of workers from all parts of the printing and mailing departments as they came to work at the nesting table during their down time. In subsequent weeks, I was also trained to help out on several different mail-processing machines and worked wherever I was needed.

The situation allowed me to observe and listen to workers for a considerable period of time. As I noted in the Preface, I believe this participation was invaluable for my understanding of some key issues. For example, it was only through lengthy observation that I *really* came to understand how little politics played a role in the lives of these workers. From listening to the ebb and flow of conversations day after day, I had a chance to learn of personal lives and crises, and of worker interrelationships in a way that simply would not have been possible by just interviewing them. Interviewing draws upon consciousness, subjectivity that is discursively accessible to an individual. Participation in a central aspect of daily life, though, helps to reach beyond consciousness to the observation of cultural phenomena that are sometimes the unconscious or unrecognized patterns of thought and behavior. The relationships I developed during this period, I believe, also improved my ability to ask relevant questions in interviews and improved the probability of my getting honest answers that were less affected by the artificiality of the interview process.

Interviews

After working at MAPS for several months, I began asking some workers to be interviewed for this project. MAPS workers make up half of the interviews. Subsequent interviews were arranged through references provided by MAPS workers. I was interested in interviewing a variety of workers of different ages and types of occupation. I attempted to keep an even number of women and men. Worker characteristics are summarized below:

Alias	Occupation	Age
Daniel	mechanic	51
Andrea	mail processing	23
Kristen	mail processing	32
Ronald	forklift operator	38
Bernice	"baum" machine operator	55

John	"burg" machine operator	48
Donna	"burg" machine operator	42
Steve	mail processing	29
Diane	mail processing	34
Helen	mail processing	56
Peter	postal employee	46
Sam	janitor	39
Nicole	"burg" machine operator	47
Judy	secretary (insurance)	33
Dorothy	"baum" machine operator	42
Cindy	hospital cafeteria worker	35
Hugh	brewery worker	36
Oscar	electrician	62
Warren	salesperson	56
Roger	public works employee	50
Ellen	data entry clerk	29
Tom	telephone company line worker	36

women n = 11   men n = 11

Age distribution:
   20s = 3   30s = 8   40s = 5   50s = 5   60s = 1   70s = 0
   Average = 41.8

Marriage/Partnership Status:
Men: 10 married, 9 with children (8 spouses employed outside the home)
   1 not married, no children

Women: 8 married, 6 with children (8 spouses employed outside the home)
   3 not married (one widow, one single mother)

Activists' interviews were arranged through a "snowball" sample that began with personal contacts in social movements. I was interested in focusing on "new social movement" activists. Although several activists were from other sorts of movements, they all had frequent interactions with middle-class movements. Thirteen of the activists worked full- or part-time in paid movement positions, whereas nine were unpaid volunteers. Again, I tried to maintain a balance between women and men. Activists' characteristics are summarized below:

Alias	*Primary Movement Affiliation*	*Age*
Sarah	Environmental	26
Patrick	Environmental	28
Carlene	Environmental	41
Carol	Environmental	34
Allan	Peace and Justice	37

Gus	Antinuclear	48
Adam	Central America/Anti-intervention	60
Karen	Peace	46
Joyce	Peace	24
Ralph	Antinuclear/Peace	44
Joanne	Labor	43
Ruth	Feminist/Lesbian-Gay Rights	31
Lynn	Peace and Justice	74
Doug	Labor	52
Phillip	Progressive Electoral Coalition	46
Jason	Housing	36
Lisa	Central America/Anti-intervention	26
Rob	Antinuclear	44
Lucy	Pro-choice/Feminist	27
Stuart	Central America/Anti-intervention	38
Mark	Central America/Homelessness	44
Norman	Peace/Labor	73

women n =10   men n =12

Age Distribution:
20s = 5   30s = 5   40s = 8   50s = 1   60s = 1   70s = 2
Average = 41.9

Marriage/Partnership Status:
Women: 7 married/partner, 5 with children
(5 employed outside the home, 7 spouses employed outside the home)
3 not married/divorced, 1 with children

Men: 9 married/partner, 4 with children
(8 employed outside the home, 8 spouses employed outside the home)
3 not married/no partner

Considering the Self and Social Science Research

Susan Krieger (1991: 1) writes that social science is based on an approach that limits discussion of the self. She observes, "We are taught to avoid attention to the authorial first person, whose view, and whose choices, a study represents. We learn to become invisible authors. If we cannot be objective, at least we should not call too much attention to the fact of our subjectivity." She argues that such an approach is problematic and suggests an alternative. Krieger (1991: 29) argues that the self is "key to what we know, and that methodological discussions might fruitfully be revised to acknowledge the involvement of the self in a positive manner. The self is not something that can be disengaged from knowledge or from research processes. Rather, we need to understand the nature of our participation in what we know." At the very beginning of this work I told the story of how I came to explore the issues in this dissertation. It seems only fitting that I conclude similarly.

Krieger (1991: 5) makes the point that "when we discuss others, we are always talking about ourselves. Our images of 'them' are images of 'us.' Our theories of how 'they' act and what 'they' are like, are, first of all, theories about ourselves: who we are, how we act and what we are like." Such is certainly the case in this work.

I identify sympathetically with both the workers in this study, who reminded me of working-class family and friends, and with the activists whose middle-class political culture is much closer to my own current status. But in thinking and writing of both groups, I found myself thinking and writing about myself. I would like to believe that the principled determination of movement activists resonates with a part of my own psyche that recognizes the small steps of progress that social-movement efforts have brought about. But more surprisingly, I found myself identifying with the skepticism and weary fatalism of the workers with whom I spoke. The unique nature of class status makes such identification extremely awkward. I do not dare call myself working class. My academic credentials and current lifestyle make me a member of an undeniably privileged middle class. Yet what is this continuing feeling of identification with workers? I learned to better understand that what growing up working class has left me is a cultural legacy more than a material one.

This realization was helpful because it illuminated the subject matter I was exploring. Clearly, material issues are central to discussing the day-to-day realities of social life, and material constraint can sharply limit an individual's prospects. But even when material conditions change, as in my own case, something remains. That "something" is the cultural legacy of class of which I write in this work. In the end, being open to exploring my own biographical relation to this topic, I believe, helped me to better understand both the people about whom I have written and myself.

Notes

Preface

1. Left movements that are dominated by the middle class also tend to be white, another limitation that calls into question their claims of universality. Working people, though, tend to see left social movements as important allies of people of color.

2. There is some debate about the identity of the "new" Republicans who voted Democrat in 1976 but then switched to Republican in 1980. Himmelstein and McRae (1984) found that, contrary to popular perception, the "new" Republicans in the 1980 election were better educated and wealthier than non-Republicans, though they differed little in terms of occupation and class (as determined by comparing employees, supervisors, and owners).

3. For example, a 1992 survey of likely voters sponsored by the Labor Research Association and Health Care Workers 1199 found that nearly half (46 percent) of all workers feel a union would "make no difference where they work" while 26 percent think "it would hurt" and only 28 percent think "it would help" ("Mixed Signals for Unions" 1992: 5). A 1990 Gallup poll found only 27 percent of Americans had a "great deal" or "quite a lot" of confidence in organized labor. "Big business" was given a 25 percent rating, Congress, 24 percent (Gallup 1991: 102). Americans do not trust labor union leaders either. A 1990 Gallup poll found only 15 percent of people rate them "very high" or "high" for their honesty and ethical standards. That was just above stockbrokers (14 percent) but well below lawyers (22 percent) and senators (24 percent) (Gallup 1991: 23).

4. See, for example, Giddens 1984 on structuration theory, Bourdieu 1984 on habitus and field, and Archer 1988 on culture and agency.

5. Three of the activists I interviewed did come from working-class backgrounds. They are identified as such in the text. One was a labor activist, one married a middle-class spouse, the other was unemployed at the time of his interview.

6. See, for example, Bellah et al. 1985 and Gans 1988, which focus on the middle class and "middle Americans," respectively. As Ehrenreich (1989: 3) observes, "in our culture, the professional and largely white, middle class is taken as a social norm—a bland and neutral mainstream—from which every other group or class is ultimately a kind of deviation." Consequently, potentially unique features of working-class experience are often ignored in political cultural studies that tend to generalize from middle-class experience.

7. For data and discussion of the biases in registration and voter turnout figures, see Piven and Cloward 1989, especially pp. 256–63.

8. The population in the primary metropolitan statistical area (PMSA) according to the 1990 census was about 200,000.

9. I chose MAPS as the site for my participant observation after exploring and rejecting several other possibilities given to me by the employment agency. MAPS offered a workforce with roughly equal numbers of women and men. The nature of the work offered me ample opportunity for meeting a wide variety of workers in the plant

and for carrying on lengthy and frequent conversations. Both were important considerations for my work.

Introduction

1. For an interesting discussion of how academics from the working class experience academia see Ryan and Sackrey 1984.

Chapter 1. The Promise of Democracy

1. For a brief introduction to the history of democracy see Arblaster 1987 and for more detailed examination of various forms of democracy see Held 1987. For a collection of essays on potentially "new" forms of democracy, see Held and Pollitt 1986. Finally, for considerations of the relationship between democracy and capitalism, see Cohen and Rogers 1983 and Bowles 1987. My discussion draws upon all of these sources.

2. Held (1987: 36–104) incorporates some of the ideas suggested by contrasting "liberty" and "democracy" in a good discussion of what he labels "protective" versus "developmental" democracy.

3. For a concise review of differing definitions of "politics," see Peterson 1990: 41–44.

Chapter 2. The Changing Face of Social Movements

1. Even these figures are inflated since they include union members who are unemployed. A more accurate figure for union members who are employed is 15 percent, with 9 or 10 percent of employed private sector workers belonging to unions. Such figures compare with those of the late 1920s and early 1930s (Butterfield 1992). For an overview of the difficulties involved in accurately determining union membership, see Chaison and Rose 1991. See also Strauss, Gallagher, and Fiorito 1991 for an overview collection of essays on the health of labor unions. For overviews of labor's decline see Goldfield 1987 and Montgomery 1987.

2. An important exception here is the struggle for racial equality that was at times interconnected with working-class movements, but that has a distinct history not addressed in this brief summary. For an excellent overview of this history see Harding 1981.

3. The following discussion is based on the American Social History Project (1992), hereafter ASHP, and Zinn 1980.

4. There is great diversity within NSM theory, which has been developed primarily in Europe. For a summary, see Klandermans 1986 and Kreisi 1988. A German variant can be found in Offe 1985, an Italian version in Melucci 1980, 1988, and a French version in Touraine 1971, 1981, 1985.

5. Examples of the collective-behaviorist approach include the structural-functionalist approach of Smelser (1963) and the mass-society theories of Kornhauser (1959). For a summary of the various strands of collective behavior theory see Marx and Wood 1975.

6. Also, European-based NSM theory is blind to some issues of class because it is limited to developed industrialized societies. This masks global economic dynamics, which, in part, allow for postmaterialist movements in "advanced" societies because of the exploitation of cheap labor and resources in developing nations. Economic conflict, therefore, has taken on an expanded global dimension that is not accounted for in movement theories focusing only on wealthy industrial societies.

7. For a discussion of the gap between the environmental movement and labor, see Seybolt 1991.

Chapter 3. Class and Politics

1. For a review of the theoretical origins for the arguments made in this chapter, and for a discussion of some competing conceptions of class structure, see Appendix One. For a more detailed discussion of varying conceptions of culture, see Appendix Two.

2. Unpaid domestic labor, usually performed by women, is a unique case that has sometimes been reconceptualized as a particular kind of production relation, distinct from general working-class relations of production. For discussions of the role of unpaid domestic labor see the collection edited by Malos (1980).

3. This middle class been variously labeled the "new" class, "knowledge" class, "professional-managerial" class, and "professional-middle" class. I generally use the latter term.

4. It is also possible to use this general schemata to theorize a fourth class, a so-called underclass of chronically unemployed who, in essence, have no direct relationship to the means of production.

5. As Derber, Schwartz, and Magrass (1990: 11) point out, it is irrelevant whether scarce knowledge is in fact "productive." What is important is that it is valued as such.

6. See, for example, Buroway's (1985) discussion of "relations in production." For similar analyses drawing upon a more Weberian tradition, see Bourdieu's (1984, 1985) analysis of "practices," and Giddens's (1973, 1984) discussion of "class structuration." The Ehrenreichs (1979: 11) argue that in addition to a common relation to the economic foundation of society, "class is characterized by a coherent social and cultural existence; members of a class share a common life style, educational background, kinship networks, consumption patterns, work habits, beliefs."

7. Recognizing the importance of lived experience helps in avoiding the traps of pure theorizing in that it is a recognition of difference amongst people who occupy a common position within the relations of production. Classical Marxist thinking suggested that common class position would create a homogenization of the working class. The development of capitalism has proved otherwise.

8. Wright is not using the three-class system I describe above, but his basic observations about workers remain valid in this context as well.

9. Women who work in the home and are not paid for their labor experience a different set of work-related experiences, an important example of how one cleavage can cut across another. Still, as Gerson (1985: 40) notes in her study of women's family and career choices, "Class position exerts a particularly powerful influence upon a woman's choices, shaping her alternatives and defining her constraints and opportunities."

10. Verba and Nie's study is limited to political actions that are "generally recognized as legal and legitimate" (1972: 3), but there is no reason that other forms of social-movement protests cannot be considered as "nonelectoral communal" actions.

11. The well-known work by Nie, Verba, and Petrocik on *The Changing American Voter* (1979) uses a study of the Eisenhower years as its baseline. Thus, evidence from earlier years that contradicts the SES model is not addressed.

Chapter 5. The Absence of Efficacy

1. Interestingly, none of the workers I interviewed cited the difficulty of voter registration procedures as a reason they did not vote. The unusually difficult process of voting registration in most states has been cited by some critics as a central reason for low voter turnout in the United States (Piven and Cloward 1989).

Chapter 6. "People Really Don't Think about It": Interests and Motivations

1. Though still the dominant perspective, the position that people are not interested in politics is perhaps underrepresented in my interviews because of the self-selection that results from a nonrandom sample. The only two people who declined to be interviewed each cited their own lack of knowledge and lack of interest in politics as their main reason.

2. See Appendix One for more details about the structure of work at MAPS.

3. The basic rules that make up this unwritten social contract can vary. Oscar talks about not breaking laws, but Andrea is a regular marijuana smoker who openly advocates the legalization of some drugs. In part, she sees drug laws as intervening in a person's private life. Drug addiction, she admits, is a problem, but it is a health problem, not a law enforcement problem. She is appalled by the antidrug program at her young daughter's school. "The other day my child came home saying, 'Drugs are bad. Drugs are not good.' It isn't that drugs are *bad*, it's that they're *illegal*. So I think you've got to do basically what I do, just talk to people and let people know that I use drugs and I'm as sane as the next person."

4. Worker skepticism is well founded. A study by the Democratic staff of the House Government Operations Committee found that between 1988 and 1992 the federal government lost over $300 billion due to fraud, waste, and mismanagement ("Waste Cost $300b, House Panel Finds" *Boston Globe*, 25 January 1993, 7).

5. Flacks (1988: 32) makes similar arguments for two motivational grounds for active political participation. First, he suggests, on the one hand, that participation may be *attractive* as a source of self-fulfillment and self-expression, as activity chosen out of the range of possible uses of free time. On the other hand, he argues, participation may be *reactive* or instrumental in that it is seen as a necessary or useful way of defending one's interests, expressing discontent, or resolving troubles. But defending one's interests, I believe, is qualitatively different than expressive political action based on values where one's interests are not directly at stake. Consequently, I distinguish between interests and values as a source of motivation.

6. Thomas and Mary Edsall (1991: 9) have similarly written of how much of the white working class has been alienated from liberal Democratic politics in part by the issue of race. They suggest that "liberalism inflamed resentment when it required some citizens—particularly lower-income whites—to put homes, jobs, neighborhoods, and children at perceived risk in the service of bitterly contested remedies for racial discrimination."

Chapter 7. "People Have Got Their Hands Full": Material Resources and Constraints

1. In an interesting variation on this, Louise, another Central America activist, suggested that poor and working people were, in fact, the originators of *all* social movements, regardless of their apparent composition. "What I'm saying is that I think that the basis for a lot of this stuff comes from the movements that were started by the very lower-class people who absolutely needed a change for survival. . . . The [Central America movement in the United States] would not exist if the very poor people in El Salvador were not fighting their government. And yes, people like us have enough time to empathize with the situation and have enough time to put into it. But all of these movements grow out of an absolute need from the lower classes. . . . I don't think people in upper classes would have jumped up and said, 'Gee, the civil rights situation in this country is horrible' if the very poor black people hadn't started the movement."

2. The evidence on work hours is complicated. Economist Juliet Schor (1991: 68) notes that "salaried workers have longer hours of work than workers paid by the hour. Half the nation's salaried workers [about 20 percent of the work force] belong to the 'managerial and professional specialty' group, the occupational category with the longest hours." But such comparisons can be misleading since many working people depend on second jobs for supplementing their income.

3. One literal attempt to act on a material-constraint analysis was described by Ruth, a thirty-one-year-old feminist activist: "I work at lesbian music festivals during the summers. . . . We recognized that we were getting very white and very middle class as far as the workers. And so what we've done about that is we've contacted various lesbian groups that are in different cities that we know to be inner-city communities and we've . . . said, 'We feel that we're losing a lot by not having participation because we're creating a festival that's getting more and more this way, and it doesn't seem helpful. Do you have any interest and if so, what's keeping you from coming?' And we got a lot of response like, 'It's too expensive. How can I spend a month not making any money?'— because that's what it is. So then what we've done is we're paying—'we' meaning the festival, and the festival is a diverse group but there are many more white and middle class women involved—so we are giving payment to women who otherwise wouldn't come." Whether "paying" for diversity is a useful or even a desirable long-term strategy seems debatable.

4. There are other approaches to explaining away the absence of workers without engaging in self-criticism. One, as mentioned earlier and as attempted by some segments of the New Left, is simply to redefine the working class to include oneself. The other approach is simply to dismiss the working class as irrelevant to the struggle, through the use of discrediting or ridiculing images of working-class conservatism or by theorizing that social change will emanate from another class.

Chapter 8. "They're Speaking the Same Language": Cultural Resources

1. It is important to distinguish this kind of fluid identity formation from another phenomenon that is sometimes called "identity politics." I am referring here to a generalized identity as a social-movement activist who is part of a political community, not to a particularized identity based on, for example, sex, race, or sexual orientation.

2. The cultural dissonance of some political messages is startling. After concluding an interview with one activist, I was perusing a table that had his group's literature. One of the items for sale was a bumper sticker that read: "Your yellow ribbon is soaked in the blood of the Iraqi people." I immediately thought of the workers I knew who had husbands or children in the Gulf and who, in some cases, displayed yellow ribbons as a sign of hope for their safe return. What would such a bumper sticker communicate to them, I wondered?

3. See Ryan 1991 for a thorough discussion of the framing of movement messages in the media.

Chapter 9. "It Takes a Special Kind of Person": Knowledge

1. Some movements have tried to bridge this gap. For example, developing a sense of civic knowledge that would enable more confidence in political matters was one goal of the SCLC "citizenship schools" led by Ella Baker, which taught African Americans, often illiterate, to read and write in order to pass literacy tests. Such efforts were started at the Highlander Folk School where students would learn to read and write by studying the Declaration of Human Rights of the United Nations. SNCC had analogous projects called "freedom schools," which also included discussions about the meaning of democ-

racy (Morris 1984). But such projects were taking place in the context of vibrant social-movement efforts where knowledge was linked to clear opportunity for participation. Most contemporary "education" efforts do not have such crucial links.

2. Sometimes these different roles are made explicit, as with a fundraising mailing for a national environmental group that assured recipients, "No, I'm not asking you to enlist in our front-line confrontations against the toxic polluters and waste dumpers. [Our] crew members and activists specially trained in nonviolent tactics will do that." What the group *did* want people to do was to "send as generous a contribution as you can."

Chapter 10. "You Do Your Work, You Pay Your Bills . . . You Hope It All Turns Out Okay": Politics, Work, and the Private Citizen

1. One classic example of this is the Wallace campaign of 1968 which was touted as an example of the conservative and racist inclinations of the working class. For example, Seymour Martin Lipset and Earl Raab (quoted in Hamilton 1972: 462), wrote that Wallace "demonstrated pragmatically and for the first time the fear that white working-class Americans have of Negroes. In Wisconsin he scored heavily in the . . . working-class neighborhoods of Milwaukee's south side." But as Hamilton points out, the percentage of Wallace voters was lower in Milwaukee's South Side than it was in the affluent North Side areas—and was higher still in the *very* affluent North Shore suburbs. As Ehrenreich (1989: 126) notes, overall, half of manual workers actually voted for Humphrey, 35 percent for Nixon, and 15 percent for Wallace. Meanwhile, only 34 percent of the "professional and business" class voted Democratic. Furthermore, northern blue-collar voters, where the conservative shift was supposed to have occurred most dramatically, voted for Wallace by only one percentage point over white-collar workers, leading conservative analyst Kevin Phillips to conclude "there was no reliable Wallace backing among blue-collar workers and poor whites as a class."

2. For background information on this fieldwork, see Appendix 3.

3. In an earlier work experience in a paper mill, where the noise level required protective ear plugs, I gradually learned an elaborate sign language workers had developed to communicate to each other about their jobs. Among the signs workers used were various signals that warned of the presence of supervisors.

4. I witnessed one dramatic version of this during my stints in a paper mill. The graveyard shift usually had few supervisors (known as "white-hats" for their distinctive white hardhats) because they usually worked the day shift. Workers on the paper machine "winders" rotated in covering each others' jobs, leaving one member of the crew free to take lengthy naps amongst the large piles of waste paper in the "broke" carts, thus minimizing the negative effects of working the graveyard shift. For an engaging description of similar processes in an auto plant see Ben Hamper's *Rivethead* (1991).

5. Recent changes had exacerbated this resentment. The mailing division had recently begun running many more "short" orders that required frequent recalibration of machines and other set-up time. Productivity, measured in raw numbers, had plummeted, and workers felt that managers still had not adjusted to the new reality in their production expectations.

6. It is interesting to speculate about how such programs might easily help support a belief in liberty. Many of the shows seemed to focus on the tales of individuals who lived unusual lifestyles. In my coworkers, the talk shows seemed to foster a sense of tolerance for people with differing lifestyles. The message was that people should be able to do what they want in the privacy of their own home—a belief consistent with a more generalized valuing of liberty.

7. One odd feature of some of these viewings was the habit some people apparently had of going to sleep while watching a movie. (Many people seemed to have televisions in their bedrooms.) Since they had to return the rental the next day, some people often saw only three-fourths of a movie, never finding out how it ended until told by coworkers.

Chapter 11. Class Diversity and the Future of Social Movements

1. In the fall of 1993, when labor forces tried to enter the public debate on NAFTA, Clinton publicly chided them for their lobbying "pressure tactics." Meanwhile, few seemed to notice the irony of the emergence of billionaire Ross Perot—rather than any union leader—as the key spokesperson for anti-NAFTA forces that were supposedly speaking on behalf of working people.

2. Verba and Nie (1972: 32) summarize participation this way:
"1. Few, if any, types of political activity beyond the act of voting are performed by more than a third of the American citizenry.
2. Activities that require the investment of more than trivial amounts of time and energy as well as those that have a short time referent (such as a single election) tend to be performed by no more than 10 to 15 percent of the citizens.
3. Less demanding activities as well as those with longer time referents (i.e., longer than a single election campaign) are performed by between 15 and 30 percent of the citizenry."

3. Gamson (1992: 163–64), for example, makes the useful points that "it is possible to frame almost any issue as, in part, a pocketbook issue" and that it is "misleading to assume that pocketbook consequences are what people really care about." He argues that proximate issues should not be equated with bread-and-butter topics and that the perceived proximity of issues is always in flux.

4. An important exception was a Central America group who had recently begun working on joint fundraising projects with a local homeless shelter. Part of their aim was to make connections between the refugees that resulted from U.S. foreign policy and the homeless who were the victims of domestic policy. The plan was part of a larger "links" orientation. Here too, though, the links were with the poor—a customary liberal ally—not with the more traditional working class. Stuart said, "I guess at its most basic it's just the realization that we can all benefit from each other's strength—and wisdom. Talking about just the class issue, if we can get involved in doing projects with the homeless group it's going to make us a lot—us being a very waspy, middle-class group—it's going to make our members a lot more aware of class issues and our own behavior and our own outlook. So I think there's that kind of benefit."

5. There is, of course, the possibility of a "radical" political approach that is, at the same time, conscious of class. Activists with whom I spoke, however, did not seem to have such an approach in mind when discussing "straights" and "radicals."

6. Perhaps the most extreme example of this was activists of the New Left era who consciously decided to "join" the working class by obtaining working-class jobs. At its best, the effort was an attempt to learn about the culture and lifestyle of workers as a starting point for political communication. For a good discussion of such issues in the New Left, see Welch 1979.

7. There is a Joe Martin comic strip, *Mister Boffo*, that sums it up. The one-panel cartoon shows an office supervisor facing a huge room with rows and rows of workers at their desks. The supervisor is pushing a button on his desk, "Click." One of the workers is exploding, "Kaboom!" The caption reads: "The world and the way it would be without unions."

8. Morris (1984: 282, n. 325–26) notes that the distinction between his indigenous perspective and the resource mobilization perspective (Gamson 1990; Tilly 1978) is

that, while resource mobilization tends to emphasize the political realm, in the indigenous perspective, dominated groups are those that are excluded from a "decision-
making process that determine the quantity and quality of social, economic and political
rewards that groups receive from society."

9. There is a cultural component to the Edsalls' argument as well. They suggest
that by being the party of outcasts and fighting for the underdogs, the Democratic Party
alienates white, ethnic, working people on culture or values issues (crime, gays, religion,
etc.). Instead of being seen as advancing the economic well-being of all voters (as in the
New Deal coalition), the party is now seen as batting for sectors of the population that
have been marginalized (criminals, gays, blacks, etc.). There is an element of truth to
this, though it is only half the equation. The workers I spoke with are also skeptical of
the Democratic Party for its embrace of wealthy elites.

10. When Gamson (1992: 150) used focus groups (seventeen white groups, seventeen black groups, three interracial groups) to study working-class discourse on a range
of political issues, including affirmative action, he found that at least one person in each
of the white groups rejected group-based reforms, asserting that "everyone should be
judged as an individual." But the same sentiment was also expressed in the majority of
black groups as well.

Appendix 1. Class: Structure and Collective Action

1. See Ossowski 1963, especially pp. 121–44, for a discussion of the evolution of
the term "class."

2. Marx, at times, suggested a similarly trichotomous class structure writing in an
unfinished chapter in Volume 3 of *Capital* (in Tucker 1978: 441), "The owners merely
of labour-power, owners of capital, and land-owners, whose respective sources of
income are wages, profit and ground-rent, in other words, wage-labourers, capitalists
and land-owners, constitute the three big classes of modern society based upon the
capitalist mode of production."

3. For some of the critiques by the Left leveled against the Ehrenreichs' idea of
"PMC," see Walker 1979.

4. The following discussion and graphic are adapted from Derber, Schwartz, and
Magrass 1990: 13.

Appendix 2. The Concept of Culture

1. See, for example, Kroeber and Kluckhohn 1963 and Williams 1958.

2. This section draws on existing reviews and analyses of culture, especially Hall
1980; Keesing 1974; and Williams 1981.

3. See Archer 1988 for a discussion of the parallels between the structure/agency
debates and a culture/agency analysis.

References

Agyeman, Julian. 1988. "Ethnic Minorities: An Environmental Issue." *Ecos* 9 (3): 2–5.

Alinsky, Saul. 1946. *Reveille for Radicals*. Chicago: University of Chicago Press.

———. 1971. *Rules for Radicals*. New York: Random House.

American Social History Project (ASHP). 1992. *Who Built America?: Working People and the Nation's Economy, Politics, Culture, and Society*. Vol. 2. New York: Pantheon.

Arblaster, Anthony. 1987. *Democracy*. Minneapolis: University of Minnesota.

Archer, Margaret. 1988. *Culture and Agency*. Cambridge: Cambridge University Press.

Aristotle. 1979. *The Politics of Aristotle*. Edited and translated by Ernest Barker. London: Oxford University Press.

Aronowitz, Stanley. 1992. *False Promises: The Shaping of American Working Class Consciousness*. 1973. Reprint, with a new introduction by Stanley Aronowitz, New York: McGraw-Hill.

———. 1984. "Labor Is the Key." In *Beyond Reagan: Alternatives for the '80's*, edited by Alan Gartner, Colin Greer, and Frank Reissman, 256–70. New York: Harper and Row.

———. 1988. *Science as Power: Discourse and Ideology in Modern Society*. Minneapolis: University of Minnesota Press.

———. 1992. *The Politics of Identity: Class, Culture, Social Movements*. New York: Routledge.

Avey, Michael. 1989. *The Demobilization of American Voters*. New York: Greenwood Press.

Baudrillard, Jean. 1983. *In the Shadow of the Silent Majorities . . . or the End of the Social and Other Essays*. New York: Semiotext(e).

Bellah, Robert, Richard Madsen, William M. Sullivan, Ann Swidler, and Steven M. Tipton. 1985. *Habits of the Heart: Individualism and Commitment in American Life*. New York: Harper and Row.

Bennett, Tony, Graham Martin, Colin Mercer, and Janet Woolacott, eds. 1981. *Culture, Ideology, and Social Process*. London: Open University.

Berger, Peter, and Thomas Luckmann. 1966. *The Social Construction of Reality*. Garden City, N.Y.: Doubleday.

Berelson, Bernard. 1952. "Democratic Theory and Public Opinion." *Public Opinion Quarterly* 16 (autumn): 313–30.

Blauner, Robert. 1964. *Alienation and Freedom*. Chicago: Chicago University Press.

Boggs, Carl. 1986. *Social Movements and Political Power*. Philadelphia: Temple University Press.

Bourdieu, Pierre. 1984. *Distinction*. Cambridge, Mass.: Harvard University Press.

———. 1985. "The Social Space and the Genesis of Groups." *Theory and Society* 14: 723–44.

Bowles, Sam. 1987. *Democracy and Capitalism*. New York: Basic Books.

Boyte, Harry. 1984. "Rebuilding the American Commonwealth." In *Beyond Reagan: Alternatives for the '80's*, edited by Alan Gartner, Colin Greer, and Frank Reissman, 316–33. New York: Harper and Row.

———. 1989. *Commonwealth: A Return to Citizen Politics*. New York: Free Press.

Braverman, Harry. 1974. *Labor and Monopoly Capital*. New York: Monthly Review Press.

Brecher, Jeremy, and Tim Costello, eds. 1990. *Building Bridges: The Emerging Grassroots Coalition of Labor and Community*. New York: Monthly Review Press.

Brint, Steven. 1985. "The Political Attitudes of Professionals." *Annual Review of Sociology* 11: 389–414.

Brubaker, Rogers. 1985. "Rethinking Classical Theory: The Sociological Vision of Pierre Bourdieu." *Theory and Society* 14: 745–75.

Bullard, Robert D. 1990. *Dumping in Dixie: Race, Class, and Environmental Quality*. Boulder, Colo.: Westview.

Buroway, Michael. 1985. *The Politics of Production*. London: New Left Books.

Butterfield, Bruce. 1992. "As Roles Drop and Ways Change, Unions Retreat." *Boston Globe*, 7 September, pp. 1, 10.

Chaison, Gary, and Joseph Rose. 1991. "The Macrodeterminants of Union Growth and Decline." In *The State of the Unions*, edited by George Strauss, et al., 3–45. Madison, Wis.: Industrial Relations Research Associates.

Clifford, James. 1986. "Introduction: Partial Truths." In *Writing Culture: The Poetics and Politics of Ethnography*, edited by James Clifford and George E. Marcus, 1–26. Berkeley and Los Angeles: University of California Press.

Cohen, Jean. 1985. "Strategy or Identity: New Theoretical Paradigms and Contempoary Social Movements." *Social Research* 52(4): 663–716.

Cohen, Joshua, and Joel Rogers. 1983. *On Democracy: Toward a Transformation of American Society*. New York: Penguin.

Coles, Robert. 1977. "Entitlement." *Atlantic*, September, 52–66.

Collins, Randall. 1977. *The Credential Society*. New York: Academic Press.

Cornfield, Daniel B. 1991. "The U.S. Labor Movement: Its Development and Impact on Social Inequality and Politics." *Annual Review of Sociology* 17: 27–49.

Coser, Lewis. 1971. *Masters of Sociological Thought*. New York: Harcourt Brace Jovanovich.

———. 1973. "Class." In *Dictionary of the History of Ideas*. Vol. 1. Edited by Philip Wiener, 441–49. New York: Charles Scribner's Sons.

Croteau, David, and William Hoynes. 1994. *By Invitation Only: How the Media Limit Political Debate*. Monroe, Maine: Common Courage Press.

Dahl, Robert. 1967. *Pluralist Democracy in the United States*. Chicago: Rand McNally.

D'Anieri, Paul, Claire Ernst, and Elizabeth Keir. 1990. "New Social Movements in Historical Perspective." *Comparative Politics* 22: 445–58.

Darhendorf, Ralf. 1959. *Class and Class Conflict in Industrial Society*. Stanford: Stanford University Press.

Davis, Kingsley, and Wilbert Moore. 1945. "Some Principles of Stratification." *American Sociological Review* 10: 242–49.

Derber, Charles, William Schwartz, and Yale Magrass. 1990. *Power in the Highest Degree: Professionals and the Rise of a New Mandarin Order*. New York: Oxford University Press.

Di Chiro, Giovanna. 1992. "Defining Environmental Justice." *Socialist Review* 22 (4): 93–130.

Dilthey, W. 1976. *Selected Writings*. Edited by H. P. Rickman. Cambridge: Cambridge University Press.

Dionne, E. J., Jr. 1991. *Why Americans Hate Politics*. New York: Simon and Schuster.

Domhoff, William. 1978. *The Powers That Be: Processes of Ruling-Class Domination in America*. New York: Random House.

———. 1983. *Who Rules America Now?* New York: Simon and Schuster.

Edsall, Thomas Byrne, and Mary Edsall. 1991. *Chain Reaction: The Impact of Race, Rights, and Taxes on American Politics*. New York: W. W. Norton.

Ehrenreich, Barbara. 1989. *Fear of Falling: The Inner Life of the Middle Class*. New York: Pantheon.

Ehrenreich, Barbara, and John Ehrenreich. 1979. "The Professional Managerial Class." In *Between Labor and Capital*, edited by Pat Walker, 5–45. Boston: South End Press.

Engels, Friedrich. [1890] 1978. "Letters on Historical Materialism: To Joseph Bloch." 1890. In *The Marx-Engels Reader*. 2d ed. Edited by Robert C. Tucker, 760–65. New York: W. W. Norton.

Eyerman, Ron, and Andrew Jamison. 1991. *Social Movements: A Cognitive Approach*. University Park, Pa.: Pennsylvania State University Press.

Fantasia, Rick. 1988. *Cultures of Solidarity: Consciousness, Action, and Contemporary American Workers*. Berkeley and Los Angeles: University of California Press.

Farber, Jerry. 1969. *The Student as Nigger*. New York: Pocket Books.

Fireman, Bruce, and William Gamson. 1979. "Utilitarian Logic in the Resource

Mobilization Perspective." In *The Dynamics of Social Movements: Resource Mobilization, Social Control, and Tactics,* edited by Mayer N. Zald and John D. McCarthy, 8–45. Cambridge, Mass.: Winthrop.

Flacks, Richard. 1972. "Young Intelligentsia in Revolt." In *Class and Conflict in American Society,* edited by Robert Lejeune, 247–64. Chicago: Rand McNally.

———. 1988. *Making History: The Radical Tradition in American Life.* New York: Columbia University Press.

Foner, Philip. 1977. *The Great Labor Uprising of 1877.* New York: Monad Press.

Foucault, Michel. 1972. *Power/Knowledge: Selected Interviews and Other Writings.* Edited by Colin Gordon. Brighton: Harvester Press.

Friedman, Debra, and Doug McAdam. 1992. "Collective Identity and Activism: Networks, Choices, and the Life of a Social Movement." In *Frontiers in Social Movement Theory,* edited by Aldon D. Morris and Carol McClurg Mueller, 156–73. New Haven: Yale University Press.

Fuentes, Marta, and Andre Gunder Frank. 1989. "Ten Theses on Social Movements." *World Development* 17 (2): 179–91.

Gallie, Duncan. 1978. *In Search of the New Working Class.* Cambridge: Cambridge University Press.

Gallup, George, Jr. 1991. *The Gallup Poll: Public Opinion 1990.* Wilmington, Del.: Scholarly Resources.

Gamson, William. 1990. *The Strategy of Social Protest.* 2d ed. Chicago: Dorsey Press.

———. 1988. "Political Discourse and Collective Action." In *From Structure to Action: Comparing Movement Participation Across Cultures,* edited by Bert Klandermans, Hans Kriesi, and Sid Tarrow, International Social Movement Research, vol. 1, 219–44. Greenwich, Conn.: JAI Press.

———. 1992. *Talking Politics.* New York: Cambridge University Press.

Gans, Curtis. 1984. "How to Expand Political Participation." In *Beyond Reagan: Alternatives for the '80's,* edited by Alan Gartner, Colin Greer, and Frank Reissman, 316–33. New York: Harper and Row.

Gans, Herbert. 1988. *Middle American Individualism: The Future of Liberal Democracy.* New York: Free Press.

Geertz, Clifford. 1973. *The Interpretation of Cultures.* New York: Basic Books.

Geoghegan, Thomas. 1991. *Which Side Are You On? Trying to Be for Labor When It's Flat on Its Back.* New York: Penguin, Plume.

Gerson, Kathleen. 1985. *Hard Choices: How Women Decide About Work, Career, and Motherhood.* Berkeley and Los Angeles: University of California Press.

Giddens, Anthony. 1971. *Capitalism and Modern Social Theory.* Cambridge: Cambridge University Press.

———. 1973. *The Class Structure of Advanced Societies.* New York: Harper and Row.

———. 1984. *The Constitution of Society*. Berkeley and Los Angeles: University of California Press.

Goldfarb, Jeffrey. 1991. *The Cynical Society: The Culture of Politics and the Politics of Culture*. Chicago: University of Chicago Press.

Goldfield, Michael. 1987. *The Decline of Organized Labor in the United States*. Chicago: University of Chicago Press.

Goldthorpe, John , David Lockwood, Frank Bechhofer, and Jennifer Platt. 1969. *The Affluent Worker in the Class Structure*. Cambridge: Cambridge University Press.

Gorz, Andre. 1964. *Strategy for Labor*. Boston: Beacon Press.

———. 1972. "Technical Intelligence and the Capitalist Division of Labor." *Telos* 12 (summer): 27–28.

Gottlieb, Robert. 1992. "A Question of Class: The Workplace Experience." *Socialist Review* 22 (4): 131–65.

Gouldner, Alvin. 1970. *The Coming Crisis of Western Sociology*. New York: Basic Books.

———. 1979. *The Future of Intellectuals and the Rise of the New Class*. New York: Seabury Press.

———. 1985. *Against Fragmentation*. New York: Oxford.

Greider, William. 1992. *Who Will Tell the People: The Betrayal of American Democracy*. New York: Simon and Schuster.

Habermas, Jürgen. 1981. "New Social Movements." *Telos* 49: 33–37.

———. 1983. "Modernity: An Incomplete Project." In *The Anti-Aesthetic: Essays on Postmodern Culture*, edited by Hal Foster. Seattle, Wash.: Bay Press.

Hall, Stuart. 1977. "Re-thinking the 'Base-and-Superstructure' Metaphor." In *Papers on Class Hegemony and Party*, edited by John Bloomfield, 43–72. London: Lawrence and Wernhart.

———. 1980. "Cultural Studies: Two Paradigms." *Media, Culture, and Society*, no. 2: 57–72.

Halle, David. 1984. *America's Working Man*. Chicago: University of Chicago Press.

Hamilton, Richard. 1972. *Class and Politics in the United States*. New York: John Wiley and Sons.

Hamper, Ben. 1991. *Rivethead: Tales from the Assembly Line*. New York: Warner Books.

Harding, Vincent. 1981. *There is a River: The Black Struggle for Freedom*. New York: Vintage.

Harris, M. 1964. *The Nature of Cultural Things*. New York: Random House.

———. 1968. *The Rise of Cultural Theory*. New York: Crowell.

Hart, Stephen. 1993. "Culture and the Left." *Dollars and Sense*, no. 190 (November/December): 28–29, 37–38.

Harvey, David. 1989. *The Condition of Postmodernity: An Enquiry into the Origins of Cultural Change*. Oxford: Basil Blackwell.

Hazelrigg, Lawrence. 1972. "Class, Property and Authority: Dahrendorf's Critique of Marx's Theory of Class." *Social Forces* 50: 473–87.

Hebdige, Dick. 1979. *Subculture: The Meaning of Style*. New York: Methuen.

Held, David. 1987. *Models of Democracy*. Stanford, Calif.: Stanford University Press.

Held, David, and Christopher Pollitt, eds. 1986. *New Forms of Democracy*. Beverly Hills, Calif.: Sage Publications.

Himmelstein, Jerome, and James McRae, Jr. 1984. "Social Conservatism, New Republicans, and the 1980 Election." *Public Opinion Quarterly* 48: 592–605.

Hochschild, Jennifer. 1981. *What's Fair? American Beliefs about Distributive Justice*. Cambridge, Mass.: Harvard University Press.

Horton, John. 1977. "A Contribution to the Critique of Academic Marxism: Or How the Intellectuals Liquidate Class Struggle." *Synthesis* (summer-fall): 78–105.

Howard, Robert. 1985. *Brave New Workplace*. New York: Viking Press.

Hoynes, William, and David Croteau. 1991. "The Chosen Few: Nightline and the Politics of Public Affairs Television." *Critical Sociology* 18 (1): 19–34.

Huber, Joseph. 1989. "Social Movements." *Technological Forecasting and Social Change* 35: 365–74.

Inglehart, Ronald. 1977. *The Silent Revolution: Changing Values and Political Styles Among Western Publics*. Princeton, N.J.: Princeton University Press.

Isserman, Maurice. 1987. *If I Had a Hammer . . . : The Death of the Old Left and the Birth of the New Left*. New York: Basic Books.

Kahn, Mark. 1986. *Middle Class Radicalism in Santa Monica*. Philadelphia: Temple University Press.

Karp, David. 1986. " 'You Can Take the Boy Out of Dorchester, But You Can't Take Dorchester Out of the Boy': Toward a Social Psychology of Mobility." *Symbolic Interaction* 9 (1): 19–36.

Keane, John, and Paul Mier. 1989. Preface to *Nomads of the Present: Social Movements and Individual Needs in Contemporary Society*, by Alberto Melucci. Edited by John Keane and Paul Mier. Philadelphia: Temple University Press.

Keesing, Roger. 1974. "Theories of Culture." *Annual Review of Anthropology* 5: 73–97.

King, Jonathan. 1989. "Yogurt-Eaters for Wilderness." *Sierra* 74 (Jan./Feb.): 22–24.

King, Martin Luther, Jr. [1968] 1986. "A Testament of Hope." In *A Testament of Hope: The Essential Writings of Martin Luther King, Jr.*, edited by James M. Washington, 313–28. New York: Harper and Row.

Klandermans, Bert. 1986. "New Social Movements and Resource Mobilization: The European and American Approach." *Journal of Mass Emergencies and Disasters* 4: 13–37.

Klandermans, Bert, and Dirk Oegema. 1987. "Potentials, Networks,

Klandermans (*cont.*)
Motivations, and Barriers: Steps Towards Participation in Social Movements." *American Sociological Review* 52 (August): 519–31.

Kleppner, Paul. 1982. *Who Voted? The Dynamics of Electoral Turnout, 1870–1980.* New York: Praeger.

Konrad, George, and Ivan Szelenyi. 1979. *The Intellectuals on the Road to Class Power.* New York: Harcourt Brace and Jovanovich.

Kornhauser, William. 1959. *The Politics of Mass Society.* Glencoe, Ill.: Free Press.

Krieger, Susan. 1991. *Social Science and the Self: Personal Essays on an Art Form.* New Brunswick, N.J.: Rutgers University Press.

Kriesi, Hanspeter. 1988. "The Interdependence of Structure and Action: Some Reflections on the State of the Art." In *From Structure to Action: Comparing Movement Participation Across Cultures,* edited by Bert Klandermans, Hans Kriesi, and Sid Tarrow, International Social Movement Research, vol. 1, 349–68. Greenwich, Conn.: JAI Press.

———. 1989. "New Social Movements and the New Class in the Netherlands." *American Journal of Sociology* 94: 1078–1116.

Kroeber, Alfred L., and Clyde Kluckhohn. 1963. *Culture: A Critical Review of Concepts and Definitions.* 1952. Reprint, New York: Vintage.

Kusterer, Ken. 1977. *Knowhow on the Job.* Boulder, Colo.: Westview Press.

Lapham, Lewis. 1988. *Money and Class in America.* New York: Ballantine.

Lepenies, Wolf. 1988. *Between Literature and Science: The Rise of Sociology.* Cambridge: Cambridge University Press.

Lipset, Seymour Martin. 1981. *Political Man: The Social Bases of Politics.* Expanded ed. Baltimore, Md.: Johns Hopkins University Press.

Luke, Timothy. 1989. *Screens of Power: Ideology, Domination, and Resistance in Informational Society.* Urbana, Ill.: University of Illinois.

Luttrell, Wendy. 1989. "Working-Class Women's Ways of Knowing: Effects of Gender, Race, and Class." *Sociology of Education* 62 (January): 33–46.

Lynd, Robert, and Helen Merrell Lynd. 1956. *Middletown: A Study in Modern American Culture.* 1929. Reprint, New York: Harcourt, Brace and World.

Mallet, Serge. 1963. *The New Working Class.* Nottingham, England: Spokesman.

Malos, Ellen, ed. 1980. *The Politics of Housework.* London: Allen and Busby.

Martin, Bill, and Ivan Szelenyi. 1987. "Beyond Cultural Capital: Toward a Theory of Symbolic Domination." In *Intellectuals, Universities, and the State in Western Modern Societies,* edited by Ron Eyerman, Lennart Svensson, and Thomas Soderqvist, 16–49. Berkeley and Los Angeles: University of California Press.

Marx, Gary T., and James L. Wood. 1975. "Strands of Theory and Research in Collective Behavior." *Annual Review of Sociology* 1: 368–428.

Marx, Karl. [1867] 1977. *Capital: Volume One.* Translated by Ben Fowkes. New York: Vintage Books.

———. [1852] 1978a. "The Eighteenth Brumaire of Louis Bonaparte." In *The*

Marx-Engels Reader, edited by Robert Tucker, 594–617. New York: W. W. Norton.

———. [1846] 1978b. "The German Ideology." In *The Marx-Engels Reader,* edited by Robert Tucker, 146–200. New York: W. W. Norton.

Marx, Karl, and Friedrich Engels. [1848] 1978. "Manifesto of the Communist Party." In *The Marx-Engels Reader,* edited by Robert Tucker, 469–500. New York: W. W. Norton.

Maslow, Abraham. 1962. *Toward a Psychology of Being.* New York: Van Nostrand.

———. 1964. *Values and Peak-Experiences.* Columbus, Ohio: Ohio State University Press.

Mattausch, John. 1989. "The Peace Movement: Some Answers Concerning Its Social Nature and Structure." *International Sociology* 4 (2): 217–25.

McAdam, Doug. 1988. *Freedom Summer.* New York: Oxford University Press.

McCarthy, John D., and Mayer N. Zald. 1987. "The Trend of Social Movements in America: Professionalization and Resource Mobilization." In *Social Movements in an Organizational Society,* edited by Mayer N. Zald and John D. McCarthy, 337–91. New Brunswick, N.J.: Transaction Publishers.

Melman, Seymour. 1970. *Pentagon Capitalism.* New York: McGraw-Hill.

———. 1974. *The Permanent War Economy.* New York: Simon and Schuster.

Melucci, Alberto. 1980. "The New Social Movements: A Theoretical Approach." *Social Science Information* 19: 199–226.

———. 1985. "The Symbolic Challenge of Contemporary Movements." *Social Research* 52: 789–816.

———. 1988. "Getting Involved: Identity and Mobilization in Social Movements." In *From Structure to Action: Comparing Movement Participation Across Cultures,* edited by Bert Klandermans, Hans Kriesi, and Sid Tarrow, International Social Movement Research, vol. 1, 329–48. Greenwich, Conn.: JAI Press.

———. 1989. *Nomads of the Present: Social Movements and Individual Needs in Contemporary Society.* Edited by John Keane and Paul Mier. Philadelphia: Temple University Press.

Michels, Robert. 1949. *Political Parties.* 1915. Reprint, Glencoe, Ill.: Free Press.

Mills, C. Wright. 1956. *The Power Elite.* New York: Oxford University Press.

———. 1959. *The Sociological Imagination.* New York: Oxford University Press.

Mitchell, Robert. 1978. "The Public Speaks Again: A New Environmental Survey." *Resources* 60 (September/November): 1–6.

"Mixed Signals for Unions." 1992. *Dollars and Sense,* no. 177 (June): 5.

Montgomery, David. 1987. *The Fall of the House of Labor.* New York: Cambridge University Press.

Morgan, Edmund. 1988. *Inventing the People: The Rise of Popular Sovereignty in England and America.* New York: W. W. Norton.

Morris, Aldon D. 1984. *The Origins of the Civil Rights Movement.* New York: Free Press.

Mosca, Gaetano. 1939. *The Ruling Class.* 1896. Reprint, New York: McGraw-Hill.

Nie, Norman, Sidney Verba, and John Petrocik. 1979. *The Changing American Voter.* Cambridge, Mass.: Harvard University Press.

Offe, Claus. 1985. "New Social Movements: Challenging the Boundaries of Institutional Politics." *Social Research* 52: 817–68.

Olson, Mancur. 1965. *The Logic of Collective Action.* Cambridge, Mass.: Harvard University Press.

Ossowski, Stanislaw. 1963. *Class Structure in the Social Consciousness.* New York: Free Press.

Page, Benjamin, and Robert Shapiro. 1992. *The Rational Public.* Chicago: University of Chicago Press.

Parenti, Michael. 1986. *Inventing Reality: The Politics of the Mass Media.* New York: St. Martin's Press.

Pareto, Vilfredo. 1935. *The Mind and Society.* 1916. Reprint, New York: Harcourt Brace Jovanovich.

———. 1966. *Sociological Writings.* Edited by S. E. Finer. New York: Praeger Press.

Parkin, Frank. 1968. *Middle Class Radicalism.* Manchester: Manchester University Press.

Parsons, Talcott. 1975. "Equality and Inequality in Modern Society, or Social Stratification Revisited." In *Social Stratification: Research and Theory for the 1970s,* edited by Edward O. Laumann. Indianapolis: Bobbs-Merrill.

Peterson, Steven. 1990. *Political Behavior: Patterns in Everyday Life.* Newbury Park, Calif.: Sage Publications.

Piven, Frances Fox, and Richard A. Cloward. 1989. *Why Americans Don't Vote.* New York: Pantheon.

Poulantzas, Nicolas. 1975. *Class in Contemporary Capitalism.* London: Verso.

Puette, William J. 1992. *Through Jaundiced Eyes: How the Media View Organized Labor.* Ithaca, N.Y.: ILR Press.

Rayman, Paula. 1983. "Labor and Disarmament: The Meeting of Social Movements." In *Beyond Survival: New Directions for the Disarmament Movement,* edited by Michael Albert and David Dellinger, 187–204. Boston: South End Press.

Reinarman, Craig. 1987. *American States of Mind.* New Haven, Conn.: Yale University Press.

Reinharz, Shulamit. 1984. *On Becoming a Social Scientist.* New Brunswick, N.J.: Transaction Books.

Roberts, Kenneth. 1978. *The Working Class.* London: Longman.

Rousseau, Jean-Jacques. 1967. *The Social Contract (1762) and Discourse on the Origin of Inequality (1755).* Edited by Lester G. Crocker. New York: Simon and Schuster.

Rucht, Dieter. 1988. "Themes, Logics, and Arenas of Social Movements: A Structural Approach." In *From Structure to Action: Comparing Movement Participation Across Cultures*, edited by Bert Klandermans, Hans Kriesi, and Sid Tarrow, International Social Movement Research, vol. 1, 305–28. Greenwich, Conn.: JAI Press.

Ryan, Charlotte. 1991. *Prime Time Activism: Media Strategies for Grassroots Organizing*. Boston: South End Press.

Ryan, Jake, and Charles Sackrey. 1984. *Strangers In Paradise: Academics from the Working Class*. Boston: South End Press.

Sanders, Arthur. 1990. *Making Sense of Politics*. Ames, Iowa: Iowa State University Press.

Schneider, William. 1992. "The Suburban Century Begins." *Atlantic*, January, 33–44.

Schor, Juliet. 1991. *The Overworked American: The Unexpected Decline of Leisure*. New York: Basic Books.

Schumpeter, Joseph. 1950. *Capitalism, Socialism, and Democracy*. 3d ed. New York: Harper and Row.

Sennett, Richard, and Jonathan Cobb. 1973. *The Hidden Injuries of Class*. New York: Vintage.

Sexton, Patricia Cayo. 1991. *The War on Labor and the Left*. Boulder, Colo.: Westview Press.

Seybolt, Susan Weber. 1991. "Of Trees and Men: Toward an Environmental and Labor Alliance." Master's thesis in Urban and Environmental Policy, Tufts University, Boston.

Shapiro, Bruce. 1990. "Connecticut LEAP: A New Electoral Strategy." In *Building Bridges: The Emerging Grassroots Coalition of Labor and Community*, edited by Jeremy Brecher and Tim Costello, 135–43. New York: Monthly Review Press.

Smelser, Neil. 1963. *The Theory of Collective Behavior*. New York: Free Press.

Snow, David A., and Robert D. Benford. 1988. "Ideology, Frame Resonance, and Participant Mobilization." In *From Structure to Action: Comparing Movement Participation Across Cultures*, edited by Bert Klandermans, Hans Kriesi, and Sid Tarrow, International Social Movement Research, vol. 1, 197–212. Greenwich, Conn.: JAI Press.

Snow, David A., E. Burke Rochford, Jr., Steven K. Worden, and Robert Benford. 1986. "Frame Alignment Processes, Micromobilization, and Movement Participation." *American Sociological Review* 51 (August): 464–81.

Snow, David A., Louis A. Zurcher, Jr., and Sheldon Ekland-Olson. 1980. "Social Networks and Social Movements: A Microstructural Approach to Differential Recruitment." *American Sociological Review* 45: 787–801.

Stout, Linda. 1993. "Why Aren't We Winning?" *Peacework*, no. 233 (September): 1–3.

Strauss, George, Daniel G. Gallagher, and Jack Fiorito, eds. 1991. *The State of the Unions*. Madison, Wis.: Industrial Relations Research Associates.

Swidler, Ann. 1986. "Culture in Action: Symbols and Strategies." *American Sociological Review* 51: 273–86.

Taylor, Verta, and Nancy E. Whittier. 1992. "Collective Identity in Social Movement Communities: Lesbian Feminist Mobilization." In *Frontiers in Social Movement Theory*, edited by Aldon D. Morris and Carol McClurg Mueller, 104–29. New Haven: Yale University Press.

———. 1993. "The New Feminist Movement." In *Feminist Frontiers III*, edited by Laurel Richardson and Verta Taylor, 533–45. New York: McGraw Hill.

Terkel, Studs. 1972. *Working*. New York: Avon Books.

Therborn, Göran. 1976. *Science, Class, and Society*. London: Verso.

———. 1980. *The Power of Ideology and the Ideology of Power*. London: New Left Books.

Thomas, W. I., and Dorothy Swain Thomas. 1928. *The Child in America*. New York: Knopf.

Tilly, Charles. 1978. *From Mobilization to Revolution*. Reading, Mass.: Addison-Wesley.

Touraine, Alain. 1971. *The Post-Industrial Society*. New York: Random House.

———. 1981. *The Voice and the Eye*. New York: Cambridge University Press.

———. 1985. "An Introduction to the Study of Social Movements." *Social Research* 52: 749–88.

Tucker, Robert, ed. 1978. *The Marx-Engels Reader*. New York: W. W. Norton.

Tumin, Melvin. 1953. "Some Principles of Stratification: A Critical Analysis." *American Sociological Review* 18: 387–93.

Tylor, Edward B. 1958. *Primitive Culture*. Gloucester, Mass.: Smith.

Vanneman, Reeve, and Lynn Weber Cannon. 1987. *The American Perception of Class*. Philadelphia: Temple University Press.

Verba, Sidney, and Norman Nie. 1972. *Participation in America: Political Democracy and Social Equality*. New York: Harper and Row.

Wachtel, Howard. 1986. *The Money Mandarins*. New York: Pantheon.

Walker, Pat, ed. 1979. *Between Labor and Capital*. Boston: South End Press.

"Waste Cost $300b, House Panel Finds." 1993. *Boston Globe*, 25 January, 7.

Weber, Max. 1946. "Class, Status, Party." In *From Max Weber: Essays in Sociology*, 180–95. Edited by Hans Gerth and C. Wright Mills. New York: Oxford University Press.

Weedon, Chris. 1987. *Feminist Practice and Poststructuralist Theory*. Oxford: Basil Blackwell.

Weingart, Peter. 1969. "Beyond Parsons? A Critique of Ralf Dahrendorf's Conflict Theory." *Social Forces* 48: 151–65.

Welch, John. 1979. "New Left Knots." In *Between Labor and Capital*, edited by Pat Walker, 173–90. Boston: South End Press.

Williams, Raymond. 1958. *Culture and Society*. London: Chatto and Windus.

———. 1977. *Marxism and Literature.* Oxford: Oxford University Press.

———. 1981. *The Sociology of Culture.* New York: Schocken.

Willis, Paul. 1977. *Learning to Labor.* New York: Columbia University Press.

Wilson, James Q. 1973. *Political Organizations.* New York: Basic.

Wright, Erik Olin. 1978. *Class, Crisis, and the State.* London: Verso.

———. 1979. *Class Structure and Income Determination.* New York: Academic Press.

———. 1980. "Varieties of Marxist Concepts of Class Structure." *Politics and Society* 9: 3.

———. 1985. *Classes.* London: Verso.

———. 1989a. "A General Framework for the Analysis of Class Structure." In *The Debate on "Classes,"* 3–43. London: Verso.

———. 1989b. "Rethinking, Once Again, the Concept of Class Structure." In *The Debate on "Classes,"* 269–348. London: Verso.

Yago, Glenn, and Kathleen Blee. 1982. "The Political Economy of Exploitation: A Revision." *The Insurgent Sociologist* 11 (2): 63–72.

Zinn, Howard. 1980. *A People's History of the United States.* New York: Harper Perennial.

Zipp, John F., Richard Landerman, and Paul Luebke. 1982. "Political Parties and Political Participation: A Reexamination of the Standard Socioeconomic Model." *Social Forces* 60 (4): 1140–53.

Index